THE READER OF GENTLEMEN'S MAIL

THE READER OF GENTLEMEN'S MAIL

Herbert O. Yardley

and the Birth of

American Codebreaking

DAVID KAHN

Yale University Press / New Haven & London

Designed by Mary Valencia
Set in Adobe Garamond type by Keystone Typesetting, Inc.
Printed in the United States of America.

Library of Congress Cataloging-in-Publication Data

Kahn, David, 1930–
The reader of gentlemen's mail : Herbert O. Yardley and the birth of American codebreaking / David
Kahn.
p. cm.
Includes bibliographical references and index.
ISBN 0-300-09846-4 (alk. paper)
1. Yardley, Herbert O. (Herbert Osborn), 1889–1958. 2. Cryptographers—United
States—Biography. 3. World War, 1914–1918—Cryptography. I. Title.
UB271.U52Y374 2004
940.4′8673′092—dc22
[B]
2003060029

A catalogue record for this book is available from the British Library.

The paper in this book meets the guidelines for permanence and durability of the Committee on
Production Guidelines for Book Longevity of the Council on Library Resources.

10 9 8 7 6 5 4 3 2 1

To Buddy and Joyce

Contents

CONTENTS

Photo gallery follows page 138

Preface

Herbert O. Yardley is the most colorful and controversial figure in American intelligence. He became a cornerstone of it when he gave America its best intelligence—codebreaking—and then, for an act to which he was driven by desperation, he became an outcast. Yet he has never had a biographer.

He deserves one. Although throughout America's history individuals had broken codes as occasion demanded, they abandoned the work when the need ended. Yardley institutionalized it. In World War I, Yardley foresaw that the United States needed the information that could come from signals intelligence, established America's first permanent agency to intercept foreign messages and break codes, and ran it well enough to prove its importance. He endowed his nation with its most trustworthy, high-level, voluminous foreign information. Then, after a secretary of state disbanded his organization on the ground that "Gentlemen do not read each other's mail," Yardley, out of work in the Great Depression, with a wife and son to feed, published a sensational memoir about his work and its successes. Titled *The American Black Chamber*, its betrayal of trust rightly drew down the wrath of intelligence and military professionals, who refused thenceforth to have anything to do with him, even during the emergency of World War II. But it awakened thousands to the value of communications intelligence. Yardley owes his significance to what he did; his fame, to what he said.

At his most successful, in his thirties, Yardley, short, balding, likeable, was quick-witted, capable, and an opportunistic self-promoter, always looking for the big buck. He did personal work on government time. He sold his soul for his book. He exaggerated his successes in his official reports and in his book, though he was honest in minor personal matters. Yet he was an extremely competent executive, dealing effectively with subordinates and superiors. He told stories well. People liked him. He drank a lot, but held his liquor. He hunted, fished, played championship golf, won at poker. Though as a codebreaker he rose only a little above the average and as a codemaker he invented no new methods, he achieved a solution that, by helping eliminate thousands of tons of warship construction, saved the world millions of dollars and eased international tensions. Later, the revelations and striking style of *The American Black Chamber* made it an instant classic of intelligence literature. Yardley is a cult figure.

This book describes the arc of Yardley's life. I have sought to embed that life into the context of its times, to infer its motivations, and to say why it matters. The book shows how Yardley's boyhood demonstrated the imagination and initiative that enabled him to achieve what he did. It describes the competition between him and a think tank near Chicago to control American codebreaking and later between him and another great cryptanalyst, William F. Friedman. It considers the stories that Yardley was a drunk and a womanizer. It discloses how Yardley obtained the foreign code messages his agency needed despite laws protecting their confidentiality. It details his greatest success: his solution of Japanese codes before the Washington naval conference of 1921–22. It corrects, on the basis of documents, the almost universal belief that the publication of *The American Black Chamber* led Japan to change its codes and ciphers. It offers a surprising positive evaluation of the effect of that book by the cryptanalyst who led the attack on major Japanese codes and ciphers before and during World War II. It debunks the slander that Yardley traitorously sold to Japan his solutions of Japanese messages. It proposes an answer to why America, alone of all the powers, closed its codebreaking agency and, by implication, deals with the morality of intelligence.

Permeating the story is the mysticism of that secret endeavor and its more esoteric subaltern, cryptology. Cryptologists' astonishing ability to reveal hidden information, to know things that the uninitiated do not, seems to give them a dark power that awes people. It confers on them the aura of the shaman, the medicine man, the sorcerer, with their miraculous black magic. This spectral atmosphere has been well evoked by Edgar Allan Poe in his stories and poems, and it is no accident that one of his best stories, "The Gold-Bug," deals with the solution of a cryptogram. Mystery has always been the attraction of intelligence, and that tone rumbles under any tale about it.

Nearly everything written about Yardley stems from his published writings. Except for a few scraps, and some letters from China, kindly provided by his sister-in-law, he left no personal papers, and his declassified technical and administrative papers are dry of almost all humanity. So the biographer must probe the archives and manuscript repositories, talk to the few remaining persons who knew him, and scratch in likely and unlikely places for a crumb or two of information. The greatest sources were the papers of his agent, George Bye, the pathbreaking studies of Louis Kruh, Esq., the back issues of the *Worthington Times,* scrutinized for me day by day from 1890 to 1950 by Wilma Shouse McBride of Worthington, Indiana, Yardley's hometown, and the investigations of David Reno.

In dealing with these sources, I have followed some conventions. Yardley sometimes misspelled words, and some Chinese place-names are now transliterated differently than in Yardley's time. Both his and the then contemporary Chinese orthography are retained. Where necessary, technical terms are upgraded to their modern, more precise form: "cryptanalysis" is used when that is meant instead of the older, ambiguous "cryptography" or "deciphering." However, sometimes I use "codes" and "codebreaking" to stand for cryptography and cryptanalysis.

This book owes much to many people. Besides those mentioned above, there are others: Dr. David Hatch, former director of the Center for Cryptologic History at the National Security Agency, brought me to the agency as the 1995 scholar in residence, fought successfully to allow me to work without a security clearance in that secrets-obsessed organization, and had Yardley's official papers declassified for me. William Crowell, the agency's deputy director, welcomed me with warmth, interest, and generosity. Jack Ingram, curator of the National Cryptologic Museum, was always ready with help. At the National Archives, Mitchell Yockelson, John Taylor, Milton Gustafson, Lawrence McDonald, and Timothy Nenninger led the team of archivists and helpers who provided that agency's excellent service. Maria deB. Waller contributed important research services. Susan Joralem provided invaluable secretarial help. Jonathan Bruck, whom I met while we were both researching at that fabulous institution, the New York Public

Library, generously telephoned one day to tell me of his find of Yardley's agent's papers at Columbia University. Kim Hastings copyedited superbly; Susan Laity shepherded the book through production enthusiastically; and Jonathan Brent managed the project with great skill. My sons, Oliver—who made the graphs—and Michael, and their mother, Susanne Kahn, helped in their ways. But my greatest debt is to Edward S. (Buddy) Miller, the author of *War Plan Orange,* and his wife, Joyce Trepel Miller, both friends from Great Neck High School. They continuously provided wonderful hospitality, interesting discussions, challenges, arguments, ideas, and emotional support. I am happy to dedicate this book to them.

David Kahn
Great Neck, New York

A Short Course in Codes and Ciphers

Codes are a way of making messages secret. But not all of what are called codes are codes. Some are ciphers. There's a difference. **Codes** are books. They are like foreign-language dictionaries, except instead of translating English into, say, French, they translate English into code. A small part of a codebook may look like this portion of one from World War I:

stop	3514
stopped	3329..4017
storm	4211
strength	1740..2329
strength of enemy unknown	3961
strengthen	1679
stretcher bearers	3166

This means that, in turning the original English message into code, the word *stop* will be replaced by 3514 and the word *stopped* by either 3329 or 4017. These numbers are what will be transmitted to the receiving station.

The receiver has a similar book, only with the numbers in numerical order:

1674	favorably
1675	make ready
1676	no patrols
1679	strengthen
1681	-nt
1684	49
1685	question mark

The gaps in the numbering make it harder for the enemy cryptanalyst to reconstruct the code. This is called a **two-part code** because it has one part for encoding, one for decoding. The code elements can be letters instead of numbers. It is harder to solve than a **one-part code,** in which the **codenumbers** or **codewords** run parallel to the plaintext elements.

While codes work mainly by words, **ciphers** work by letters. They use not books but tables or mechanisms to convert their messages, letter by letter, into secret form. The simplest cipher—one found in the Bible—replaces the individual letters of the plaintext message with other letters:

plain   a b c d e f g h i j k l m n o p q r s t u v w x y z
cipher   L B Q A C S R D T O F V M H W I J X G K Y U N Z E P

The message *attack at dawn* would be enciphered into LKKLQF LK ALNH.

The weaknesses of this **monoalphabetic** system are evident. The **ciphertext** reflects the letter pattern of the underlying **plaintext.** And since each plaintext letter is represented by a single ciphertext letter, the system is vulnerable to frequency analysis. This technique is based on the fact that—given several different pieces of writing of about two hundred letters or more in a single language—the percentage of each letter in each piece stays about the same. Thus, in English, the number of *e*'s—the most common letter—will average around 12.5 percent. The next most common, *t*, will stand around 9 percent, and on down to *z*, at around 0.5 percent. These frequencies hold whether the text is a military telegram, the Gettysburg Address, or "To be or not to be." So a codebreaker, faced with a cryptogram enciphered in this system, can count the letters in the cryptogram and can assume that the most frequent cryptogram letter stands for the most frequent letter of the language of the plaintext. He can then insert this guess into the cryptogram and try to fill in the missing letters. Sometimes the guess is wrong, so the cryptanalyst must try another possible plaintext letter. Cryptanalysis involves much trial and error; it is not as straightforward as proving a theorem in plane geometry.

Because frequency cryptanalysis has been known in the West since the

Renaissance, cryptographers have proposed systems that would defeat it. One uses several alphabets, so that a single plaintext letter would have different ciphertext representations, according to the alphabet used. Such systems are called **polyalphabetic;** the best known, published by a French diplomat in 1586 and named for him, is called the **Vigenère.** A mnemonic, usually called the **keyword,** specifies which alphabets are to be used and in which order. Both the encipherer and the decipherer must hold the keyword. For example, if the keyword is COMET, the alphabet beginning with the letter C will encipher the first plaintext letter, the alphabet beginning with O the second, and so on, repeating the keyword until the entire message has been enciphered. To avoid the weakness caused by the regular repetition of the keyword, cryptographers use a long text, such as a poem or novel, as a **running key.** Some **cipher machines** generate extremely long incoherent keys for polyalphabetic cryptosystems. Other machines create many different cipher alphabets. Solving repeating-key polyalphabetics requires the cryptanalyst to first determine the number of alphabets used, to separate out the letters enciphered in each alphabet, and then to apply frequency analysis to each such set. Other polyalphabetics demand more complicated solutions.

While these partake essentially of mathematical and statistical analyses, solutions of code messages more resemble the reconstruction of lost languages. It is not surprising that the ace French cryptanalyst of the 1890s, Commandant Etienne Bazeries, was called the Champollion of codebreakers. Code solutions require many more messages than cipher solutions, and their cryptanalysts often begin by determining, from their frequent appearance and their positions in the cryptogram, the codewords that represent *period* or *full stop.* This outlines the structure of the plaintext. Then, events in the world, such as the sailing of a warship from various ports during a cruise, are related to intercepted messages, guesses are made and confirmed and other guesses added to them. Gradually the code is built up.

Codes and ciphers form one of the kingdoms of cryptography, the **substitution** kingdom. Letters or words are replaced by other letters or numbers. The other kingdom consists of **transposition** ciphers. In these, the letters of the plaintext message are scrambled: *enemy* might become NEEYM. The cryptograms of transposition ciphers retain the original letters and thus may be seen as weaker than substitution systems, where the plaintext has to be recovered. Transposition cryptograms are more difficult to decipher correctly than substitution systems if a letter is dropped in transmission. So they are used less often than substitution systems. Substitution systems may operate in a continuous stream; transposition systems must run in batches.

Cryptographers apply substitution or transposition systems to codes to double the work of those trying to break a code. These systems conceal the codewords or codenumbers. For example, the letters of the codeword PEDED may be replaced, either individually or in pairs, as agreed on, with other letters or numbers. Thus PEDED might become, in one system, RBIBI. In a different system, the PE might become RL, the DE might become MI, and the D, X, so that PEDED becomes RLMIX. This is **enciphered code,** or **superencipherment.**

Cryptanalysis is a practical, not an abstract, technology. Many cryptosystems fail not because of their own flaws, but because they are poorly used. Commanders repeat themselves. Cipher clerks err. Generals begin messages with "To the colonel of the 14th Regiment," diplomats with "I have the honor to. . . " Cipher clerks send messages in the wrong key that they have to redo in the right key, creating two cryptograms with the same plaintexts that cryptanalysts can work like a crossruff in bridge. Codes may list many different code equivalents for *stop,* but the clerks quickly remember one or two and use them instead of looking in the codebook for the others. Even when codes or ciphers change, the habits of the communicators do not. And often messages are not solved at all.

The terminology of cryptology has become more precise since Yardley's time. In those days, "cryptography" ambiguously meant both making and breaking codes and ciphers. Today **cryptography** means only making. Breaking is **cryptanalysis,** a term that came into general use only in the 1930s. Cryptography plus cryptanalysis now combine into **cryptology.** Likewise, under Yardley, **decoding** and **deciphering** stood both for the authorized turning of a cryptogram into plaintext by the legitimate receiver and for the unauthorized solution of a cryptogram by the enemy. Popular writing often prolongs this confusion. But in the modern taxonomy, "deciphering" means only the legitimate reconversion of a cipher message from its secret form into its plaintext; "decoding," of a code message. The term for solving a message is "cryptanalysis." I use the clearer modern terminology except in quotations and sometimes, when the meaning is plain, I use "codes" to stand for all cryptography, as in the first sentence of this glossary, and "codebreaking" for all cryptanalyses. The modern term **encrypt** usefully means either "encipher" or "encode"; likewise **decrypt** for the restoration to plaintext.

How Yardley Wrote His Best-Seller

In 1929, when Secretary of State Henry L. Stimson withdrew his department's funds from codebreaking on the ground that it was immoral, Yardley's agency, quartered in New York, was closed down. Unable to find a job in the Depression, Yardley decided to use his sole asset—his knowledge of his secret activities—to support his wife, their boy, and himself by telling that story. In a memorandum for literary agent George T. Bye he set down how he wrote his book, The American Black Chamber, *which became a best-seller and one of the most famous books in the literature of intelligence. The memorandum gives a good insight into Yardley, including his misspellings.*

I was a cryptographer, not a writer. Friends suggested that I return to New York and consult you. They told me that you could make anyone write, no matter what his training. So I came to New York with my last few dollars, took a room at the Commodore Club Hotel, and called you up. Your suave secretary told me that you were not in; so I left my telephone number and sat around the rest of the day waiting for a call from you. None came. The same thing happened the next day, and then the next. I was a bit discouraged, not only because my funds were low, but because no one seemed to recognize that I had a story to tell.

Well, this went on for about two weeks. Finally I found FPA [columnist Franklin P. Adams], whom I had known during the war, and asked him to recommend a literary agent. He asked me if I could write, and I told him no, but that perhaps someone else would oblige me. He suggested that I see you, and I said that was what I had been trying to do for two weeks without success.

I said, "Bye must be drunk; he's never in."

He replied, "No, he isn't drunk all the time."

"What's the matter with him?" I asked.

"He's busy—out selling stuff."

"Perhaps he is," I said, "but can't you get me another agent? Bye won't see me."

"There is no other agent," FPA retorted. "I'll fone him and tell him to see you."

Well, George, by this time, the seat of my pants was quite thin, and I went to bed and sent them out to be mended. I foned and foned and foned. Finally I caught you unaware and you said to come up.

I had had some tough spots in my life, but talking to you for the first time was the toughest of all. I was conscious of my patched trousers, and though I had rehearsed the glowing terms in which I would recite my tale of romance, adventure, and intrigue, I was confused by the sudden interruption of telephones and your conversations with the Great.

But I think you took pity on me. Anyway, you told me to come back the next day to interview Mr. Costain of the *Saturday Evening Post* [Thomas B. Costain, later the best-selling author of *The Silver Chalice* and other books].

I was a good half hour early and sat in your anti-room while your secretary wrote checks and introduced me to the successful as they streamed into your office. For two hours I waited, most of the time listening through closed doors to the exchange of conversation between Mr. Costain, you, and Mr. Franklin, the American bull-fighter, who was negotiating for a series of articles.

Finally, in despair, I started to pick up my hat and ragged coat, when suddenly Mr. Franklin ended his conversation, and you asked me to come in and tell my story to Mr. Costain.

Mr. Costain has an overpowering personality, and I felt very small in my rags and could scarcely open my mouth. Poverty had done strange things to me, though only a few months before I had stood at the top of my profession. Now I suddenly found myself with no voice, no matter, no confidence. Mr. Costain, however, was polite enough to listen for a few moments, then rushed from your office to catch a train. I followed, discouraged, and to tell the truth, in a hopeless mood.

I presumed this ended my association with you, but much to my surprise you telephoned me the next day to catch a train to Philadelphia, as the *Saturday Evening Post* wished to talk to me there.

I saw Mr. Costain again, whose distinguished head and restless eyes intrigued me. He introduced me to their most distinguished writer, Mr. Stout. To the latter I told my story. He seemed not particularly impressed, and I wondered at his chubby face and round eyes. He asked me if I could write the articles, and I told him no, that I was, I believed, the only person in America who couldn't write. This statement warmed him to me a bit.

Mr. Costain finally came back, and after discussing the matter with Mr. Stout, told me that he would take three articles, but that Mr. Stout was engaged on another series and could not do mine for several weeks.

This was a bit discouraging, for I wanted quick action. I came back to New York and we discussed the matter. You told me to write the articles myself, and I said I couldn't. You then promised, in order to save time, to get someone else to write them at once.

I waited several days, but did not hear from you. Finally I came back and had the nerve to show you a chapter that I had scribbled. You took it home with you and read it, or at least you said you did (I doubt if you even looked at it), and told me that all I needed was a typewriter and some paper.

These I had within a few hours, and moved from the hotel to a dark cheap room. Before me sat a typewriter, and [by] my side laid 500 sheets of paper. But I could do no more than stare into space. For days I pecked out a few lines and threw them into the fire. I utterly detested the job of writing what seemed to me one of America's greatest episodes. All that I had done in life had been done well. I had in my possession hundreds of letters testifying to my ability as a decoder of cryptograms. But I knew nothing about writing. And, George, it seemed to me that I had a thrilling story to tell. You cannot know what it means to sit before a typewriter with a tremendous story with no training, no craftsmanship to tell it. I was desperate.

At last I began to write whole paragraphs, then pages, and I cared nothing for words, for form, for structure. Often after working all night I timidly handed you a chapter, and the next day you told me to keep at it. I doubted then, and I still doubt that you read the MS, but you gave me the desire to continue in my poor, illiterate manner.

For relief from the grind you asked me to come to your Thursday Afternoon Culture Club which you hold on Friday afternoons. I met many famous writers and journalists there, and by way of conversation told them what I was trying to do. They dismissed my words with, "You might have a story; I doubt it."

Well, no one could make believe that I did not have a story, I knew that I had one of the most dramatic stories in American history. But I trembled lest I could not tell it.

I said nothing to you about these contacts, but went back to my dark room and kept pecking away at my rented typewriter.

At last you told me that Bobbs-Merrill, the publishers, wanted to see me. I called on Mr. Shively, the New York representative, and sketched my tale. He thought I had something, but wanted a written outline of the entire book.

Well, I was writing without an outline, but I called up two stenographers and for 48 hours dictated to them. The result was a terrible mess, for there was no time for second guesses. Anyway, George Shively sent my outline to Mr. Chambers in Indianapolis, and indicated that they would take the book.

This was good news, for I had only a few dollars in my pocket and was cooking my own meals. To conserve my street suit, since it was thread-bare, I worked in my dinner clothes. I came to see you again and again, as I needed encouragement and advice. But the long hours of waiting in your office discouraged me, and though you were always courteous, I somehow felt that you had your tongue in your cheek. Aside from this, you seemed always just returning from a party. And I was so anxious to forget it all and do the same. How could it be possible for one with no training to tell a story? You really had asked the impossible.

For New Year's [1931] I drank an ice cream soda and worked all night. I ground out a thousand words a day, then two thousand, then three thousand; and on occasions when the room got cold and I could not sleep as many as seven thousand. Messy, yes. Humiliating, yes. I, a person who had once stood at the top of my profession, now trying to enter another—enter another with no background, no words to express myself. I wanted to weep for words and the training for expression. These I could not acquire. So I simply pecked away, day after day, night after night.

At last after four weeks I gave you about three quarters of the book and Bobbs-Merrill asked that I come to their office to discuss advance royalties and a contract. Before they would sign, they said I must complete the MS within one month. I was already dead on my feet and hollow-eyed but desperate for an advance. So I promised I should not fail them.

I came to your office with this information. After telephoning to the *Saturday Evening Post,* you told me that I must complete the book within two weeks, instead of a month, in order to give them sufficient time to run a few articles before the publication of the book.

I don't believe you realize what a slave driver you are. I thought I had been working before, but I now began to work in four shifts, sleeping two hours, working four; sleeping two, working four. And then you told me that the book must be complete by Monday at 10 a.m., so that the MS could go to the typist's. By working all night Saturday and all night Sunday, going to bed at 10 p.m. and setting the alarm for 2 a.m. Monday, I managed to finish the last chapters within your time limit.

After delivering the MS I sat around in my room in trembling and fear. Then when the typist delivered the MS to you and you were kind enough to read it and telegraph "Congratulations on magnificent book which is ten times better than my most optimistic expectations"; then all the hours of drudgery slipped from me, and I felt that perhaps I had told my story not too poorly.

In any case, George, for you it must mean something to pick up a person from the street and by your genius for encouragement and criticism inveigle this person to produce a book within a few weeks.

No wonder you have New York by the tail!

1

All-American Boy

In 1890, the center of population of the United States moved into Indiana. That brought it ninety miles east of, and approaching, a small rural town sixty-five miles southwest of Indianapolis. This was Worthington, a grain terminal. Hills rose to the north, but the town and surrounding fields of corn, wheat, and oats lay flat. At its eastern edge flowed the Eel River. Worthington, population 1,448, was laid out in a grid, although two railroad lines and the parallel Commercial Street cut its southern end diagonally.

The station agent and telegrapher for one of those railroads, the Indianapolis and Vincennes, was Robert Kirkbride Yardley. A short, heavyset, well-dressed man, he could trace his family to a Thomas Yardley who had come from England to Pennsylvania in 1703. Robert had been promoted to Worthington in 1886 from nearby Freedom, where he had met and married Mary Emma Osborn, a quiet, self-effacing woman. The family lived in a two-story wooden house at 127 West Union Street, the southeast corner of Union and Dayton Streets. A Quaker, Yardley was a deliberate and not particularly friendly man. He never arrived at work early but, as customers fretted and fumed, he unhurriedly and thoroughly got the job done. Though a member of several fraternal organizations, he was regarded as a bit of a character. But he was kind: once, when a farmer's boy came by offering three baby owls in a basket, he bought one for 25¢, perhaps as a pet for one of his three children.

On 13 April 1889, a dry, calm Saturday that was the busiest day Worthington merchants had had in several weeks, the Yardley's second surviving child, Herbert, was born. (The oldest boy had died in a fall from a tree.) He grew to resemble his father in both looks and personality. Neither did things ahead of time. Herbert would start for the town's sole school—a block away—as the bell began ringing and drop into his seat at the final peal. He was regarded as somewhat moody. But he was fun to be around. If, while hunting—he was a good hunter and fisherman in the bottomlands around the river—he could find no game, he would sometimes throw his hat into the air and shoot at it. He also skated on the frozen river; one female companion said he was "a rhythmic figure on the ice. . . . I had many a good skate with him." One day Herbert decided to bake a pie from the blackbirds that abounded in Worthington. The result was a legendary disaster that left blackbird feathers all over the house. Herbert and his friends adored the school janitor, who regaled them with stories; one fall day they filled the basement with firewood for him.

Herbert didn't think only of good times. He was bright. Several teachers remarked on his exceptional keenness of mind and ability to grasp and retain new concepts. A friend from a nearby town shared the general impression that Herb was "the smartest boy in the county." Another friend called him "very brilliant"; a third, "a genius." Still another said, "His mind was on a different level than anyone in town." Herbert read omnivorously. He beat everybody in a word-building contest.

Then, on 9 February 1903, when Herbert was thirteen, his mother died of a heart attack. For a while, his own health declined, and he grew obstreperous, leading his schoolmates in pranks—a situation exacerbated by the mutual dislike between him and the school principal. But Herbert soon curtailed his rebelliousness, joined the Presbyterian church two blocks away—and learned poker.

All seven of Worthington's saloons, with their dim interiors and mysterious odors, irresistible to teenage boys, ran poker games. Herb, fascinated by the game at first sight, determined to learn it. He haunted the bars and, at home, dealt himself hands and studied possible plays. Concluding that a particular bar offered the most action, he befriended the owner and used him as his instructor. He took one lesson particularly to heart: "I figure the odds for every card I draw, and if the odds are not favorable, I fold. This doesn't

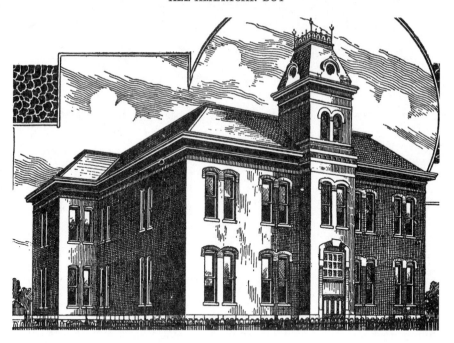

The Worthington grammar and high school Yardley attended

sound very friendly. But what's friendly about poker?" Then, with $200 left him by his mother and some extra money from odd jobs, Yardley, at sixteen, began playing. In a back room with a green-cloth-covered round table, seven chairs set around (each with its spittoon) and a shaded lightbulb hanging over it, he watched men sell farm implements, horses, hogs, a sawmill to play poker. He saw a shoe salesman lose all ten trunks of his shoes. A farmer literally bet the farm against a tent show and died of a heart attack at the call—though he held four aces and had won. Yardley learned how cardsharps cheat. He learned not only about poker but about life. At the saloon he met traveling salesmen, circus owners, magicians, actors, preachers, and atheists, as well as Worthington's own bankers, businessmen, farmers, cattlemen, village idiots. He saw one girl, made pregnant by a chicken picker, turn into a drug addict when the physician who had botched her abortion relieved her pain with too much morphine.

At the same time, Herbert engaged in more respectable activities. The high school literary society elected him attorney; whatever that title meant, it recalled his ambition at the time of becoming a criminal lawyer. He sang baritone in the quartet. He played Lemuel in *The Union Depot* and Bob in *Our Jim.* He was invited to many young people's parties, and traveled—

perhaps on his father's passes—to friends in towns near and far. He and a friend in the county seat at Bloomfield, Don Herold, later a syndicated columnist, pored over the best-selling book *What a Young Boy Ought to Know.* He organized a sandlot baseball team, running it from his position as catcher; he also pitched.

And Herb was an outstanding athlete. He quarterbacked the high school football team, and on defense played safety because he was fast and the best tackler, even though he was small. In 1905, when he was a sophomore, Worthington won two games out of six. The next year, when he had been elected captain, the purple and white won three out of four. When a succession of plays advanced the ball for the second touchdown in the 23–5 victory over Bicknell, Herbert was one of the players. And when he was no longer in school and the team had gained the Southern Indiana football championship, the newspaper commented that "Clay Adkins and Herbert Yardley, too, must be given some of the credit of the remarkable showing made this season."

In May 1906, at age seventeen, Herbert rode the rails to Denver, and the following summer repeated the trip with his good friend John Owen. Their money was gone long before they reached their destination and they resorted to knocking on back doors for food. But whenever a pretty girl answered the door, Herbert, apparently shy, mumbled something and turned away. Among other jobs in Denver, Herbert tended bar. He made John promise not to tell anyone in Worthington about it. The next summer, he worked at the Worthington rail depot. He toted baggage, checked freight to and from the draymen, sealed freight cars, and delivered telegrams for $21.20 a month. And he learned telegraphy from his father—his main reason for working there. He picked it up "like I learned to talk," he said. When he expressed dissatisfaction with his telegrapher's paraph, or signature, HY, protesting that he wanted three letters, his friend Rose asked him what his mother's maiden name was. "Osborn," Yardley replied—and HOY was born.

The Worthington school tradition of rivalry between juniors and seniors over class flags celebrated Herbert, the ringleader, in his junior year and disgraced him the next. In April 1906, when he was a junior, the seniors' green-and-white banner flew from the school for a few minutes, taunting the juniors. By recess, it had disappeared. Rumor had it that Herbert had stolen into the school belfry and spent the night there, waiting for the right moment to drop the flag to Floyd Clifford. The following year, with Herbert now a senior and president of the class, its members raised a six-by-eleven-foot flag over the high school. It bore the painting of a mule with a man leading it and two women whipping it. The five seniors involved in the prank insisted that it was not intended to insult the principal or the high school teachers but merely to tease the juniors. When they refused to take it down, the principal climbed the belfry and removed it himself. He then suspended the five and sent them home. Leading the list was Herbert Yardley. Three seniors apologized to the school a few days later—but not Herbert or John Owen. Two teachers resigned to protest the principal's move, and Herbert and John were given until 9 a.m. Monday to apologize. They refused, and their suspensions became permanent. The following week, at the end of April, the fourteen other members of the class graduated. Herbert went to Eaton Rapids, Michigan. He graduated from the high school there and was home by 25 June; a week later he was pitching the Worthington baseball team to a 12–8 victory.

Herb got into more serious trouble in the summer of 1909. A few days before the Fourth of July, he and some friends were setting off firecrackers. Shortly before midnight, Mrs. Mattie Cox called the town marshal to complain that the smoke was suffocating and the reports deafening. The marshal went to the scene. The revelers fled, so he hid himself. Then he heard another firecracker and saw four young men running. Chasing them, the marshal stumbled and his gun went off. The bullet struck Herbert in the thigh. "I regret that he was shot," the marshal said later. "I had no intention of shooting anyone." The injury was not serious: by November Herbert was watching a football game at nearby Linton.

Mischievous he may have been, but he was also honest. In a football game between Worthington and Odon, he served as referee. Once he was caught not at work when a friend was covering for him; his boss tried to give him an excuse but he refused to lie, saying he had left deliberately. He expected to be fired; instead he was promoted. A friend said he never knew Herb to lie or cheat.

So in those sunny years in the heart of America, which had beaten Spain, grabbed the Philippines, sailed its Great White Fleet around the world, dug the Panama Canal, sold horseless carriages, gaped at the airplane, embraced its manifest destiny, prospered, and burst with optimism, Herbert O. Yardley grew to smart, energetic, in-charge young manhood.

After graduation, Herb took a job as a railroad telegrapher, building on the training and experience he had gained while working for his father. The job consisted essentially of acknowledging and transmitting the orders of a railroad dispatcher to control the movements of trains in his district. The

OATH OF ALLEGIANCE AND OFFICE.

I, *Herbert O. Yardley*, of *Indiana*,
appointed, *on probation, a Clerk in the Department of State* of the
United States at *$ 900 per annum*, do
solemnly swear that I will support and defend the Constitution of the United
States against all enemies, foreign and domestic; that I will bear true faith
and allegiance to the same; that I take this obligation freely, without any
mental reservation or purpose of evasion; and that I will well and faith-
fully discharge the duties of the office on which I am about to enter. So
help me God.

Name as above **Herbert O. Yardley**

Sworn and subscribed before me, a Notary Public in and for the District
of Columbia, this **23** day of **December**,
A. D. 191**2**.

Miles M. Shand
Notary Public.

Yardley's oath of office into government service

dispatcher would, for example, direct one train on a single track to wait on a
siding while a more important train used the track. The telegrapher often
worked in the bay window of a depot, with views up and down the track.
The primary requirement for a telegrapher—besides, of course, fluency in
Morse code—was a high degree of literacy, which Yardley certainly possessed.
He or she (a few telegraphers were women) also had to be conversant with
railroad terminology and often utilized codes or abbreviations, such as "DS"
for *dispatcher* and "73" for *best wishes*. Yardley worked at different depots
around the state, ending up in Indianapolis, whence he visited home from
time to time.

In 1912, he took a civil service examination for a government telegrapher.
Three men, of whom Yardley had scored the highest, were certified. He was
hired for a job in Washington, and on 23 December took the oath of office as

a clerk in the Department of State. Herbert traveled home several times, and on one trip proposed marriage to the girl next door. She was Hazel Milam, who lived across the alley between her family's house, at the southwest corner of Union and Edwards Streets, and the Yardleys'. Born 4 March 1889, she was five weeks older than Herbert, tiny at five feet, quiet, and plain, but her father, Abraham Lincoln Milam, an undertaker and owner of a furniture store—and an outstanding fisherman—was one of the town's civic leaders. In 1900, he served as a delegate to the Democratic district convention. Later he and his wife helped start Worthington's first library; their daughter became the town's first librarian. As a teenager, Hazel had hosted parties, been invited to others, and served as a member of a girls' group. She had shared the spotlight with Herb on several occasions; when he was elected attorney of the literary group, she gave a speech. She was not the first girl Herbert was interested in—he once visited an Ellen Piel in Vincennes.

By 1 April 1914, when Herbert got a raise from $900 to $1,000 a year, many of the other girls his age—Hazel's friends—had left Worthington. Hazel, moreover, was a bit of a belle, and Herb may have gazed longingly at the parties she and her parents held in the house across the alley—and at the Milams' money. She may have adored him from a distance, and may have been as lonely in Worthington as he was in Washington. Their engagement was announced 12 May. Hazel quit her job and a week later left for Washington, her father accompanying her to Indianapolis. On the day she arrived, Wednesday, 20 May 1914, the Reverend James H. Taylor, at 1464 Newton Street, Northwest, married Hazel Milam and Herbert Yardley, both age twenty-five.

2

His Life's Work

After their wedding, Herbert and Hazel returned to his northeast Washington home at 1009 Seventh Street, a three-story brick house where he probably rented a room. They did not then take a honeymoon. Ties with Worthington remained strong. Hazel visited her parents in September; the following July, 1915, the couple's kid brothers, Dick Yardley and Pat Milam, visited the pair; in 1916 Hazel, wisely escaping Washington's heat, spent the summer with her parents. In 1917 she took a job in a depot of the quartermaster corps as a typist at $1,000 a year. She and Herbert later moved to a small, two-story row house with an attic and a porch at 542 Shepherd Street, also in northeast Washington.

Herbert took correspondence courses from the University of Chicago, declaring English as his major. He had apparently abandoned his earlier ambition to be a lawyer in favor of writing—perhaps influenced by the success of one of the most popular authors in America, Booth Tarkington, like Yardley a Hoosier. Yardley got Bs in English I and III and a B minus in The Short Story in English and American Literature. He began English IV with a young instructor, Carl Grabo, but never completed the course. His work, meanwhile, was in the State-War-Navy (now Old Executive Office) building, a baroque gray sand castle of a structure next to the White House. Nobody has caught the feeling of its code room, Room 106, better than Yardley:

> This spacious room with its high ceiling overlooked the southern White House grounds. By lifting my eyes from my work I could see a tennis game in progress where a few years earlier President [Theodore] Roosevelt and his tennis Cabinet had played each day.
>
> Along one side of the room ran a long oak telegraph table with its stuttering resonators and sounders; cabinets containing copies of current telegrams almost blocked the entrance. In the center sprawled two enormous flat-topped desks shoved together, about which a few code clerks thumbed code books and scribbled rapidly, pausing now and then to light cigarettes. The pounding of typewriters specially constructed to make fifteen copies of a telegram mingled with the muffled click of the telegraph instruments. The walls were covered with old-fashioned closed cupboards filled with bound copies of telegrams from and to consular and diplomatic posts throughout the world. In the corner stood a huge safe, its thick doors slightly ajar.
>
> There was an air of good-fellowship in the room and I was soon at home. However, I was mystified at the casual attitudes of these overworked code clerks. Daily history passed through their hands in one long stream and they thought less of it than of the baseball scores.

Yardley, however, liked history. When, on the night shift, work eased and the department's officials gathered to relax, he enjoyed listening to their exploits—diplomatic and amorous. He was especially fond of the no-nonsense William T. S. Doyle, the chief of the Latin American division and the author of dollar diplomacy. He spellbound Yardley with stories of his machinations in Latin America, and Yardley would afterward pull down the cables and read, on the yellow Telegram Received forms or the green Telegram Sent forms, the contemporary record of his exploits. Disclosure of some of these might have been fatal to Doyle's intrigues, or at least embarrassing, and Yardley began to ask himself whether those secrets were safe from prying eyes. Did American codes truly protect these messages? He thought other countries might have people to try to break these codes and he wondered why America didn't have an agency of its own to solve and read foreign messages.

"As I asked myself this question I knew that I had the answer to my eager young mind which was searching for a purpose in life," he wrote. "I would devote my life to cryptography. Perhaps I too, like the foreign cryptographer, could open the secrets of the capitals of the world. I now began a methodical plan to prepare myself."

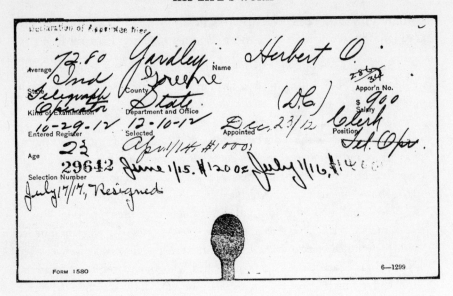

Card on Yardley from his personnel file

Knowing of Poe's short story "The Gold-Bug," he searched through the author's letters for more information about cryptology. Aside from Poe's elementary essay "A Few Words about Secret Writing," Yardley found only boasts. He perused the books on cryptology in the Library of Congress, most of them in French, and, though he could read foreign languages but poorly, if at all, gleaned some information from their diagrams of cipher systems. He read the U.S. Army's manual—the first book on cryptology published in the United States since 1874.

The manual revealed that the army had advanced more in the field than Yardley had suspected. In 1911, a year before he joined the State Department, the Army Signal School at Fort Leavenworth held a conference on cryptology. A captain of Britain's Royal Field Artillery read a paper titled "Military Cryptography," and students responded with papers of their own. One of them, Lieutenant Joseph O. Mauborgne, a tall, good-looking, outgoing man who had participated with Lieutenant H. H. (Hap) Arnold in the world's first ground-to-air radio transmission and who was an excellent artist and a cellist whose playing "would wring your heart out," later whiled away the tedium of a transpacific crossing by solving a long test message from the captain in the British field cipher, the Playfair; the U.S. Army published his exposition in 1914, making Mauborgne's the first known solution of the system. Another student, Captain Parker Hitt, an instructor at Leavenworth, had an aptitude for cryptanalysis. A six-foot-four-inch native of Indianapolis, Hitt had solved insurgents' ciphers during the Aguinaldo-led insurrection against American rule in the Philippines after the takeover of 1898. Later, he and other army officers in the Southwest solved Mexican messages intercepted or captured during the Pershing punitive expedition and other troubles along the border. Hitt deepened his experience—greater than that of any other person in the country at the time—with theory and information from European books on cryptology and with teaching elementary cryptanalysis at the Signal School. He molded this into an excellent book, clear and succinct, which the army published in 1916 as the 101-page softbound *Manual for the Solution of Military Ciphers.* When the War Department asked the Army Signal School for the names of persons who might solve cryptograms that came to it, Hitt's led the list as "undoubtedly the best cipher man in our service." Seven others were named, including Mauborgne. But army cryptanalysis was not centralized, and Yardley seems not to have known of it.

Hitt's book completed Yardley's search for instruction. Nothing else was available. And Hitt's work, valuable as it was, explained breaking only ciphers, not codes. Field forces used ciphers, he believed, as did the United States Army, the Mexicans, the Filipinos. But the World War I armies of both sides on the western front were even then shifting to trench codes. These books of a few score pages, giving the codewords or codenumbers for a few thousand plaintext words and phrases, were easier to use than the complicated cipher systems then in service. Their chief defect—that capture of one copy would compromise all messages using that code—was obviated by making them small and replacing them frequently. Hitt did not know of this development, then just getting under way, and cryptanalysis of the thousand-page codes used by navies and foreign offices exceeded both his knowledge and his mandate. So he omitted information about the breaking of codes.

Yardley had therefore to study on his own. Friends brought him the encrypted communications of foreign embassies in Washington, and he began with the unavoidable drudgery: counting how many times groups of letters or numbers appeared. Some countries, particularly in Latin America, used primitive ciphers. Yardley solved some messages and failed with others.

"One night, business being quiet," he recalled, "I heard the cable office in New York tell the White House telegraph operator (we used the same wire to New York) that he had five hundred code words from Colonel House to the President. As the telegram flashed over the wire I made a copy. This would be good material to work on, for surely the President and his trusted agent would be using a difficult code." President Woodrow Wilson had sent

Edward House to Europe to propose a peace conference. Within two hours Yardley had discovered that the president and his confidant had merely renumbered the central pages of a State Department code in reverse order, starting on printed page 739 by handwriting in number 113. The cable, of 29 March 1915, stated that "The situation in Germany is this: Peace is desired generally. . . . The problem is to save the face of the authorities." Yardley was shocked at how easily he solved the message—though of course he had the codebook and had only to determine the renumbering. "Colonel House must be the Allies' best informant!" he exclaimed. And with so simple a code he may well have been.

This perhaps spurred Yardley's major project: an analysis of the American diplomatic codes. Three then existed. The RED—so called from the color of its binding—had been compiled by John H. Haswell, an Albany-born lawyer. As chief of the Bureau of Indexes and Archives, the unit that handled communications, he had examined State's older systems and proposed a new one, which he introduced in 1876. The twelve-hundred-page RED would encode *The President directs me* into either the codeword PLANT or the codenumber 44384; the clerk could choose whether he wanted to transmit letters or numbers, perhaps on the bases of cable economy or security. Either numbers or letters could be further disguised. In 1898, four years after his retirement and almost a quarter of a century after the RED began to serve, Haswell, insightfully warning the secretary of state that other powers copied and tried to solve American diplomatic messages, urged a new code. He got the job, being paid $3,000. The BLUE code, with fifteen hundred pages, entered service in 1899 (it was the one Wilson and House renumbered). But it proved inadequate for the new worldwide range of American diplomacy, for in 1910 the department issued its fourteen-hundred-page GREEN code.

These codes were known to Yardley from his work, so his study presumably concerned their weaknesses and how these might be exploited by a foreign cryptanalyst. Eventually, he handed his hundred-page "Solution of American Diplomatic Codes" to his boss, David A. Salmon, the new chief of Indexes and Archives. A native of Westport, Connecticut, with a club foot, Salmon had been brought from the War Department to State to improve Haswell's outdated filing system. At thirty-six, Salmon seemed insecure in his job, possibly because its organizational difficulties overwhelmed him, and he certainly recognized his lack of knowledge in cryptologic matters. Salmon studied Yardley's paper, which he generously called "a masterly piece of analysis," and a month later introduced a new method to preserve cryptologic security. It divided State's five-letter codegroups in a variety of ways according to a key and then replaced the two-letter groups and the single letters with other letters. State assumed that the codebook and the replacement tables were known to the enemy—and thus to Yardley—but that the points of division were kept secret. Solving this problem does not appear to have been tremendously difficult. Yardley eagerly attacked it. "My fingers itched to tear it apart. . . . It was the first thing I thought of when I awakened, the last when I fell asleep," he wrote, describing what is now called the "Yardley symptom" in cryptologic literature. In March 1916, he succeeded. He believed his to be "the first successful attempt to solve a problem in enciphered code." It was certainly such in the United States, but European powers may have been doing it earlier.

Tension with Germany had been mounting at least since the sinking of the *Lusitania*. On 6 April 1917, Wilson, concerned about German aggression, asked Congress to declare war on that empire, and Congress did so. This offered Yardley the opportunity of his life. He had looked into the vulnerabilities of American codes and had wondered whether foreign codes might not be vulnerable as well. Now that the United States was at war, should it not attack enemy codes? And shouldn't he, who had studied cryptography, head an organ to do this? He spoke first to Salmon, who eventually wrote a letter commending him as a cryptologist. He got recommendations from some army and navy officers he knew. Finally he was steered to one Major Van Deman.

3

A History of American Intelligence
before Yardley

Ralph Van Deman was in charge of military intelligence. But neither he nor Yardley knew much about the background of that activity.

It had begun even before the nation came into being. As head of the Continental Army, General George Washington sought information about British activity. He dispatched one of his first spies only eleven weeks after independence was declared. The mission failed. Nathan Hale was captured while trying to return to American lines, but he immortalized himself by saying that he regretted that he had only one life to lose for his country. Washington improved as spymaster as the Revolution proceeded. By 1779, he was all but running the Culper ring, which operated out of Long Island. One spy, Culper Jr., he directed "to remain in the City [of New York], to collect all the useful information he can—to do this he should mix as much as possible among the officers and Refugees, to visit the Coffee Houses, and all public places. He is to pay particular attention to the movements by land and water in and about the city especially." He warned too of the need for security: dispatches should be delivered only to those assigned to receive them and forwarded "to no one but the Commander-in-Chief." The ring's spies encoded their reports, wrote some in invisible ink, and hid them for pickup in a hollow tree trunk—what would later be called a "dead drop." They told Washington how many Redcoats were stationed where, what warships were anchored in New York harbor, what provisions were entering the town, and the like. He found their reports "intelligent, clear and satisfactory." But though he avidly sought spy information, none of it helped him win any battles. It seemed to provide him with a general picture of the situation—not as dramatic as a victory, but useful, if only in preventing a possible defeat.

Washington's most valuable information came from communications intelligence. America's first cryptanalyst, James Lovell, a Harvard graduate, teacher, and member of the Continental Congress, solved a British dispatch revealing that a Royal Navy fleet planned to relieve Lord Charles Cornwallis, blockaded in Yorktown. Delivered to the French naval force, it scared off the British, ending any hope of rescuing Cornwallis, who had just surrendered. This set the seal of final victory on the American Revolution.

But as useful as this intelligence was, and as enthusiastic and wise as Washington had been in seeking and exploiting information, the new American army did not incorporate a permanent unit for seeking and evaluating intelligence into its organization. Neither did any other army or navy of the time. For though commanders always sought information, often it arrived too late to be useful, seldom could it be trusted, and almost never did it award them victory. The military had little confidence in it. In only one of Edward Creasy's *Fifteen Decisive Battles of the World: From Marathon to Waterloo* did foreknowledge of the enemy matter—the battle of the Metaurus River in Italy in 207 B.C., in which an intercepted Carthaginian message enabled the Romans to concentrate and defeat Hasdrubal before his brother Hannibal could reinforce him. The other fourteen battles were won by strength, brains, and will. Carl von Clausewitz epitomized this historical insignificance of intelligence when he gave it but three scornful paragraphs in *Vom Kriege*.

This situation did not change during the Civil War. Most information about enemy forces came, as it had for millennia, from scouts on foot and on horse and from larger cavalry reconnaissance troops. Prisoner and civilian interrogations filled in details, which sometimes were even accurate. The more glamorous tools of balloon observation, intercepted signals, and espionage rarely added anything of value. It is true that Rebel spy Rose Greenhow learned of the Union decision in 1861 to advance on Manassas, leading to the Confederate victory at First Bull Run. And Yankee spy Elizabeth Van Lew forwarded reams of occasionally correct spy reports to the Federals. Allan Pinkerton, head of a detective agency, set up a Secret Service of the

Army for the Union's Army of the Potomac. He did well in counteres-pionage, arresting Greenhow, but less well in espionage. The reports from the spies he sent behind Confederate lines led him to overestimate Rebel strength, encouraging Major General George B. McClellan's tendency to procrastinate. The North lofted tethered balloons in 1861, using them pri-marily to spot enemy positions and movements. In a typical case, aerial observation told General Charles Stone that the Rebel force across the Poto-mac that he was surveilling consisted of only four Mississippi infantry regi-ments and a Virginia battery. The South had no balloons. Both sides fre-quently tapped one another's telegraph wires and read one another's optical signals, most messages being sent unencrypted. Of those that were en-crypted, the South's polyalphabetic substitutions were often solved by Union telegraphers, while the North's route transposition system defied Rebel at-tempts to break it. All in all, intelligence made but trivial contributions to the battles of the Civil War, on either side.

With the end of that struggle, the army forgot intelligence. Because in-telligence units had varied from corps to corps, from department to de-partment, no one pattern could suggest itself to the postwar army. Most importantly, the war had been won without intelligence, and no obvious intelligence targets presented themselves afterward. So the army did not establish any agency for intelligence. It went back to subduing the Indians.

But military technology had by then begun to advance at a dizzying rate. Muzzle-loading guns were replaced by breech-loaders. Smooth-bore cannon gave way to rifled ones; cannonballs, to explosive shells; wooden ships, to ironclads. Steam had already replaced sails at sea and horses on land. Pro-pellers took the place of paddlewheels and rails, that of roads. The machine gun intensified firepower. The telegraph facilitated control. The railroad enabled nations to mobilize and deploy their large armies with timetable precision and to supply them in the field. Intelligence was needed more than ever to keep up with these developments. It also gained for the first time a target of great value: war plans. Knowledge of these gave commanders more specifics about enemy mobilization and likely offensives than older, more generalized campaign plans and consequently allowed more time to prepare defenses than ever before.

As these technological horizons were expanding, so were America's politi-cal and economic ones. California had become a state in 1850; Japan was opened to trade in 1854; China, in 1858. Alaska had been bought in 1867; the transcontinental railroad was completed in 1869. The nation paid in-creased attention to the Pacific—and then to the world, as the European nations scrambled for colonies in Africa, Asia, even distant Samoa. In 1874, U.S. exports permanently exceeded the value of imports.

These currents pushed the American army and navy toward establishing intelligence sections. But for a while countervailing tendencies deflected that trend. The nation was protected physically by oceans and politically by the Monroe Doctrine. The United States didn't need intelligence. Moreover, collecting information reeked of spies and militarism—dishonest, undemocratic concepts. The United States didn't want intelligence. Conservative officers opposed the concept, in part because it had never been done, in part because new specialists would compete with them for promotions. They rejected intelligence.

But the pressures of technology and the nation's growing interaction with the world drove the armed forces finally to see that more and better information was needed. The secretary of the navy established the Office of Intelligence on 23 March 1882. Three years later, the army's adjutant general, Brigadier General R. C. Drum, acting, it is said, on a suggestion of the secretary of war because foreign information for which he had asked was not available, assigned an officer and a clerk to collect information about foreign militaries. On 12 April 1889, the secretary formally authorized a Military Information Division within the adjutant general's office, and Congress the following year appropriated $1,500 "for the pay of a clerk attendant on the collection and classification of military intelligence from abroad." At last the United States had formal intelligence agencies in its armed forces—a permanent institution for the first time.

In three years, the Military Information Division grew large enough to be reorganized into four branches, in part because much of its work dealt with American mobilization plans and instruction. Yet no spies sought secret intelligence about other countries. No American company or government agency intercepted cablegrams, much less solved any that were encoded. Since the United States was not at war, no cavalry or infantry patrols fed information to field commanders and thence to the intelligence agency. The only foreign intelligence that it obtained, apart perhaps from maps, came from the military and naval attachés newly dispatched to the major European capitals.

Despite the Military Information Division's organizational suffocation— it lay not under the commanding general of the army but under one of the secretary of war's bureaus that dealt with logistical, fiscal, and administrative matters—it quickened for a while under the command of an excellent leader, one of the first in the American army to recognize the importance of intelligence. Colonel Arthur L. Wagner, an outstanding personality who had helped the School of Application for Infantry and Cavalry evolve into the General Service and Staff College, had published in 1893 the first American work on intelligence, *The Service of Security and Information.* As tensions grew with Spain, he asked for permission to send one of his officers "to examine and report on the military situation" in Cuba. When the Spanish-American War broke out, he dispatched Lieutenant Andrew W. Rowan on his famous "mission to Garcia"—a reconnaissance that brought back maps and other intelligence from the insurgent Cubans. Wagner wangled himself into a cavalry unit, fought in Santiago, and after the war returned to the staff college before directing the Army War College. He died in 1905. But he and his missionary zeal for intelligence had excited a subordinate.

Lieutenant Ralph Van Deman first walked into the three-room office of the Military Information Division on the main floor of the State-War-Navy building in June 1897. Tall and gaunt, with big ears, he had been born in Ohio the last year of the Civil War, had graduated from Harvard in 1888, spent a year in its law school, and accepted an infantry commission in 1891. The army let him complete a medical degree from Miami University in Ohio. During the Spanish-American War, he had charge of the White House war map. Wagner's evangelism for intelligence persuaded him of its importance, for when, sent to the Philippines to help fight the Aguinaldo insurrection, he was assigned to convert the Bureau of Insurgent Records into a Military Intelligence Division there, he accepted the job not reluctantly, as did most officers assigned to intelligence, but with interest and effectiveness. Van Deman discovered a plot for an attack on Manila, which was thwarted.

In the United States, meanwhile, Congress and the press were exposing the army's embarrassing lack of planning during the Spanish-American War, with its insufficient and rancid rations, its distribution of Civil War winter uniforms for a July campaign in Cuba, its employment of black powder instead of smokeless, its bungled troop embarcations, its inadequate medical supervision. The outraged nation and the new secretary of war, Elihu Root, demanded a better system. The English writer Spenser Wilkinson's *The Brain of an Army* and General Emory Upton's *The Armies of Asia and Europe* publicized the idea of the general staff. Prussia had proved its effectiveness when it engineered the speedy and efficient victories over Denmark in 1864, Austria in 1866, and France in 1870–71. Though America's fear of militarism joined the army's bureau chiefs and the commanding general in opposing the idea, an ethos of progress and new concepts of scientific management helped Root convince Congress of its soundness. The bill creating a general staff was approved by President Theodore Roosevelt on 14 February 1903.

Where should the intelligence function be put? Britain merged it with operations. Prussia incorporated it into its two war-planning sections, east and west; it formed a separate intelligence element only on mobilization, reverting to the peacetime amalgam after hostilities ended. France, however, specified intelligence as the second bureau of its general staff. When the U.S. army organized its staff, the Americans copied this numeration, making intelligence the second division of their staff, the later G-2. But in 1908, intelligence was joined with the third division, ending its separate identity. Van Deman, who had held several intelligence posts in the normal rotation of army duties, arrived at that division in July 1915. Then, in 1916, despite World War I in Europe, Congress in effect cut the Washington staff, leaving Van Deman as the only officer there with any experience in intelligence. But neither he nor any of the American observers abroad recognized the tremendous changes that activity was undergoing during the conflict.

Intelligence was expanding enormously, not only in volume, but in value, primarily from a new form of information. This was not spies, long regarded as a chief source. Their information was slow and infrequent; it was subjective; it came from untrained observers and so was often erroneous; and it was suspect—the agent may have reported correctly in the past only to set up a deception. Trench warfare produced volumes of prisoners, but they could tell about little more than the units to which they belonged and the weapons they served. Captured documents and matériel likewise yielded mainly order of battle information and technical detail. Aerial reconnaissance—by eye or camera and from balloon or airplane—indeed became so good that after 1917 neither the Allies nor the Central Powers dared move troops in daylight hours.

But though photographs may persuade best of all, radio intelligence proved the most valuable. Radio has the great military advantage of being able to communicate quickly, easily, and cheaply. The disadvantage is that those communications can also be intercepted quickly, easily, and cheaply. And the intelligence produced from communications is extraordinarily trustworthy: it consists of the very words of the enemy. (Commanders have almost never tried to trick the enemy with fake messages, because they can too easily be mistaken for real.) Usually, it is not sporadic but voluminous and continuous. Moreover, the intercepts often consist of plans and orders. As a consequence, communications intelligence—in particular its cryptanalytic branch—gave skeptical commanders confidence in intelligence for the first time. Though no one in American intelligence then knew it, that source had helped Germany defeat czarist Russia, paving the way for the Communist revolution. It enabled France—the war's greatest cryptanalytic power—to block Germany's supreme offensives on the western front in 1918. It had produced the greatest intelligence coup of all time, the disclosure that German foreign minister Arthur Zimmermann was offering Mexico three American states if it would join with Germany in warring on America—a plot that, when made public, helped push the United States into the war and into world power. So communications intelligence was making intelligence into a significant instrument of war, no longer mistrusted but accepted and even welcomed by admirals, generals, and statesmen. This was the source that Yardley wanted to bring to America. But since it was not yet known or accepted there—the army's *Field Service Regulations* never mentioned it among the forms of information—he faced a struggle against ignorance and inertia.

On 11 April 1917, five days after the United States declared war on Germany, the head of the Army War College proposed that the general staff organize a military intelligence unit. He thought it should be a division separate from his. But the chief of staff directed instead that the War College supervise military intelligence. On 3 May the secretary of war approved. Van Deman, the only person in Washington who knew anything about the subject, was chosen to head the section, and thus became the individual to whom Yardley was directed.

Van Deman's office was in the War College building. This handsome McKim, Mead and White structure, with its elegant semicircular entrance entablature, rose in solitary splendor at the end of a parade ground on the shores of the Anacostia River where it joins the Potomac. Yardley went to it by trolley, bearing with him the idea that would forever change American intelligence.

Van Deman's face reminded Yardley of that of a beardless Lincoln. He looked tired, but he grew intensely interested as Yardley outlined the need for codebreaking services in Washington to solve foreign diplomatic messages and on the western front to break enemy military messages. Van Deman knew that "neither the State Department nor the War Department has any real experts on cipher work," yet the possibility of the army's having its own codebreaking agency in Washington seems to have surprised him. Of the memoranda about setting up an intelligence unit only one had even mentioned "analyzing the enemy's codes and ciphers"—and that in passing, within a list—and did not propose a separate unit for it. Hitt, Mauborgne, and the army's other significant cryptanalyst, Frank Moorman, had duties elsewhere, so Van Deman had accepted an offer from a private research organization near Chicago to solve ciphers for the government. But Yardley's conviction of his mission intensified his normal persuasiveness. Though young and inexperienced, he convinced Van Deman that the general staff needed its own cryptanalytic unit.

And the major did something about it. He arranged for Yardley's release from the State Department and for his commissioning. On 29 June, Yardley became a first lieutenant in the Signal Corps in the National Army—the organization into which draftees and volunteers were enrolled—with serial number O-159744. On 5 July, he was assigned to active duty. On 11 July, he was ordered to report to the War College Division, and soon thereafter he established and, as its sole officer, took charge of MI-8—military intelligence, section 8. Thus began America's first official cryptologic agency. No guns boomed, no drums rolled, no troops paraded. But, unnoticed though it was, it marked one of the most significant steps in American intelligence.

For an office, Yardley was given a few square feet on a narrow balcony on the north side of the west wing of the War College building overlooking the library stacks. Lit by one of the wing's semicircular lunettes, it had barely enough space for a desk for Yardley and a clerk or two. No walls or partitions set it apart. The floor was a grating. This was the cradle of American cryptology. Rocking it was its father, Herbert Yardley.

He was twenty-eight years old, five feet five inches tall, 125 pounds. His head was round atop a short neck. His nose was straight and small; his hair was light brown, but his early baldness gave him a high forehead. He walked with short quick steps. He was convincing when he talked, tending to dominate a conversation, and he told stories well. He was bright. He had gained self-confidence and experience in organizing and running things from his presidency of his high school class, his captaincy of the football team, his acting in school plays, his creation of the sandlot baseball game, his leadership of many high school pranks, and his general popularity. He had broken some codes and believed he could crack others. He was ambitious. And now he had, via cryptology, a chance to be not an underling, but a boss. Sure that he could handle the opportunity, he seized it.

But he had no personnel, no organization, no clout. And so the code-breaking went by default to the think tank outside Chicago.

4

A Rival

George Fabyan usually wore riding or yachting attire, though he never rode a horse or sailed a boat. He parroted the phraseology of the learned, even though he was a high school dropout. At fifty, he was tall and thickset, with a high forehead, a straight nose, a dark Vandyke beard, and an imperious manner. Instead of speaking, he bellowed. Instead of laughing, he guffawed. He used profanity. He bossed people around. He butted into their private lives. He was rich.

Fabyan was the multimillionaire owner of a cotton-goods business inherited from his father. Around the turn of the century, he acquired an estate, which he called Riverbank, that straddled the Fox River in Geneva, Illinois, twenty-five miles southwest of Chicago. He hired Frank Lloyd Wright to remodel the house. He built tennis courts, a gazebo, a sunken pond, a Japanese garden, and a zoo with an aviary, monkeys, ten-foot snakes, and alligators; he also brought in a windmill, reconstructed a lighthouse, and farmed, maintaining a staff of one hundred to run the place. Fabyan studied—or, rather, paid for the study of—acoustics, genetics, and the theory that Francis Bacon wrote the works of William Shakespeare. For this, he hired a team of eight or ten women to investigate the messages that he thought Bacon had cryptographically hidden in the plays to prove his authorship. The women dined well at formal dinners each night and could play tennis and swim in the icy, spring-fed waters of the pool but were underpaid and controlled by Fabyan. He bought a number of seventeenth- and eighteenth-century books on cryptology. On 15 March 1917, as America's entry into World War I grew increasingly likely, Fabyan, who held an honorary colonelcy from the governor of Illinois, offered military intelligence his books and any information on cryptology that he had and invited a man at his expense to see the work. He visited Van Deman to discuss military cryptography. Yardley had not yet contacted Van Deman.

Lieutenant Mauborgne, head of the Army Signal School and one of the army's three top cryptologic experts, came to Riverbank a few weeks later, after the United States had entered the war. Impressed, Mauborgne urged that the government "take immediate advantage of Col. Fabyan's offer to decipher captured messages." Van Deman, who then knew nothing of Yardley or of his plans, did so at once. At Van Deman's invitation the Justice and Navy Departments, postal censorship, and other organizations participated, most importantly State. Van Deman dealt there with Leland Harrison, a career diplomat, a polo-playing but "mouselike" and unusually reticent individual.

Soon intercepts were being mailed, or, if urgent, telegraphed to Riverbank. The now four men and three women on the first floor of Riverbank's Engledew Cottage, whose Baconian work had not yielded much knowledge of cryptanalysis, learned by doing. And, with the screeches and yowls of Fabyan's exotic menagerie in the background, they often succeeded in breaking messages. On 22 June, for example, Fabyan sent Van Deman some Mexican cryptogram solutions that, he said, were "finished in the wee, small hours by a lot of people who are happy when they get results. This was a particularly hard nut, and they want to know 'If I supposed any one beat them to it'; 'if the work they have done will accomplish any good,' and a thousand and one things of this kind such as children might ask." A month later, Fabyan boasted that "We have had a bully run of luck with work from your friend Mr. Harrison in securing solutions of everything that he deemed important, and for which he was in a hurry. In each case we have been able to send it by return mail." Fabyan reported on 28 July that the previous day's mail had brought seventeen messages for solution and that four had gone out that morning. Much of the work consisted of correspondence between Mexico and Germany, for which Fabyan brought in one German and two Spanish translators. Yardley was then only beginning to organize and staff his new unit.

Fabyan villa at Riverbank, remodeled by Frank Lloyd Wright

One of the Riverbank cryptanalysts was William F. Friedman. A graduate of Cornell, specializing in agriculture, he had been hired by Fabyan in September 1915 to genetically improve the products of his farm. But he turned out to be good with a camera, and the Baconians utilized him to photograph and enlarge pictures of the letters in Shakespeare's First Folio that played a major role in one theory of hidden messages. Another crypt-analyst, Elizebeth Smith, had been brought to Riverbank in 1916 to help read these alleged messages. In the restrictive atmosphere of Riverbank, where there was little for young people to do in the summer, Smith and Friedman discussed their growing skepticism of the Baconian theory. Elizebeth disliked Fabyan, with his coarse, bullying ways, but she considered Friedman handsome, gentle, considerate, polite; he was indeed fastidious in dress, manner, and mind. They wed on 21 May 1917—he was twenty-five, she twenty-three. Cryptology had come to fascinate him— not surprisingly for a geneticist, for, as has been written, "there is no fundamental absolute line between the types of transmission which we use for a telegram and the types of transmission which are theoretically possible for a living organism such as a human being." Elizebeth became "more than a helpmate," though her attraction to cryptology was never as strong as his and never produced the results that his did. To one of their coworkers, it seemed that "They lived and ate ciphers all day long." Friedman abandoned genetics and became head of the Department of Ciphers, which grew in nine or ten months from the original seven members to between twenty-five and thirty-five.

Bliss, Fabyan & Co.

Chicago July 19, 1917.

Dear Major Van Deman:

I beg to acknowledge receipt of two photostats of cipher messages received by the State Department and yours of July 16th.

We will go to work on them, and try to prove that I am mistaken in thinking they are code, but I am afraid that without the code book we will be up against it.

We have had a bully run of luck with work from your friend Mr. Harrison in securing solutions of everything that he deemed important, and for which he was in a hurry. In each case we have been able to send it by return mail, and I hope it has served its purpose. It has meant night work, and burning the candle at both ends.

If you send us anything that you are in a hurry for, and it is more important than any other which we have on hand, please so signify.

The work is coming in bunches, but we manage to get a little out every day.

Loyally yours,

Rec'd W.C.D., G.S., JUL 2 1 1917

Major R. H. Van Deman
Chief, Military Intelligence Section,
Washington, D. C.

Fabyan indicates Riverbank Laboratories will attack intercepts sent to them

Working on the second floor of the Riverbank building that housed the water well, Friedman wrote technical papers. Published by Fabyan on glossy paper with heavy white covers and known as the Riverbank Publications, these became landmarks in the literature of cryptology. Friedman also solved cryptograms, and one of his jobs saved the Allies from a cryptographic calamity—and embarrassed Yardley. The British planned to introduce a cipher device as a new field cipher. The system had been invented around the 1860s by the British scientist Sir Charles Wheatstone (who had, curiously, also invented the field cipher that the device was to replace, the Playfair), but a wartime British army cryptanalyst, J. St. Vincent Plett, had improved the mechanism by utilizing two concentric rings. The outer one, for the plaintext, bore on its circumference the twenty-six letters in jumbled order plus a blank to be used as a word space. The inner one, for the ciphertext, had just the twenty-six letters in a different mixed order. Gears controlled indicators for each alphabet. These made the cryptosystem an irregular polyalphabetic substitution. The British had of course tested the device, as had the French. So had Yardley's MI-8. None could solve cryptograms enciphered in it. By April 1918, the United States was also considering adopting the Plett device. It was regarded as invulnerable, and indeed one argument against it was that, if the Germans captured one and used it, the Allies would be unable to read their cryptograms.

As a final check, the device was submitted to Riverbank. Five sample cryptograms enciphered with the device came to Friedman. He determined that one of the two mixed alphabets was jumbled using the keyword CIPHER. He thought the second would be associated with that word, but he could not get it. He asked Elizebeth Friedman, who was working across the room on another message, to, as she said,

> lean back in my chair, close my eyes, and make my mind blank, at least as blank as possible. Then he would propound to me a question to which I was not to consider the reply to any degree, not even for one second, but instantly to come forth with the word which his question aroused in my mind. I proceeded as he directed. He spoke the word "cipher," and I instantaneously responded, "machine." And in a few moments Bill said I had made a lucky guess. The officer in Washington had broken a fundamental rule, that is, when choosing a key word, never choose one which is associated with the project . . . Bill had not attempted to use it because his meticulous mind's eye saw a device, not a machine. . . . The five test messages were solved and on their way back to Washington within three hours of the time they had been received.

An embarrassed Yardley had to cable a frantic warning to Britain "that messages enciphered by Plett machine have been broken by method of attack different from any considered by inventor, and that system is considered dangerous in presence of enemy."

In the fall of 1917, Yardley lectured at the War College to young military intelligence officers. His speech so fascinated four—not surprising, considering his captivating way of talking—that they volunteered for work in cryptology with the American Expeditionary Forces. Riverbank accepted them for training in November 1917. Friedman handled at least some of the instruction, and the four did well enough to be sent to France. By the end of the year, with Yardley's organization on its feet and solving cryptograms on its own, Riverbank had less to do. The training of the four second lieutenants had gone well, and Fabyan, perhaps sensing the loosening of his grasp on intelligence power, perhaps wishing to continue his patriotic efforts, generously offered to teach codes and ciphers for two or three weeks to two to three men from each army division. The War Department accepted. At his own expense, Fabyan put up seventy-eight men in February and early March at the Aurora Hotel, just south of Riverbank. The men were taught the principles of cryptology with emphasis on the proper use of codes and ciphers. In March and April, a half dozen more men were taught.

But Fabyan increasingly alienated Van Deman, who no longer needed Riverbank as much as before because MI-8 was operating. Besides trying to tell the army how to run its cryptology and taking credit for work that MI-8 had done first, Fabyan was pushy. He pressed Van Deman to give Friedman a commission and to bring another officer into MI-8. Fabyan was also indiscreet. He encouraged a cryptologic society of officers, advertised for books on cryptology and for someone "acquainted with both cipher and code," and pressed to distribute Friedman's Riverbank Publications to people who might be interested. This led to an explosion, then an apology from Van Deman's office, but no change in Fabyan's attitude.

By then the relationship between military intelligence and Riverbank had all but dissipated. In May 1918, Friedman was commissioned and went to France; he became a member of the American Expeditionary Forces' cryptanalytic unit. And Van Deman and State stopped sending intercepts to Riverbank. Yardley had set up the Code and Cipher Solution Subsection, recruiting and organizing a staff for cryptanalysis. The unit was nearby and it was the army's own. So Van Deman forwarded the intercepts that came in from all government departments to MI-8 for solution. Yardley had shifted the center of American cryptology from Chicago to Washington.

5

Staffers, Shorthand, and Secret Ink

When he began, Yardley wanted to break foreign codes, but four things stood in his way. First, Riverbank was doing that work. Second, the British reported that the War Department code was unsafe (probably because they themselves had solved or stolen it), and Yardley was ordered to drop everything and revise War Department cryptosystems. He had Altus E. Prince, a former State Department official with experience in code work, commissioned to take charge of this endeavor. Soon Prince was efficiently running a ten-man code and cipher compilation subsection whose work Yardley had to spend only an hour a day reviewing. Third, although encoding and decoding army correspondence was the job of the adjutant general's office, military intelligence insisted that it handle its own correspondence for security reasons; it dumped this work on its new cryptologic unit, swamping Yardley and his few assistants. Yardley reacted energetically. He had a former private code-room clerk, James E. McKenna, commissioned to run a subsection for these communications. Direct wires were cut in to the cable points, telegraphers and code clerks were hired, a twenty-four-hour office was opened, and eventually almost one hundred messages a day were being handled expeditiously, with exceptionally fast service to the American forces in France.

Yardley's fourth obstacle was the most difficult to overcome: lack of cryptanalysts. Though the Selective Service Act of 18 May 1917 allowed the general staff to expand and permitted branch officers to request that the necessary civilians be commissioned, Yardley faced the same challenge as every other recruiter: to find not just people but good people. "Judging from the letters I found in the files of the War College," he said, "nearly every one in the United States had dabbled in ciphers." Probably many had only invented "unbreakable" ciphers and wanted to give or sell them to the government. They knew nothing about cryptanalysis. Yet even when individuals who seemed to know something about the field appeared, Yardley could not always obtain them. He wrote to Captain Otto Holstein, who had demonstrated a good knowledge of cryptology, that "We sure would welcome you with open arms," only to be told that Holstein's commanding general had said that Holstein "will" stay with the field artillery. One Oswald Jensen of Minnesota applied to aid the war effort as a cryptanalyst, but Yardley had to turn him down because he was not a native-born American. So his hiring efforts were slowed. The recruitment problem was never fully solved.

But Yardley did find some outstanding people. His first hire proved exceptional. John M. Manly was the head of the English department at the University of Chicago. Manly was fifty-two, small, quiet, and stern-looking. He had been interested in cryptology since he was a teenager and had collected some nineteenth-century French works on the subject—the best then available. Around 1915, Manly had been invited by Fabyan to investigate the cipher-based claims that Bacon wrote Shakespeare. This perhaps alerted him to the army's needs, for in March 1917 he visited Van Deman. University business detained him after war was declared, but Manly was commissioned a captain on 3 November. Yardley said he "had the rare gift of originality of mind—in cryptography called 'cipher brains.' He was destined to develop into the most skillful and brilliant of our cryptographers." He became Yardley's chief assistant.

Manly's academic connections helped recruit a staff. He brought in his Chicago colleague in Chaucer studies, Edith Rickert, forty-six, a brilliant and hard-working woman with a countenance of great nobility. The skill of Charles H. Beeson, forty-seven, an associate professor of Latin at Chicago, in detecting sources of error in medieval Latin manuscripts led Manly to invite him to Washington. Curiously, Beeson's dissertation, from the University of Munich, dealt with the *Etymologiae* of the church father St. Isidore of Seville, which is one of the rare medieval writings to mention cryptology. Beeson may also have found a connection to Yardley as a fellow Hoosier and through his official cataloging of the fish in the Eel River, which runs past Worthington, when he was in his early twenties. Another specialist in Middle English, Thomas A. Knott, had studied under Manly. Edgar H. Sturtevant, an authority on Hittite, had received his Ph.D. from Chicago. Not all the academics were from that university. Of bearded Yale professor Frederick Bliss Luquiens it was said "the study of Spanish appears to satisfy every craving of his soul." But codebreaking seemed to gratify it as well, for he proved good at it.

Charles Jastrow Mendelsohn, a soft-faced, bespectacled man, came from a distinguished intellectual family. His father was a rabbi in Wilmington, North Carolina; his mother was a cousin of the phenomenal linguist Morris Jastrow, professor of Semitics at the University of Pennsylvania and the university's librarian; Morris's brother's Ph.D. in psychology was said to have been the first awarded in the United States. Though Mendelsohn had obtained his Ph.D. in classics from the University of Pennsylvania and taught that subject at the City College of New York, he also excelled at mathematics and had won the class prize his freshman year. He had long been interested in cryptology and in war service got himself moved from censorship to MI-8. He later wrote some of the first scholarly articles on the history of the field and eventually assembled one of the finest collections of antiquarian books on it.

One of Yardley's finest cryptanalysts was Victor Weiskopf, a short, stocky man with a crewcut and a pince-nez. He had immigrated from Bavaria when he was sixteen, and had gone to Mexico. There he sold stamps, showed motion pictures from town to town, lost a valuable lead mine in the Mexican Revolution, and, after narrowly missing death when a sniper's bullet was deflected by a trolley wire, joined the Department of Justice as an agent in the Southwest. He solved a number of Mexican ciphers and, when war broke out, began working for MI-8.

Yardley chose as his clerk John C. Meeth, a graduate of Baltimore College, a high school, where he claimed to be a classmate of Babe Ruth. Meeth attended but never graduated from Fordham Law School, where he was a good-enough student to sell his class notes to other students. Short, with a toothbrush moustache, witty, likable, opinionated, charming when he wanted to be, an excellent story teller, he had a beguiling smile and was efficient enough for Yardley to keep him after the war.

Later in the war the future poet Stephen Vincent Benét, still a Yale undergraduate, moved from the State Department code room to MI-8. But his eyes proved too weak for the work, and he lasted only a few weeks.

The navy, which had no cryptanalytic organization of its own, detailed to MI-8 its sole person known to be interested cryptanalysis. Though this naval reservist, Yeoman H. E. Burt, claimed some cryptanalytic results, he conceded that he had not made "the complete and exhaustive study and analysis" that would be necessary to determine whether the German naval code could be solved. He seems never to have attacked it.

By then MI-8 had expanded from the War College balcony to the Colonial, a just-completed apartment house at 15th and M Streets, Northwest. After a brief stay it moved to the top floor of an office building in the 1800 block of F Street, Northwest, where it remained for the rest of the war.

MI-8's neophyte staff had not yet grappled with cryptanalysis when Yardley was faced with an immediate problem. Van Deman summoned him to his office and flourished a letter of several pages that had been sent from the Department of Justice.

"What is this, Yardley? Cipher?"

"Looks like shorthand to me," he replied.

"I've already shown it to my secretary. She says it isn't Gregg or Pitman." Van Deman said it came from a German prisoner of war in America. Yardley got a car to the Library of Congress, learned that the most widely used German shorthand system is Gabelsberger, located a specialist in it, and got the letter translated. It revealed that the POW planned to communicate with his wife by invisible ink and to escape from the prison camp by digging a tunnel. It was the first flake in a blizzard of shorthand letters and other documents, including writings in Yiddish and Arabic, looking to the untutored eye like shorthand, that began arriving at MI-8 as reports of its skill spread to the censorship and other intelligence agencies. Yardley had to organize a subsection to deal with them.

He found Franklin W. Allen, a partner in Hulse and Allen, a widely known firm of law reporters with headquarters in Manhattan and branches in Washington and other cities. Allen not only served for free, even advancing expenses and donating office space; he also leaped energetically into the work. He compiled a list of the foreign shorthand collections in several public and private libraries and collected texts not only in the widely used shorthand systems, such as Gabelsberger and Stolze-Schrey in German and Martí in Spanish, but also in those for Hungarian, Turkish, and the southern Slavic languages. Eventually the unit compiled recognition charts for fifty-four systems. When these failed, Allen sent photocopies of the mysterious missives to experts he thought might recognize the shorthand. If that too failed, the staffers analyzed the document as if it were a cryptogram. This enabled them to transcribe documents in unknown systems. Allen organized and directed the subsection, which employed six persons—not always at the same time—three of whom dealt with German, and two with Spanish documents. Allen also found half a dozen cryptologists for Yardley; Luquiens was one. Censorship, Justice, and others sent dozens of documents to the subsection. Each was transcribed, translated, and forwarded to MI-8. Most proved innocuous. A few suspicious ones led to further investigation, but no prosecutions ensued.

Around the time MI-8 was coming into being, Van Deman became concerned about detecting invisible inks used by German spies, though he may also have considered having some concocted for possible American agents. Brought onto the scene was America's first Nobel Prize winner in chemistry, Theodore W. Richards of Harvard. In his Wolcott Gibbs Memorial Laboratory in Cambridge, Richards was joined by Emmett K. Carver, a twenty-four-year-old Iowan who had just gotten his Ph.D. in chemistry under Richards. They had fun playing with secret inks, though they seemed more interested in inventing new ones than in finding ways of spotting unknown ones. Carver reported happily on 10 September 1917 after a week of work that "We have developed two new methods of invisible writing which are not detected by the general tests." One utilized a $\frac{1}{500}$th solution of blood, developed by dissolving some Rhodamine B extra (an indicating agent) in alcohol with zinc dust and sodium hydroxide; in the other, the agent wrote with a smooth piece of gold. The ink was developed by exposing the writing to vapors of mercury. "The only defect apparent in this method of writing," Carver said, "is that exposure to mercury vapors is a very excellent general method for developing sympathetic inks, and it may be one of the methods used by the Germans." Later they considered using spores that would react with chemicals, and Carver devised a method using rennin as an invisible ink; the developer was milk, which the rennin would curdle. Government agencies sent Richards and Carver suspected items to be tested for secret ink. The two had little luck. Richards early in November 1917 reported that a document sent by Harrison of State "is still under investigation; the small amount of substance indicates that it is either a catalyst or a germ—but thus far we have found neither. Perhaps it is really nothing at all." Of one sent by Van Deman, Richards disclosed that "No. 50 has now been subjected to all the regular tests and some extra ones: e.g., mercury vapor, electroscope for radium, Rhodamine B, etc., with absolutely no outcome."

In November 1917, MI-8 set up a laboratory in the postal censorship office at 541 Washington Street, Manhattan; Carver came from Cambridge to direct it. In July 1918, a second laboratory was set up at military intelligence headquarters at 1330 F Street, Northwest, Washington, headed by Aloysius J. McGrail, a twenty-seven-year-old Harvard graduate who had gotten his Ph.D. in chemistry from Catholic University. Stanley W. Collins, chief chemist of British censorship, came to Washington for two months that summer to instruct the Americans in secret inks, particularly those used by German agents trying to evade censorship, and their detection. He explained that Allied chemists had discovered what amounted to a general reagent that would develop any secret ink. Iodine vapor, blown into a closed cabinet containing a letter suspected of having writing in invisible ink, would settle more heavily into those fibers in the paper that had been disturbed by the ink and make the writing visible, no matter what the ink. It was not necessary to find a specific reagent for each ink.

The New York office examined an average of two thousand suspicious letters a week from the New York censorship, and the Washington office those mailed in from the stations at Seattle, San Francisco, San Antonio, New Orleans, and Key West. With that volume, the iodine vapor test was not practicable. Instead, laboratory assistants—in New York, four women—striped them with chemicals for indications that secret ink might have been used. Only fifty such instances were found.

But secret-ink letters found through detective work helped indict a woman whom Yardley called "the most daring and dangerous spy encountered in American history." Madame Maria de Victorica had been born Baroness Maria von Kretschman, the daughter of a Prussian cavalry officer; her grandmother had been the illegitimate child of Jenny von Pappenheim and Jérôme Bonaparte, one of Napoleon's younger brothers and king of Westphalia. Maria had been reared in garrison towns in Germany. At twenty-five, while visiting relatives in South America, she married. When her husband died, she began a successful career writing for periodicals, being sent to Chile and then to Russia, where she stayed seven months. In 1913, she married an Argentine, whose name is given variously as Manuel Gustave Victorica and as José Manuel Victorica. In Bulgaria when her fatherland went to war, she returned home and began translating articles for the government. In 1916, with the help of naval intelligence, the German Foreign Office sent her to the United States. She was then thirty-eight, intelligent, cultured, with attractive features and blonde hair, but overweight and addicted to morphine.

Her chiefs assigned her to write pro-German articles, to work for an embargo on food and munitions to the Allies, to encourage pacifists among Catholics (she was a convert) and to support Irish nationalists, who were bitterly anti-British. Then she was instructed to run a ring to place bombs on British and Allied merchant ships. After the United States entered the war, the ring planned to sabotage American munitions plants. Her chief associate was Herman Wessels, then thirty-seven, an officer of the Hamburg-Amerika steamship line. He proposed importing explosives hidden in toy blocks. Victorica apparently considered sneaking them in hidden in altars for Catholic churches, but nothing ever happened. Wessels visited a hotel near Lake Hopatcong, New Jersey, perhaps to scout three nearby gunpowder plants, but none was ever sabotaged. Indeed, most of the spies' energy seemed to be spent not on blowing up ships or factories but on planning, organizing, financing, moving, and communicating.

Invisible ink concealed many of the important messages. The ink—which looked like water to one agent—was impregnated into stockings and into a muffler of mixed cotton and silk so it could be transported without arousing suspicion. Many letters covered one page with visible, innocuous writing and left another page blank for the secret writing. Once a Bible contained a secret-ink message. But the spies encountered problems. Sometimes the ink could not be read because the spy had not received the developer. One message became visible by accident when the spy carried the paper next to his skin. Victorica tried but failed to develop the ink in a letter two or three months old. And some of the letters were obtained by military intelligence from German couriers, British and French intelligence, an American postmaster, and arrested suspects. They submitted them to Carver to be developed. He could bring up only portions of the two- or three-month-old letter because the ink had deteriorated with age. He failed, despite many tests, to find any secret writing in a letter from Madrid. But he succeeded brilliantly with the two blank pages of an undated four-page typewritten letter signed "Maud." It gave six cover addresses in neutral countries and instructed the addressee to destroy docks, war industries, and mercury mines. This information, intelligence said, "was the most important that we had had since the outbreak of the war." It alerted the War Industries Board, which took steps to protect mercury plants throughout the country.

Such information as this helped bring some of the conspirators to trial, though not all were convicted. Victorica was arrested on 27 April 1918 in the Hotel Nassau in Long Beach, Long Island. At first she talked freely to the arresting agents, giving, for example, some of Wessels's aliases, which led to his arrest. But she also told a lot of lies. When her interrogators threatened that unless she told the truth she would not have the morphine for which she used to drive to New York two or three times a week, she revealed the entire story. This broke up the ring. By then her addiction required the removal, a physician said, "of large quantities of pus from places on her body made sore by use of the needle." Victorica was never brought to trial. She died of pneumonia in 1920. But military intelligence said hers was the "most important" ring discovered after American entry into the war. And the agency Yardley was running had played a role in revealing it.

MI-8 occasionally had to invade the sanctity of sealed correspondence—as the British were doing. It developed methods for counterfeiting wax seals that might be damaged in opening the letters. Once, after opening a letter to a high Mexican official, MI-8 found that the duplicate seal was too defective to be used. Fortunately, McGrail discovered that the seal had been made with an old Mexican centavo. MI-8 obtained a coin and used that to reseal the letter.

But the agency's main job was Yardley's first love: breaking foreign cryptosystems.

6

The Executive

During these early months of organizing and running America's first communications intelligence agency, Yardley rapidly grew in confidence and decisiveness. In September 1917, for example, in dealing with an inventor's proposal for an improvement in a cipher mechanism that had been solved earlier by Hitt, he directed that "his device really should not be examined" and "we should not return the papers to him." He won his staff's loyalty and credence. Van Deman regarded him and his work as "outstanding" among the military intelligence people. A former subordinate said retrospectively that "Yardley possessed unusual organizing and executive ability. It must be remembered that he started without any organization whatsoever. In addition to his ability as a cryptographer, his foresight in executive work was essential to our success in M.I.8. I know of no one else there in my time who could have built up the organization or perfected it as he did."

Yardley vigorously championed his people. When Friedman's technical Riverbank Publications reached MI-8, he angrily defended its priority. Friedman's first pamphlet was titled *A Method of Reconstructing the Primary Alphabet from a Single One of the Series of Secondary Alphabets*. But Manly had reconstructed such an alphabet in a system dealing with a Mexican cipher. Based on information from Yardley, Van Deman reported to Fabyan that MI-8 had achieved the same results in a way "earlier and more rapid than his." He jabbed that although "the subject has recently been regarded as sufficiently important to justify the publication of a special treatise, . . . we do not regard this discovery as very useful." When on 1 December 1917 six test messages in a system hitherto regarded as unbreakable, the running key Vigenère, were submitted to MI-8, it took only five days to break them. This was a month before Friedman dated the foreword of his second pamphlet, *Methods for the Solution of Running-Key Ciphers,* which Yardley called a "deliberate steal." In April 1918, MI-8 solved a cryptogram produced by a device called the Bazeries cylinder apparently a month or two before the appearance of the Friedman Riverbank Publication that described such a solution. And after Friedman had concluded that the chances of cracking an enciphered code were "too insignificant to be worth consideration," MI-8 solved such a problem the very day it was submitted. Van Deman pointed out that Friedman, though a cryptologic star, was not a wizard. While recognizing Friedman's "excellent work," he told Fabyan that he overestimated the value of Friedman's studies and that "they have not thus far contributed anything essential that had not already been worked out and placed on record here." The question of priority in these matters began a lifetime of rivalry between Yardley and Friedman, at first insignificant and masked by outward friendliness, later all but vitriolic, at least on Friedman's part.

MI-8 was now taking over the solution work that Riverbank had done. Intercepts that had been sent to Illinois were now handled in Washington. Some came from State, some from army or navy radio stations, some from censorship. The navy, which hadn't been able to solve its German intercepts, abdicated its short-lived cryptanalytic effort to MI-8. Some of the cryptograms were solved. But not until about August 1918 were enough cryptanalysts available to seriously dent the pile.

As MI-8's first target, Yardley chose Chile. He made this surprising choice perhaps because he did not have enough German intercepts and because Chile had close ties to Germany—many Germans had settled there and Germany had molded Chile's educational and military structure, including the goose step. Unlike other Latin American countries, Chile had not declared war on Germany, nor even broken diplomatic relations with it. Yardley put Luquiens in charge of attacking Chilean cryptosystems. He and the other cryptanalysts were helped by much collateral information from State, the War Shipping Board, and other agencies and by Chile's felicitous habit of mixing plaintext and code in a single cryptogram. Working on what seemed at first to be three distinct codes, designated A, D, and G, they discovered that the three were but different encipherments of the same one-part code. Though other messages were solved before Chile's, the codebreakers eventually read some eight hundred Chilean cryptograms. The first was a message of 28 January 1918 from Santiago to the embassy in Washington, requesting it to "Advise when the submarine squadron will leave." It referred to five submarines being constructed in New London, Connecticut. They sailed in March and reached the Chilean port of Arica in June.

Yardley oversaw attacks on the cryptosystems of other countries as well. Only one country whose codes were solved could be construed as threatening to the United States: Argentina, which remained neutral. Other solutions were those of countries that either had declared war on Germany, such as Brazil, Nicaragua, and Cuba, or had severed diplomatic relations, such as Peru. The codes of Costa Rica, which had declared war, were obtained by theft. MI-8 never tried to solve the intercepts of Ecuador and El Salvador, perhaps for lack of manpower. And in some cases the agency failed. One such instance involved a Norwegian five-digit code. Captain David H. Stevens thought he saw a crib to such a code in 1918. The U.S. Commission for Relief in Belgium issued a statement 28 August saying that one of its ships, the *Gasconier,* carrying food to Belgium, had been sunk by a U-boat in Norwegian territorial waters; the submarine then fired on the lifeboats, killing six crewmen and wounding several others. Norway protested on 5 September to the United States that the vessel had in fact been sunk by mines outside Norway's waters. Stevens had the Norwegian memorandum, which had been presented in English, translated back into Norwegian to match it with the original cable from Oslo. But the censor could not locate cable 1320, the putative original. Without a match, MI-8 gave up trying to solve Norwegian cryptograms—not, in any event, the highest priority.

Yardley designated Mexico MI-8's second most important target. The government wanted information about that neighbor, still in the turmoil of its revolutions, which hated the imperialistic gringos who dominated its economy, had bombarded Vera Cruz, had invaded it in search of Pancho Villa. Victor Weiskopf, who had been solving Mexican cryptograms on the border before coming to Washington, and cryptanalyst Claus Bogel led the attack. The cryptosystems proved juvenile. The consul general in New York used a monoalphabetic substitution—the simplest kind of cipher, used as puzzle cryptograms in newspapers. One of the ambassador's three systems was also monoalphabetic. The immigration, postal, and telegraphic bureaus of Mexico employed polyalphabetic substitutions with short repeating keywords—

ACTIVO, ROJINA—and straight numerical cipher alphabets. Since the cipher clerks often left parts of the message in plaintext, giving clues to the enciphered parts, MI-8 cracked these messages with minimal effort. Eventually it was reading them at a rate of two or three a day. On 30 September 1917, for example, MI-8 solved a message from Venustiano Carranza, the man who had claimed for himself the leadership of the Mexican Revolution and who hoped for support from Germany. On 7 February 1918, Yardley returned to State's Harrison nine intercepts that MI-8 had solved; on 25 February, he sent back twenty; on 4 March, nineteen. Such solutions gave the government insight into happenings south of the border.

Germany was of course the main enemy. Yardley did not deal with military messages on the western front. These were handled by the radio intelligence section of the American Expeditionary Forces, G.2 A.6, headed by Major Frank Moorman, one of the army's three early cryptanalysts. MI-8 obtained the German diplomatic messages that interested it from a government radio station in Houlton, Maine. Most passed between Berlin and Madrid, Spain being neutral in favor of Germany. Yardley put Charles Mendelsohn in charge of solving the messages, which were in four- and five-digit groups. Mendelsohn and his team, which included Weiskopf and Edith Rickert, were greatly helped by Britain's having given MI-8 a partial reconstruction of 13040—a code of the Zimmermann telegram—and other codes. They took advantage of a large number of typists, unexpectedly and temporarily assigned to MI-8, to prepare statistics about the messages. MI-8 eventually solved six German diplomatic codes, which Mendelsohn and his coworkers determined derived from an unknown original that they called XX.

Two messages exposed German intrigues in Mexico. The first was transmitted from Nauen, the German transmitter in an exurb of Berlin, to Mexico at least sixty-four times between 23 January and 2 February 1918. It discussed a plan for providing Mexico with arms, machinery, and technicians for manufacturing weapons and airplanes. Nothing came of it. The second, likewise from Nauen and intercepted in February, authorized the German minister in Mexico to offer the Mexican government 10 million pesetas as a "preliminary amount" "on supposition that Mexico will remain neutral during war." But the minister, who had been urging that Germany loan Mexico twenty times that amount to resist American pressures, never even mentioned the proposal to the Mexican government, and no significant German capital ever passed to Mexico. Though the United States merely watched these developments, the intercepts deepened its knowledge of Germany's machinations in a neighbor.

A radiogram from Madrid to Berlin in Code 9700 revealed a plot to infect

DEPARTMENT OF STATE

OFFICE OF THE COUNSELOR

S.D. 318—10531-139

Confidential.

February 1, 1918.

Lieutenant H. O. Yardley, U.S.A.R.F.,

Army War College.

Dear Lieutenant Yardley:-

Here is the message which I have been expecting for some time from the Argentine. It may be of extreme importance and I should be very grateful if you could turn your staff on to it and let me know over the 'phone if it is anything requiring immediate action. Please return the copy when you are through with it.

Very truly yours,

[signature]

Enclosure:
    Balboa's 12030.

Enclosure CB 1605 withdrawn

State's Leland Harrison sends message to Yardley for solution

horses that the Allies planned to buy. MI-8's reading of a fifteen-hundred-word prewar message validated its cryptanalyses, for the solution proved identical to a memorandum by the German ambassador to the secretary of state that was in the files. And MI-8 felt gratified, for while it found German diplomatic codes better than those of any other government it studied during the war, it broke them.

S. D. 518

-5-

connected with our voyage. Later we shall try to say something in regard to the interior situation of Mexico. In an interview with Irigoyen independent of the international situation and in view of the fact that the Congress could not be held, the idea was expressed that by direct relations between the Governments it might be possible to achieve a closer understanding between this country and ours, especially with respect to direct interchange of products and to the establishment of regular communication between the two countries. We believe it possible to arrange for ships to go regularly to Mexico for petroleum, taking corn and wheat at least during three or four voyages. We greet you affectionately, Cabrera. Ugarte.

Please acknowledge receipt of the foregoing.

FREYMANN.

Copies to State Dept by Mayr Feby 3, 1918 RCy

Yardley sends solution to Harrison

At 10 A.M. on 1 February 1918, American officials arrested a young man with a ruddy complexion, fair hair, and striking blue eyes just after he crossed from Mexico into Nogales, Arizona. A double agent had tipped them off that the twenty-two-year-old was a German saboteur. The arrestee insisted that he was Pablo Waberski, a Russian American—he presented a Russian passport—returning to San Francisco to report to his draft board.

W.C.9.
105!—9
m28

OFFICE OF STAFF.
WAR COLLEGE DIVISION.
10531-131
CAPT. D.
WAR DEPARTMENT

February 4, 1918.

CONFIDENTIAL

Mr. Leland Harrison,
State Department,
Washington, D. C.

Dear Mr. Harrison:

Referring to your confidential letter of
February 1, enclosing a twenty-six page Mexican cipher from
Freymann, Buenos Aires, to Perez, Mexico City, dated Jan.
30th, and asking, because of the importance of the message,
that the Cipher Bureau make every effort to decipher it as
quickly as possible, I beg to inform you that the message
was completed Sunday afternoon and immediately delivered to
the State Department by messenger.

As of possible interest to you, I wish to state
that the message was enciphered in a new table, probably taken
to South America by Cabrera. Having discovered about sixty
per cent of the values of the five mixed alphabets, we discovered the "master word", which is CARTONES. From the
"master word" we constructed the table, and then discovered
the key, which is INTER. The rest of the work then was
purely mechanical.

The Mexicans are now using twenty-three different single alphabets, and three tables, each table, we
believe, having one hundred different keys. In addition
to the foregoing, there are an unknown number of figure
alphabets; both single and multiple.

The original cipher is returned herewith as
requested.

Very sincerely,

R. H. VAN DEMAN,

Colonel, General Staff,

By
H. O. Yardley,
1st Lieutenant, U.S.R.

1 encl.
erl.

Yardley and Van Deman cover letter for the solution

He stuck to his story despite intensive interrogation and the statements of
the double agent and a colleague. But found sewn into the upper left sleeve
of his jacket was a slip of paper with a 424-letter cryptogram on it. It had
neither address nor signature, only a date of 15-1-18. "Waberski" said he
didn't know how it got there. He was taken to Fort Sam Houston. The secret
message was forwarded to MI-8.

It arrived at MI-8 on February without any indication of its source or its significance. Several cryptanalysts, including Yardley, failed to read it. The message was put aside for a couple of months. Then MI-8 was asked whether it had been solved and was told of its significance. At the end of April, Manly took it up.

Manly was an excellent cryptanalyst. One observer ascribed this not to lucky guesses but to his disciplined powers of deduction and his close attention to the question at hand. In the Washington heat, he worked in puttees and high collar until 5 P.M., when he took them off—and then worked on until 10. Some people thought that, despite his distinguished academic career, he was never happier than in this work.

The Waberski cipher proved to be an immensely complicated system; one wonders how the German officials worked it. From its frequency count, Manly recognized it as a transposition cipher, probably in German. He began to reconstruct it by bringing together letters that had been adjacent in the original—in German, for example, *c* is usually followed by *h* or *k*. Counting and trial brought together groups of four letters that were parts of German words. At noon on a Saturday, Manly and Rickert began searching for the system that underlay the disarrangement of these groups.

"There was a special stimulus to complete the solution that very day, for Colonel Van Deman had informed Captain Yardley that the Chief of Staff accompanied by members of the congressional committee would make a visit of inspection on Sunday morning," Manly wrote. But the work "was not completed at six o'clock, the usual close of the working day. The two experts could see that success was just at hand, and therefore decided to take dinner near the office and continue their work in the evening. To cut a long story short, the complete solution was obtained, a translation made, and numerous typewritten copies of the cipher message as received, the solution of it, and the translation, were prepared before the experts left the office late in the evening."

The message stated, in part, that "The bearer of this is . . . a German secret agent." It confirmed that a real spy, and one of some importance, had been captured, and that MI-8 had furnished indisputable and damning evidence against him. "The triumphant feelings of Colonel Van Deman as he awaited the visit of inspection can easily be imagined," Manly wrote. "Not only was he able to point to a well-organized, smoothly-working division, he could cite a fresh achievement of the Code and Cipher Section, which, in the opinion of the Chief of Staff and the other members of the visiting committee, would alone have justified the whole organization."

The two cryptanalysts were sent by train on the long, hot, August journey from Washington to San Antonio, where Waberski was to be court-martialed in a bare room on the second floor of a hastily constructed wooden building at Fort Sam Houston. For Manly, who had never appeared in a court of any kind, "the occasion was not without its excitement. He felt that he was summoned to a task of unusual importance and solemnity. A fellow man was being tried for his life before one of the highest special tribunals in the world. The decision reached would be reviewed only by the president of the United States himself." Manly testified that the secret message read, in English translation: "To the Imperial Consular Authorities in the Republic of Mexico. Strictly secret. The bearer of this is a subject of the empire who travels as a Russian under the name of Pablo Waberski. He is a German secret agent. Please furnish him on request protection and assistance, also advance him on demand up to one thousand pesos Mexican gold, and send his code telegrams to this embassy as official consular dispatches. Von Eckardt." Heinrich J. F. von Eckardt was the German minister to Mexico.

Nothing could be more condemnatory. With Manly's solution before it, the court convicted Waberski and sentenced him to death—the only enemy agent so sentenced during the war. He proved to be Lothar Witzke, a sailor in the Imperial German Navy. He had been interned in Valparaiso, Chile, when his light cruiser, the *Dresden,* cornered by the British, sank in Chilean waters. But Witzke broke his parole and escaped to San Francisco. There, hoping to be of further use to his fatherland, he reported to the consul in San Francisco, who headed German espionage on the West Coast. Sent east, Witzke and his intelligence superior blew up Black Tom—the munitions depot in New York harbor—at 2 A.M. 30 July 1916 in one of the most spectacular sabotage incidents of all time. Witzke couriered confidential messages between Germany's consulates in the United States and built a cover, obtaining, for example, a California driver's license. The American declaration of war drove him to Mexico. There he planned to set the huge oil fields of Tampico on fire. When this failed, he concocted a scheme to draw troops to the Southwest by fomenting an uprising and a mutiny by black soldiers, thereby preventing them from being sent to France. He was returning from Mexico to make more mischief when he was betrayed and caught.

The Waberski solution was MI-8's most spectacular achievement. Yardley held that it was its greatest.

In all this, Yardley was participating in the World War I evolution of intelligence and cryptology. Radio's cheapness and flexibility in the million-man war had generated enormous quantities of messages. In Germany's case, it helped overcome Britain's cutting of its overseas cables. But because wireless transmissions could be heard as easily by the enemy as by one's own communicators, they had to be encrypted. The enemy naturally tried to solve them. But many were encrypted in complicated modern systems whose solution often required multiple messages and ancillary information, such as knowledge of the circumstances in which the messages had been sent. And the greater volume of communication led to a greater volume of communications intelligence. Overnight, cryptology outgrew the form of cryptanalysis that had dominated the field for four hundred years: chamber analysis, in which an individual wrestled with a single cryptogram in an isolated room. This shift from artisanal piece work to mass production expanded the functions of the chief cryptologist. No longer was he simply first among equals, solving along with his colleagues and occasionally assigning intercepts to them for solution. Now he managed them. The heads of the belligerents' main cryptologic agencies—Britain's Sir Alfred Ewing, France's Colonel François Cartier, Germany's Captain Ludwig Voit, Austria's Major Andreas Figl—rarely attacked a cryptogram themselves but rather spent their time hearing, from the other branches of the army and the government, what information was needed, disposing staffers to get it, acquiring material to help them, and passing the results to those who would use them. Chief cryptologists had to demand more personnel, find and instruct them, augment and accelerate the supply of intercepts, preserve security, consider new cryptosystems, and deal with superiors. Yardley was doing the same. Like his counterparts, he had to be an executive. And he was a good one. As of 25 February 1918, he was promoted to captain.

In July, orders came from General John J. Pershing, commander of the American Expeditionary Forces, for Yardley to visit the French and British cipher bureaus. Manly took charge of MI-8, presiding over the agency at its largest: 18 officers, 24 civilian cryptographers, and 109 typists and stenographers, for a total of 151 men and women in November 1918.

Yardley arrived in London 29 August. He passed his first night at the Ritz for 12 shillings 6 pence and then prudently moved to a lodging for 3 shillings a day at 70 Comeraugh Road. But what he saved on room he spent on entertainment. He took four British officers to dinner at the Ritz on 3 September "to obtain military information" at a cost of 78 shillings 6 pence. He entertained others a few days later at the Savoy for 71 shillings 6 pence "in exchange for courtesies" and climaxed this spree with a dinner costing 114 shillings 6 pence for five British officers and himself at the Ritz. How productive it all was is questionable: Yardley himself later said that he "received no information." But he could not have known this beforehand— and besides, it was fun. When he proved himself by cracking a proposed

British field cipher, he was admitted to the War Office's cryptanalytic bureau at 5 Cork Street, London. There he studied its techniques and collected its reports—"finishing my education," he called it.

He had much less luck with the Admiralty. Its Room 40 solved not only naval codes but diplomatic ones—American as well as German. The intelligence produced by these feats gave Captain Reginald Hall, the director of naval intelligence, extraordinary influence. He had masterminded the solution and disclosure of the Zimmermann telegram, which helped push the United States into the war, and Yardley's remark that he "stood next to [British Prime Minister David] Lloyd George in power" was not far wrong. But Hall disliked Yardley, making his name "anathema" to the Admiralty on the ground that he was talkative. He not only put off Yardley's request to visit but steadfastly refused him admission to Room 40. Yardley, giving up, went to France to visit the cryptanalytic section of the British Expeditionary Forces. He met Captain O. T. Hitchings, the music teacher turned codebreaker, of whom his superiors said, in one of the most striking phrases about the value of cryptanalysis, that he "was worth four divisions to the British Army." But Van Deman, who had been kicked over to France to take charge of AEF intelligence because he had infringed on Americans' rights in his counterintelligence overenthusiasm, felt that Yardley could not learn more there than he had in London and sent him on to Paris.

The French repeated the London scenario. Yardley met with Colonel François Cartier, the head of the French War Ministry cryptanalytic agency, along rue St. Dominique, on Paris's Left Bank, who granted him access to the cryptanalysts dealing with German field codes and ciphers. There he befriended Captain Georges Jean Painvin, the greatest cryptanalyst of the war, who told him about his solution of the war's most difficult cryptosystem, called the ADFGVX because only those letters appeared in the cryptograms. But, like Hall, Cartier stonewalled Yardley's attempts to learn about his agency's solution of German diplomatic or military attaché codes. He felt that Yardley was indiscreet—a feeling reinforced by a member of Room 40 who told Cartier that Hall had warned them to be on their guard about Yardley. The American exaggerated his importance and that of his work, a trait that irritated his transatlantic allies. His openness had been intensified by his need to sell his program, and no harmful effects had taught him to boast less. Moreover, though the French had indeed cooperated with Moorman and Yardley on the tactical level, they weren't going to teach the Americans how to break diplomatic codes—which they themselves were using and whose solution produced their best intelligence.

> Washington, D. C., June 4, 1919.
>
> RECEIVED from L. L. Winslow, two Red Code Books, Nos. 1 and 2, also explanatory sheets designated as "55515", under conditions as set forth.
>
> *H O Yardley*

Yardley signs a receipt to State's L. Lanier Winslow for two code volumes—presumably the Spanish code given by Britain's director of naval intelligence, Captain Reginald Hall, to U.S. Embassy secretary Edward H. Bell

Yardley had pressed Hall for a Spanish code, but Hall waited until Yardley was in Paris to gave the Americans, through Edward Bell, the American embassy liaison official, whom Hall trusted, the two red-bound volumes Yardley wanted and a German naval code. Hall told Bell he "wouldn't have parted with it [the package of codebooks] to any other man living"—an implied rebuke to Yardley. Yardley returned to London at the beginning of December to get the books, which went to Washington via State Department channels. By then the Armistice had been signed and preparations had begun for the peace conference. In January, Yardley was advising the head of military intelligence at the American Commission to Negotiate Peace; he named as his assistants Lieutenants Frederick Livesey, a Harvard graduate who had broken codes for more than a year for the AEF, and J. Rives Childs, a round-faced Virginia aristocrat who had solved ciphers and superencipherments for G.2 A.6 after doing poorly at Riverbank. They worked in a building on the corner of Paris's rue Royale facing the Place de la Concorde. The Germans had introduced new substitution and transposition ciphers, presumably for their delegates to the conference. The Americans failed to solve them. They massaged their egos with reports that the French and British hadn't broken them either. They assuaged their superiors by issuing a twice-daily German Wireless News Service—a couple of pages of press reports. And they salved their ids in the social whirl of the conference.

For Paris was wild and they had little to do. Yardley came in for a couple hours in the morning and Childs for a brief spell in the afternoon, though Childs later wrote a two-hundred-page study of German military ciphers. They assigned Livesey, who applied himself, to the 4 p.m.-to-midnight shift. The Parisians, exploding with joy after four years of death, ignored the government edict to respect the dead by not dancing and threw clandestine parties, called dancings, all over the city. Yardley and Childs went to many. To have more spending money, they quit the Hotel Crillon, the headquarters of the American commission and one of the most elegant hostelries in an elegant city, and moved first to separate rooms with French families and then to a pension on the avénue Wagram near the Arc de Triomphe, where they took their meals. One day, after lunch, as they were hailing a taxicab, they saw two attractive young Frenchwomen running for the same cab. They offered to take them downtown; the girls laughingly agreed. One of them, who said she was a dancer named Jacqueline, was slim and lively with jet black hair. She and Yardley took an immediate liking to one another and rapidly became inseparable.

This led to a desire for a place where, as Childs put it, "we would be freer to receive our acquaintances." They soon found a roomy and attractive furnished flat at 18, rue Gustave Zédé, a five-story apartment house in the Passy section of Paris, and, with two other officers, moved in. There they held dancings on alternate Sundays, beginning at 5 and lasting until midnight. At other times, they attended other dancings, many of which Jacqueline seemed to know about. One party that Childs never forgot took place New Year's Eve at the mansion of the Mumm champagne family, to which they had been invited after a dinner at the home of a Roosevelt family member. The Mumms had invited six hundred; fifteen hundred showed up, stampeding in their smart clothes for the food and getting themselves so drunk on three thousand bottles of champagne that ambulances had to take some of them home. Needing a respite from all this activity, Yardley and Childs decided to visit Brussels. To authorize the trip, Yardley signed Childs's orders and Childs signed Yardley's. Staying at the Palace Hotel, they repeated their Paris experiences. Their pleasures were marred only by the sobering train-window vistas of devastated landscapes and former battlefields.

The party could not last. They were solving nothing and seemed unlikely to solve much more. Yardley's cryptologic advice seemed unneeded. He was ordered home via Italy, where he might learn something from the Italians or from their British and French advisory groups. He departed Paris from the Gare de Lyon, forgetting his briefcase on the counter of the station's transportation officer. An agitated American colonel telephoned Childs to say he had found it and would never have opened it had it not been necessary to identify the owner, for the briefcase held some highly confidential documents. Childs picked it up and couriered it to Yardley in time for the MI-8 chief to have it when, on 31 March 1919, he sailed from Genoa. Big things were in prospect back home.

7

Morning in New York

In the eighteen months of its existence, MI-8 read 10,735 foreign messages and solved about 50 codes and ciphers of eight governments (though Yardley, in a characteristic exaggeration, claimed the solution of 541 Mexican cryptosystems by counting each mono- and polyalphabetic key as a separate system). Its flashiest result had condemned a German spy to death, but, as Yardley said, "The chief value of all this work has resided in the large and constant stream of information it has provided in regard to the attitudes, purposes, and plans of our neighbors." He was expressing the conclusion that not only the United States but other countries had reached about the new significance of signals intelligence. Nations that had learned the value of cryptanalysis during the war wanted to preserve that value for themselves in peace. Britain, Germany, and Italy, which had not had cryptanalytic agencies before the war, established them afterward. The United States did too.

Though Yardley may have had inchoate thoughts that the breaking of foreign codes should be pursued in peacetime and that the work should be handled by a single central agency, others had proposed the idea before him. As early as 16 November 1917, Leland Harrison of State, who handled much of its secret intelligence, wrote to Van Deman that it would be "most desirable that we should have an organization along the lines now existing at Riverbank Laboratories." It was not empty talk: the secretary of state, Robert Lansing, "promised me any financial assistance that might be required for this purpose." And "it would seem desirable that the staff be selected with a view to keeping them on after the war." At the same time, Fabyan suggested that a central cryptanalytic bureau be set up in Washington, apparently under military intelligence. A. Bruce Bielaski, chief of the Justice Department's Bureau of Investigation, agreed with Van Deman that "at least in war times your office is the proper place for such an organization." The navy, which had been sending messages to the army for solution since February 1918 and one year later had dissolved its failed codebreaking agency, approved the centralization of cryptanalysis under military intelligence. The new intelligence chief, Brigadier General Marlborough Churchill, cabled from France, "I consider the establishment of M.I. 8 on a permanent peacetime basis most essential and believe that both Yardley and Manly should be included, with Yardley as Chief." Van Deman had earlier summed it all up by saying that the central cipher bureau "should handle the cipher messages of all government departments" and that it "should be a permanent one to be maintained after the war." By the end of January 1919, Harrison and Churchill had agreed on such an organization and had even tentatively decided it would have thirty cryptologists.

State's L. Lanier Winslow, who had worked with Harrison on intelligence matters, began planning State's role in the new agency. He acutely foresaw that getting cryptograms from the cable companies would present a problem and wrote Harrison, then in Paris, of that problem and others:

> Just at present, there is great difficulty in procuring material. This is due to the fact that the Navy [cable] censorship has been practically abolished and any material would have to come from the telegraph companies who are afraid to make any move without orders from Burleson [Postmaster General Albert Sidney Burleson], largely owing to the law which that gentleman had passed making it a penitentiary offense to divulge to anyone the contents of messages [while the president had control of wire communications under a congressional resolution]. . . .
>
> The question of the carrying on of our work was all beautifully settled and squared up until a few days ago when it became apparent that it could no longer be continued along the same lines as heretofore. This is primarily due to the fact that the general staff does not think a group of specialists can be permanently kept in the War Department. This would mean that a regular officer would

have to be put in charge in M.I.8 and it does not seem feasible to have a lot of civilians working under a man who in the usual course of events would know nothing about the work. No one who is any good or wants to make a reputation for himself would act as a figurehead, and anyone who really tried to run the job would put it on the blink. There are many other ramifications to this and I am discussing it with all parties concerned. I think a solution has been found and the entire matter may be handled in another city. This also might appear necessary in view of the fact that the necessary moneys might not be expended in the District [under the State Department appropriations act for fiscal 1920], in further view of the fact that the proper kind of personnel would be very limited in Washington and would be much easier procured and kept in some other center. I am going to have another confab with General Churchill in a few days and hope to definitely settle the matter. I have given it my most earnest attention and have had the cooperation of the chief and Mr. Carr [Wilbur J. Carr, who as chief clerk administered the department] in this regard. It has been practically left to me and I have no kick. Don't worry about it as it will be fixed up one way or another satisfactorily.

At the same time that Winslow was writing his letter to Harrison, Yardley, who had returned from Europe in April and almost certainly consulted with Churchill, plunged into drafting a memorandum of his own, "Plans for M.I.8." He listed the foreign cryptosystems that he had broken and demonstrated the value of the work with some case histories. Then he argued the need for a codebreaking agency more sharply than anyone else had: "If it is worth while to know exactly what instructions foreign powers give to their representatives at Washington, . . . it seems imperative that this Government should maintain in time of peace as well as in time of war an organization of skilled cryptographers sufficient in number to carry out the program of deciphering promptly all foreign code and cipher messages submitted to it, of solving new codes, of developing new methods and of training an adequate personnel." He placatingly observed that MI-8's achievements owed much to the corollary information it obtained from the army and State while it served these two departments. "Therefore after consultation with the Director of M.I.D. [Military Intelligence Division] and with responsible officials of the State Department it seems desirable to recommend continued cooperation between the two departments, with acceptance of the financial assistance heretofore approved by the State Department, and with administrative control vested as heretofore in the Director of M.I.D." Yardley provided details on which officials could make organizational and financial decisions. The unit should consist of civilians, he wrote, because the thinkers with language qualifications needed for cryptanalysis are difficult to find in the army or, if found in civilian life, to induct into the army. With an eye to his own future, he commented that "Men and women of the high qualifications necessary can hardly be attracted to the work and—what is equally important—retained in it for smaller salaries." He projected annual expenses at $100,000, divided as follows: rent, light, and heat, $3,900; reference books, $100; salary of chief, $6,000; ten cryptanalysts at $3,000; fifteen at $2,000; twenty-five clerks at $1,200. The proposed staff size was about two-thirds that of MI-8, which had by then shrunk to seventy-seven people, about half what it had been at the Armistice. As for the money, $40,000 could come from State and $60,000 from the confidential funds of military intelligence. This amounted to about a quarter of a percent of State's budget and about a hundredth of a percent of the peacetime army's.

Yardley submitted his seven-page proposal to Churchill, who signed it as its author and forwarded it to the chief of staff on 16 May. He covered it with a memorandum stating that the acting secretary of state concurred in the plan and requesting authority to establish the organization and pay for it with $60,000 a year from military intelligence funds.

The next day, Frank L. Polk, who was acting secretary of state while Lansing was at the Versailles peace conference, marked "OK" in brown pencil on the memorandum and initialed it. Two days after that, Chief of Staff General Peyton March signed it as "Approved: By order of the Secretary of War." This document may be regarded as the certificate of conception of what was officially called the Cipher Bureau but has become known as the American Black Chamber. And Yardley, who had founded America's first official codebreaking agency, now had established himself as its permanent peacetime leader.

Conceived the agency was, but born it was not. Whence would the money come for it? Who would staff it? How was it to be organized? Where was it to be situated? These were the problems Yardley had to resolve.

The army obtained an extra $60,000 from the Military Intelligence Division for the agency. State perhaps shifted funds around to provide its $40,000.

As Winslow had said, Yardley could not put the organization in the District of Columbia: appropriations acts since 1916 prohibited the expenditure of any additional funds there for State personnel. Washington had no suburbs. Yardley was compelled to locate in New York City—Baltimore, Philadelphia, and Richmond, though nearer, could not compete. Moreover, an operation involving codes could be concealed more easily in a port and communications center. Yardley did not mind the move. Supervision would

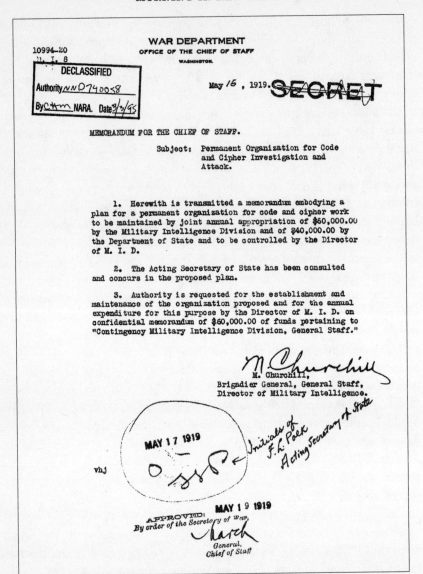

Certificate of conception of the Cipher Bureau—the "American Black Chamber"

be looser. He could exploit business opportunities in commercial codes there. He was ordered to New York on 8 July 1919; a few weeks later, Hazel quit her $1,400 typist's job.

Yardley recommended to Churchill that the government rent a building at 17 East 36th Street. But it turned out that Yardley's wartime friend, the court reporter F. W. Allen, who had headed MI-8's shorthand section, had a three-story building that he owned or controlled at 3 East 38th Street, a few feet off Fifth Avenue. He was willing to rent this for the same amount agreed on for the 36th Street building. Yardley substituted Allen's building without informing Churchill. For security reasons, Yardley signed as lessee. Alterations converted the building from a house to an office. The rent was $5,500 a year; Hazel and Herbert were to live on the third floor for $900 a year. Mail was addressed to P.O. Box 354, Grand Central Station. The telephone number was Vanderbilt 7539, but army leased lines connected the office directly with Washington. Yardley urged callers to use the army line, simply asking for Major Yardley in New York, since calls using it took less than three minutes to connect whereas the commercial line needed about half an hour.

By the end of August, the two-dozen-odd staffers were working normal office hours in their parquet-floored new quarters—though those on the second floor were perhaps distracted by their view into the women's fitting room of the upscale Bonwit Teller department store.

Although Yardley's original proposal had budgeted fifty people, he hired only about twenty-five. Nine professionals came from the personnel of MI-8. Charles Mendelsohn, who had headed the German diplomatic code-breaking section, was demobilized 1 August and returned to teaching Greek and Latin in New York, but worked a few hours each day for Yardley. He would be paid for the number of hours worked each month based on a rate of $3,000 a year. Frederick Livesey, who had been at G.2 A.6 and with Yardley in Paris, was also hired at $3,000. Claus Bogel, who had been solving Mexican ciphers for a year, was to head what Yardley grandly called the French department for $2,000. Victor Weiskopf, still on the Department of Justice payroll, came to New York as well. Yardley also employed sixteen typists and clerks. A lovely but shy sixteen-year-old from New Jersey, Edna Ramsaier, sent there by an employment agency, stood nervously at the door, afraid to enter because a man was standing guard, until a woman crypt-analyst, Ruth Willson of Scarsdale, accompanied her. Yardley, who had an eye for women, hired Ramsaier. Extremely intelligent and hard-working, she became more than a clerk, assisting with cryptanalysis. But, like the other clerical help, she received $1,100. Yardley himself, never timid about asking for money, got a princely $6,000—$1,000 more than the principal assistant secretary of state.

The team began work, and on 4 June 1920 submitted its first report from New York. The lodging on 38th Street lasted less than a year, however, because the lease was sold. By May 1920, Yardley had found a four-story town house on the top floor of which he and his family could live rent-free. Though it rented for $1,000 more a year, Yardley pointed out that the

STEER HIDES [continued]

96234	zciho	65% steers
96235	zciip	70% steers
96236	zcikr	75% steers
96237	zcils	80% steers
96238	zcimt	85% steers
96239	zcioi	90% steers
96240	zcipj	95% steers
96241	zcirl	5% steers 95% cows
96242	zcism	10% steers 90% cows
96243	zcita	15% steers 85% cows
96244	zciub	20% steers 80% cows
96245	zcivc	25% steers 75% cows
96246	zciwd	30% steers 70% cows
96247	zcixe	35% steers 65% cows
96248	zciyf	40% steers 60% cows
96249	zcizg	45% steers 55% cows
96250	zcoao	50% steers 50% cows
96251	zcodr	55% steers 45% cows
96252	zcoes	60% steers 40% cows
96253	zcoft	65% steers 35% cows
96254	zcogu	70% steers 30% cows
96255	zcohv	75% steers 25% cows
96256	zcoiw	80% steers 20% cows
96257	zcojx	85% steers 15% cows
96258	zcoky	90% steers 10% cows
96259	zcolz	—% steers —% cows
96260	zcomn	African
96261	zconc	agrupacion
96262	zcood	agrupacion abasto
96263	zcope	agrupacion steers and cows
96264	zcorg	air dried
96265	zcosh	air dried firsts
96266	zcoti	air dried firsts heavy
96267	zcouj	air dried firsts light
96268	zcovk	air dried firsts medium
96269	zcowl	air dried heavy
96270	zcoya	air dried light
96271	zcozb	air dried medium
96272	zcuaj	air dried seconds
96273	zcubk	air dried seconds heavy
96274	zcucl	air dried seconds light
96275	zcuea	air dried seconds medium
96276	zcugc	all weights
96277	zcuhd	Allahabad
96278	zcuie	Allahabad air dried
96279	zcujf	Anglo South American
96280	zcumi	Anglo South American frigorificos
96281	zcunv	Anglo South American wet salted
96282	zcuow	Antofagasta
96283	zcupx	Antofagasta salted
96284	zcuqy	Antofagasta salted steers and cows
96285	zcurz	Antofagasta steers and cows
96286	zcusn	Argentine
96287	zcuto	Argentine and Uruguay
96288	zcuup	Argentine and Uruguay saladeros
96289	zcuwr	Argentine campos
96290	zcuyt	Argentine campos steers and cows
96291	zcuzu	Argentine city
96292	zcyaf	Argentine city mataderos
96293	zcydi	Argentine city special
96294	zcyej	Argentine city special mataderos
96295	zcyia	Argentine freezer

STEER HIDES [continued]

96296	zcyme	Argentine frigorificos
96297	zcyos	Argentine frozen
96298	zcyqu	Argentine mataderos
96299	zcyuy	Argentine mataderos and campos
96300	zcyxo	Argentine ordinary
96301	zcyyp	Argentine ordinary campos
96302	zdaae	Argentine ordinary mataderos
96303	zdabf	Argentine ordinary mataderos and campos
96304	zdadh	Argentine ordinary steers and cows
96305	zdaei	Argentine river saladeros
96306	zdafj	Argentine saladeros
96307	zdagk	Argentine special
96308	zdahl	Argentine special mataderos
96309	zdaim	Arica
96310	zdaja	Arica salted
96311	zdalc	Arica salted steers and cows
96312	zdamd	arsenicated
96313	zdaor	Artigas
96314	zdaps	Artigas frigorificos
96315	zdaru	Assam
96316	zdasv	Asuncion
96317	zdatw	Asuncion campos
96318	zdaux	Asuncion campos steers & cows
96319	zdavy	Asuncion city mataderos
96320	zdawz	Asuncion city mataderos steers & cows
96321	zdaxn	Asuncion frigorificos
96322	zdayo	Asuncion salted
96323	zdazp	Asuncion salted campos
96324	zdeaz	Asuncion salted campos steers & cows
96325	zdebn	Asuncion salted city mataderos
96326	zdeco	Asuncion salted city mataderos steers & cows
96327	zdeeq	Austrian
96328	zdefr	badly damaged
96329	zdegs	Bage
96330	zdeht	Bage campos
96331	zdeiu	Bage campos steers and cows
96332	zdejv	Bage city mataderos
96333	zdekw	Bage city mataderos steers and cows
96334	zdelx	Bage salted city mataderos
96335	zdemy	Bage salted city mataderos steers & cows
96336	zdena	Bage steers and cows
96337	zdeob	Bahia Blanca
96338	zdepc	Bahia Blanca salted
96339	zdere	Bahia Blanca salted campos
96340	zdesf	Bahia Blanca salted campos steers & cows
96341	zdeuh	Bahia Blanca salted steers and cows
96342	zdevi	Bareilly
96343	zdewj	Bareilly air dried
96344	zdexk	Bavarian
96345	zdeyl	Benares
96346	zdezm	Bhopal
96347	zdiav	Bhopal air dried
96348	zdibw	big
96349	zdicx	Bogra
96350	zdidy	Bohemian
96351	zdiez	Bombay
96352	zdifn	branded
96353	zdigo	branded No. 1
96354	zdihp	branded No. 2
96355	zdiiq	branded packer
96356	zdijr	branded packer No. 2
96357	zdiks	Brazil

172

A page of the Tanners' Council section of the commercial *Universal Trade Code* compiled by Yardley and Mendelsohn and sold by them for private profit

money was available: although by 1 July, the end of the fiscal year, he would have spent all $40,000 of State's funds, he would have disbursed only $11,700 of the army's. He got his way, and by 1 July 1920, the bureau, Yardley, and his wife were in the twelve-foot-wide, gray sandstone building at 141 East 37th Street.

To camouflage his operation, to give his employees and himself a business address, and to make money, Yardley created a company to produce and publish commercial codes. The Code Compiling Company was incorporated in New York City on 3 May 1920 with $500 as its capital and with Yardley getting forty-nine of its one hundred no-par shares, Mendelsohn getting forty-nine, and their lawyer getting two. All three became directors. The certificate of incorporation specified only that the principal office was to be in Manhattan, the addresses given being those of the three principals. The firm's first job was to compile a code for the Tanners' Council that included hundreds of codewords for the great variety of calfskins (Dacca slaughtered = uwtez or 78210). In 1921 it produced the *Universal Trade Code* "under the supervision of Herbert O. Yardley and Charles J. Mendelsohn." It supplied seventy-five thousand codewords for use with its printed words, phrases, lists, and tables and twenty-five thousand for handwritten private meanings. These codewords utilized two up-to-date principles not always employed in other commercial codes to detect and help correct garbles: (1) each codeword differed from all others not by just one letter but by at least two (if AAAAA is a codeword, AAAAB cannot be one but AAABB can be), and (2) codewords that differed by the transposition of adjacent letters were excluded (if FIEND is a codeword, FEIND cannot be). It is said to have sold well.

Finally, Yardley cleaned up a loose end by obtaining his honorable discharge on 30 September 1919. He remained a civilian until he accepted a commission as a major in the Military Intelligence Reserve Corps on 28 May 1921.

Yardley then plunged into the essential preliminary: getting telegrams to solve. This was a challenge. Though the so-called Burleson law had expired with the repeal of the congressional resolution giving the president control of the wires, an older law prohibited revealing those messages. In 1910, the Mann-Elkins act extended the jurisdiction of the Interstate Commerce Commission to telephone, telegraph, and cable communications by defining as "common carriers" companies "engaged in sending messages from one State, Territory, or District of the United States . . . to any foreign country" or "from a foreign country to any place in the United States." It then forbade "any officer, agent, or employee of such common carrier . . . knowingly to disclose . . . any information concerning the nature . . . of any property tendered or delivered to such common carrier for interstate transportation, which information may be used to the detriment or prejudice of such shipper." It added that "it shall also be unlawful for any person or corporation to solicit or knowingly receive such information." Though it did permit "the giving of such information . . . to any officer or agent of the government of the United States . . . in the exercise of his powers," this provision was either forgotten or viewed as not applicable to intelligence or as risking security, for Yardley did not invoke it.

So how could he get the raw material without which his agency could not function? The cable companies knew the legal prohibitions; they also knew disclosure would contravene their longstanding promise of confidentiality to their customers. "For fifty years telegraphic service has been maintained between this country and Europe," the president of Western Union, Newcomb Carlton, told Congress in 1921, "and up to the time of the war there never had been a case of disclosure of cable messages to the detriment of the United States trade and commerce that was ever made and proved." Yardley got the cables he needed through simple candor. He himself approached, or had a State Department official approach, high officers of the cable companies with a frank statement of what he wanted. Their reactions varied.

One readily acceded to the request. W. E. Roosevelt of the All-America Cable Company declared, "The government can have anything it wants." The head of the Postal Cable Company, in contrast, granted access to the telegrams only until 30 June 1920—and that in a veiled manner, through his lawyer to the wife of the director of military intelligence. The vice president of the Western Union Telegraph Company instructed his general superintendent in Washington, H. F. Taff, to let military intelligence copy the messages. Each morning, Robert S. Duncan, a civilian clerk—Taff did not want an officer in uniform coming around—collected the messages from Taff. Duncan brought them to another military intelligence civilian, Helen J. Neville, who, working in the telegraph room, copied them. Duncan returned them to Taff before the end of the day. The messages that Neville copied were sent to Yardley by registered mail every evening. Some problems arose. At least one other member of the Military Intelligence Division also sought the telegrams, perhaps causing the cable officials to wonder about the efficiency and secrecy of the organization. And when the division wanted to get cables to discredit a Hearst journalist, Yardley objected. "There are limits to the kind of material the companies will furnish us without feeling they are being imposed upon," he wrote, warning that "If we are going to start an investigation of each man that criticizes officials of the United States Government where will we land?"

A couple of days after Yardley arranged for the copying, he received "a distinct shock" when the executive assistant of the Military Intelligence Division wrote that Neville had told several acquaintances that she was working for Yardley. The executive assistant ordered that she not be employed and that she be told that the work had fallen through. Yardley responded decisively the next day, demonstrating his executive ability in a forceful letter with no bureaucratese. He explained that Neville had been taken on in the fall of 1917, when he was organizing what became MI-8. She "practically ran the communications office" and "gained the well-earned reputation of being not only discreet and efficient, but a girl who had unusual executive ability." After a tour as a code clerk in London, she returned to New York and visited with friends in Yardley's office. "Late Tuesday afternoon I gathered indirectly that she was uncertain of her status and, seeing an opportunity to retain in M.I. 8 one whom I had come to regard as both discreet and efficient, I dictated the letter that has brought up the present situation." He discovered that Meeth, his assistant, to whom he had dictated the letter, had told her what she would be doing. "Mr. Meeth has proved himself to be unusually discreet and his action in this case though wrong, can be understood, for his opinion of her was that held by everyone before her departure for London, and he felt that she was sufficiently on the inside to be informed of the nature of her work." Yardley went on:

> I feel that I should take some of the responsibility for recommending Miss Neville, for I hardly talked to the girl, assuming that she was as discreet and competent as she was when she left for London. . . . I believe that her statements to other people about her work were prompted by wishing to appear important in the eyes of her associates; and that her trip to Europe has so turned her head that she has lost all sense of discretion. I heartily approve of your decision not to employ her. If I were you I should call her to Washington and tell her . . . that when she divulged this information she was under oath and that if she did not put some restraint on her tongue, action would be taken against her. . . . If you decide to follow my suggestion and I am sure that you will feel that I have written the foregoing merely as a suggestion, please inform me so that I can cite to the clerks in this office the example of Miss Neville as a strong plea for greatest discretion.

Neville was probably discharged. Despite occasional glitches like these, the cable-copying system worked well.

The demobilization of many MI-8 members had compelled Yardley to abandon some fruitful codebreaking activities even before the move to New York. He had to drop his successes against Peru, which was participating at Versailles and whose cryptosystems were rendered more vulnerable by a sudden influx of intercepts, and against Costa Rica, which faced subversion by America's puppet, Nicaragua.

SECRET

4131-549
3

3 East 38th Street,
New York, Sept 22, 1919.

MEMORANDUM FOR BRIGADIER GENERAL M. CHURCHILL:

       1. Some time in June I informed you that M. I. 8 had broken the German diplomatic code used between Berlin and Madrid.

       2. We have now broken three of the codes, having identified approximately one thousand words in each. Hundreds of messages are partly deciphered but it is only now and then that we find a message that we can decipher completely. I am enclosing two such messages.

       3. Work is progressing rapidly and it should not be very long before we are able to decipher all of the messages.

       4. As you probably know we receive our material from the intercepting station at Houlton, Maine.

H. O. YARDLEY,
Major, U. S. A.

2 encl.

jam

SECRET

Yardley reports the solution of three German diplomatic codes

While the United States was technically still at war, the codebreakers in Washington had recovered one thousand words in one German code. They were helped by a person—never identified, but possibly a former member of an imperial Russian cryptanalytic bureau—who in the Netherlands in April 1919 offered to sell information on German codes to the United States. There was no honor among thieves. The material was brought to Washington, photocopied, marked "Not Wanted," and returned. One of the codes had in any event already been reconstructed by MI-8. The Cipher Bureau continued its work in New York and eventually reconstructed thirteen German codes, which Yardley called "wheels within wheels," and had done so "sufficiently to enable us to read any messages almost as quickly as the Germans." General Churchill congratulated the unit for "this splendid work." Yardley claimed in a report that his unit had solved twenty German codes. It was a typical exaggeration. One had been given to MI-8 by the British and the remainder consisted of only five or six basic codes, the others deriving from them or using different discriminants. But soon after the Cipher Bureau arrived in New York, and long before the president had signed a congressional resolution on 2 July 1921 ending the state of war, it abandoned German cryptanalysis because it was receiving no current intercepts.

Churchill also expressed appreciation for the bureau's solution of Spanish codes. The bureau continued its work on Chilean codes when the State Department forwarded it a Chilean superencipherment, apparently extracted by the British from a sealed diplomatic envelope. But it pumped out more Mexican solutions than any other. The United States anxiously watched the tumultuous Mexican scene as rebels assassinated President Carranza and as its government in effect nationalized oil. Cryptanalysts, eager to demonstrate their prowess and productivity, fed on Mexico's feeble cryptosystems. One message, intercepted and solved in six days, revealed that Mexico was considering opposing a proposed article for the Versailles treaty that would allow the United States, under the Monroe Doctrine, to intervene in Latin affairs. Two days later, the Mexican ambassador iterated in Washington that Mexico did not recognize that doctrine. Though this hardly surprised American officials, it eased their minds. They were getting early and accurate information. This was the major contribution of Yardley's Cipher Bureau.

When Yardley had been in New York almost a year, he looked ahead. "My plans for the future, when greater confidence is established between us and the various cable companies," he wrote on 4 May 1920, "call for a bureau that can read messages of the following important governments." He listed five. The fifth and least in importance was Communist Russia. While fear that it would export its Red bacillus was so strong that the United States, with other countries, had invaded Siberia and contorted itself with the Palmer raids to extirpate domestic Communism, Russia was too weak and too far away to attack the United States, and so its diplomatic and military cryptosystems did not demand priority. Fourth was Germany. Though past its abortive, often Communist postwar revolts, American troops still stood on its soil and fears of Prussian aggression had faded. Third was Mexico, always a concern. Second was Britain, growing antagonistic over worries— justified, in fact—that the United States would build a fleet larger than the Royal Navy and would steal some of its markets. The most important target was Japan. Its belligerence toward China jeopardized America's Open Door policy. Its emigrants exacerbated American racism. Its naval growth menaced American power in the western Pacific. Its commercial expansion threatened American dominance of Far Eastern markets. Yardley focused the Cipher Bureau on the rays of the Rising Sun.

8

Yardley's Triumph

Yardley was then thirty-one. His frame was slight but his physique was wiry, enabling him to get on with little or no exercise and to endure stress. His forehead was prominent, his nose straight. Though, as an acquaintance said, he "characteristically had an emotionless expression . . . on his immobile face," he was energetic, ambitious, effective as an administrator, fair but determined. If things had to be done, he made sure his people did them. He thought he had broken "enough codes to awaken the government to a sense of responsibility in this sort of work even in peace times." He dealt smoothly with his superiors. He looked ahead. He was extremely interested in—if not fascinated by—his work. This was the man who was running the American codebreaking agency as the United States—and the world—looked forward to peace and prosperity.

But the nation's military leaders had to plan for war. They had been anticipating conflict with Japan since the United States had seized the Philippines. Japan's defeat of Russia had made it feel it could—and should—expand. It tried to boss around China, which it had also beaten in war. It planned a major naval expansion program. Its actions at the end of the Great War intensified American concerns. It was going to obtain as League of

Nation mandates former German islands in the central Pacific that could sever America's sea route to the Philippines. It was resisting returning to China the peninsula of Shantung, the birthplace of Confucius, which it had seized and which America felt it should give back. Japanese emigration to the western United States irritated many Americans. So it was not surprising that Yardley's military intelligence bosses urged him to turn all his efforts "to the unraveling of Japanese secrets."

While he was abroad during the war, MI-8 had attempted several times to solve Japanese codes. But these tries had failed, perhaps for lack of manpower, or intercepts, or ability, or interest, since Japan was then an ally, or perhaps because—as the Japanese loved to believe—their language was too difficult for any foreigner to understand, much less cryptanalyze. Yardley, however, believed that any code or cipher could be solved. In an access of enthusiasm in his new job, he promised his bosses "a solution or my resignation in a year."

Not knowing that German and British cryptanalysts were even then solving Japanese codes, he soon regretted his optimism. Japanese, he came to think, was "the most difficult of all languages." But he manfully grappled with it. He discovered that much of Japanese may be expressed in some seventy-three syllables, or kana. For telegraphy, these are written in one, two, or three Latin letters, thus: *n, go, ru, ba, tsu.* Yardley had about twenty-five plain language telegrams—one began *beisikan nankinjuken kaiketu*—comprising about ten thousand kana. He had clerks count the kana. He also had a number of code telegrams. He hoped that he could equate the most frequent plain language kana with the most frequent codegroups in the code telegrams and thereby break into the code. But he could not do this without knowing the length of the codegroups. Since all the messages consisted of ten-letter codegroups, the codegroup length could not be three. And if the codegroups were two-letter, on average only one codegroup in every five of those at the end of a message would have ten letters—yet every message ended in a complete ten-letter group. This threw the two-letter hypothesis into doubt. Moreover, most commercial and many diplomatic codes used five-letter codewords. So was the codegroup length, the starting point for all work, two or five? Yardley noticed that the codegroup EN mostly appeared in the last ten-letter group of a message. Perhaps it stood for *stop.* This would suggest a codegroup length of two letters; the letters following EN would be fillers, or nulls.

While he was still puzzling over this problem, help came from Frederick Livesey, the G.2 A.6 codebreaker and Paris colleague whom Yardley had invited to New York as his principal assistant, probably because, as a promotion recommendation stated, besides speaking Spanish and French, and reading German, Russian, Italian, and Portuguese, he "has shown a special talent for finding the true reading of messages of foreign languages, the cipher text of which has been garbled." Livesey observed that the codegroups BA IL LY, which often appeared as a group in the messages, started only in the odd-number positions. This all but proved that the codegroup unit was two. He had also bought a Japanese-English dictionary in a store on Fifth Avenue with 75¢ of his own money. Its Japanese was written in the Latin alphabet. Studying it, he found that the Japanese word for "conclusion" was *owari,* and he connected this with some codegroups near the end of the cryptograms. The kana *ri* was a common one because it served often as a verb ending, and Yardley and Livesey "went on prowling through the texts for various possible identifications of the more frequent symbols preceding *ri* but three identifications [*o, wa,* and *ri*] were an insufficient basis to write into the texts" to make skeleton words that would lead to further identifications. The cryptanalysts were stymied.

Yardley considered what is sometimes called practical cryptanalysis. He checked out the Japanese consulate in Manhattan to see whether the code could be stolen, thought the job might be done, but never pursued the matter. He concocted a scheme that—though he did not know it—was like one French cryptanalysts had used to confirm their solution of an Italian code during the Dreyfus affair. American officials would ask Japanese authorities for some information that had to be referred to Tokyo; this would plant in a Japanese telegram a name that Yardley felt he could recognize though it was encrypted. He could then use this to break into the code. At his request, military intelligence asked the Japanese about a man whose name was given variously as Vladislaus Filofei and Wenceslaus Filofi; the name Gortinski was also mentioned. Whie awaiting the reply, Yardley pressed on.

To keep his spirits up, Yardley reread the story of Champollion's decipherment of Egyptian hieroglyphics, which, he noted, took twenty-three years from the discovery of the Rosetta stone. "And if it took this long, was it not silly of me to be so quickly discouraged?" he asked himself. Though some people laughed at his efforts, he received encouraging letters from his superiors and from Manly, back in academe: "your method is fine and your results are probably right. . . . How I wish I were with you." His wife, Hazel, gave him emotional support. No matter how late into the evening he worked, she waited up for him in their apartment on the top floor of the building on 38th Street, made dinner for him, never asked questions, listened to his pessimistic prognostications, encouraged him, and repeatedly urged him to get some sleep.

"The damned stuff may not even be Japanese. I don't believe it is a two-letter code. What do you think?"

"I think you ought to go to bed."

"I doubt if I'll ever solve this code. Do you think so?"

"Of course you will."

"Why 'of course'? The whole thing is an absolute blank."

"You always talk that way when you are close to a solution. Don't you think you should get some sleep?"

Yardley would go to bed after drinking lots of black coffee, which alone let him sleep, awaken two hours later with a brilliant idea, rush downstairs to his office, open the safe, test his hypothesis—and find it was just another false lead. This went on for months.

By now he "had worked so long with these code telegrams that every telegram, every line, even every code word was indelibly printed in my brain. I could lie awake in bed and in the darkness make my investigations—trial and error, trial and error, over and over again." Livesey did the same, despite being distracted by work on Russian cryptosystems. Yardley hypothesized that AS FY OK, which occurred near the end of some messages, stood for *o wa ri* and was used to mean "period." The two fit these tentative equivalencies back into the cryptograms. But they proved too sparse to confirm or to lead to further equivalencies. As new words to look for, Livesey proposed *beikoku*, meaning "American," and *eikoku*, "British." But these seemed not to help either. Yardley, avid for recognition, kept his guesses to himself. Because the Irish troubles were then much in the news, Livesey suggested trying a Japanese transliteration of "Ireland," which he regarded as amusing because it could have no letter *l*: *Airurando*. If this were followed by *dokuritsu*, meaning "independence," the plaintext would have *do do,* and Livesey suggested testing every doubled two-letter codegroup. He further noted that three of the kana in these two words would appear in different order in *Do i tsu*, which, he told Yardley, was the kana form of "Deutsch." Night after night Yardley sought these patterns. Then,

one night I wakened at midnight, for I had retired early, and out of the darkness came the conviction that a certain series of two-letter codewords absolutely *must* equal *Airurando* (Ireland). Then other words danced before me in rapid succession: *dokuritsu* (independence), *Doitsu* (Germany), *owari* (stop). At last the great discovery! My heart stood still, and I dared not move. Was I dreaming? Was I awake? Was I losing my mind? A solution? At last—after all these months!

He stumbled down the stairs to his office, opened the safe, and tested his hypotheses. The repetitions of the codetext matched those of the proposed plaintext perfectly. "The impossible had been done," he wrote. "I felt a terrible let-down. I was very tired." He climbed the stairs back to where Hazel was awake and said that he'd done it. "I knew you would," she replied. He told her to "Get on your rags" so they could go out and get drunk. It was 1 A.M. on Saturday, 13 December 1919.

When Livesey arrived for work that morning, Yardley called him in and announced that he had broken the code. The two spent the morning inserting his equivalents into the codetexts, but none stood close enough together in the texts to obtain confirmation through new identifications. Then, just as Livesey was about to go to a late lunch, he found the plaintext kana group *kuan*. He knew just enough Japanese to prefix *jooya* to it to make *jooyakuan*, "draft treaty." A moment later he divined *jooin*, "senate." These joined the previous assumptions to verify all the earlier work and nail down Yardley's identifications of the night before. By nightfall, aided by some regularities in the construction of the code, they had added seven or eight more identifications. They had cracked their first Japanese code. Livesey "felt like a world champion." The logjam was broken, and the way stood open for subsequent solutions.

On Monday morning, 15 December, Yardley reported his success to the chief of the Military Intelligence Division, General Churchill. He explained how he had done it—omitting Livesey—and went on, "I may, because I am so interested in this code, overestimate its value, but I cannot but feel that if you go before an executive committee with this information, you will have no small argument for MID." Then he added, "I am sure you will overlook the tone of this letter, if it seems overzealous. With the exception of clerical assistance I have worked practically alone, and it is the first thing that I have ever done which I really feel proud of."

He designated this code Ja—the *J* for Japan, the *a* for the first code solved—and, probably with the help of Livesey and Ruth Willson, a thirty-one-year-old graduate of Syracuse University who had taught Romance languages in several schools and had worked for MI-8, began expanding the equivalents. But Yardley needed a translator for whatever solutions he and his team might eventually make. It wasn't easy to find one. The language was difficult and the country xenophobic. He had in fact begun the search before he achieved his solution, sending out more than five hundred letters. Finally he found an available competent translator: the Reverend Irvin H. Correll, an Episcopal priest, who was believed to have had the longest continuous service of any Christian missionary in the Japanese empire, having started there, with his wife, right after their marriage in 1873. He knew Japanese well enough to write books in it. He also understood the secular world well enough to press for the then substantial salary of $5,000 a year. He eventually settled for $4,000 on a three-month contract. This enabled Yardley, on 28 February 1920, to send to Churchill, "with a great deal of pleasure and pride," "the translations of the first Japanese messages that were ever deciphered by this Government." Two days later, an exultant Churchill praised Yardley and his assistants on "the most remarkable accomplishment in the history of code and cipher work in the United States." He had shown the solutions to the chief of staff, General Peyton March, who extended to Yardley and his workers his official congratulations and his personal regards. Yardley replied that he believed that this work would "eventually surpass in importance any former work done by M.I.8." And indeed it did. He had secured the future of codebreaking in America.

After Ja was solved, Livesey found that another code, Jb, was merely a rearrangement of Ja into eight alphabetical sequences; he solved it in a few days. Ja itself, once filled out, apparently proved to be a simple code used merely for low-level communications and was dropped. By the end of February, the Cipher Bureau had solved three codes. On 1 March, Yardley mailed Churchill the translation of a long dispatch of 16 February from the Japanese ambassador in London to his colleague in Washington and to Tokyo giving his views on the Shantung amendment to the proposed Versailles peace treaty and dealing with other matters. He also forwarded a shorter message about a $7 million loan.

Correll translated these and many subsequent messages. He eventually concluded, however, that the work was unethical, and, six months after he had been hired, he resigned. But Livesey had by then accomplished the unbelievable: he had mastered written Japanese. The flow of translations did not abate.

Nor did the flow of solutions. By May 1920, at least two other codes had been solved—apparently Jc, a two-letter code, and Je, which the cryptanalysts worked on for two months without any success until they guessed it might be in English (for transmitting documents without the need for translation), whereupon they solved it in two or three weeks. (Jd appeared to be a naval code and was not then solved.)

Japanese codes were growing bigger, which meant more codewords to recover. The first codes solved consisted of only some 200 to 250 codegroups, for the seventy-three kana and some common words, but Jg was thought to contain 1,000, many of which proved to be three-letter code-groups, which threw off the codebreakers for a while. Jh was first thought to encompass one hundred thousand groups and Ji, Jj, and Jl thirty thousand to fifty thousand. These figures were later halved, but were still orders of magnitude greater than anything Yardley's team had ever tackled before. In a memo to the Military Intelligence Division on 3 June 1921, he described how the Cipher Bureau worked with these larger codes by detailing his cryptanalysis of Ji:

> All of the material that we had in Ji comprised about 25,000 five-letter code-words. These were first typed, for purposes of indexing, filling about 800 pages. Each code-word with its two prefixes and two suffixes was then typed on a card. This work required 25,000 cards which were then alphabetized. The data on these cards was then typed in manuscript form which required about 1100 pages. Next in order to try to discover the system upon which the five-letter code-words were constructed, which if possible would give us the exact size of the code, each code-word with the number of times it appeared was copied in manuscript form in alphabetical order. This required about 200 columns of code-words.
>
> All of this work of course was required before any attempt was made to make identifications. So far we have discovered the days of the months, numerals from 1 to 50, Roman alphabet from A to Z, and quite a number of the more frequently used Japanese words. . . .
>
> Ordinarily the Japanese spell English words according to the Japanese phonetic spelling but now and then they follow the English spelling. In the latter case they are required to use a five-letter code-word for each letter. In examining our manuscript carefully we ran into one curious repetition which turned out to be p-r-o-t-o-c-o-l (note the repetition of the letter "o"). The discovery of this identified the entire Roman alphabet.

Ji was a naval attaché code, as was Jj, which was never solved because of its considerable size. When the Cipher Bureau ascertained that Jh, a diplomatic code, was only about half as big as the cryptanalysts had thought and had an English vocabulary, its staff began making progress. Soon it stripped the encipherments, where they were used.

In the summer, the Japanese Foreign Ministry adopted a more complicated form of diplomatic code. Yardley's Cipher Bureau first intercepted a message in this system, which the Japanese called YA and which the bureau dubbed Jp, on 18 July 1921, and at once began an intense effort to break it. The code resisted strongly, however. Even work after hours and on at least one Sunday, 8 August, did not at first disclose its secrets. But three days later, eveg-kanaraju

(eboné)				eveh-
abab-	amew-	eb- *(-S)*	ehok-	eves-
abak-	amex-	ecab-	ehor-	evet-
abam-	amid-tashi	ecak-	ehow-	evev-
abas-	amij-tari	ecam-	ehoy-	evew-
abec-23 nichi	amin-tame	ecaz-	ehul-	evex-
abeg-16 *nichi*	amob-*tashika*	ecec-hakari	ehup-	evid-
abeh-17 *nichi*	amof-tatsu	eceg-guu		evij-kettei
abes-	amok-teikoku	eceh-	ej-gai	evin-ketsu
abet-	amor-	eces-hatsu	ek-yu	evob-
abev-	amow-taku	ecet-*haka*	el-"(open)	evof-kin
abew-aida	amoy-tadashi	ecev-*kanakata*	em-shuu	evok-
abex-31 *nichi*	amul-teikoku	ecew-hiki	en-o	evor-kono
abid-	seifu	ecex-hen	ep-ju	evow-kei
abij-	amup-tada i	ecid-hei	er-N	evoy-kata
abin-		ecij-hatashite	esab-mooniron	evul-kon
abob-	an-	ecin-han	esak- mokka	evup-
abof-	ap-oyobi	ecob-	esam-	ew-H
abok- *akin*	ar-soo	ecof-	esaz-moku	ewab-
abor-	as-	ecok-hin	esec-	ewak-shigataki
abow-	at-I	ecor-hoka	eseg-mitsu	ewam-
aboy-21 nichi	av-bi	ecow-haku	eseh-mizukara	ewaz-shitagatta
abul-ai	aw-pa	ecoy-hai	eses-mooshisningi	eweg-shikarubeki
abup-ai	ax-mu	ecul-Hitsu	eset-moo	eweg-
	ay-te	ecup-	esev-	eweh-shidai
ac-juu	ay-V		esew-	ewes-shikyuu
ad-ru	azab-aru	ed-ki	esex-moshi	ewet-serareta
af-e	azak-arita	ef-ya	esid-	ewew-
ag-fu	azam-boku	eg-x	esij-motome	ewew-
ah-koku	azaz-aruiwa	egab-	esin-	ewex-shita
aj-nikansuru	azec-Bai	egak-	esob-	ewid-shin
ak-x	azeg-ari	egam-	esof-nai	ewij-shiki
akab-8 getsu-	azeh-	egaz-	esok-naki	ewin-
akak-7 getsu	azes-beki	egec-	esor-nan	ewob-shina
akam-12 nichi	azet-baai	egeg-	esow-mooshiire	ewof-shitsu
akaz-9 getsu	azev-*katsu*	egeh-	esoy-mon	ewok-
akec-12 getsu	azew-betsuden	eges-	esul-naku	ewor-
akeg-	azex-beshi	eget-	esup-moyozuki	ewow-
akeh-2 *getsu*	azid-beku	egev-	et-T	ewoy-
akes-5 *nichi*	azij-bei	egew-	etab-futsu	ewul-shoku
aket-	azin-*kano*	egex-	etak-fun	ewup-
akev-3 nichi	azob-ben	egid-	etam-gokuhi	ex-K
akew-10 nichi	azof-*kin*	egij-	etaz-*fuu*	exab-ran
akex-8 *nichi*	azok-	egin-	etec-gainu	exak-raku
akid-7 nichi	azor-botsu	egob-	eteg-	exam-roo
akij-4 *nichi*	azow-	egof-	eteh-fuku	exaz-rare
akin-2 *nichi*	azoy-atsu	egok-	etes-*gatsu*	exec-rei
akob-9 *nichi*	azul-boo	egor-	gatsu	exeg-
akof-	azup-betsu	egow-	etet-geikoo	exeh-rai
akok-13 *nichi*		egoy-	etev-gan	exes-*riku*
akor-15 *nichi*	ba-ooden	egul-	etew-	exet-
akow-2 *nichi*	be-joo	egup-	etex-geki	exev-
akoy-10 *getsu*	bi-n	eh-y	etid-gawa	exew-*roku*
akul-	bo-5	ehab-	etij-gataki	exex-rin
akup-9 nichi	bu-ra	ehak-	etin-gaku	exid-riku
	by-itashitashi	eham-	etob-*gi*	exij-retsu
al-shakkan		ehaz-	etof-*gi*	exin-ren
am-F	ca-de	ehec-period	etok-*jo*	exob-*ritugun*
amab-	de-ri	eheg-	etow-gun	exof-ron
amak-	ci-	eheh-	etow-gaikoku	exok-
amam-tei	cu-3	ehes-"(open)	etoy-gagtoki	exor-rui
amaz-tadachini	cy-se	ehet-	etul-gotoki	exow-*rei*
amec-taki	da-ninmatte	ehev-(open)	etup-gen	exoy-raru
ameg-	de-denpoo	ehew-	es-P	exul-rokku
ameh-taido	di-seifu	ehex-	evab-	exup-ritsu
ames-taru	do-ka	ehid-"(close)	evak-*kangae*	
amet-taka	dy-narabini	ehij-)(close)	evam-	ey-jin
amev-tan	dy-4	ehin-	evaz-	ez-taishi
		ehob-	evec-katsu	
		ehof-		

Part of the Cipher Bureau's reconstruction of Japanese diplomatic code Jp on Wednesday, Yardley discovered that Jp was "24 different small codes instead of the usual 1." What he meant by this is not entirely clear, since the code is a single entity, but perhaps he was referring in an exaggerated or obfuscatory way to the phenomenon that, while some two-letter codewords existed in Jp only as those pairs—DO, for example, which stood for *ka,* never appeared as parts of other codewords—some two-letter codewords existed both as separate pairs and as parts of four-letter codewords. Thus while EW as a two-letter codeword stood for *h* and AK as a two-letter codeword for *z,* EWAK as a four-letter codeword meant *shigataki.* To a cryptanalyst examining the cryptograms, this double usage of some two-letter codewords blurred their behavior and made it more difficult to determine their meaning. Of course, it offered dual meanings to the decoding clerk as well. Now, many Western ciphers avoid this confusion by prohibiting any group that introduces a longer group from acting as an autonomous group. But the Japanese cryptographers suffered ambiguity to gain security. Their code clerks differentiated between the two- and four-letter codewords not in the codetext but in the plaintext. In other words, though EW, AK, and EWAK were all ciphertext elements, the four-letter EWAK alone made sense in Japanese whereas joining EW and AK would make the senseless *hz.* Thus the double-meaning two-letter codegroups would probably not trouble the Japanese decoders much, but caused the American cryptanalysts to stumble. Not for long, however. Working with just fifteen intercepts, the Cipher Bureau reconstructed the 700-plus-element, partially two-part, enciphered code so quickly that on 23 August, less than two weeks after the breakthrough, the Cipher Bureau had its first translation in Jp.

Perhaps Japan had put Jp into service as a routine change of code. But it may also have wanted to secure its communications for an international conference that loomed ahead.

9

The Fruits of His Victory

The war to end all wars had left the world abhorring war. But warship programs continued in Japan, Britain, and the United States. They cost millions. As the postwar recession struck, budgets tightened. More and more people wanted to stop the programs. The war had altered the global constellation of power. So in Great Britain, as the time for reconsideration approached under the Anglo-Japanese pact of 1902, sentiment for abandonment grew. The two countries had originally supported each other against Russia, which menaced both India and the western Pacific, and later against Germany. But both those threats were gone, and Britain had come to worry more about the growing assertiveness of Japan, which challenged Britain's political and economic position in Asia. Britain felt increasingly that its interests paralleled those of the United States, despite commercial and naval rivalries.

In March 1921, the first lord of the Admiralty proposed a face-saving way both to reduce naval expenditures and to dump the Anglo-Japanese treaty: an international conference to settle arms and Pacific questions. The United States eagerly assented. Japan was unhappy at the thought of ending the treaty, which had certified it as a great power—the only nonwhite one. And it had just proudly launched the *Mutsu,* the world's largest battleship, paid for in part by the pennies of schoolchildren. But it saw no way out. Six other nations were invited—France, Italy, China, Belgium, the Netherlands, and Portugal. The conference was set for November.

Britain wanted the event to be held in London. The incompetent American ambassador initially seconded this idea, then offered Havana. The British foreign secretary later proposed Bar Harbor, Maine, as a venue. Neither Tokyo nor Paris nor Rome seems to have been suggested. Eventually, the nations settled on Washington, which would make this the first conference of world powers ever held in the United States. Political considerations led to this decision; nobody took into account that the location would confer an intelligence advantage on the host. The Congress of Vienna in 1815 had yielded Austria a great deal of information from betrayers, pilfered documents, and intercepts. France had probably gained similar benefits during the more recent conference in Versailles. Of course, visiting countries could hire spies, but espionage would be easier for the host, and only the United States would be able to read the instructions to and reports from each nation's plenipotentiaries. Yardley exploited this advantage as best he could.

President Warren G. Harding opened the Washington Conference on the Limitation of Armament at 10:30 a.m. on the cold and windy Saturday of 12 November 1921. In the colonnaded Continental Memorial Hall across from the south lawn of the White House, he addressed many of the delegates who, the previous day, had heard him plead with the world to give up war as he solemnly interred America's Unknown Soldier. Then Secretary of State Charles Evans Hughes, dignified, bearded, a former governor and former presidential candidate, stepped up to speak. The delegates were expecting a pro forma welcome. He stunned them. He proposed not only that their governments not build major warships for ten years, but that they scrap sixty-six of their capital ships. A British correspondent wrote that Hughes had proposed sinking more tonnage than all the admirals in history together. Hughes began with his own country. Thirty of the scrapped ships would be American. He then compassed the other navies. When he urged canceling the new pride of the Royal Navy, four *Hood*-class super–battle cruisers, Admiral David Beatty, the victor of Jutland and first sea lord, looked "slightly staggered and deeply disturbed." The first lord of the Admiralty "turned the several colors of the rainbow and behaved as if he were sitting on hot coals." In contrast, the Japanese delegation's impassive faces revealed no emotion but they continued "looking straight ahead" as Hughes's proposal to reduce Japan's navy included junking the *Mutsu.* But at the end of his talk the delegates applauded stormily, and his proposal won the enthusiastic support of the nation.

Under Hughes's formula, the remaining size of the navies would be based on their existing strength. The United States would have 500,000 tons, the United Kingdom 500,000, and Japan 300,000—a ratio of 10:10:6. The two major powers quickly agreed on their parity, but Japan was unhappy. It wanted 350,000 tons. This would make the ratio with the Americans 10:7. Those figures were based not just on national pride but on solid technical reasons, though these seem never to have been mentioned in the discussions. They stemmed from naval experience and the famed gunnery equations of British theoretician Frederick Lanchester.

Naval planners assumed that a fleet lost 10 percent of its effectiveness for each one thousand miles it sailed from its base. This would be caused by wear and tear, bottom fouling, and enemy attacks. They expected that the U.S. fleet would steam five thousand miles from Pearl Harbor to the Philippines. There it would engage the Imperial Japanese Navy, fifteen hundred miles from Japan. If the Americans sailed with ten battleships, they would arrive with a strength equivalent to five. If the Japanese sailed with six battleships, they would lose 15 percent of their power and would arrive with a strength roughly equivalent to five. The fleets would be of equal strength. If, however, Japan sailed with seven battleships, it would arrive with a strength of six, outnumbering the Americans. This advantage was exacerbated by the Lanchester gunnery equations. Lanchester hypothesized that the fleets fired in salvos, that the accuracy of fire was 10 percent, and that each hit destroyed an enemy gun. Working this out, he concluded that the power of the two forces was not in the ratio of the number of ships but in the ratio of the square of the number of ships. This meant that under the Japanese plan the strength of the two forces would be not just 6:5 but (rounding) 35:25. In other words, instead of a 20 percent advantage, the Japanese would have a 44 percent advantage. The United States could not stand for a 10:7 ratio; Japan insisted on it. This became the hardest fight of the conference.

Yardley hoped to provide the American negotiators with information about the other nations' negotiating positions and intentions. He had a good start with Japan. But he did not fare as well with the cryptosystems of the other two major powers. Though Britain had abandoned its two-power standard, in which the Royal Navy would be larger than any two other fleets combined, it could not accept naval inferiority. Yet the United States had called for "a navy second to none." Foreknowledge of Britain's intentions would help American diplomats. But Britain was alive to the need for security in its communications. So although the Cipher Bureau solved some codes for trivial messages—such as one urging a Philadelphia Orchestra concert for the delegates—it read no significant cables. The same happened with France, which possessed the world's third largest navy. Work on its cryptosystems, as on Britain's, started belatedly and without any background, for neither MI-8 nor its successor had studied them. Moreover, French cryptology, with decades of success behind it, was one of the best in the world. Even though the Cipher Bureau's Claus Bogel made a few tentative identifications (as 1272 = *experts*) and discovered that France was using four two-part codes for the conference, it never advanced much beyond that.

But Japan was the main target, and here Yardley had succeeded. The Cipher Bureau had been reading the two main codes, Jo and Jp, since before the opening of the conference. The intercepts reached the Cipher Bureau on 37th Street in bunches of half a dozen to a dozen around six days after transmission, delayed that long because couriers brought them from Washington. At first the typists merely copied them on legal-sized sheets of paper and handed them to Livesey and Ruth Willson for cryptanalysis. Soon two of the typists—one was Edna Ramsaier, whose married name was now Hackenberg—became so proficient and so familiar with the Japanese system that they themselves mentally divided the cryptograms into the two- and four-letter groups and then decoded them almost as fast as they could type. Livesey and Willson recovered unknown groups, translated the Japanese plaintext, and returned this to the typists to be turned into fair copies. These were given to Yardley. Sometimes during the conference the staff worked twenty-four hours in twelve-hour shifts; work until midnight was not uncommon. Once, before Thanksgiving, Hackenberg told Yardley she could not work on the holiday. Yardley retorted, "I can't play golf either"—and she knew she'd have to come in that Thursday.

Most intercepts were solved and translated the day they were received. A few took a day longer; even fewer, more. Originally the solutions in Washington were delivered in weekly batches by forty-four-year-old State Department officer William L. Hurley, a former newspaperman who had served with the military attaché in London during World War I; a later evaluation gave him a rating of "Fair—as clerk. For secret service work, apparently very good." When the conference began, couriers—among them Tracy Lay, a Foreign Service officer recalled from abroad—brought the solutions down daily. They reached Washington the day after they were solved and translated. The volume was impressive. Many of the telegrams, such as reports of meetings or of press reaction, ran five or six single-spaced pages, sometimes more. For security, they bore no markings as "For State Department" or "For

Military Intelligence Division." Most went to FE—State's Far Eastern Division—which was deeply involved in the negotiations. Interestingly, few or none went to Hughes. He was too busy meeting with American and foreign delegates, chairing committees, talking to subordinates, studying position papers, and holding daily press conferences to read many of them.

An episode early in the conference convinced doubtful officials of the solutions' veracity. On 18 November, Hughes granted an interview to newspaper correspondents on the condition that the information not be attributed to him. Several days later, the codebreakers furnished State with the Japanese report of the meeting, and the officials could see for themselves that it was correct, as well as a clear, fluent translation. As further intercepts came in, American officials chuckled over Tokyo's query whether the American government, in the throes of Prohibition, would object if liquor were brought to the conference. They observed that the auditor mentality was not confined to the West when they read a Tokyo message beginning, "The expenditure of a year's rent for a building which is to be used for a few months would ordinarily not escape the censure of accountants." Their moral concern about reading others' messages ebbed when they saw Japan wiring $30,000 for secret service work during the conference. And although, somehow, the head of the Far Eastern Division thought the intercepts were "very difficult to read" and "almost never of real value," he conceded that they did keep "the members of F. E. currently informed of Japanese feelings."

But cryptanalytic evidence was not the only information available to the American negotiators. The press, though less authoritative, was quite accurate and sometimes faster, particularly on the key issue of the 10:6 or 10:7 ratio. Thus the *New York Times* reported on 25 and 26 November that Japan remained resolute on its 10:7 demand. However, on Monday, 28 November, three days after Crown Prince Hirohito had been named regent and was expected to surround himself with moderates, it front-paged a change in Japan's attitude. "Tokio Is Prepared to Yield on Ratio," the headline ran, over a story that "It is understood that Admiral Kato [Baron Tomosaburo Kato, navy minister and delegation head] received from Tokio today very explicit instructions. . . . The report was in circulation today that Japan, failing to have her own standard of measurement accepted, would be quite disposed to accept the '5-5-3' arrangement."

The Cipher Bureau lagged. The next day, it solved a four-day-old Jp cryptogram implying that Japan would not yield. Tokyo was reminding Kato that he himself had once said that "the ratio of 10 to 7 between the American navy and our navy should be the limit. We understand that you will work to maintain this limit without any change."

For events were outrunning Yardley. While the Cipher Bureau was forwarding this days-old message, the *New York Times* was front-paging a story that conference opinion held that Japan's acquiescence in a 10:6 ratio was only days, if not hours, away. The next day, Wednesday, 30 November, it headlined "Crisis on Naval Ratio Plan Passed; Agreement Likely in Session of Dec. 5."

Thus up-to-date but unverified evidence conflicted with authentic but outdated evidence. The American negotiating staff perhaps agonized over the discrepancy as, on Friday, 2 December, Hughes, Kato, and Arthur Balfour, the chief British delegate, discussed the naval ratio. Kato repeated what he had told Balfour the day before: an agreement by America not to fortify Guam and the Philippines and by Japan not to fortify its mandated islands would help in getting Japan to accept the 10:6 ratio. This was the first official hint that the empire might yield. But the meeting ended with Kato saying only that he would ask for further instructions.

That very day, as he was cabling Tokyo, a telegram arrived at the Cipher Bureau. Dated 28 November and consisting of sixty-four ten-letter groups, it began: "Koshi, Washington URGENT 0073 vrxpm dozoorupuh uteletamme fuinofridy." It was copied triple-spaced on a legal-sized sheet and its Cipher Bureau serial number, J6204, was penciled in the upper right corner; someone jotted JP above it. A clerk typed out the plaintext between the lines. "ka too zen ken he 'gokuhi' kiden kai i 7 4," the plaintext began. It was translated later that day. The result showed that Tokyo had softened.

"We are of your opinion," the Foreign Ministry was telling Kato,

that it is necessary to avoid any clash with Great Britain and America, particularly America, in regard to the armament limitation question. You will to the utmost maintain a middle attitude and redouble your efforts to carry out our policy. In case of inevitable necessity you will work to establish your second proposal of 10 to 6.5. If, in spite of your utmost efforts, it becomes necessary in view of the situation and in the interests of general policy to fall back on your proposal No. 3 you will endeavor to obtain a wording which will make it clear that we have maintained equilibrium with the American fleet by limiting its power of concentration and maneuver in the Pacific through a guarantee of reducing, or at least maintaining in status quo, the Pacific defenses. No. 4 is to be avoided as far as possible.

The codebreakers scrupulously noted that "6.5 [is] reconstructed from a garbled passage." They did not say what either No. 3 or No. 4 was.

Despite that omission, this solution, when it arrived in Washington on Saturday or Monday, solidified the American delegation's sense that the Japanese would abandon 10:7 and accept 10:6.

No. 784

Reference No. J-6507

From: Tokio, December 10, 1921.
To: Washington, Conference No.155

Type: JO Diplomatic Code.

Received December 14, 1921.
Translated December 14, 1921.

      Forwarded to London as No. 646.

      Very Confidential. Urgent.

      Referring to your cablegrams Nos. 142
and 143 (Note. Neither received), in
consideration of the close relation which
the question of the ratio of the Japanese
and American navies has to the question of
Pacific defenses and to the question of the
quadruple agreement, and in view of the
extreme importance of all three questions, the
Japanese Government has given it exhaustive
consideration on the basis of your cablegrams.

      We have claimed that the ratio of
strength of 10 to 7 was absolutely necessary
to guarantee the safety of the national defense
of Japan, but the United States has persisted
to the utmost in support of the HUGHES proposal,
and Great Britain also has supported it. It is
therefore felt that there is practically no
prospect of carrying through this contention.
Now therefore in the interests of the general
situation and in a spirit of harmony, there is
nothing to do but accept the ratio proposed by
the United States.

First page of the Cipher Bureau solution of a Japanese diplomatic
intercept reporting that Japan will agree to America's proposal for a
10:6 ratio in capital naval warships. But it was solved after Japan
agreed to the proposal on 12 December.

This message, Yardley believed, was "the most important and far-reaching telegram that ever passed through its [the Cipher Bureau's] doors." He was right about that. But he failed to look at the press and the negotiations when he added, "It is the first sign of weakness on the ten-to-seven Japanese demands," and he exaggerated when he claimed, "This telegram was definitely to determine the respective strength of the fleets of Japan and the United States." He did summarize the contents correctly:

"It shows that if America presses Japan vigorously, Japan will give up proposal 1, then proposal 2, and that provided the status quo of the Pacific defenses is maintained, she will even accept a ten-to-six naval ratio.

"With this information in its hands, the American Government, if it cared to take advantage of it, could not lose. All it need do was to mark time. Stud poker," he concluded with a metaphor dear to his gambler's heart, "is not a very difficult game after you see your opponent's hole card." The skeptical head of State's Far Eastern Division concurred. The one intercept that provided help "made it clear that the Japanese would finally give in on the naval ratio." This, he said, "stiffened Mr. Hughes' attitude." Thus fortified, Hughes let time work against the Japanese. Intercepts undergirded his strategy. In one message Kato moaned that "they put pressure on us by arguing that if we do not accept the American plan . . . the whole plan will break down. . . . It is extraordinarily hard to persist in our proposal." In another, he warned that some newspaper articles charged that Japan's failure to accept the American proposal would mean that it "would block the success of the conference." He added that "even British correspondents in America are as a rule reporting unsympathetically on the attitude of our country regarding the naval question." And Tokyo itself appeared to be weakening. In a message solved on Saturday, 10 December, the Foreign Ministry confessed that now "many of our own people . . . appear to desire the reaching of an immediate agreement through some compromise." None of this appeared in the *New York Times*.

Finally, Japan capitulated. Good relations with the United States were more important than the battleship and a half that the greater ratio would have given it—and which it concluded it would not get anyway. At a late afternoon meeting at the State Department on Monday, 12 December, Kato agreed to the 10:6 figure in return for the face-saving agreement he had proposed: that neither party fortify its possessions in the Pacific. The intelligence provided by the codebreakers had bolstered Hughes's toughness and helped win the day.

The Cipher Bureau staffers had worked nights and weekends turning out thousands of intercepts. At Christmas, their government gave them bonuses:

a procedure rarely seen among federal employees but not unprecedented among cryptanalysts—those of the absolutist monarchs' black chambers had been given extra money for solutions. The U.S. Army could pay this money because the Cipher Bureau funds were unvouchered. The bonuses, a little more than a week's salary for each of the fifteen persons receiving them, ranged from $37 to $184, with the latter amount going to Yardley. They were accompanied, he said, "by personal regards and assurances that our long hours of drudgery during the Conference were appreciated by those in authority." And the hard-working typists, codebreakers, and translators had as well the secret satisfaction of having helped their government to win a major diplomatic victory and save hundreds of millions of dollars—and the world to enjoy more peace.

10

The Busy Suburbanite

The exhilaration of the Washington conference was followed by exhaustion. Yardley went to Arizona to recuperate from a mild case of tuberculosis. Staff members were so overworked they had nightmares—one dreamed that she chased a bulldog around and over and under the furniture in her bedroom and that when she caught it she found the word "code" written on its side. A couple resigned. But these negative aspects of their line of work were countered by two positive ones.

One came from Secretary of State Hughes, whom Yardley's work had so helped during the disarmament conference. In gratitude, Hughes supported a military intelligence appropriation. The "daily contact between this Department and the Military Intelligence Division, . . . which has developed its facilities to a very high degree, is of the utmost value to the Department of State through the information which it is able to supply," he wrote.

A few months later, the director of military intelligence recommended that Yardley be awarded the Distinguished Service Medal. The War Department's highest noncombatant honor, it could be conferred only for acts during hostilities, so the commendation dealt not with his conference results, which in any event had to remain secret, but with his wartime work.

Distinguished Service Medal, awarded to Yardley on 30 December 1922

Yardley had developed, the director said, "out of a practically unknown field of mystery and doubt, a science by which he was able to translate the most secret messages and obtained information of vital importance to the War Department." This statement precisely articulated Yardley's fundamental contribution to the nation. The chief of staff, General John J. Pershing, saying that "I am familiar with the remarkable work of Major H. O. Yardley," agreed. The award was made "For exceptionally meritorious and distinguished services in a position of great responsibility as Chief of the Communication Section of the Military Intelligence Division, War Department General Staff, during the World War." The citation did not mention Yardley's cryptanalytic successes, but when the tall and convivial secretary of war, John Weeks, pinned the medal on Yardley's lapel, he winked at the cryptologist. "The wink," Yardley admitted, "pleased me immensely."

Still, neither of these acclamations kept the Cipher Bureau's funds from being cut more deeply than those of its parent organizations when Congress set the budgets for fiscal 1924, which began 1 July 1923. Congress was in a peacetime mood, eager to economize and put war behind it. It was confident of American military prowess and felt safe behind twin moats. So while it trimmed the budget of the State Department 5 percent, it cut that of the War Department 10 percent, which in turn sliced that of the Military Intelligence Division a proportional 10 percent. But the Cipher Bureau lost 30 percent. Its budget fell from $50,000 to $35,000. The army, probably unaware of the role the bureau had just played in brightening the future, and believing that spying was immoral, un-American, and unnecessary, disdained codebreaking and opted to save a pittance.

As one consequence of the cut, the bureau's personnel was more than halved. Of the sixteen on the payroll, ten resigned or were let go. One was Livesey, who had been unhappy about his pay; he joined State as an economist. Yardley had to dismiss Serena B. Laning, "a very clever girl" who knew Japanese. Claus Bogel went to the navy's Code and Signal Section for a couple of years, where he was regarded as "a nice old duck," then to the Library of Congress Reference Room. The chief clerk, John Meeth, went to work for the New York City utility Consolidated Edison. Their departures were sweetened by a bonus of four months' salary or, in one case, six months'. In the fall of 1923 another clerk was dismissed, and later another.

Six people remained. They comprised the staff during the remaining years of the Cipher Bureau. Besides Yardley, three were cryptanalysts. Victor Weiskopf, on the payroll of the Justice Department, increased his income by running a stamp business on the side, specializing in old U.S. and Confederate covers. The brilliant Ruth Willson, who in 1925 had married accountant Howard L. Wilson, thus changing her name from two *l*'s to one and causing endless misspellings, commuted from the wealthy Westchester suburb of Scarsdale. Charles J. Mendelsohn, who taught Latin and Greek at the College of the City of New York and at its associated high school, Townsend Harris, continued to work part-time. Yardley's secretary was Marguerite O'Connor, an elegant, five-foot-eleven-inch blonde who later married John Meeth. Two women were clerk-typists, Alice Dillon and Edna Ramsaier Hackenberg, by then desperately in love with Yardley.

Despite the layoffs, budget pressures persisted. Driven by them, and perhaps also by a burglary in the 37th Street brownstone, from which only three bottles of liquor were stolen—it was Prohibition—but which apparently worried Yardley about security, he moved the office on 24 October 1923 to smaller quarters in Room 229, later to Suite 814, of a twenty-story office building at 52 Vanderbilt Avenue, corner of 47th Street, near Grand Central Terminal. The cryptanalysts worked in secret in the back; the front, to which the public could be admitted, quartered the Code Compiling Company, the cover firm that published Yardley and Mendelsohn's *Universal Trade Code.* It was listed in the Manhattan telephone directory with telephone number MURray Hill 9912. Though funds had shrunk, Yardley coolly asked for a raise—and got $600 more, to $7,500—the same as the undersecretary of state. Moreover, since he now had to rent an apartment, instead of living for free on the top floor of the brownstone, he also asked for and received a housing allowance of $150 for eight months. Hazel and he moved out of Manhattan across the East River to what was then suburbia— the New York City borough of Queens.

The shrunken agency continued on its more modest scale. Even more severe than the financial problem was the growing difficulty of obtaining intercepts. This posed no problem in other countries. In Britain, a 1920 act of Parliament required "any person who owns or controls any telegraphic cable or wire" to produce any telegram that a government official requested under a warrant. This brought in sacks of telegrams daily whose governmental messages went to the codebreakers. In Germany, a commissioner granted codebreakers the legal right to copy foreign telegrams entering or leaving Berlin. France's administration of post, telegraph, and telephone continued to give messages to the various codebreaking agencies. But in the United States, as the wartime spirit evaporated, American carriers grew less and less inclined to patriotically give Yardley cablegrams. Revelation of the practice not only could invite prosecution; worse, it could hurt business! Eventually all the carriers refused the Cipher Bureau access to traffic. Yardley was faced with a life-and-death situation for his agency. With no help from his superiors in resolving the problem, and probably telling himself that the nation's security demanded the information he produced, and doubtless with his own job security in mind, he bribed employees of Postal Telegraph, Mackay Radio, All-America Cable, and Western Union. He put them on a regular "salary" and paid them in cash. They gave him the cablegrams he needed to survive.

What was he doing with them? Not much. International relations were calm. Germany had been defeated and disarmed. Communism had been contained within Russia's borders. The United States was concerned only with the behavior of its Latin neighbors. So the bureau solved the codes of Mexico, which always stood at or near the top of the list of American external concerns. It read messages of Nicaragua, where the United States had staioned troops, and of Peru, whose dispute with Chile over the border areas of Tacna and Arica the United States was arbitrating. Cryptosystems of China were read, perhaps because a betrayal made them available, since relations with China were not troubled.

At the end of the Washington conference, in March 1922, Yardley reported that "We have temporarily given up the French code," because the bureau had "been instructed to concentrate on the Japanese." But on 3 February 1923, with the conference long ended and work on French resumed, he admitted that he had had "very little success" with the code he had attacked. A month later, he optimistically said that "We have only identified 15 or 20 words but as you know once a few words are identified the rest comes rapidly." It didn't happen. The land of the Sun King's great cryptologist, Antoine Rossignol, had preserved its cryptographic secrets. In mid-March 1927, the Cipher Bureau obtained a handful of British intercepts in a diplomatic code. Not until a year later did Yardley send in the solutions, which consisted of the text of non-British documents. "The City of Tokio," one began, "has entrusted to the Industrial Bank of Japan, Ltd., the power to sign [words missing] the Loan Contract." The others were equally exciting. While during the Anglo-Japanese-American conference in Geneva of 1927 to extend the Washington conference's results to cruisers, destroyers, and submarines, the British solved dozens of messages dealing with the negotiations, Yardley obtained only French press reports on the speech of the British foreign minister and on the conference's prospects. Those results were as feeble as the conference's, which failed.

In one critical area the Cipher Bureau did continue its success: the cryptosystems of Japan. Though Japan had withdrawn its troops from Shantung and Siberia, eliminating two points of contention with the United States, and though the Washington treaties had engendered an era of good feeling, Japan remained the focus of America's codebreakers, as it did of naval planners, because—with the unlikely exception of Great Britain—its policies alone could involve the United States in war.

Even before the Washington conference, Yardley wrote in a memorandum, the Cipher Bureau had begun attacking new Japanese army codes in which

there were practically no repetitions of sequences of groups such as are necessarily present in small codes. Finally an index was made of the groups in one long message and it was found that all of the groups had been used about an equal number of times and that there were practically no repetitions of two or more groups in the same order. In other words the message offered against attack a surface as smooth and perfect as a billiard table.

After a considerable number of messages had accumulated, a careful analysis was made and three codes designated as JN, JQ, and JR were identified by various similarities and differences between messages. JR was taken for close study and ultimately it was found that JR (and similarly JN and JQ) consisted of eleven different code vocabularies which we designated as JR 1, JR 2, etc. The system of operation was to number the messages serially and transmit this number in plain text. In encoding the message the operator added the digits of the serial and encoded the first part of the message in the corresponding subcode, e.g., cablegram 52 would begin with JR 7 code. After ten, twenty, forty or whatever number of words the operator pleased, he would put in a code indicator, a group indistinguishable from any other code group, and would then shift to JR 8 code, etc. Thus no consecutive messages would begin with the same code and one message might be in eleven codes so that any code group might appear eleven times in a message and have eleven different meanings.

When this principle was discovered, and it took us six months of patient labor to make the discovery, a careful search was made for the code indicators. When they had been tentatively discovered it was possible to isolate the material in the sub-codes JR 1, JR 2, etc., and attack these sub-codes as code problems comparable to the old JF, JK, etc. . . . ultimately a breach was made.

The effort, completed by May 1922, proved all but worthless. The Jn messages did not warrant translating, the Jq messages were routine, and only a few Jr intercepts were submitted to the Washington policymakers.

In 1924, clerk Edna Hackenberg, who read the *New York Times* every day, suspected that the Japanese were sending press reports based on it to Tokyo encoded in an English-language code, probably Jw. She had assimilated a lot about cryptanalysis—almost nobody in those days was trained in it anyway—and she matched the cryptograms against probable news stories in the *Times*. She found a rich source of equivalents in the citations that began with *open quote* and ended with *close quote.* Though the same method didn't work when she tried to expand her code vocabulary by using the *Christian Science Monitor* because the Japanese apparently stuck with the *Times,* she did well—and, by September, she had broken the code. Then she kept up with its new editions—Jwa, Jwb, and so on—every two months. She thought it was "marvelous work" in which "You could feel your brain was expanding." And not only her brain: her wallet too. Yardley gave her a $200 raise (to $1,400 a year) for the solution.

Her success was offset somewhat by a decline in the cryptanalysis of Japanese army messages, which began in February 1923. This was partially due to the loss of funds and the concomitant loss of Livesey and Laning. It may also have been attributable to a reduction in intercepts. And it may have been owing to the improvement in Japanese military cryptography made by a remarkable Polish cryptanalyst.

Captain Jan Kowalewski was a tallish, broad, handsome man, with a wonderful sense of humor and great intellectual intuition. He had created cryptanalysis when the new Poland was fighting for its existence during its 1919–20 war with Communist Russia. He was helped when the Japanese military attaché gave Poland some Communist cryptosystems seized by the Japanese during their 1918 invasion of Siberia. Kowalewski and his dozen-man team solved Russian radiograms—among them one of 24 June 1920, read the next day and signed by Kowalewski, that mentions Stalin—which contributed to Poland's repulse of the Reds. After the war, when one of his many girlfriends, unhappy over their affair, killed herself, Kowalewski, believing that honor necessitated it, shot himself. But he merely paralyzed his left side. A superior, seeing him with his arm in a sling and his left coat sleeve empty, waiting to talk to the head of intelligence, thought it would be good to assign him less strenuous duty. The two higher officers knew of their country's good relations with Japan—Russia was their common enemy—and of Japan's cryptologic interests. To the Japanese military attaché, they broached the idea of sending Kowalewski to Japan as an instructor. On his return to Tokyo, the attaché persuaded his chief of the value of cryptology. Kowalewski arrived in Japan in January 1923 and, staying for a couple of months, taught four Japanese army officers codebreaking, particularly of Red Army systems. He also advised them on cryptography, for the military systems suddenly improved, depriving Yardley's Cipher Bureau of one of its principal points of entry.

That point was the start of messages. The drafters of military (and diplomatic) communications, believing—rightly—that security is the job of the cryptographers, usually begin their messages with such phrases as "Re your telegram 123" or "To the commander of the 25th Division." These stereotypes offer cryptanalysts the probable meanings of the first few codewords of a cryptogram and thus the opening wedge to solution. Kowalewski, aware of this, had the Japanese code clerks divide a plaintext message into two, three, or four sections, depending on its length, mark them, rearrange them, and then encode them. This procedure hid the vulnerable opening. It indeed delayed the cryptanalysts in New York. But they eventually discovered this procedure, ascertained the marking indicators, and then resumed its solutions. And when other codes began using this method, the cryptanalysts quickly recognized it, searched for and found the marking indicators, and solved the codes. Still, solutions never achieved the earlier volume.

The Cipher Bureau's codebreaking results were distributed chiefly to the State Department—the information seldom interested the War Department—in a "Bulletin" that concealed the source of the information. These began with the phrase "We have learned from a source believed reliable that . . ." and continued with the text of the message in indirect discourse. Yardley sent them to his liaison at the department, who forwarded the information to whomever he thought should get it. From at least 1920, his contact was William Lee Hurley, who had delivered messages before the Washington conference. He was replaced in May 1924 by Arthur Bliss Lane, who occasionally visited the bureau in New York; Lane was replaced in turn by Alexander Kirk.

Yardley's move to Queens made him a suburbanite. In the age of the flapper, the Charleston, and the Great Gatsby, he installed his family in a

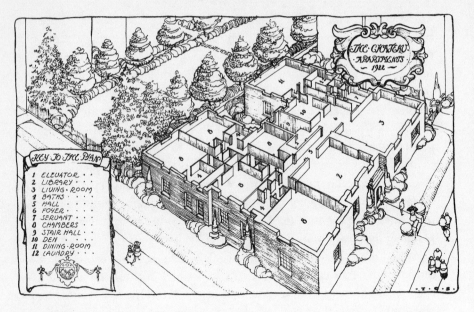

Plan of the elegant Chateau garden apartment house where Herbert, Hazel, and Jack Yardley lived in the 1920s

new community called Jackson Heights. Twenty minutes by the new subway from Grand Central Terminal, it had been developed by the Queensboro Corporation on what had been farmland. The corporation, which had a sales office at 50 East 42nd Street in Manhattan, two hundred yards or so from Yardley's office, targeted people from small towns who had moved to New York and were making between $3,000 and $7,000 a year. This was Yardley's category. Advertisements warned that the Jackson Heights development was a restricted community—meaning no blacks and no Jews—whose genteel anti-Semitism Yardley shared. All the residents had what one historian has labeled "easily pronounceable last names." The development boasted the nation's first garden apartments: instead of covering the nearly three-quarters of the plot allowed by law, they used only one-third to one-half. Lawns and shrubs behind the buildings greened the rest. The occupants paid not rent but mortgage installments as owners of perhaps the world's first cooperatives. The corporation constructed the apartments expensively, with fine details, and offered many amenities. A special bus line carried shoppers to elegant Fifth Avenue stores. Residents could play on a nine-hole golf course and on tennis courts, could join many clubs, and could participate in plenty of activities, including a winter festival. Herbert and Hazel moved at first into one of the dozen apartments in Linden Court, 95 28th Street (now 37–

18 85th Street). By 1927, after a son, Jacky, born in 1925, needed a room for himself, they transferred to the newer and classier Chateau, at 195 24th Street (now 34–06 81st Street). This six-story building was advertised as having walls "of a coppery red brick, capped by roofs of purple and golden slate, an ensemble of picturesque towers and gables" with two five-, six-, or seven-room apartments on each of five floors, which were served by one of the first automatic self-service elevators in New York. And it was across the street from the golf course.

Yardley was an excellent golfer. He claimed his skill came from practicing as much as he played. He was a perfectionist. In golf, at least, he had an explosive temper—throwing his clubs and cursing when things didn't go right. It was an age when golf mattered. Men wore plus fours and tried to play like Bobby Jones. In Yardley's first year at Jackson Heights, 1924, he showed himself a golfer to be reckoned with, winning the second round in a tournament. The following year, he won the local spring tournament and the so-called Governor's Trophy in Jackson Heights, becoming the club champion. The winner of the spring tournament was supposed to have played the winner of the Fall Scratch Tournament, but Yardley won both. When he said that the Jackson Heights course "is the best course on Long Island and requires the most accuracy. It takes a real golf shot to place the ball on the green and hole it. Every hole is well trapped," the club secretary remarked that the best players are the most enthusiastic. Yardley won the championship of the Cold Stream Golf Club on Long Island, where he was a member, and in August 1926 he broke the course record of 72 at Sound Beach, farther out on Long Island, becoming the first first-time player to come in under 78.

Herbert and Hazel participated in many activities the community offered. She lay atop him on a sled as they raced down a wooden slide during a winter carnival. They made friends in the development, particularly with the Koukols. Clem Koukol was a telephone company engineer; his lean and attractive wife, Beatrice Koukol, played in the No. 1 position as captain of the women's tennis team and never lost a team match. She and Yardley were close; they went to speakeasies together in the wee hours and may have had an affair.

Like many American communities, Queens boomed during the 1920s. On average, more than 150 people a day moved there. Its population doubled during the decade. Speculators bought farms to put up housing developments. Though its real-estate prices did not go as ballistic as Miami's, Yardley saw prices soar as apartment blocks and rows of houses sprang from the ground, followed by businesses and schools. "Twenty-foot building lots rose

GRANTOR	GRANTEE	DATE	RECORDED	LIBER	PAGE	PROPERTY
Herbert O. Hazel	Sarah Robinson	Aug 19 1926	Aug 21 1926	3942	97177	

Portion of real-estate index book diagramming location of land in Queens County sold by Herbert and Hazel Yardley to Sarah Robinson

from $100 to $5000, and business frontage from $10 a front foot to $2000 a front foot," he said. He called it a gold rush and he wanted in. As boss of the Cipher Bureau, whose activity had declined, he could and did spend only an hour or so each day in the office. He used the rest of his time to become a real-estate broker, working as an associate or a syndicate member with Cody Realty, Randall Real Estate, Willis Realty, and McKay Real Estate. With them, he assembled land and arranged for financing for private houses, apartment houses, and stores, profiting on the purchase or sale of the land and receiving brokerage fees. He and his partners constructed apartment houses in the Queens neighborhoods of Astoria and Woodside and built blocks of one-family houses. He speculated in land, sometimes successfully. He bought and sold "a number of two-story brick attached homes on 82nd Street, Jackson Heights (which rapidly became the principal business street) while their price rose rapidly from $10,000 to as high as $50,000 before they were torn down and replaced by business structures." He and his associates cleaned up titles, lifted old restrictions, rezoned many small gores, appraised rentals, and leased space, especially to chain businesses—all for fees.

And he dealt in land for his own account. On 15 October 1925, as the rush gained strength, he bought a plot of land fronting on Roosevelt Avenue, a main throughfare, from Fredwill Realty, which had bought it from the families of two of the original settlers. Yardley gave Fredwill a two-year mortgage of $26,250. The next year he and Hazel sold some property in the same lot to Lyle T. Alverson. Either Yardley alone or Yardley and Hazel made four other purchases or sales in the same lot between 1925 and 1927. In a series of deals involving some neighboring plots in Woodside, he bought or sold seven times in 1927 and 1928. Elsewhere in Queens, he purchased two plots in August and September and disposed of both in November. He bought a couple of plots from his colleague Charles Mendelsohn in December 1928 and, the following year, sold a plot to another former colleague, John Manly of Chicago. And there were many other deals.

In addition to real-estate profits and his $7,500 in salary, Yardley was making some $5,000 a year as a consultant in codes for businesses. He was also profiting from the commercial code he and Mendelsohn had published. But his concentration on outside activity hurt the Cipher Bureau. All it was producing in the later 1920s was its Bulletin every few days of a few diplomatic messages, mostly Japanese. And these were often tardy. For example, a JCC code message of 26 February 1929 was not read until 2 November. It is true that cable intercepts were hard to get and that the international scene was quiet. Nevertheless, Friedman had already begun trying to intercept Japanese radio messages to cryptanalyze and Navy Lieutenant Laurance F. Safford had, in 1924, established a radio intelligence unit within the Code and Signal Section, likewise concentrating on Japanese communications. And this was a golden age of codebreaking. As a German cryptanalyst of the time put it, "By the end of the war in 1918, there was no cipher system in the world that was unbreakable. . . . The cryptanalysis of the ciphers and codes then used was . . . only a question of time, which depended upon the quantity of material and the range of cryptographic elements on the one hand and the number of personnel available for cryptanalysis on the other." In contrast to the handful of solutions per month that Yardley was putting out, Great Britain's Government Code and Cypher School and Germany's Chiffrierstelle were producing scores or hundreds. The worldwide shift from breakable codes to unbreakable cipher machines was getting under way, with Swedish, German, and American inventors offering such systems and the Reichsmarine and the U.S. Navy adopting them. Yardley was not interested. He never cryptanalyzed them nor considered them for military or diplomatic use. Moreover, though he knew of the weakness of State Department cryptography, had criticized its systems as "sixteenth-century codes," and had once proposed the American Telephone and Telegraph Company's Vernam-Mauborgne online unbreakable cipher machine as the answer and could have known that it could take paper-and-pencil form, he never battled the bureaucracy of the State Department—admittedly an all but hopeless task—to improve its cryptosystems. American cryptology stagnated. Yardley had failed to lead it energetically.

He contrasted sharply with his rival, William Friedman, then a civilian army employee with a staff of one clerk. Their motivations differed fundamentally. Yardley sought money; Friedman, knowledge. Friedman was driven not by egoism but by intellectual curiosity. "When it came to the cryptology," he said of his first contact with it at Riverbank, "something in me found an outlet." He loved the field not for its rewards, but for itself. And he changed it. A landmark study written while he was at Riverbank, *The Index of Coincidence and Its Applications in Cryptography,* empowered cryptology with new statistical weapons. Using them, Friedman reconstructed

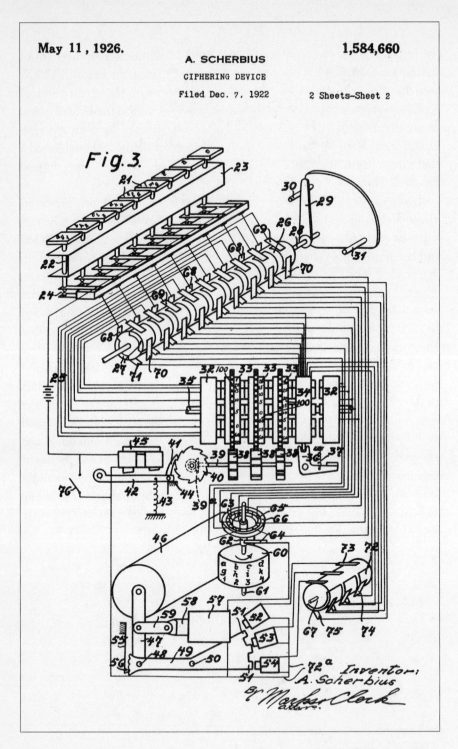

May 11, 1926.

A. SCHERBIUS

CIPHERING DEVICE

Filed Dec. 7, 1922

1,584,660

2 Sheets—Sheet 2

Fig.3.

Inventor:
A. Scherbius

By Marker Clerk
Attor:

Part of the patent of a version of the Enigma cipher machine—one of the modern cryptosystems ignored by Yardley in the 1920s the settings of a rotor cipher machine, the most advanced cryptosystem of the day (and which, in the form of the German Enigma, the British TYPEX, and the American SIGABA cipher machines, became the major form of high-level cryptography in World War II). He thus moved the United States to the forefront of cryptanalysis. In 1923, his textbook, *Elements of Crypt-analysis,* organized the field more logically than ever before and established a clarifying terminology that has become universal. He constantly looked forward, seeking to improve things.

Yardley, in contrast, wanted to maintain the status quo, which preserved his privileges. From the start, he moved politically. When war came, he saw what the country needed; he proposed himself to fill that need; he got the job and the money and power that came with it. Afterward, he continued on that track. He was never disinterested. He did not hunt for opportunities to improve codebreaking. Germany had had mathematicians breaking codes since World War I; Poland was foresightedly hiring them; Friedman, when he had the opportunity later, did so as well. Yardley never looked in that direction. The U.S. Census Bureau and the army's surgeon general's office were using Hollerith tabulating machines to deal with volumes of statistical data; the farsighted director of naval communications, Captain Stanford C. Hooper, was beginning to think about codebreaking machines. These devices would have reduced much of the Cipher Bureau's clerical work and would perhaps have made possible solutions that its limited staff could not undertake. Yardley never considered them. Improvements like these might have led eventually to promotions and raises, but seeking and implementing them would have distracted him from the outside work that was bringing him money. Thus he never sought them. While Friedman became the wave of the future, Yardley languished, and so did his agency.

11

End of a Dream

Soon after Major Owen S. Albright of the Signal Corps took charge of the Military Intelligence Division's communications division in July 1928, he surveyed its work. That included supervising Yardley's agency. Albright concluded that the Cipher Bureau was not doing what the army needed. It produced material of use to the State Department but not to the War Department. Most important, it was not training people for wartime use—the army's main requirement. "The expert staff of three were getting older each day and there was no arrangement for replacement or addition by young blood," he wrote. Nevertheless, even though the army did not need the agency, Albright did not propose abolishing it, perhaps because he did not want to encroach on State's work. He observed, however, that the army's cryptologic functions were split among three elements—military intelligence for solving intercepts, the Signal Corps for compiling codes and ciphers, and the adjutant general for the printing, storage, and issuance of cryptosystems. Albright suggested that they be assembled within the Signal Corps. Another officer, supporting this view, pointed out that "in technique the solution of enemy codes and ciphers is very closely related to the compilation of codes and ciphers for use by our own forces." Still another remarked that running a cryptanalytic office "is not a normal General Staff function as contemplated by the National Defense Act, but is an operating [line] function which should be performed by an existing service branch if practicable." The adjutant general objected to the proposed loss of control, but in support of his position he could argue only that his office had been doing that work for a long time and doing it perfectly—which nobody believed. The assistant chief of staff for intelligence, who would also lose an area of authority, did not concur in the proposal. The Signal Corps liked this growth in power and prestige. A colonel in the War Plans and Training Section, a disinterested unit, supported Albright's argument. On 4 April 1929, a memorandum recommended that the secretary of war order the reorganization for wartime operation.

Yardley knew about these proposals. Friedman wrote to him on 23 April that "Things are moving very slowly around here and nothing has yet been done toward organizing the business here." It did not concern Yardley very much. Moving the Cipher Bureau from one part of the army to another was a nuisance, perhaps, but not much more: agencies in bureaucracies are often shifted around. And since the draft proposal called for the move to take place only in case of war, it might not affect him for years. So starting at 9:30 a.m. on Monday, 6 May, Yardley attended a two-week course in cryptanalysis run by Friedman in Room 2469 of the temporary Munitions Building on Washington's Constitution Avenue. On Friday, 10 May, the army issued Changes No. 1 to Army Regulations 105-5, making the chief signal officer responsible "in time of war" for "the solution of intercepted enemy code and cipher messages." Yardley continued in the Friedman course. A week after it ended he complimented Friedman, said the course should be given annually, and offered to put together a cryptology "bible" of between two thousand and five thousand pages that would give examples of the importance of codes and ciphers in history and detail different cryptosystems.

The naval rivalry between the United States and the United Kingdom, stemming in part from their economic conflict in the western Pacific, had grown acute by 1929. The United States wanted "a navy second to none"; Britain, to protect its empire, had long sought the two-power standard—a fleet bigger than the next two largest together. Though the Cipher Bureau had contributed little if any intelligence to American diplomats at the 1927 Geneva naval conference, which had failed to come to an agreement, Yardley wanted to provide them with what he could for a new parley expected in London at the end of 1929 or the beginning of 1930. To do his best, he felt, he needed to get intercepts as regularly and as frequently as foreign codebreakers, and for this he had to free himself from the fetters that restrained his getting them. He remembered that J. Rives Childs, who had been with him in Paris, later worked for the American Relief Administration that Herbert Hoover had organized after World War I and had been impressed by Hoover's understanding of international affairs. Yardley therefore decided to present directly to President Hoover a plan that would "take full advantage of the skill" of his cryptanalysts. He conferred with Manly, who concurred.

"My plan was a bold one," he said, "and I would not move until I was confident of success. . . . It was therefore with some trepidation that I awaited the first speech of our new president." Hoover was to speak for the first time since his inauguration at a luncheon of Associated Press editors in New York City on 22 April.

The newspapers announced that the speech would be broadcast and I left the office searching for a radio. Belonging to no club where I could listen to the speech, I dropped into a speakeasy and asked the bartender to tune in. For half an hour I impatiently listened to a music program, then suddenly the President was announced. As he began to talk my heart beat faster for I had a premonition that this speech would shape the destiny of the Black Chamber. His voice was solemn and very serious, and I listened closely to every word.

His reference to those "who have not the intelligence and moral instinct to obey the law as a matter of conscience" made me uneasy [though Hoover was referring to Prohibition], for the United States Government had required me to do things which if known would send me to the penitentiary.

Then when he said, "Every citizen has a personal duty to order his own actions, to so weigh the effect of his example so that his conduct shall be a positive force in this community with respect to the law as law," I felt the doom of the Black Chamber.

No matter whether this was a political speech or whether it expressed the true sentiments of our President—in either case no official could afford to support the activities of the Black Chamber, for our very existence depended on the violation of Federal laws.

I would not now dare to present my memorandum. I was discouraged, and returned to my office in a cloak of gloom.

The next day I managed to shake off some of my pessimism. After all, the Black Chamber had won the Conference of 1921–22. We could do this again.

Perhaps by our skill we could retain our place, in spite of the necessity for breaking laws.

Yardley waited for an opportunity to demonstrate that skill.

A month earlier, on 28 March 1929, Hoover's secretary of state had taken the oath of office in the larger outer room of the department "before a galaxy of newspapermen and photographers who dictated how we should stand, look, and appear." Henry L. Stimson, a New York lawyer, gray-suited, gray-moustached, gray-haired, was well qualified for his new post. He had served as secretary of war and as governor-general of the Philippines and had run for governor of New York in 1910 on the Republican ticket. But though some felt that he was "not a great man," he was regarded as upright and principled—more so than many Washington officials. One journalist wrote of his "moral fastidiousness"; another said that "He is never under the slightest temptation to do anything slick or smart"; a third predicted that "there will be no trickery at the State Department while Stimson is in command."

He took charge at a time when his president saw in the world "the most profound outlook for peace today than we had at any time in the last half century." The world was sick of fighting. The Senate had just ratified the Kellogg-Briand pact renouncing war. Britain's Admiralty thought the world so calm that it could maintain maritime security with a smaller navy. The "spirit of Locarno," whose cluster of treaties had secured borders in Europe and required arbitration of disputes, warmed that continent. Hitler was a fringe politician, and Germany had in any event acceded to Kellogg-Briand. Mussolini was signing treaties with Spain, Hungary, Albania. Russia was preoccupied with its internal problems. Only Japan continued to act aggressively.

Those were the times and that was the man who held in his hands the fate of the Peeping Tom of the American government. Stimson started his secretaryship by preparing for the same naval disarmament conference for which Yardley wanted intercepts. The officials at the State Department wisely allowed Stimson to become familiar with his new job, including its realities and deceptions, before telling him about the Cipher Bureau. Yardley, who perhaps knew Stimson from the three months they had both worked in the little military intelligence unit just after America's entry into World War I, was likewise no fool, and in June, when his bureau had solved what he thought was "a series of important code messages," he thought the time ripe "to acquaint the new Secretary with our skill." With previous secretaries of state, he had not felt anxious. With Stimson he did. And he was right. When told about the bureau and its work, Stimson exploded.

In part the codebreaking undermined a practice that had worked for him. Stimson had had to deal with lies, deception, and prevarication as a secretary of war, a politician, a lawyer, and a human being. He could not be regarded as naive, yet he concluded that "The chief lesson I have learned in a long life is that the only way you can make a man trustworthy is to trust him; and the surest way to make him untrustworthy is to distrust him and show him your distrust." This principle guided his foreign policy as well. "We will do better by being an honest simpleton in the world of nations than a designing Sherlock Holmes."

This rule reinforced his belief that honor, in the form of diplomatic principle, outweighed any advantages that codebreaking would bring. He discussed the matter with his old friend Joseph P. Cotton, whom he had chosen as undersecretary and under whose purview the Cipher Bureau came. Cotton, a fellow lawyer, competent, and brilliant, explained that the crypt-analysts had been reading cryptograms to foreign ambassadors. Stimson and he agreed that this was "highly unethical." Stimson would have objected less if the War and Navy Departments were reading foreign code messages. "If we have to do it, it would be far less a mistake to do it through our military and naval services than to do it through our State Department. . . . Information which would tend to make him [the secretary of state] to have to carry on the functions of the head of the War Department ought not to be put in his hands." He explained, "The ambassador is the guest of the country he goes to. He is awarded diplomatic privileges"—such as immunity from arrest—that, under international law, Stimson said, include "absolute free-dom to communicate with his country free of espionage." Diplomats, he continued, "are the only class of officers who are supposed to deal interna-tionally on a gentlemen's basis. . . . The secretary of state doesn't act as a spy on the people he is receiving as brothers." He summarized this view in the lapidary phrase "Gentlemen do not read each other's mail."

Stimson told Hoover that he planned to stop the codebreaking; Hoover replied that it was the secretary's responsibility to run his department. And so, notifying the Military Intelligence Division of his action, Stimson de-cided to stop State's payments for the Cipher Bureau.

This doomed the bureau. Its expenditures stood then at about $23,000 a year, with State paying a slightly larger share than the War Department. Stimson wanted to discontinue payments at once. But the army pointed out that Cipher Bureau employees, none of whom had retirement benefits or civil service protection and whose work was secret and had little relevance to the commercial world, needed time to find other jobs. Moreover, an abrupt dismissal might drive employees to sell revelations. Stimson understood

117

June 1, 1931 - page 3

unethical thing for this Government to do to be reading the
messages coming to our ambassadorial guests from other
countries. So then and there, in 1929, I discontinued these
payments and that put an end to the continuing of this group
of experts who subsequently disbanded. Yardley now in his
book tells about this and also tells the fact that I put an
end to the practice. The newspaper men are very keen to
find out about it. The reasons why I cannot tell about it
must be manifest to anybody. I do not know how far my
predecessors knew of the facts which were brought to my
attention in 1929 and on the basis of which I stopped the
contributions; but if I should tell that story, it would seem
to make a reflection upon both Mr. Kellogg and Mr. Hughes.

In the afternoon I stayed at home trying to get over
my lumbago which I am very tired of. During the afternoon
Eleanor James came in and later her husband and Blanton
Winship came in and we had tea together and a very nice
reunion.

Then in the evening Mabel and I dined at the Klots's,
where Mr. Bundy, the new Assistant Secretary, and his wife
were visiting. We had a very pleasant dinner and we both
enjoyed the Bundys very much. Mrs. Bundy is particularly
attractive.

Page of Secretary of State Henry L. Stimson's diary, telling why he stopped State funds for codebreaking

and compromised. Cryptanalysis would cease at once, but the employees were paid and the office rented until 31 October.

For several years, only six persons had been on the payroll: Yardley, at $7,500 a year; Ruth Wilson, a cryptanalyst, at $3,750; Victor Weiskopf, also a cryptanalyst, at $3,660; and three clerks or secretaries, Marguerite O'Connor, $1,800; Edna Ramsaier, $1,600; and Alice Dillon, $1,320. Mendelsohn may have worked occasionally. Friedman, head and sole member of the Signal Corps' Signal Intelligence Service, whose job was to train, not solve, offered jobs in Washington to Wilson and Weiskopf. Both turned them down. Wilson had a husband and daughter in the New York suburbs; Weiskopf, a business in Manhattan. The three clerks, lacking civil service status, could not be transferred. Yardley resigned from the War Department and was rewarded with a fulsome letter that "regretfully accepted" his resignation, recalled the "outstanding and much coveted honor" of the Distinguished Service Medal, and thanked him for his "long and faithful services" and his "excellent record." He remained in the army reserve assigned to the G-2 communications section.

Thus was broken up the small band who had cracked codes in their small office for a decade and were bonded by their secrecy. America's first venture into peacetime codebreaking ended not with eulogies or the blowing of taps but, in Washington, with Yardley's sad handshakes with the State Department officials with whom he had worked, and, in New York, with sad smiles, hugs, and tears.

The question of what should be done with Yardley was discussed at a July meeting of Friedman and Signal Corps officers. A lieutenant colonel cold-bloodedly suggested that Yardley "be offered a definite proposal that he come here at a salary considerably below his present, with whatever other personnel from his section he wishes, the total to be within the funds available, which is $10,000. It is highly probable that this offer will be inacceptable, in which case this office is free to go ahead and reorganize from the very bottom, with no entanglements from the past." And in fact the army proposed $3,750, half of what Yardley had been getting and substantially less than Friedman's $5,600—and Friedman had less experience and less responsibility. Perhaps insulted, and probably confident that his real-estate and commercial code ventures would bring him enough money until he could find more lucrative work, Yardley turned the offer down.

In October 1929, Friedman went to New York for the chief signal officer. The pungent blue smoke of burning autumn leaves hung in the air as he packed up the Cipher Bureau's records—at least those that Yardley had not kept. He brought them to Washington and incorporated them into the files of his Signal Intelligence Service. The agency formally expired on Thursday, 31 October. Two days earlier, on Black Tuesday, the stock market had crashed. The Great Depression had begun.

During its existence, the Cipher Bureau had cost State $230,404 and the War Department $98,808.49. This third of a million dollars constituted less than one one-hundredth of a percent of State and War's combined budgets from 1919 to 1929. Over the entire decade codebreaking cost each American less than half a penny. What had the United States gotten for it? The Cipher Bureau had not contributed any significant information about several major international events of the decade—not the Rapallo pact of 1922 between the two pariah nations of Germany and Russia; nor the 1923 Franco-Belgian occupation of the Ruhr, occasioned by a claimed default of Germany's reparations payments and their connection with the Allied failure to repay war debts to the United States; nor the antiforeigner demonstrations in China that led to the 1927 American and British shelling of Nanking; nor the rupture of diplomatic relations between Britain and Russia that raised fears of war in 1927. But in many cases America's diplomats provided no forewarnings of these events either. Whether America would have done anything about any of these events is beside the point: intelligence is always welcome. Even though the Latin American codes were weaker and the nations closer, the Cipher Bureau did not provide details about the Honduran and Nicaraguan revolutions, which led the United States to land troops in those countries. It gave some details about the Mexican convulsions of 1919 and 1920. It provided information about the Tacna-Arica dispute between Chile and Peru, which the United States arbitrated to a successful settlement. It seems not to have offered much information that could help with America's main foreign policy problems—tariffs, immigration, foreign debts, the naval race with Great Britain, the diplomatic recognition of the Soviet Union. But it did help the United States compel Japan not to build as many warships as it wanted, thus relieving tensions, and so it saved the United States and the other Washington signatories millions of dollars by not building warships, instead, it may be hoped, using that money to advance the welfare of their peoples. This was the chief contribution of Yardley's Cipher Bureau. And this alone made it worth the money spent on it.

Yet Stimson abolished it, and though he claimed to base this on diplomatic protocol, he did not say "Diplomats do not read each other's mail" but "Gentlemen do not reach each other's mail." For actually his point was larger. Reading another's mail was theft and therefore wrong, not just for diplomats, but for everybody. Gentlemen exemplify man's moral obligations. At the root of Stimson's observation lay not a legalism but a Commandment: Thou shalt not steal. As Martin Luther, several of whose letters had been opened, said, "A thief is a thief, whether he is a money thief or a letter thief."

Yet other nations coolly broke the messages of diplomats who enjoyed immunities, who were gentlemen, and whose religions, like Stimson's, venerated the Ten Commandments. The 1921 British foreign secretary, Earl Curzon of Kedleston, had no qualms about profiting "by information which his own Department had secretly acquired." The foreign ministers of France, Germany, Italy, the Soviet Union read intercepts without a moral quiver. Why did only the United States ban codebreaking?

Because it flouted a creed peculiar to the nation: Puritanism. America claims for itself a morality greater than that of other nations, because it believes that it has a mission to redeem the world and that in fulfilling this it is doing God's will. This righteousness, or self-righteousness, which turns its wars into crusades and decrees that American presidents may not have mistresses, explains as well why Americans may not read other people's mail, even if foreigners do. Congress's 1792 law establishing the post office forbade its agents from illegally opening mail entrusted to them. Americans do not meddle. They do not deceive. They do not spy. President Woodrow Wilson, who said that America had "a moral obligation" to make good its "liberation and salvation of the world," maintained also that "Americans . . . condemned spying." A 1921 "Guide for Military Attachés" stated that "a military attaché shall not take any action, either directly or through agents, detrimental, or obnoxious to the government to which he is accredited." In 1928, the director of military intelligence told Army War College officers that the United States ran no spies and collected foreign information through its attachés only "with the knowledge and consent of the officials of the foreign government." When the Philadephia *Public Ledger* later heard of "the obtaining and decoding the messages passing between its guests here," it denounced the activity as "discreditable." The *Boston Post* called it "a mighty low-down business for the United States to be engaged in. . . . Certainly no honest American negotiator would have allowed this country to be put in the position of taking so unfair an advantage." Senator Hiram Johnson likewise learned of the codebreaking later and, while clear-sightedly recognizing that the United States was probably "the only first-class power in the world not doing this sort of reprehensible thing," he praised Stimson for closing the agency: "Be it said to the credit of the government of the United States and to the credit of the secretary of state who came into office in 1929 that when that practice was found existing in our country he stopped it forthwith." Just as Yardley's rise symbolized one of America's most characteristic qualities— optimism—so his fall spotlighted the other—Puritanism. The ethics of the nation demand purity; they reject lying. This is one of the reasons that F. Scott Fitzgerald called America the "greatest of human dreams," that

Abraham Lincoln called America "the last, best hope of earth." This morality helps make America a beacon for much of the world.

Of course, morality is conditioned by circumstance. It is as right during a war to break enemy codes as it is to kill enemy soldiers. During World War II, the man who had closed the Cipher Bureau championed codebreaking. But in the 1920s, nothing threatened the United States. The Cipher Bureau was then thus immoral. Henry Stimson said that closing it was the best thing he ever did. It was probably one of the most American.

12

The Best-Seller

Yardley had to support a wife and a four-year-old son. He made no money from his real-estate or codebreaking ventures in 1929 and he lost money in 1930. Never a saver, he had few or no resources to fall back on. Codebreaking jobs did not exist; his talent was "lodged with me useless." He gave up his fancy apartment in Jackson Heights and by October 1929 had retreated to Worthington, where he could live in his old house. His father was still alive; Yardley's well-to-do in-laws had just died and left Hazel and him some money, but Herbert soon spent it all. In April 1930, he applied to the navy for work as an instructor in cryptanalysis; it rejected him. His part-time code business did not bring in much money. As the Depression deepened, his real-estate business failed.

"I gave up an apartment house I held, an eighth interest in a real estate corporation, and sold nearly everything I had for less than nothing. I still have three pieces of property in my name that I surely hate to give up but I simply cannot afford to carry them. Rather than face a foreclosure I have offered to transfer the property to the holders of the mortgages." To Manly he wrote despairingly, "I'm not at all certain what I shall do." In the fall of 1930, on Manly's suggestion, Northwestern University's Scientific Crime

Detection Laboratory appointed him an associate staff member for "Decoding of Code Messages." A part-time lectureship, it could not have brought in much money. Yardley, broke and desperate, turned to his main marketable asset: his secret knowledge.

He had had the idea of a book since the Cipher Bureau had been closed, and had kept, illegally, many of its documents. He had long been interested in literature. As a code clerk at State, he had taken correspondence courses in English from the University of Chicago. In 1924, he considered writing some kind of religious story; it never went anywhere. He was not the only person interested in writing about American codebreaking. In 1927, Manly had asked military intelligence for some documents for six or seven articles he planned to write for *Collier's* magazine. "I believe I can be of some service to the Division in helping the public to understand the need for maintaining a military intelligence division." He would submit them before publication. But the War Department responded that present policies "covering use of confidential files make it impossible to grant your request."

Despite his ambitions, Yardley had never written anything except memoranda and letters, knew no one in the publishing business, and felt that "I was a cryptographer, not a writer." But he needed money. In the spring of 1930, apparently at the suggestion of the famous columnist Franklin Pierce Adams, known as FPA, who had worked in military intelligence during World War I, he proposed to Viking Press that he write the story of his activities, both during and after the war. But the publisher, after conferring with Colonel Stanley H. Ford, the assistant chief of staff for intelligence, decided that such a book would not serve the national interest and turned it down.

Yardley, discouraged, did nothing for a few months. Then he heard about an agent in New York, George T. Bye, who, friends told him, "could make anyone write, no matter what his training." Two years older than Yardley, Bye was one of the most powerful literary agents in New York, boasting as clients Charles A. Lindbergh, Governor Franklin D. Roosevelt, General John J. Pershing, and FPA, among others. After Yardley repeatedly telephoned him, Bye invited him to his office. He met the next day with Thomas B. Costain, the editor of the *Saturday Evening Post*, who later offered him a contract for three articles based on the work of MI-8 and the Cipher Bureau. A few days later, Bye proposed the idea to the Bobbs-Merrill Company, which was headquartered in Indianapolis. The editor, D. Laurance Chambers, who said "It is my job to keep in touch" with Indiana authors, suggested that Bye talk to the New York editor, George Shively. Yardley visited him on 20 December 1930. That afternoon, Shively wrote excitedly to Chambers:

"Bye may have dug up that best seller. This morning he sent in a chap named Yardley, who was chief of a secret bureau of the Intelligence Dept. during and for some time after the war. . . . It's an amazing story, and if true ought to make the front page of every paper in the world," although he recognized that "In a sense the whole thing was illegal." Shively indicated that "Yardley has done his best to meet my rather stiff requirements for an outline at once, and he asks that we give him as prompt an answer as we possibly can, as he is staying here on dwindling funds. He seems considerate, in that he is willing to sacrifice three Satevepost articles from the ms. if we think they would hurt the book." After reading the outline, Shively said that he was "more impressed even than I was before by its possibilities." He sent it off the day after Christmas even though he told Chambers that he knew he was "up to your eyes in the problems of the [sales] Conference." He warned that "it is likely that some careful maneuvering will be necessary. . . . Maybe we'd all be charged with treason and shot at sunrise." Yardley returned to New York and talked to Bye, who told him to write the book himself.

Yardley rented a second-floor room, called Apartment 14, at the back of 21 Jones Street in Greenwich Village, near Sixth Avenue, and began writing. As he told Manly:

> I sat for days before a typewriter, helpless. Oh, I pecked away a bit and gradually under the encouragement of Bye I got a bit of confidence. Then Bobbs Merrill advanced me $1000 on outline. Then there was a call to rush the book. I began to work in shifts, working a few hours, sleeping a few hours, going out of my room only to buy some eggs, bread, coffee and cans of tomatoe juice. Jesus, the stuff I turned out. Sometimes only a thousand words, but often as many as 10,000 a day. As the chapters appeared I took them to Bye who read them and offered criticism. Anyway I completed the book and boiled down parts of it for the articles all in 7 weeks.

On 11 February, Bye telegraphed Yardley with relief, pride, and hope: "Congratulations on magnificent book which is ten times better than my most optimistic expectations." Yardley was overwhelmed. "I cannot tell you how deeply your very kind and understanding telegram touched me STOP," he replied. "It has erased all the hours of drudgery necessary to the writing of this episode in American history STOP I have tried in my illiterate manner to write a history not of sensation but of human accomplishments STOP Your messages makes me feel that I have not struggled in vain."

But publication lay several difficult months ahead.

Yardley had, on 31 January 1931, submitted his resignation as a major in the Military Intelligence Reserve. He stated that "I do not approve of the policies of [the] Military Intelligence Division and therefore no longer wish my name identified with this division." The true reason was fear of a court-martial. The resignation was not accepted immediately. Friedman grew suspicious when he heard of it—a suspicion that deepened when Yardley asked him for some bits of World War I information that Friedman "could not very well withhold because they seemed innocuous." Friedman then took up the matter with the Military Intelligence Division. Its Lieutenant Colonel Albright, who in 1929 had proposed amalgamating Yardley's bureau into the Signal Corps, got in touch with Yardley. When the cryptologist admitted that he was considering writing a book, Albright warned him that disclosure of his peacetime activities could lead to international unpleasantness and, more pointedly, reminded him that he was a reserve officer—a veiled threat that he could be prosecuted for disclosing official secrets. Yardley promised vaguely to be careful but said neither that he would reveal no secrets nor that he would submit his articles to the War Department before publication.

Meanwhile, the army's judge advocate general was asked whether Yardley could be prevented from publishing anything. His office thought it could not act, because, despite Albright's threat, a reserve officer not on active duty was considered a civilian. The associate chief of section said, "There is no law known to this office which would render this individual liable to any prosecution or penalty as a Reserve Officer for any disclosure." Yardley's resignation wouldn't change this, he wrote. The Department of Justice might enjoin publication, but he doubted that this would succeed. The Espionage Act of 1917 indeed prescribed that "whoever, lawfully or unlawfully having possession of . . . any document . . . relating to the national defense, willfully communicates . . . the same to any person not entitled to receive it, . . . shall be punished by a fine of not more than $10,000, or by imprisonment for not more than two years, or both." But this penalized after the fact, and was in any event not specific to army officers. A prepublication prohibition seemed not possible because of the First Amendment.

Albright suggested to his boss, Ford, the assistant chief for intelligence, who had dissuaded Viking from publishing Yardley's book, that he alert the State Department and Charles Evans Hughes, by then chief justice of the United States. Ford perhaps spoke with State's Arthur Bliss Lane, a former liaison with the Cipher Bureau. The chief signal officer failed to get any information from Yardley about missing records of the Cipher Bureau. The army discussed the matter thoroughly but decided that nothing could be done. Yardley's resignation was accepted on 1 April 1931.

When the manuscript came in, Bye and Bobbs-Merrill each hired lawyers. Bye's team trembled. They had not seen the manuscript, but, they feared, "various individuals . . . might bring civil suits for libel. . . . The book might be held to be a criminal libel under New York law, . . . the publisher might be guilty of a misdemeanor" for publishing a document taken or copied without authority. They contended that "if the Attorney General applied to a Federal Court he would meet with slight difficulty in persuading it to issue an injunction against the publication and sale of this book." They concluded, "It is a reasonable assumption that the publication of this book would be opposed with the utmost possible vigor by a number of very powerful interests, and as indicated above we believe that such efforts would be likely to meet with success."

Bobbs-Merrill's lawyer was feistier. He argued that "there should be no criminal liability attached to the publication of this manuscript. I do not feel that it comes under the statutes defining treason, sedition, or espionage. Yardley may be guilty of dishonorable conduct and the violation of his oath of office, but I do not see where this would let the Bobbs-Merrill Company in for liability under the criminal laws of the country." He pointed out that "The information . . . was, in the main, obtained by the government by improper methods" and that Yardley's unit constituted "a left-handed appendage to the War or State Department which was not regularly organized and recognized as a bureau or department of the government. . . . Consequently, owing to the method by which the information was obtained and the fact that it was not obtained by a regularly constituted department of the government, I do not believe that there would be any liability on the part of the house in publishing the manuscript."

Bobbs-Merrill accepted it and, on 23 February, paid Yardley an advance of $500—not the $1,000 about which Yardley had boasted to Manly, and not on outline but on delivery of the manuscript. Bye deducted his commission of $50 plus $75 for legal fees, half of the $150 he had paid. Yardley's net was $375. On Sunday, 22 February, he left New York for Worthington, but not before telegraphing Bye, "Sorry I could not know you better as a person STOP FPA told me you were greatest literary agent in NY STOP Now I know it."

In Indianapolis, editing began. The copyeditor, Miss Kersey, was extremely conscientious. As one example, she counted some of the letters in a cryptogram, found that the tally differed from the count given in Yardley's manuscript, and queried it. Bobbs-Merrill continued to worry about possible legal consequences. Yardley defended his book. It "is proof that the United States is through with these criminal practices. I doubt if we will receive any protest from the present administration for they have washed their hands of my bureau. I can see that the publication of this book will force our government to use codes and ciphers that cannot be read by other governments. To me this is more important than the reading of foreign governments' messages," he wrote, expressing the unsensational and therefore rarely mentioned but utterly valid fact that keeping one's own secrets is more important than learning someone else's. He went on, "We will receive no protest from the Japanese Government . . . no government ever protests at this sort of thing."

But to ease the publisher's anxieties, Yardley made changes in his copy. In an anecdote about a possibly identifiable military intelligence officer who got a young society woman to steal code secrets, he switched the name from "Captain Pimp" to "Captain Lothario"; it wound up in the book as "Captain Brown." The publisher hired more lawyers. After more conferences with them, Yardley deleted all references to Hughes, a few personal letters, and the suggestion that one of Captain Pimp's girls might have sold her virtue for a code. He took out a reference to All-America Cable and replaced some names with titles. Thus Leland Harrison became "my correspondent at the Department of State" and Undersecretary Joseph Grew turned into "an important Department of State official who dealt directly with the Secretary on matters that affected my bureau." He deleted a crack that "Whatever the trouble, it must be serious indeed, for this was the first time I had ever heard of an Under Secretary of State arriving at his office as early as nine o'clock in the morning." He changed "break Federal laws" to "use embarrassing means." During a week in Indianapolis, he wrote thirty pages of revisions and then another twenty. He cut an introductory first chapter.

"This has hurt the book a great deal," he wrote to Manly, "but the publishers still think we have something. I'm not so sure. I finished the galleys yesterday. It seems to me the life has been taken out of the book. The original I believe had some fire. But we shall see." He lied in a more optimistic tone to Bye. "The story hasn't been hurt any. In fact, since I have had more time I have built it up here and there. Chambers and I were much pleased at reaction of lawyers. One sat up until 2 a.m. to finish the tale." And indeed, the firm's board of directors was "quivering with excitement." Yardley fought with Chambers over the price of the book. Chambers had originally promised to price it at around $3 but then tried to raise it to $5; Yardley made "a hell of a scene" in Indianapolis and Chambers reduced it to $3.50. On 23 March, Chambers wrote to Bye that the publishers were about to start setting type on the book. It was off the press by 3 May—a very fast job indeed.

One reason for the rush was that the *Saturday Evening Post*, with its circulation of 2.8 million the most popular magazine of the day, had bought

THE CURTIS PUBLISHING COMPANY
INDEPENDENCE SQUARE
PHILADELPHIA

February 17, 1931

George T. Bye, Inc.
535 Fifth Avenue
New York City

We inclose herewith our check

Twenty-two hundred and fifty dollars *in payment for*

Three articles at $750.00 each
by Herbert O. Yardley $2250.00

IMPORTANT

This check is offered and accepted with the under-standing that The Curtis Publishing Company buys all rights in and of all stories and special articles appearing in its publications and with the further understanding that every number of these publications in which any portion thereof shall appear shall be copyrighted at its expense. After publication in a Curtis periodical is completed it agrees to reassign to the author on demand all rights, except American (including Canadian) serial rights.

MOTION-PICTURE RIGHTS

Please note that our purchase of American serial rights covers new story versions based on motion-picture scenarios of short stories and novels that have appeared in Curtis publications, and that we do not permit the use of such versions in any peri-odical or newspaper. When selling motion-picture rights of stories that have appeared in a Curtis publication, you should notify the producer to this effect, so that there may be no misunderstanding on his part and no infringement of our rights.

THE CURTIS PUBLISHING COMPANY

Voucher for payment to Yardley for three *Saturday Evening Post* articles three prepublication excerpts, amounting to about a third of the book, and was scheduling the installments for the early spring. Stout, the *Post*'s leading writer, touched them up a bit. The first article led the issue of 4 April. Under the headline "Secret Inks," in the *Post*'s distinctive shaded typeface, and with a big byline, the first page displayed a photograph of the Army War College, which had been MI-8's first home, an oval vignette of Yardley, and a reproduction of a spy letter with the developed secret ink between the lines of the open letter. A two-page spread followed with more photographs, and then the article jumped to the back of the issue. The text began as the book did, with a description of the State Department code room. That first article was succeeded two weeks later by "Codes," with a reproduction of a page of a partially solved British code, and three weeks after that by "Ciphers."

The articles elicited some immediate fan letters. Van Deman, his old boss, wrote that "I have enjoyed your two articles very much indeed and congratulate you on the way they are written. I have heard many people here talk about them." A friend said that "All Jackson Heights is following your stuff in the *Post*." Two former colleagues, MI-8's David H. Stevens, by then vice president of the University of Chicago's General Education Board, and longtime Cipher Bureau cryptanalyst Ruth Wilson, also complimented Yardley.

Still others balanced praise with criticism. Mendelsohn wrote to Yardley that the articles were clear and "interest-holding" but revealed too much secret material. Manly, too, wrote that "I approve the articles and think they are well done," but he had always felt that "you might incur very serious criticism if you disclosed the fact that you had been reading the official messages of the Foreigners, and it seemed to me that your articles would not be saleable unless you did disclose that fact." He told Friedman that "I myself would not have revealed the fact that we were at any time reading, or attempting to read, the messages of a friendly nation, and I urged him not to do this." Friedman, while acknowledging that "You did a fine job of writing" and that "Mrs. F says you write in a thrilling style," was surprised at the amount of valuable information disclosed, in particular the reproduction of the British code, which showed that the United States was solving British messages.

Friedman solicited the views of World War I colleagues. Major Frank Moorman, head of G.2 A.6, the overseas codebreaking agency, replied: "I started to read the Yardley articles, but finding that their object seemed to be exaggeration of the importance of the writer with little respect for the truth, I did not finish. I have been surprised at the number of individuals who can write quite plausibly on the subject, 'How I Won the War,' and it was with some regret that I discovered Yardley had joined them." Colonel Parker Hitt, one of the giants of early American cryptology, declared, "I have never seen in a reputable magazine any series of articles so full of misstatement of fact, uncalled for criticism and innuendo as those by Yardley. A great national weekly has permitted him to pose before its readers as one of the outstanding heroes of the war, poor fellow, and he had to lie to do it."

This did not dismay Yardley or his editors. Costain was pleased. "The articles were a complete surprise to us. Yardley has a naturally clear and interesting style." The articles perhaps impelled Northwestern University's Scientific Crime Detection Laboratory to invite its new associate staff member to lecture, which he did early in May. Yardley said he had not realized that "this organization was so well thought of by both Chicago papers and Chicago police" and as a consequence "I lost a real opportunity for publicity" by not arranging for reporters to hear his talk.

Bound books became available in May. Yardley sent copies to his friends. The famous columnist Heywood Broun, who had gotten an advance copy and had apparently heard some of Yardley's tales of woe, wrote, "It's too bad that you couldn't write your book as you wanted to. But even with the deletions I think it is an impressive document."

The book ran 375 pages, with a frontispiece photograph of Yardley, eleven halftone tip-ins, and some line cuts in the text. It was bound in black, with the author's name and title stamped in red on the cover and the spine. The dust jacket was black with a red hexagon and black lettering. The list price was $3.50. With his flair for the colorful, Yardley named his book for the secret institution that in the eighteenth century had unsealed letters and cracked codes for the ministers and monarchs of absolutism. He called it *The American Black Chamber.*

He opened with a description of his work in the State Department's code room, his release from that department, and his staffing of MI-8. His work started when Van Deman summoned him and presented him with a letter in a shorthand that his secretary couldn't read. Yardley's discovery at the Library of Congress that the letter was in a common form of German shorthand led to the establishment of the shorthand section; he follows his story of how, with the help of a chemist, he brought out invisible writing on a blank piece of paper with a fascinating lecture on secret inks by a British expert that Yardley quotes at length. He provides the technical details of iodine vapor as a general reagent and the mechanics of counterfeiting a wax seal on official documents. This led to his setting up a section to detect and develop invisible ink. The case of German agent Madame de Victorica involved that technology, and Yardley tells the story in rich detail—more of it having to do with gumshoe tracking, however, than with the ink. He twice wrongly calls her "the beautiful blonde woman of Antwerp," adding in one case that it was she "for whom the British had searched in vain since the stirring days of 1914." He was thinking of Dr. Elsbeth Schragmüller, called Fräulein Doktor because she had obtained a Ph.D. in medieval history from the University of Freiburg with a dissertation on medieval guilds. She herself never spied but ran the German spy center in occupied Antwerp capably and except for Mata Hari was the most famous female intelligence personage of the war. Though Yardley believed "Fräulein Doctor is more or less a myth," meaning the tales about her activities, that did not prevent him from conflating the legend with Victorica's facts and glamorizing the spy. Nor did the invisible ink about which Yardley makes so much play a role in her capture.

Two chapters describe cryptanalysis—one of a one-part code used for two German wireless intercepts, the other of the Waberski cipher. In opening a section on Latin American espionage, Yardley deftly limns Harrison, though he never names him, as one of the "most brilliant leaders" of the "small clique in the diplomatic corps" that controls the State Department, whose "voice was so low that I had to strain my ears to catch the words." He offers Yardley a cigarette without any greeting and waits a minute in silence before almost whispering, "The Spanish code?" Spanish Code 74 is later photographed in Panama by a secret agent, enabling MI-8 to read it and the related codes.

Yardley reports his successful connections with the military cryptanalysts in London and in Paris and his rebuffs by the diplomatic cryptanalysts in those two cities. He titles his chapter about the French "La Chambre Noire," which to a Frenchman means "the black bedroom" (the French term is *le cabinet noir*). His chapter on the Versailles peace conference divulges nothing about the paucity of his work or the plenitude of his play but asserts sensationally that he solved a message reporting "an Entente plot to assassinate President Wilson either by administering a slow poison or by giving him the influenza in ice."

He sketches the demobilization of MI-8 and the establishment of the Cipher Bureau. He teases the reader: "Our problem was to obtain copies of messages. How? I shall not answer this question directly." And he never does, either directly or indirectly. Instead he digresses into an official's telling him the State Department wants some Soviet cryptograms solved "at the earliest possible moment." Yardley promises to do his best but warns him, in a phrase that evokes the mysticism shrouding cryptology, "don't give them the idea that all we have to do is to go into a trance to reveal hidden secrets." And he pleads: "Soviet agents, please note. Yes I once had copies of these

Old Balance	Posting Date	Invoice Date	Dept.	TERMS	Amount	Deductions	Balance	
	AUG 8 31	AUTHORS		ADVANCE AGAINST ROYALTIES	500.00		500.00	1
								2
								3
								4
								5
								6
								7
								8
								9
								10
								11
								12
								13
								14

MANAGEMENT SERVICE INC. (INDPLS.)

PLEASE DETACH BEFORE DEPOSITING

AUG 8 1931   19

THE BOBBS-MERRILL COMPANY

Check stub for an advance payment to Yardley for *The American Black Chamber* documents, but I don't care to have my throat cut and do not plan to publish them. In fact they have been destroyed. So be reasonable."

The next three chapters give a reasonably accurate account of the solution of Japanese codes and the Washington disarmament conference. Yardley camouflages Livesey as "Charles Mundy" because "he now holds a position that might be jeopardized were his past history known" and says that when Yardley asked whether he wanted to study Japanese, "I could see his little eyes burn with desire." At the end, he exults that "America at last had won her point."

With this, the book reaches its climax. Yardley skims over the next seven years of the bureau's existence in three chapters—70 percent of its life in 15 percent of the text. He claims to have solved forty-five thousand cryptograms from 1917 to 1929 and to have broken the codes of twenty countries. A blonde tries to seduce him. When Yardley starts to say he is considering attacking Vatican ciphers, the new director of military intelligence, Major General Dennis E. Nolan, a Catholic, turns pale—and Yardley finishes lamely with, "I personally feel that it is unethical for us to inquire into the Vatican secrets." He explains to a shocked Leland Harrison of State, whom he had known since World War I, that "Your codes, your point of view, belong to the sixteenth-century." He then refers to the on-line cipher machine invented in 1917 by engineer Gilbert S. Vernam and says accurately that its bastardized version using repeating keytapes "was not indecipherable." Then he points out, again accurately but obscurely, of the never reused keytape that Signal Corps Major Joseph O. Mauborgne had conceived for it and that made it unbreakable, "The only indecipherable cipher is one in which there are no repetitions to conceal." He predicts presciently: "Sooner or later all governments, all wireless companies, will adopt some such system." But, forgetting how often cipherers' errors lead to solutions, he adds prematurely, "And when they do, cryptography, as a profession, will die."

As he leaves Harrison's office, he reflects how his "whole life had been devoted to destruction. I should like to leave a monument to constructive cryptography . . . I mused how proud one might be to leave to the United States Government a method of communication that would insure the secrecy of her dispatches throughout the ages. . . . But why dream? After all, weren't all diplomatic representatives just funny little characters on a stage, whispering, whispering, then yelling their secrets to the heavens as they put them on the cables!" Finally, Yardley relates how he informed his uncomprehending little staff of the decision to close the Cipher Bureau and how he himself visited officials in Washington to say good-bye, the last of whom, his immediate superior, Assistant Secretary for Administrative Affairs Wilbur J.

Carr, "was visibly relieved when I shook hands and said good-by. He walked with me across the spacious room and even opened the door for me. Thus ended the secret activities of the American Black Chamber."

Though not the most significant work on cryptology published up to then—Friedman's monographs in particular far outweighed it—*The American Black Chamber* was the most memorable. It owes this star quality in part to its shock value but in larger part to Yardley's writing. Of course, the competition was sparse. Most books on the subject dealt with the technology. But even those—most of them antiquarian—that told about the effects and the people of cryptology could not rival Yardley. Blaise de Vigenère told only a few anecdotes in his 1587 tome; John Davys did little better a century and a half later. Johan Ludwig Klüber's historical examples merely salted his outstanding 1809 survey, and Etienne Bazeries barbed his few stories and opinions with Gallic cynicism in 1901. In their years, however, cryptology did not have a persistent significant effect on events. Yardley enjoyed the advantage that in his time it did. Still, other post–World War I writers did not match *The American Black Chamber* in excitement. André Langie, a Swiss cryptanalyst, merely related half a dozen cases. André Lange and E.-A. Soudart, deputy heads of the French military codebreaking agency, added a historical perspective. Yardley alone provided a continuous narrative. And he was a better writer than all of them. His book races along. Although it lacks the creamy elegance and patrician worldliness of that great American autobiography, *The Education of Henry Adams,* it has a tightly focused story, told well. Yardley was not literary. The entire book has not one biblical or poetical allusion, not one historical reference, not one simile out of his small farmtown boyhood. But he had the soul of a poet. He evokes scenes or people in unforgettable images. A photocopy operator has a "face the color of death under the dim green lights of the photostat room." The reticent Leland Harrison is "a human sphinx." Victorica "fenced cleverly" with her interrogators. During his break of the Japanese codes, "words danced before me." He brings an agents' rendezvous in Manhattan to life: "On this April evening, just as the street lights were switched on along Fifth Avenue and the Cathedral [of St. Patrick's] chimed the quarter-hour, this slender schoolgirl, barely sixteen, a folded newspaper held tightly under her left arm, carefully picked her way through the jammed busses and squawking automobiles, and without so much as turning her head, squeezed a path through the late shoppers, and quickly disappeared into the grim Cathedral."

The American Black Chamber is presented as history. How truthful is it? Yardley himself admitted that some of the material was "bunk" and "hooey" and that "To write saleable stuff one must dramatise. Things don't happen in dramatic fashion. There is therefore nothing to do but either dramatise or not write at all." And he did exaggerate, err, and fictionalize. How else but by imagining it could he have known how the schoolgirl went to the cathedral? The "old and rare Spanish coin" used to counterfeit a seal was merely an old Mexican centavo. Madame de Victorica was not "of royal birth" but the daughter of a Junker officer. An account of the breaking of Spanish codes is fiction. And there are others.

The most knowledgeable evaluation of the book's accuracy was written by an insider, Charles Mendelsohn, Yardley's longtime colleague and friend. He dealt less with the minutiae than with larger issues, and he was fair in judging the work as a whole.

"The American Black Chamber" is an account of the cryptographic activities of the United States Government during the World War and the years that followed. Its author, Herbert O. Yardley, was in charge of these activities with the exception of those conducted at the front in France. He has unlocked the doors and opened the windows of the secret room and has shown us without reserve how the wheels of the machinery revolved and what the products were.

We need not here enter into the question of whether the author is justified in making these exposures. There will be some, and the present writer is among them, who think he was not. Mr. Yardley's point of view is that since the United States have now discontinued the work of the Black Chamber there is no reason why secrecy should be further maintained.

What we are concerned with is the book itself. The author has told his story more than well, and has skillfully avoided two temptations that must have assailed him—the technician's wish to write of the details of his subject as a specialist, and the opposing desire to write down to a public that craves sensation above all else. Thrills there [are] and thrills aplenty; but for the most part they are legitimately provided by the subject matter and only at times by red fire.

Mr. Yardley obviously set himself a three-fold task, which it was none too easy to accomplish. In the first place he has given a history in outline of the organization and subsequent progress of the Black Chamber. At the same time he has been at pains to present some of the most important messages deciphered; and, in addition, to give, in sufficient detail for the lay reader to follow, the analysis of some of the most interesting cryptographic problems that arose during the course of the ten years of work.

Accordingly we follow the growth of the Chamber from its very inception shortly after America entered the war to the point where it comprised at one [point] we are told, two hundred workers. We see how it deciphered messages written in many different systems of shorthand, documents written in secret ink, and many different kinds of codes and ciphers.

In the way of dramatic stories we have that of Waberski, the captured German spy, and the hair-raising accounts of the activities of Madam Victorica and Patricia [a suspected German spy]. We have German transposition ciphers as used by the Germans and the Soviet Government of Russia, the Mexican modification of the Vigenere or Beaufort Cipher, the German use of a Dictionary Code, and other cryptographic devices, with brief references, mostly worked in, to German Trench Code[s] as used at the battle front, and the diplomatic codes of Spain and Peru.

But the climax in dramatic interest as well as in code and cipher achievement is reached with the account of the decipherment of the Japanese messages and the verbatim reproduction of a number of those messages sent in 1921 on the occasion of the Washington Naval Disarmament Conference.

It is not often that decipherment and message content are alike dramatic. Most of the high moments of drama during the World War were missed so far as American cryptographers were concerned because the Black Chamber was not organized until we were already in the war. The famous Zimmermann note endeavoring to associate Mexico and Japan with the German cause—loud evidence of the complete bankruptcy of German diplomacy—was deciphered by the British and turned over by them to our Government. The message in which [German] Ambassador Bernstorff, informed of Germany's approaching unrestricted submarine warfare, and convinced that America's entrance into the war was unavoidable, ordered the captains of German ships in American waters to make their vessels unseaworthy, was read in Washington—but it was read more than a year after the event had taken place, and aroused but passing interest.

With these Japanese messages, however, the case is different. Their decipherment was indeed a beautiful cryptographic achievement, and even to one who, like the writer of these lines, saw the work in progress, the account of it in Mr. Yardley's book, rudimentary as it necessarily is, brought a new thrill and a new sense of admiration. One need not share the author's feeling of the relative merits of this decipherment and Champollion's decipherment of the Rosetta Stone to feel this thrill—the reading of these messages challenges wonder quite apart from any such comparison.

The contents of the Japanese messages reproduced is likewise fascinating in the extreme. We are put behind the scenes in Japan's diplomatic work-room, and see how the delegates were instructed to work day by day—what they were to demand, and with what part of their demands they were to be content. We are told that the American representatives received these messages daily "before they have their morning coffee." (Page 305) It is easy to see how the work of the latter was facilitated, and how the United States finally obtained a ten-to-six naval ratio instead of the ten-to-seven ratio which the Japanese had originally demanded. As Mr. Yardley puts it, "Stud poker is not a very difficult game after you see your opponent's hole card." (Page 313)

We have said that Mr. Yardley has only occasionally yielded to the temptation to use red fire. He has, however, done so at times, and quite unnecessarily. He had attempted to make the story of Pablo Waberski more dramatic by leaving the reader under the impression that Waberski suffered the death penalty; as a matter of fact he was convicted and sentenced, but ultimately pardoned. We are told (page 331) of a sensational raid on the Black Chamber with papers found in disorder etc. What actually happened was the theft of a few bottles of booze—and nothing else. We are left in suspense on page 139 with the whole Black Chamber under suspicion and an unknown German spy in their midst—a situation to which Mr. Yardley never returns. This is unpardonable.

The speed with which the Waberski cipher was read is very greatly exaggerated. And in two instances the author has erred more gravely. The analysis of the two German wireless intercepts (Chapter VI) and their decipherment is a pretty narrative, but the facts in the case are far more prosaic: no such decipherment was made and none was necessary, because the Chamber ascertained by underground railroad how the messages had been encoded [in an English-French bilingual dictionary whose name had been given to MI-8]. Still we are told that what we are witnessing is an "actual decipherment." (Page 121) Again in his account of the decipherment of the Spanish Diplomatic Codes, Mr. Yardley has forgotten a certain advertisement in the personal columns of a newspaper informing him that his uncle had the Spanish influenza—a neat way of imparting the news that a Spanish code or two awaited him in London (the neutral government's codes referred to on page 218), and this influenza germ, by pretty cryptographic work developed into the whole Spanish code system.

"The American Black Chamber has never had an equal," says Mr. Yardley (Page 20). This may be an exaggeration. In any case, however, its work, climaxing in the Japanese achievements, was sufficiently outstanding not to require claims for more than it did.

Mr. Yardley dedicates his work "to the personnel of MI-8 and the American Black Chamber and to our skillful antagonists, the foreign cryptographers, who still remain behind the curtain of secret diplomacy." Among his associates in the Black Chamber he is enthusiastic in his praise of Dr. John M. Manly:

"Fortunately for us, Captain Manly had the rare gift of originality of mind—in cryptography called 'cipher brains.'" (Page 39) Everyone who worked under and with Captain Manly will understand and heartily echo those sentiments.

As for the other cryptographers, the success of the Black Chamber would seem to have been attained more in spite of than because of their assistance. Of those sent abroad we are told "I regret to say that not more than two of all those we sent to France distinguished themselves, but this was not the fault of MI-8." (Page 120) Of the choice of personnel we are informed that from applicants who had dabbled in ciphers "I quickly selected a few scholars who appeared to have a superficial knowledge of ciphers, and ordered them commissioned." (Page 38) To judge from the description given of their behavior they seem to have been a supercilious crew, and one is not surprised to learn that "most of them proved dismal failures." One worker, we are told, "became expert" (Page 348), and another was obviously still better, for he is called "My cleverest cryptographer." (Page 272) But we must not too quickly assume that even those two amounted to much, for of the second—the "cleverest"—we are told a little later (Page 279) that "he had no originality of mind as a cryptographer and needed assistance when a new cipher problem confronted him."

Were the American cryptographers really such a rotten lot as this? The present writer has never thought so. In any case, the document PQR [a German order to destroy all secret service papers], the reading of which earned the special thanks of General Churchill, (Page 153) was deciphered by one of this aggregation, though nothing in the text of the book would lead one to suppose it.

If among all the thousands engaged in cryptography with the British, French and Italians, "there were no more than a dozen who had 'cipher brains'" (Page 121), the failure of the Americans outside of a very, very few cannot have caused any great surprise. The rest of us got a great "kick" out of the work and now get another out of Yardley's corking good story.

Mendelsohn is correct in saying that the faults of the work, though irritating and reducing its value as evidence, do not detract much from its merit. Its revelations, its narrative thrust, its distinctive writing overwhelm its defects. The book is a classic. And it stamped Yardley unforgettably into cryptology and intelligence.

13

The Critics, the Effects

T**he** *American Black Chamber* exploded into the consciousness of the world on publication day, Monday, 1 June. All three Washington dailies—the *Post,* the *Herald,* and the *Evening Star*—front-paged their stories about it. So did the Chicago *Tribune* and the *New York Herald Tribune.* The *New York Times* put its story on 3, as did the *Brooklyn Eagle* and the Atlanta *Journal.* Some papers ignored the story, among them the *New York World-Telegram* and the *New York Evening Post.* The news was not the publication of a book but Yardley's statement that he had solved a coded message revealing that the Allies had planned to poison President Woodrow Wilson at the Versailles peace conference.

The *New York Times* and the *Herald Tribune* probed beyond the allegation. The *Herald Tribune* reported that the then chief of the general staff said he had never heard of the conspiracy. The *Times* said that some army correspondence bore on Yardley's statement but that no officers could remember anything about it. In follow-up stories the next day, both papers reported that officials in the State and War Departments denied the existence of the Black Chamber—though State's officials left themselves an out by saying that they "had never heard of a decoding room for the purpose intimated" and were "disposed to discredit" Yardley's statements. The Chicago *Tribune* said that no one at State "ever had heard of any move to decode the secret telegrams" and that War Department officials had failed to find any documents substantiating Yardley's Wilson report. The story stayed alive for a few days in Washington. Wilson's physician, asked by the *Evening Star* about it, denied that Wilson had died from poisoning. And Yardley provided the *Herald* with the solved text of a message by an informant reporting the alleged poisoning plot.

The actual reviews of the book varied. Harry Hanson of the *World-Telegram,* claiming to have known Manly and J. A. Powell, also of MI-8, raved, "Necromancy is certainly what these men used, and yet Yardley tells about it as if you and I could go out tomorrow and, by dint of patience and some application, decode the secret messages of the Soviet. But to me Yardley is nothing short of a living Sherlock Holmes." The *Herald Tribune*'s Lewis Gannett was cooler. "As an international diplomat Mr. Yardley is an over-excited amateur. He takes seriously a theory that the Allies poisoned President Wilson at the Paris Peace Conference; he thinks his decoding of Japanese confidential messages was almost exclusively responsible for Secretary Hughes's success at the Washington Arms Conference, and that the recent London [naval disarmament] conference failed because he was out of the picture; he consistently over-sensationalizes his revelations; and one marvels a little at the code of ethics which permits a professional decoder to keep copies of the messages he decodes and later to publish them, without authorization from any government, apparently solely to tell a good story and to get back at those who banned his bureau." But he conceded that "Yardley does tell rattling good mystery stories."

"*The American Black Chamber* is one of the most gripping and exciting mystery stories I ever came across. And it actually happened," enthused the Chicago *Tribune.* The *Philadelphia Ledger* proclaimed that Yardley "has written a book of intense importance to all those interested in safeguarding world peace and honor." In the *New York Times Book Review,* which led the issue with an extensive review of the memoirs of the pre–World War I German chancellor, Prince Bernhard von Bülow, Uffington Valentine capsulized some of Yardley's stories but never offered an overall judgment of the book. The *Saturday Review of Literature* wrote that "Simply as entertainment this exposé . . . is well worth the price, for it is written with sprightliness and insperded with startling and amusing tidbits. To a person with curiosity to know something of what goes on behind official draperies, it provides more than entertainment, and this even though it is quite impossible to check up on many of its statements and incidents."

Famous friends and acquaintances sent blurbs for the dust jacket. Best-selling author Christopher Morley declared that "A phase of international relations hardly suspected by most citizens is here revealed in full candor." William Allen White, the Kansas editor who was the most famous journalist of the day, called it "The most important book of the year." It even inspired the flattery of a satire: Corey Ford, writing as John Riddell, revealed "the secret operations of a similar organization in the field of American Critical Intelligence, known as the Literary Black Chamber," which was "written with the same charming modesty and reserve which characterized the style of the retiring Major Yardley."

The book took off. Within a week, the clipping bureau sent Bobbs-Merrill "an amazing bunch of clippings." Advertisements ran in the *Washington Post* and the *Evening Star*. By mid-June the book was in its third printing—though the printing was small because, the publisher claimed, it needed to keep the inventory down when its fiscal year ended 30 June. A Bobbs-Merrill sales bulletin of 16 July proclaimed that the book was first on the best-seller list of eight of eleven New York bookstores, and second or third on the others. A bulletin 28 July put it at eight of twelve bookstores and listed fifteen cities whose newspapers carried it on their best-seller lists. Some stores were selling three copies a day. Putnam's, on 45th Street near Fifth Avenue, one of two Manhattan bookstores that displayed piles of the book, put up a large photograph of Yardley accompanied by the review quote "A living Sherlock Holmes." The display included a photocopy of a page of a German trench code, a strip cipher device, and photocopies of a dozen secret-ink documents. By 31 July, the book had sold 7,456 copies. Still, the publisher griped. Chambers noted to agent Bye "that we have *incurred* extremely heavy lawyers' fees, that we have been spending generously for publicity and advertising, so that our investment in the book is a bit stagger-ing, and it will take a whole lot of business to cover it. Your lawyers' opinion made it necessary for us to proceed warily at every step, and consult, consult, and consult again. Only by that course could the book have been published at all." Bobbs-Merrill had spent $4,736.89 for advertising alone, and so it had not yet shown a profit, Chambers said.

Yardley, however, was ecstatic. Mail inundated him. People sent crypto-grams to see if he could solve them. Former colleagues got in touch. Mark Ryan, a former coworker in the State Department telegraph room, wrote,

THE AMERICAN BLACK CHAMBER !

NOW CLOSED AND BOLTED —

July 28, 1931

THE AMERICAN BLACK CHAMBER
Bulletin No. 3

THE AMERICAN BLACK CHAMBER, still holding its own on best seller lists, now occupies the following positions according to reports from stores in New York and Brooklyn the past week:

The Store	The Position
Abraham & Straus	First
Frederick Loeser & Co.	First
Arthur R. Womrath, Inc.	First
R. H. Macy Book Department	First
Carroll's Book Store	First
Kleinteich Book Store	First
Doubleday, Doran Book Shops, Inc.	First
Ball & Wild	First
American News Company	Second
Charles Scribner's Sons	Second
Brentano's	Third
Putnam's Bookstore	Third

The newspapers in cities outside of New York and Brooklyn that are now listing THE AMERICAN BLACK CHAMBER as a best seller are as follows:

Best Seller In:

Jersey City, New Jersey	Charleston, West Virginia
Minneapolis, Minnesota	New Orleans, Louisiana
Los Angeles, California	Indianapolis, Indiana
Philadelphia, Pennsylvania	Chattanooga, Tennessee
New Bedford, Massachusetts	Cleveland, Ohio
Paterson, New Jersey	Lewiston, Maine
Quincy, Illinois	Waterbury, Connecticut
Seattle, Washington	

A full page story of how Madame Maria de Victoria was captured, appeared in the Pittsburgh Press and the Philadelphia Record, Sunday July 12th.

The Literary Guild of America, Inc., in Wings, lists THE AMERICAN BLACK CHAMBER first among the recommended books.

The Spots News Bulletin, published by the New York Evening Post, says THE AMERICAN BLACK CHAMBER "is one of the few titles that are both selling and renting well."

R. R. Bowker Company include THE AMERICAN BLACK CHAMBER in their list of best selling books during June.

Sales bulletin for *The American Black Chamber*

"You've put your personality into it so definitely that I'm sure I'd know you were the author even if it had been anonymous. It's typical Yardley. . . . The characters stand out very plainly—from Buck [John R. Buck, head of Indexes and Archives, under whom telegraph and cipher communications came] to Dick Tanis, including [Jordan H.] Stabler, Harrison, and the others. You've shown real talent and I hope you won't stop with this one." The Leigh Lecture Bureau contracted with him.

All this attention turned Yardley's head. After *Liberty* magazine wrote about Reginald Hall, the head of British naval intelligence in World War I, Yardley boasted, "The more he talks of Hall the better the book, for I am the Admiral Hall of America." The man who was always broke had stationery printed: "Herbert O. Yardley Worthington, Indiana." But he went overboard. Chambers said that "Yardley is crazy to get his name in the papers. . . . This sort of thing is not going to help the sale of The American Black Chamber. It is calculated to involve us in obloquy if nothing worse." He warned an executive: "I trust that I made it perfectly clear to you that we could not directly or under any form of subterfuge or indirection pay one cent of Yardley's expenses to Chicago, New York or anywhere."

Some observers criticized Yardley for having revealed secret information. The *New York Evening Post* editorialized that *The American Black Chamber* "betrays government secrets with a detail and clarity of writing that makes one gasp. Rarely has there come out here a book with such dramatic and important official revelations. We wish Theodore Roosevelt were alive to read to the author of this book a lecture on betraying the secrets of one's country." The *Brooklyn Eagle* told the government to strengthen its legal restraint against betrayal by former servants. The *Boston Post* said that "We do not believe for a moment that a man like Secretary Hughes would countenance such treachery." The *Japanese American*—not surprisingly—blasted Yardley for writing "an immoral book. It is immoral because it boastfully narrates the pilfering, the snooping, the stealing, the spying practiced by agents under his supervision." The same paper urged worldwide abolition of black chambers, but conceded that "Japan is not the proper nation to advance the proposal." Of Stimson's action, the Christian Science Monitor said that "This fine gesture will commend itself to all who are trying to develop the same standards of decency between governments as exist between individuals."

A clandestine roar came from the intelligence community and some cryptologists. They fumed at Yardley's breach of confidence, envied his fame, and resented his revelations, which they thought would make more work for them. Lieutenant Colonel Albright reviewed the book for his boss, Colonel Ford, the assistant chief of staff for intelligence. "The book is a self-glorification of the author's activity. . . . While most of the basic facts in the book are correct, the narration of details is in most cases so distorted that the exaggerations would seem to be apparent to the casual reader. . . . they may cause protests from foreign governments." War Department records did not bear out in full Yardley's claim of solving the codes of more than a dozen nations named in the book. Aloysius J. McGrail, who had handled secret ink in MI-8, wrote to the director of military intelligence that "I cannot protest too strongly against Yardley's action" and then listed several technical details—such as the use of iodine vapor to detect secret ink—that should never have been made public. He went to see MI-8 colleague Thomas A. Knott, who pronounced Yardley's activities "dishonorable."

One anecdote in the book particularly angered Friedman. Yardley had written of a test in which an American student cryptanalyst in France had had American radio messages intercepted and, without any knowledge of the American cryptosystem, had solved the messages in a few hours. Yardley went on to claim that the Germans intercepted all Allied messages and that their experienced cryptanalysts "without question had also solved and read these telegrams." Learning that the Americans were planning to flatten a bulge in the German lines, the St. Mihiel salient, the Germans consequently withdrew before the American attack. According to Yardley, this "represents only a small part of what might have been a tremendous story in the annals of warfare."

Friedman felt this account maligned the late Captain Howard R. Barnes, who had run AEF codemaking. Yardley and Barnes, who had clerked in the State Department (though not in the code room) at the same time, had not gotten along, but Friedman liked him and told Yardley that Barnes "did a very creditable job. His memory does not deserve such ill-treatment. Moreover, he left some children. The boy is about 15 now, and, doggone it, I put myself in Barnes' place and I wouldn't want my youngster to get the notion that I fell down on the job, which I didn't. As I look at it, you place a stigma on Barnes' record, without any warrant whatsoever." Friedman circularized former colleagues about it. The chief clerk of G.2 A.6, Edward J. Vogel, replied that "My best recollection is there was not a word in the files indicating that the elimination of surprise in the St. Mihiel offensive was due to any fault in the construction of our code." He quoted from the memoirs of the German commanding general, Erich Ludendorff: "movement had been noticed as early as the end of August, and an American offensive seemed probable there." Ludendorff ordered the withdrawal 8 September, but it

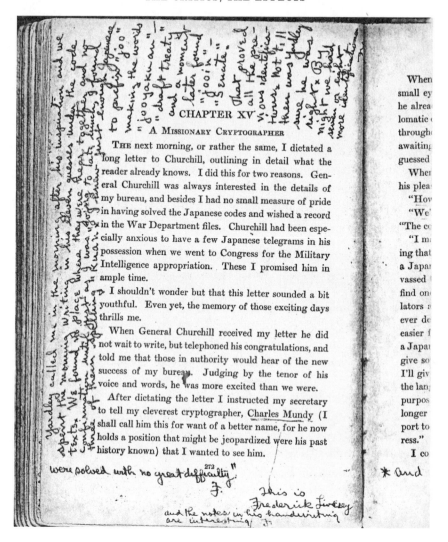

A page of *The American Black Chamber*, annotated by former Yardley coworker Frederick Livesey and by William F. Friedman ("F")

had not been carried out very far when the American offensive began on 12 September, his memoirs stated. Vogel and some colleagues felt that Yardley had invented the story to sell books.

In fact Yardley had jumbled two episodes. In one, Lieutenant J. Rives Childs, a Riverbank graduate, had tested an enciphered American code, found he could strip the encipherment from it, and reported the danger of this system; no messages were transmitted in it and the system was dropped. The other episode involved a 1930 talk by G.2 A.6's chief, Moorman, before

officers of the Military Intelligence Division. He told how American monitoring of American messages—"every one of which could be copied by the
Germans"—had enabled an American cryptanalyst to test-solve the code and
notify superiors of an attack. Moorman later admitted "that he put it on a
little thick at that lecture, to make the impression he wanted." Still, Yardley
had again erred and exaggerated. Childs's test took place in May; the St.
Mihiel attack came in September. And Yardley had no evidence that the Germans had intercepted, solved, and utilized American messages. Still, he was
not as unprincipled in this matter as Friedman made him out to be. And
Manly defended him. He explained the matter to Friedman, put it into the
context of the book, and put the book into the overall political picture. He
and Yardley

> had before us information which I thought justified our understanding of the
> occurrence. I recall that this was in part the stenographic report of Col. Morr-
> man's [sic] address, and I am under the impression that we had also some
> information from Childs himself, . . . I do not believe Yardley intended to
> reflect on the A.E.F. code and cipher staff, but only to emphasize the very great
> importance of an undecipherable means of communication. He has, however,
> for the sake of a heightened effect, given an entirely false impression of the
> equipment of the officer whom he represents as deciphering the codes. . . .
> Yardley's articles and book are, of course, often inaccurate in details, and I
> think he has made a serious mistake in not giving due credit to the men who
> actually did the work in many of the instances he relates. I have, of course, no
> personal complaint, as he has written of me in terms more complimentary than
> I deserve. I should, in fact, have preferred to receive the same treatment as
> other men who were equally deserving. But I do not think Yardley distorted
> the facts for the sake of personal aggrandizement, but with the aim of writing a
> dramatic story which would command attention and lead to some effective
> action on the part of the government to secure and maintain an effective code
> and cipher bureau. In doing this, he has invented conversations, changed
> details, and made revelations which I do not think he ought to have made.
> Whether any good will come of what he has written I do not know. It is, of
> course, perfectly certain that such leading nations as Great Britain, Germany,
> and France maintain at all times effective organizations for reading codes and
> ciphers, and actually do read the messages of friendly nations. There can be no
> question that the United States is at a fatal disadvantage in negotiations when it
> refuses to do what the others are doing, but I fear that in spite of the excitement
> which Yardley's book has caused, our government will take no steps to re-
> establish the bureau which Mr. Stimson has dissolved.

Yardley had other defenders. Mark Ryan, his code room colleague, said, "I can hear you laugh at those reviewers who suggest that a question of ethics may be involved. I don't see the question—and if I did I'd say that your purpose amply justified the means." Ezra Neff, a Los Angeles lawyer, urged his senator, Hiram Johnson, to "rectify" the situation—the closing. Johnson replied he would read the book and would be "very greatly interested in it."

Yardley also defended himself vigorously. He asked the *New York Evening Post,* which wanted Theodore Roosevelt to lecture him, that since the Black Chamber had been closed, "what valid reason could there be for withholding the knowledge of the work of this bureau from the general public?" And isn't "an airing, publicly, of the condition" a first step toward eliminating such practices? He told Friedman that he had written the book not to avenge himself on those who had thrown him out of work, but only to pay his grocery bills. When Friedman asked whether it was not unpatriotic to publish the book, Yardley riposted that "it was very questionable who had acted unpatriotically: Mr. S[timson] when he closed the bureau and thus shut off the government's source of authentic information in critical situations, or he himself who exposed what Mr. S had done to blind the government's secret eyes and deafen its secret ears." After Friedman criticized him for having abandoned his longtime position as the "fountainhead of secrecy," Yardley replied, "The only grounds that I ever made for secrecy, was that publication would make the job of supervising foreign telegrams more difficult. The State Department no longer supervises telegrams; therefore there are no grounds for secrecy." And when Friedman said that McGrail, the secret-ink specialist, "is quite sore at you for disclosing" the iodine test, he retorted, "McGrail is a pretty good friend of mine and . . . we got pretty drunk together a few times but I can't recall appointing him my guardian."

"If you will look at the sun tomorrow morning," he told Friedman, "you will see that it still rises in spite of the Post articles. . . . Is America ashamed of her history? Are the voters entitled to know something of what goes on behind the scenes. . . . And the picture of the British code. What of that?" He sounded weaker after a speech at the Harvard Club when he was asked whether he had ever pledged not to reveal something of a confidential nature and he said that he had never so pledged. The questioner remarked that Yardley must be the only person never to have done so. He wrote to Manly that "I sure got my belly full of the War Department, Ford, Friedman, et al. But I think I have wiped the bitterness from my mind."

In fact, Yardley's disclosures ruptured his previously friendly relations with Friedman. Though in technical terms Friedman was the greater cryptologist, he looked up to Yardley. Yardley, two years older, had founded and run organizations, which Friedman had never done. Yardley was senior enough to try to get him commissioned into MI-8 and to offer him a job in New York. Yardley had solved codes for the peacetime government, dealt with policymakers, affected world events. He outranked Friedman. He had made more money. But most of all he was likable. Friedman was not unpleasant, but he did not have Yardley's attractive personality, which, if not truly charismatic, had elements of charisma. Friedman, like many others, was fond of Yardley. In December 1930, after the closing of the Cipher Bureau but before the publication of *The American Black Chamber,* he wrote to Yardley, "I wish I could keep in closer touch with you. Please, when you are next in Washington, even if you have only an hour or two, give me a ring. You have no idea how badly I feel at the way things turned out for you, not that you need my sympathy, but that I can appreciate what a raw deal you got, and that I was powerless to avert it." Of course, Friedman could be expected to disclaim responsibility and express regret, but this sounds genuine. A couple of months later, he wrote, "I would like to see you because I really miss our former contacts of a personal nature." He regretted that Yardley would not participate in reserve activity duty with him in Washington. He tried to obtain for Yardley's brother "whatever information he wanted for you. . . . Please do not hesitate to call upon me for anything further." But this began to change on publication of the *Post* articles, and then of the book. "Of course, I read your two articles and found them interesting from several points of view. You have always found me to be frank and outspoken, so I will be now. The first article rather surprised me as a whole in regard to the amount of valuable information disclosed." He told the undersecretary of state that he "had always liked Yardley and thought he was entirely to be trusted and that it was a terrible blow when Yardley published his book." Though he wrote to Yardley that "I guess we will never agree on the question of secrecy now, but that oughtn't to be any bar to our continued friendship," in fact it was. The correspondence tapered off. The friendship between the two titans of American cryptology died.

The book ignited a firestorm in Japan. A leading newspaper, the *Osaka mainichi shimbun,* recognizing a story when the American edition was published, printed excerpts as *Buraku chiemba* on 10 August. Very soon the book was published in a Japanese translation, and in October the *Yomiuri shimbun* of Tokyo published three articles about it. That Yardley had broken Japan's secret codes and that the United States had used the information to inflict a painful diplomatic injury caused that proud empire to lose face. Parliamentarians hurled charges and countercharges. Ministers exculpated themselves.

The press reported the story and editorialized about it: one English-language paper said that the solving was "a thing which is distinctly not done," while another said exactly the opposite: it "is part of the game." The Foreign Ministry bore the brunt of the criticism. A member of the House of Peers charged that the then foreign minister "must be held responsible." Another declared that "The Japanese authorities are really foolish." A naval officer assured everyone that the navy "has taken great trouble to preserve the secrecy of wireless telegrams." The army, after swatting the crestfallen Foreign Ministry for its "serious blunder" in not changing codes, promised to give it advice. The Foreign Ministry later conceded that the American solution "was due to failure of the Japanese Government to effect a change in ciphers occasionally." Though it had itself started cryptanalysis in 1921, it sought to save face by hypocritically calling the solution "a dishonor" and by tarring Yardley with the false accusation that at the time of the disarmament conference he had "visited the Japanese embassy in Washington and stated that Japan's cipher telegrams were all deciphered and then proposed to sell the translations."

Book sales skyrocketed. On a per capita basis, the Japanese total of 33,119 copies in the first year was almost four times better than in the United States. The American ambassador, who had been instructed to keep the State Department "fully informed" about the matter, reported that "The 'Black Chamber' evidently made a great impression in Japan. I often hear reference made to it in conversation with various classes of Japanese." When Japan accused two American round-the-world fliers, Clyde Pangborn and Hugh Herndon, of espionage in August 1931 for overflying fortified islands, a Japanese correspondent for an American magazine, *The Commonweal,* ascribed it in part to the sour taste left by *The American Black Chamber.* The book lastingly impressed Japan—ten years later the foreign minister mentioned it in connection with a communications matter. It infuriated many Japanese and embittered relations between Japan and the United States.

Some writers have said that *The American Black Chamber* caused Japan to change its codes, suggesting an immediate conversion and a blackout in intelligence from that source. William Friedman asserted in December 1931 that "every nation had spent time since the publication of the book in revising its codes." But both the writers and Friedman were wrong. The writers did not understand cryptologic practicalities. Nations rarely stock backup cryptosystems because of expense and the dangers of theft and obsolescence, and when they want a new one, they must devise it, test it, produce it, distribute it, and teach it before they can use it. All this makes overnight replacement impossible. Friedman of course understood these

October 8, 1931, in the YOMIURI SHIMBUN, a second rate
and sensational daily newspaper of Tokyo, in regard to
the Yardley disclosures.

These articles, it should be noted, were written
by an employee of the Japan Wireless Telegraph Company.
They are obviously propaganda in favor of the transmission
of messages by wireless telegraph, and were quite likely
inspired by officials of the company. They do, however,
reflect to a considerable extent the reaction of the
Japanese public to the disclosures made in Yardley's
book.

The "Black Chamber" quite evidently made a great
impression in Japan. I often hear reference made to it
in conversation with various classes of Japanese. According
to the publishers of the Japanese edition, more than 40,000
copies have been sold. It remains a best seller at the
present time.

I am, Sir,

Respectfully yours,

W. Cameron Forbes

W. Cameron Forbes,
Ambassador.

Enclosure: 3
Translation of newspaper articles.

Embassy's File No. 110.2

WTT/SR

4 Carbon Copies .
Received F. P........
3 Carbons destroyed
7-18-34 met

Last page of a dispatch from the U.S. ambassador to Japan telling of the effect of Yardley's book realities. But how did he know what "every nation" or, allowing for hyperbole, many nations were doing? The army was not intercepting the messages of other nations, and Friedman was not attacking any; he was training cryptanalysts. Moreover, his own country did not change its codes. Would other countries be any different? The writers' remarks stem from ignorance; Friedman's, from animosity. Neither is based on fact.

The facts depict a more nuanced, less negative situation. Japan, which had been updating its diplomatic cryptosystems every couple of years, did not immediately change to new ones. An internal history of the United Kingdom's cryptanalytic agency, though observing sourly that Yardley gave away "all the secrets" of the Cipher Bureau, does not complain that his revelations made solving Japanese codes harder. For they did not. The number of Japanese solutions submitted to British officials soon after *The American Black Chamber* was published did not decline either at once or in the year following. In fact, they rose (owing in part to Japan's takeover of Manchuria in 1931 and 1932, which increased traffic, and in part to Britain's adding two diplomats experienced in the Far East to its Japanese codebreaking section). Likewise, the German Defense Ministry felt no cryptanalytic repercussions from *The American Black Chamber*. While the quarterly reports of its Chiffrierstelle do not list solution volume by country, they do describe nations' new systems, and they mention no change of Japanese codes. Its solution statistics disprove Friedman's allegation of worldwide code revisions. The Chiffrierstelle, which in the last quarter of 1930 distributed 434 solutions from its attack on the cryptosystems of thirty-eight countries, distributed 1,070 from forty countries in the last quarter of 1932, when Yardley's book might have been expected to start having an effect.

In his memoir, the German Foreign Office cryptanalyst and Japanese specialist Dr. Rudolf Schauffler wrote that soon after the publication of Yardley's "indiscreet, sensational book . . . we could observe that the Gaimushō [Japan's Foreign Ministry] planned the development of a cipher machine, which came into service in 1933 [actually, 1932] in addition to other, more developed systems." This was no overnight change but was part of a long-term development in Japanese diplomatic cryptosystems that Setsuzo Sawada, head of the Foreign Ministry's cable section, had begun in 1929 and that in turn was part of the global trend toward automation in cryptography— toward cipher machines, which provided greater speed and greater security. The change was neither sudden nor total but gradual. And consequently it crippled neither the American nor foreign codebreaking agencies. The machine to which Schauffler referred, called the RED machine by American codebreakers, was solved by both the Germans and the Americans.

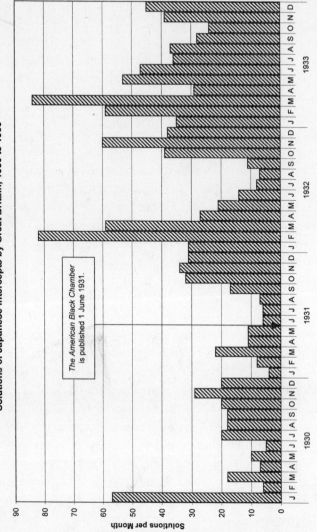

Solutions of Japanese Intercepts by Great Britain, 1930 to 1933

The American Black Chamber is published 1 June 1931.

Solutions per Month

1930   1931   1932   1933

This graph shows that the publication of Yardley's *The American Black Chamber* did not impel Japan to immediately change its cryptosystems, thereby preventing other countries from solving its secret messages, as some people have charged.
Source: Solutions submitted to higher authority from Great Britain's Government Code and Cypher School, in United Kingdom, Public Record Office, Files HW 12/127 to /174.

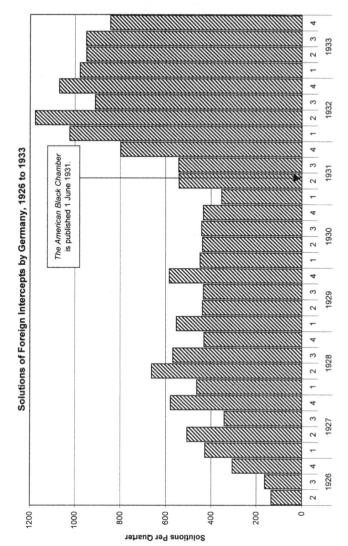

Solutions of Foreign Intercepts by Germany, 1926 to 1933

The American Black Chamber is published 1 June 1931.

Solutions Per Quarter

This graph shows that the publication of *The American Black Chamber* did not prod many countries into changing their cryptosystems, causing a worldwide blackout, as is sometimes claimed.

Source: Quarterly totals of solutions of all cryptosystems attacked by the German Defense Ministry's Cipher Center, in U.S. National Archives and Records Administration, Microfilm T-77, Roll 1575 E[ntzifferungs]-Berichte der Chiffierstelle, 1926–1933. In 1931 and 1933, the Cipher Center combined second- and third-quarter statistics; these have been halved and shown in two quarters.

In 1931, Friedman wrote that "the great harm he [Yardley] has done our country will not become fully apparent for many years to come." Near the end of World War II, he said that, owing to Yardley's book, the United States was "put up against more and more difficult things which probably would not have happened if the book had not been published." He forgot that all technologies advance, including cryptology. The "more and more difficult things" would have taken place even if *The American Black Chamber* had never been published. The book very likely did sting the Foreign Ministry into initiating additional improvements to its cryptosystems earlier than it otherwise might have. This led, however, not to what Friedman said was the "losses of thousands of lives" but to a boon for the United States. Japan's ten-year progression from untransposed to transposed codes and from the simple RED to the complicated PURPLE machine gave American codebreakers experience in solving these increasingly difficult systems and time to do so before America entered World War II. That is why the American cryptanalyst who led the 1939–41 attack on the PURPLE machine, Frank Rowlett, said that the publication of *The American Black Chamber* was a "terrific" thing. "It helped us a lot more than it hurt us. . . . I am so glad that Yardley published that book that I could shout about it." he said. "Yardley did us a favor and he'll never get credit for it of course because the other angles are rather reprehensible but in the simple act of publishing these results he really promoted U.S. cryptanalysis more than he could have in any other way." Though the solutions did not (and could not) prevent the tragedy of Pearl Harbor, they did spare thousands of men and women later in the war. As General George C. Marshall said, referring in part to the PURPLE messages, "They contribute greatly to the victory and tremendously to the saving in American lives." So to Herbert O. Yardley and his indiscretions these people owe their survival, their fortunes, their hopes, and their children.

14

Grub Street

Though *The American Black Chamber* had made Yardley famous, it hadn't made him rich. On 15 July 1931, six weeks after publication, he told Bobbs-Merrill that he was broke and needed $500. The publisher advanced the money to him. Small payments, apparently from sales of excerpts to various publications, trickled in: $122.64, $18.32, $100, $25, $67.80. He got a check for $532.01, and in March 1932 he received his biggest payment: $3,694.21. Three $500 advances had been deducted before Yardley got that money. In August 1932, the publisher advanced him $250, saying it could not give more because of the "large number of delinquent accounts from the trade." But soon thereafter it nevertheless sent $576, the remainder of a royalty payment.

A little more money came from sales abroad. The London house of Faber and Faber bought the British rights, paying $245.28 in advance, half of which went to Yardley. Before the British edition was published, Commander Alastair Denniston, the head of the British codebreaking agency, getting wind of the plan, lunched with "an American subject" of the publisher, probably in an attempt to discourage publication. Denniston asked why Yardley's disarmament conference disclosure was permitted. The editor explained that there was no Official Secrets Act in America and then offered astonishingly erroneous reasons for Yardley's disclosures and for Stimson's decision: Yardley "early in his cryptographic studies fell foul of the Navy because he showed that their ciphers were childish. As a result, . . . he was dismissed with his staff by Mr. Stimson when he became Secretary of State in the United States, because Mr. Stimson had been in the United States Navy." In fact Stimson had been secretary of war from 1911 to 1913 and in World War I a colonel in the army. But though Denniston had gotten Admiral Hall's proposed memoirs suppressed, he seems to have realized that it was hopeless to try to block a book already published; in any event, he did not press the matter. To cut costs and so the price, Faber set its own, smaller type for the book, reducing it from the American 375 pages to 266, and published it 17 September at 15 shillings, or $3.60. Though its sales of seven hundred in the first three months were, Faber said, "disappointing," that didn't stop it from reissuing the book in 1937 and again in 1940, that time as *Secret Service in America*.

Later, *The American Black Chamber* was published abroad in foreign languages. It was, oddly, translated twice in France. R. L. Claude put it into French for six 1934 issues of the weekly *Les annales politiques et littéraires,* and Emmanuel Rinon translated it for a book, *Le cabinet noir américain,* published in 1935 by the Editions de la Nouvelle Revue Critique, where the book's editor Gallically—and correctly—doubted Yardley's assurance "that the American government no longer has any codebreakers." In Sweden in 1938, the translator of *Amerikas Svarta Kammare,* Johan O. Lilliehöök, formerly Swedish consul general in Helsinki and Shanghai, thanked the Swedish cryptologist and historian Yves Gyldén for help with terminology. (The book also inspired Norway to set up a cryptanalytic bureau.) A German translation was contemplated, for which Yardley received $23.08 in advance, but it never materialized. Nor did a Chinese version.

By the beginning of December 1931, sales had risen to 11,616 copies. In the next six months, however, following the customary curve, only 1,640 more copies were sold. Some copies were sold later and some abroad, and in June 1933 Blue Ribbon Books reprinted forty-five hundred copies. The book used the original printing plates, but the page size was slightly reduced, some of the tipped-in halftones were moved, and others eliminated. Altogether, then, *The American Black Chamber* sold in the neighborhood of eighteen thousand American copies. The British, the French, the Swedish, and especially the Japanese editions totaled perhaps another forty thousand—three-quarters of them Japanese. So almost sixty thousand copies of Yardley's book went into the world. He received perhaps a total of $10,000 in royalties for it.

Herbert O. Yardley at the top of his fame, in Los Angeles during the summer of 1931 to publicize *The American Black Chamber*

(Top) The Worthington (Indiana) High School football team, 1905. Yardley is the fifth from the left in the top row. His good friend John Owen is second from the left in the same row.

(Bottom) A Worthington pool hall. It was in the back room of establishments like this that Yardley learned to play poker.

Herbert Yardley and his bride Hazel Milam during a visit to their hometown, Worthington

(Inset) Hazel Milam when she was Worthington librarian, probably in the 1940s

The State-War-Navy (now Old Executive Office) building, next to the White House, where Yardley first worked in cryptology as a State Department telegrapher and code clerk

(Inset) David Salmon, Yardley's superior in the code room at State, who acknowledged his subordinate's cryptanalytic ability and released him to the army in 1917

(Top left) George Fabyan, owner of Riverbank Laboratories, Geneva, Illinois, placed the lab's cryptanalysts at the service of the government in 1917

Engledew Cottage of Riverbank Laboratorites, ca. 1915, where the cryptanalysts worked

Leland Harrison of the State Department, "a human sphinx" who handled much of its secret intelligence. Fabyan and Yardley passed their solutions of intercepted foreign messages to State through him.

(Bottom left) Major Joseph O. Mauborgne of the Signal Corps, an early influential figure in the development of American cryptology. He was a friend of Yardley and Friedman, a painter, a cellist, a cryptanalyst, and the inventor of the one-time cipher system.

(Bottom right) William and Elizebeth Friedman, the young couple at Riverbank who "lived and ate ciphers all day long"

(Top) The Army War College, which housed America's first permanent official codebreaking agency. Yardley's desk was under one of the semi-circular windows in the right (west) wing.

(Left) Colonel Ralph Van Deman (seated), the father of American intelligence, who brought Yardley into the army to establish the cryptologic section. Standing behind him is a fellow member of the staff of the American Commission to Negotiate Peace in Paris in 1919, a young diplomat later not unknown to intelligence fame: Allen Dulles.

(Right) Herbert O. Yardley as a second lieutenant, at about the time he founded and headed the army's cryptologic unit, Military Intelligence, Section 8: MI-8

Some of the officers of MI-8. Seated, from left: Captains David H. Stevens, instructor in English; John Manly, professor of English; Thomas A. Knott, professor of Middle English; Charles H. Beeson, professor of Latin; and Charles J. Mendelson, instructor in Latin and Greek. Standing, from left: Captain Robert B. Marvin, high school language teacher; Lieutenant Paul B. Woodfin, lawyer; Captain Frederick B. Luquiens, professor of Spanish; Lieutenant William M. Barlow, high school language teacher; Lieutenant George W. Bicknell, construction inspector; Captain Emmett K. Carver, chemist; Captain Joel Hathaway, teacher; and two unidentified officers.

(Left) Captain John Manly, deputy chief of MI-8 and solver, with Edith Rickert, of the Waberski cryptogram

(Bottom left) Victor Weiskopf, a cryptanalyst, originally from the Justice Department

(Below) Lieutenant J. Rives Childs and Captain Yardley, army cryptologists at the Paris peace conference

(Top left) Edna Ramsaier, Yardley's future lover and wife, at about the time she began work as a clerk in the Cipher Bureau in New York City

(Inset) Ruth Willson, one of America's first woman cryptanalysts, who worked in the Cipher Bureau during the 1920s

John Meeth, Yardley's chief clerk, and his wife, the former Marguerite O'Connor, later Yardley's secretary

The office building at 52 Vanderbilt Avenue, Manhattan, on the corner of 47th Street, where Yardley's Cipher Bureau worked from 1923 until its closing in 1929, first in Room 229 and then in Suite 814

A session of the Conference on the Limitations of Armament, Washington, 21 November 1921. Fifth from the left at the table facing the camera is Charles Evans Hughes, U.S. secretary of state and host of the conference.

Frederick Livesey, who expanded Yardley's work into the Japanese code and later taught himself enough Japanese to translate the intercepts

The Rev. Irvin H. Correll, who translated Japanese code telegrams during the Washington conference before deciding that the work was immoral and resigning

(Top left) Yardley in 1925 with his infant son, Jack, in Jackson Heights, Queens. Yardley was then head of the Cipher Bureau.

Herbert and Hazel Yardley preparing to take a toboggan slide at a Jackson Heights winter carnival, January 1925

The elegant newly developed community of Jackson Heights in which the Yardleys lived in the 1920s. Their apartment was in the tall building, the Chateau.

Yardley is visited in New York by Georges Jean Painvin of France, the greatest codebreaker of World War I, who taught Yardley a great deal and was then in the process of building a successful business career

William R. Friedman of the War Department, Yardley's great rival, with the Hebern cipher machine he analyzed. During the 1920s, Friedman broke new ground in cryptology; Yardley solved foreign cryptograms but did not train personnel or explore the field or advance it.

(Left) Secretary of State Henry L. Stimson, who in 1929 effectively closed Yardley's Cipher Bureau on the grounds that "Gentleman do not read each other's mail"

George T. Bye, Yardley's literary agent and friend

(Left) Marie Stuart Klooz, the ghostwriter of Yardley's *Japanese Diplomatic Secrets*, which was seized by the Justice Department and later outlawed by an act of Congress

Carl Grabo, a professor of English at the University of Chicago, who co-wrote novels with Yardley

Yardley dedicated *The American Black Chamber* to "The Personnel of MI-8 and The American Black Chamber and to Our Skillful Antagonists, The Foreign Cryptographers, Who Still Remain behind the Curtain of Secret Diplomacy." Here are some of them, out from behind the curtain. The Chiffrierstelle of Germany's War Ministry posed at the retirement in 1925 of its founding chief, Major Erich Buschenhagen, seated in the front row with plaque. In the same row, third from left, is a former Russian codebreaker, Novopaschenny, who fled after the Communist revolution. At extreme right, wearing glasses, is Wilhelm Flicke, author of *War Secrets in the Ether.*

Yardley shows part of a cryptogram to a trying-to-look-interested Rosalind Russell, female lead of *Rendezvous*. Publicists claimed the film was based on Yardley's best-selling *American Black Chamber*, but it had nothing to do with that or with any of Yardley's novels or stories.

(Top) Yardley in China with some of his cryptologic students

(Left) Yardley in his room during a Chungking summer

Yardley at a press interview in Los Angeles on his return from China in 1940

(Top) Codebreakers at work in Canada's Examination Unit, founded and led by Yardley. This picture was taken just after Yardley left.

Herbert and Edna in Reno just after getting married on 28 August 1944

(Top) Edna, Herbert, and friends May Read and Layton Fordham relaxing at Beverly Beach, Maryland, July 1944

(Left) Yardley building a house in Silver Spring, Maryland, helped by a young friend, Robert Mabie

Yardley with his 16-gauge Remington model 11 shotgun

The poker player

Yardley saw writing as his best way of surviving in an America sunk in depression. Even before *The American Black Chamber* had been published he was proposing new projects. "I had a burst of energy today," he wrote to George Bye on 15 April 1931, "and started something I've had in mind for a long while: namely, a text book on Codes, Cipher and Their Solution. There is a tremendous interest among youngsters in the solution of codes and ciphers but there is nothing in print in any language"—not exactly factual. He thought the Boy Scouts might be interested, and pointed out that their manual was the second best seller in the world. But he soon dropped the project. Two months later he sent Bye a two-thousand-word piece because "I wanted to get rid of the idea." It never appeared. Three articles he had promised Bye had been delayed because "my boy got sick. . . . But they will be along soon." Bye sold two by the now best-selling author to *Liberty* magazine. "Double-Crossing America" in the 10 October 1931 issue described Yardley's solution of some May 1927 Japanese messages, during Japan's intervention with twenty thousand troops in Shantung, that "created such a stir in Washington." In "Are We Giving Away Our State Secrets?" on 19 December he published two of his letters to the State Department urging that it improve its cryptography systems and proposing the Vernam-Mauborgne on-line device. After praising Bye for these sales, he pitched another idea: "How about a story for a woman's magazine showing what wonderful cryptographers women are?" It never materialized.

But he did sell six of what he called "cipher squibs" to *Liberty* for $150, or $25 each; later, he asked $100 apiece. Each, presented in a typographical box, consisted of a simple—very simple—cryptogram ensconced in a brief story that explained the cipher system. The reader was challenged to solve the cryptogram. Called Yardleygrams, they began on 26 December 1931 and ran every other week until 5 March 1932, when *Liberty* replaced them with a short detective mystery. Yardley liked the idea of embedding puzzle cryptograms in stories. He planned to compile some into a book, which would be called *Yardleygrams*. "I can't tell you how bullish I am about this little book," he wrote to Bobbs-Merrill's Chambers on 1 September 1931, "but the hell of it is that I have to do it with my left hand for Bye has my nose to the grind stone on other matters."

In fact his left hand was his friend from Jackson Heights, Clem Koukol, who wrote the book for him. An engineer of the American Telephone and Telegraph Company, Koukol knew nothing more about cryptanalysis than what he had read in a navy textbook Yardley had given him, but Yardley probably helped with both the cryptanalytics and the spy stories, which ran only a page or a page and a half long. The fictional theme of the book—

YARDLEYGRAM

By Herbert O. Yardley

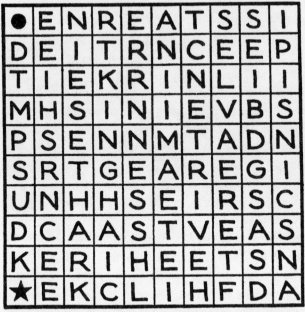

●	E	N	R	E	A	T	S	S	I
D	E	I	T	R	N	C	E	E	P
T	I	E	K	R	I	N	L	I	I
M	H	S	I	N	I	E	V	B	S
P	S	E	N	N	M	T	A	D	N
S	R	T	G	E	A	R	E	G	I
U	N	H	H	S	E	I	R	S	C
D	C	A	A	S	T	V	E	A	S
K	E	R	I	H	E	E	T	S	N
★	E	K	C	L	I	H	F	D	A

**There is a complete message hidden in the square above.
It can be found by drawing a continuous pencil line through
the correct letters, vertically, horizontally, or diagonally.
The pencil lines, when done correctly, will give a symmet-
rical design. No letter may be used more than once.
Start at the ●
Finish at the ★**
  The solution will appear next week.

Letter square of a Yardleygram

which sounds so like Yardley, who had used it in the *Liberty* squibs—was that
Alan Crossle, a former member of the American Black Chamber, was giving
his nephew a course in elementary cryptology at his country home on Long
Island. The cryptograms in the twenty-five chapters were monoalphabetic
substitutions and route and columnar transpositions. Each chapter included
a square-ruled page or two on which the reader could analyze the cryptogram; the method of solution and the plaintext were given at the end of each
chapter. Chambers, who had bought the book, thought the puzzles "too
difficult for us morons who make up the bulk of the American public." But,
he said, "We shall continue to get options and reactions." Bye forwarded the

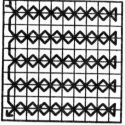

YARDLEYGRAM ANSWER

LAST WEEK'S PROBLEM

Drawing your pencil line as indicated at the left will give you this message:

Entente spies carried their invisible inks impregnated in garments, such as ties, scarfs, handkerchiefs, and the like.

Solution to the Yardleygram

introduction in January, and Bobbs-Merrill published the book—190 pages, yellow-bound—in the spring of 1932, with an advance of $300. By June, Yardley was energetically seeking to promote it. He obtained the addresses of 2,365 people whose names were listed in a detective magazine as having solved its cryptograms and wanted to send them a letter advertising *Yardleygrams*. He drafted it and got Koukol to do the donkey work of filling in the names and addresses and Bobbs-Merrill to stamp and mail the letters. It seems not to have helped: unlike books of crossword puzzles, then the rage, the book didn't go anywhere. Though Faber turned it down for Britain, Hutchinson there bought it, publishing it as *Ciphergrams*. It too vanished into the great limbo of unsuccessful books.

The failure did not discourage Yardley. Nor did the fact that he reluctantly turned down an idea of Bye's for a series of articles because "I have not available sufficient accurate material for the articles you want. Two years ago I could have done a swell job, but men who could have furnished me with the dope I'd want are no longer in Washington." He had, however, written three short stories based on a single character, managing "to map out the plot in ten days and write the story in four." These seem never to have been published. Yardley wanted to know what Bye thought of the suggestion of "a very fine critic in Chicago" that he complete a dozen stories before selling them, though he warned that "I'm such a lazy devil I'm afraid if you sell a story or so I'll lay down on the job and never complete the dozen." He apologized to Bye "for the [insufficient] amount of work I have turned in for I think we both feel that we should make hay while the sun shines. I don't seem able to arrange my hours. There is so much detail and I have been accustomed to having others tend to details. But I am learning. Some of these days I'll surprise you with some original articles."

During the summer of 1931, he gave luncheon talks in Indianapolis and elsewhere, which he said "cuts in on writing, but damned good practice for

December 19, 1931   Liberty   9

Our State Secrets?

THE HONORABLE HENRY L. STIMSON,   JULY 11, 1931.
SECRETARY OF STATE,
STATE DEPARTMENT,
WASHINGTON, D. C.

MY DEAR SIR:

In Chapter XIX of my book, The American Black Chamber, a copy of which I am sending you under separate cover, I have described a conversation I had with a responsible official of the Department when he asked me to analyze the State Department's code messages to determine whether or not they were soluble. The conversation grew from the fact that the State Department had received information that another government was intercepting and reading our diplomatic messages.

It is not necessary for me to detail here as I have in my book the various points discussed. Suffice it to say that I advised your official then that your codes were soluble by skilled cryptographers; that it was not only possible for the agents of foreign governments to read our confidential code and cipher messages, but that they were undoubtedly doing so; that the methods of the Department for encipherment were slow and cumbersome, being no great improvement over those employed in the sixteenth century.

I was asked at that time whether it was possible to devise a system of encipherment which would render our messages indecipherable by even the most expert cryptographers of other governments. I assured your official then that it was possible to do this, but that it could only be done by a consideration of the fact that *no code or cipher is impregnable to attack unless it is insoluble by the inventor himself.*

All existing codes now employed are broken in the end by the fact that the inventor attempts to conceal repetitions. The only indecipherable means of communication is one in which there are no repetitions to conceal. The adoption of

[CONTINUED ON NEXT PAGE]

"I SENT the code word meaning ten million dollars. Two letters were transposed, which changed it into the word meaning eleven million dollars!"

Illustration for a Yardley article in *Liberty* magazine

me. Reactions so far have been very favorable." New York lecture agent W. Colston Leigh offered talks by Yardley on wartime espionage, the place of the Black Chamber in history, and why the American "defeat" at the 1930 London naval conference "was inevitable." A brochure, embellished with pictures and anecdotes from the book, called the Black Chamber "the strangest phase of American history." But Yardley complained to Bye that

Another illustration for the Yardley article in *Liberty*

Leigh "has me in the air. So has his agency in Chicago. I have a number of letters from different sources for lectures this fall. All want to know my plans." But something better supervened.

The unexpected success of *The American Black Chamber*—not only its sales but also the publicity and word of mouth—had attracted that ultimate money-making and fame machine: Hollywood. As screenwriter Herman J. Mankiewicz had once wired a friend: "Millions are to be grabbed out here and your only competition is idiots. Don't let this get around." But it got around. When RKO Pathé contacted Yardley several weeks after the book had been published, he put off Leigh and others clamoring to have him lecture until he knew whether anything would happen with the movies. "I think we will both make a great deal more money in getting me out there," he told Bye. Bye made the deal. Pathé wanted him badly enough to rearrange a lecture date for him so that he could "report our studio Culver City October twentysixth STOP We willing engage you to write as directed by studio officials commencing October twentysixth at salary five hundred week we to guarantee you five weeks work" plus transportation to and from California.

It was every writer's dream. Yardley of course accepted, saying, "I sure as hell need the money." He was laid low by illness in October after hunting ducks, but reached Los Angeles by the beginning of November. At first he was delighted. Newspapers, he exulted, wrote about him. Columnist Lee Shippey forecast in the *Los Angeles Times* that "There is no danger" that *The American Black Chamber* "will fade from memory as does the average book of the month. It will be preserved in the secret service departments of every country under the sun." He misstated Yardley's height and nature. "He is above medium height, well knit, slightly bald, confident as a sales manager but not at all given to eloquence or dramatics. When asked about his discoveries and achievements, he tells about them about as enthusiastically as a business man tells his wife about an ordinary day at the office." Yardley told Bye happily that "Everyone here treats me swell—have been accepted as a writer—and book will have a great deal of publicity now and when picture is finally done."

He was quickly disillusioned—not the first writer to be disenchanted with screenwriting. "Studio is cockeyed," he wired Bye less than two weeks later. "Asked for a love story now they don't want a love story they want a spy story with cryptography I see what they do not see STOP Cryptography no good unless I write dialogue Ill be leaving in two weeks but they will have to have me to make cryptographic pictures successful. . . . You must play your part to knock them out for real money. . . . Im licked unless you can impress them with fact are [am] under contract for lectures etc. Im the key to situation sounds egotistical but am reporting facts STOP Today I called [*sic*] them to go to h and they like me for it Three weeks and nothing done Have never known such a cockeyed situation." Bye replied: "That's Hollywood They had opportunity to get you for longer period and knew of your lecture engagements STOP Tell them they will have to see me about indemnifying lecture agent and suitably rewarding you STOP You will probably be happier away from Hollywood where only a peculiar type of brain can stand the strain." By the end of the month, Yardley told Bobbs-Merrill, "Story a complete flop until last Wednesday when I turned in original story My true collaborators have been canned STOP My story accepted and I demanded four weeks contract with screen credits and fifty percent increase in salary STOP." But Bye had apparently found that, after five weeks on the payroll, he "actually is working at the Pathe Studios without a salary."

And when Bye heard that the new contract would require Yardley's being on the Coast for another month and meant that he would have to cancel his schedule of lectures in Chicago, Cleveland, and Buffalo, he warned his client, "I am terribly afraid you are getting deeper and deeper into some kind of a bad muddle. . . . The lecture tour will help sell more books, and it would keep you in the public eye. In Hollywood, you are buried deeper than you will be when you solve the greatest cryptogram of all. Your [lecture] agent is just about ready to resign." He told Chambers that "I have been after Yardley to come out of his Hollywood trance." Chambers, for his part, while courteously congratulating Yardley on all the publicity and on the new contract, seconded Bye's regret about Yardley's canceling his lecture dates. Their criticism led Yardley to reconsider his cancellation. He telegraphed his lecture agent that he would "positively" honor his engagement dates for January and February "but since can make thousand dollars a week here expect that you arrange profitable tour." But he warned the agent not to book any dates for March and April because he had to be in Hollywood to complete a film. "This to your advantage as well as mine as my name will be featured." He said he was "finishing up cryptographic"—probably a screenplay—for actress Constance Bennett, who had starred in four films in 1930, four in 1931, and three in 1932. If Bye wanted more Yardleygrams—a term that he said was "copywrited"—they would cost $100 each for about five hundred words. He informed Bye that the "type of cipher I have in mind for future features deals with transposition"—as if Bye even knew what a transposition cipher was, much less cared.

He left Hollywood in time for his lecture series, which began on 2 January 1932 in Grand Rapids. He spoke in Evanston, Cleveland, South Bend, New York, Boston, and Buffalo, where he ended on 29 January; after a ten-day break in Worthington, he went to Detroit, Indianapolis, Bloomington (Illinois), Chicago, and Denver. A dispute erupted with lecture agent Leigh—a "god dammed Jew"—over payment for the South Bend lecture, but Leigh eventually admitted his mistake and paid the money. And on 18 August 1932, Yardley crowed to Bye, "Haven't had a drink now for three months."

More than most people, Yardley always needed money. His greatest—almost his only—asset was his spymaster image. Early in 1933, he moved to profit from it by selling secret ink. He made two kinds. One was for a game; the other, for direct-mail advertising. The game used two perfume-sized bottles—a green one for the ink, written with ordinary dip pens, and a brown one for the developer, spread over the paper with a cotton swab. The secret message came up brown. Yardley mixed the ingredients himself. He kept the formula secret—it included an acetate and cottonseed oil—and filled the bottles himself in a separate room. Worthington High School juniors and seniors, paid 10¢ an hour, seated around a table in a four-room bungalow at 104 Union Street, pasted the labels on the bottles, made swabs out of toothpicks and cotton, and packaged the bottles, the swabs, and the instructions in a box about six inches by nine. Wilson Dyer had drawn the label art; Esther Falk kept the books; Wilma Shouse and Peter Bussard made swabs and packaged; even Jacky Yardley, then eight, helped. The place reeked of the oil.

The invisible ink for advertising was developed by dipping the paper that had the message on it in water. If the paper was allowed to dry after wetting, the message could be brought out repeatedly. Experiments to get a satisfactory product took until June. Bond paper never worked well; a heavier stock as absorbent as blotting paper had to be used. In May a salesman sold five thousand sheets; Yardley boasted that "We are selling quite a lot of this form of advertising" and that his secret-ink letters were "sweeping [the] country." He brought into the business Virgil Vandeventer, a Worthingtonian in his early twenties, who, like him, had been a telegrapher and worker at the railroad depot.

To the youngsters, Yardley appeared a commanding figure: he was, after all, the boss and owner. He watched prices carefully. When a supplier charged him $3.50 per thousand for small cartons, which he called "unreasonable," he turned to Bobbs-Merrill, which told him of a manufacturer that would make boxes at $2.25 a thousand. Yardley thanked the publisher for the prices, which he said were "25 to 30% lower than what I got the job for." He sent a sample of the product to Bye, who told him, "Yesterday my wife wrote the menu for dinner out of the green bottle, and the cook later used the brown bottle to find out what it was all about."

At the end of April, while compounding an experimental batch of secret

Magician letterhead for Yardley's secret-ink business

ink, Yardley cut his right palm on a piece of glass. The injury caused an infection that put him on his back for ten days. "I had a hunch that I'd be lucky to escape with my life," he wrote Bye, "—this because Jack's little dog cried when I went to bed." The infection worsened, and he had to be taken to the hospital. Staff there soon got him out of danger, but the second finger of his right hand had turned black—"has died on you," the doctor said—and would have to be amputated. "But what's 1 finger among 10!" On 21 May, he wired Bye, "Finger whittled off this morning Am OK" and signed it "Three-Fingered HOY." The hand was slow in healing. Ten days later it was still draining in three places, but it did not endanger him. It was not a healthy time for Yardley. In July poison ivy left him bedridden and he had to turn down an invitation to attend the national meeting of the Association of College Book Stores only twenty miles away.

His usual need for cash suddenly became acute. The day before the amputation he told Bye that "A discouraging angle is that I put my money in secret ink but am in no position to sell it until I get up." And he needed the money because "Another specialist [is] coming down from Indianapolis to see me [and] will have me cleaned. To see me thro will take another $500. . . . Do you suppose we could get the $250 from Liberty real soon? . . . I've never borrowed a dime in my life—so you know how I feel. If you can let me have it—great—if not, I'll understand. The matter is so urgent that I'm having a man drive to Terre Haute so this will reach you Monday. Pls write me as soon as possible." He signed it "Apologetically." Bye sent him $250. The day of the amputation he telegraphed Bye: "You will receive hot article in Mondays mail STOP If you cannot sell it quickly am stuck for cannot escape from hospital until I pay surgeon and hospital bill STOP." He escaped.

CONFIDENTIALLY

Post Card

Dip This Card In Water
And Message Will Appear.

After Card Dries —
Message Disappears —
Dip Again.

Blue secret-ink postcard

The ink business staggered along until he sold it to Vandeventer. Yardley's venture in commerce had failed.

Neither secret ink nor *The American Black Chamber* nor the brief sally into Hollywood had made Yardley the money he needed. So he produced a new kind of Yardleygram for *Liberty*—the transposition type he had mentioned to Bye. These consisted of squares of letters, usually ten-by-ten or eleven-by-eleven, in which a secret message was concealed in a complicated route. They ran for twelve weeks from 27 May to 12 August 1933. And he lectured. A talk 26 February 1933 at the Cincinnati Country Club was announced in a long article on the front page of the *Cincinnati Enquirer* society section. Yardley's speech before the Los Angeles Athletic Club in August 1934 recounted his life story. When at its end he was asked rhetorically, "Would you invite a gentleman to your home and over the weekend rifle his mail?" he felt he could say nothing, but he remarked afterward that he might have responded, "When is a diplomat a gentleman?"

But mainly he wanted to write. The *New York Herald Tribune Magazine* and the Washington *Sunday Star Magazine* bought the factual "Spies inside Our Gates." Then, however, Yardley abandoned nonfiction, perhaps because, as he had told Bye a few years earlier, his sources had left Washington and so he no longer had "available sufficient accurate material," but more

MAJOR YARDLEY'S SECRET INK

INCORPORATED

WORTHINGTON, INDIANA

May 20, 1933

Dear George:

Here is a tale which I think is a 'knock out.' Since Cosmopolitan telegraphed me about the book I think it might be the smart thing to try to sell it to them. Howevever, use your own judgment. I hope you will consider this article in good taste. I have received a couple dozen letters from my friends wanting to know why in the hell I did not defend myself.

Am going to have my finger whitled off to-morrow.

Am anxious to hear from you to know whether you think I have a good story,

Cordially,

HOY

WHAT do you think of this as a dictator job?

Yardley tells Bye about his finger amputation. The circled F means "file."

likely because he thought he could make more money from fiction. He wrote two stories, which Bye sold to *Liberty* in May 1933. "I shall feel quite proud of myself when I see my name on fiction, but I am not so simple minded as to let it go to my head, for I fully realize that I am in the hands of a master salesman. I do believe, however, that this sale will give me some badly needed confidence and that the next tales will be decidedly better." A few days later he told Bye that "I will have another fiction story for you in a few days. It deals with my stock hero, who solves a case for the Commissioner of Police. I also have an outline for another story dealing with Japanese spy activities in America. Our hero foils them when they attempt to steal the state department code just before an international conference. It is thinly veiled fiction of a fact story. Please destroy this letter on account of this last paragraph." For a nonfiction book of seventy- to seventy-five thousand words, he signed a contract for a $500 advance, to be paid on delivery of the manuscript. He contended that "I don't NEED the advance for financial reasons but I NEED it to maintain my ego. Advances are the life blood of an obscure writer—advances mean inspiration to do better because some one else believes in you." Though he had insisted that "no matter what happened I'd finish the book," it never came out. Probably he never wrote it, for in August he was wiring Bye, "Just recovered from poison ivy and have the itch to write STOP Am naturally lazy but if have contract will meet obligations STOP Do you think we could get contract from Schuster for novel guaranteeing that it would pass standard set by my short stories STOP . . . I have the writers itch and a swell tale please get me started."

One of the short stories Bye had sold to *Liberty*, "The Beautiful Secret Agent," is so inane that it seems as if *Liberty* published it only to keep the powerful agent's good will. Its main character—"hero" is too strong a word—is Nathaniel Greenleaf, from the Revolutionary War hero Nathanael Greene, who gave his name to Yardley's home county, Greene. His job is never identified, though he moves, oddly, in diplomatic, intelligence, and police circles. At a party in Washington, the beautiful secret agent is shot and wounded. She whispers to Greenleaf to "Find the man with black shoe laces." Greenleaf solves an improbable cryptogram warning that a German spy, charged with destroying the Panama Canal, has invisible ink impregnated in his shoelaces and that the beautiful spy is actually a double agent working not for the fatherland but for America. During a gala party, the lights are doused and shafts of ultraviolet rake the room. The shoelaces of an attaché glow! Confronted with this evidence, he shoots himself. Greenleaf visits the recovering spy, who wants to date him.

Yardley improved—it could hardly be otherwise—with his second story. "H-27, the Blonde Woman from Antwerp," stems from Yardley's confusing the German agent Maria de Victorica with the spymistress Fräulein Doktor. Greenleaf is now the "chief of the Black Chamber," a World War I U.S. organization. The president urges Greenleaf to solve German messages that are telling U-boats where in the Atlantic American troop transports will

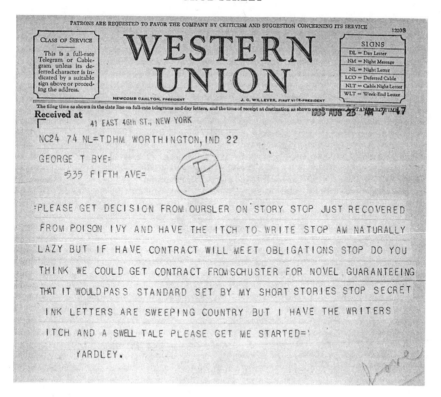

Yardley seeks work

assemble for the crossing. Greenleaf cracks first a simple cipher for latitude and longitude and then a columnar transposition giving the meeting date and the size of the convoy. Rigging up an improbable lens-and-tube device that projects the image of a room in the White House onto a screen, he sees a charwoman removing the ribbon from a typewriter and replacing it with a fresh one. Agents follow her and catch her exchanging her cleaning clothes for a tailored suit and removing her wig and shaking out blonde curls. It is H-27! When accosted, she takes a poison pill and falls dead into Greenleaf's arms, saying, "We all make mistakes—*c'est la guerre.*" The story has more interesting characters and a better plot than the first—despite its idiotic ending—but can't be called literature.

Yardley also tried novels. As usual, he collaborated. At first he sweated "blood . . . for many a month" with dramatist Charles E. Whittaker, author of *Apron Strings,* in writing what he called a seventy-five-thousand-word serial about arms makers titled "Eaters of Men." He told Bye on 1 December 1934 that "I shall be in New York only a week or so and therefore hope that you will do me the special favor of reading this at once. . . . You will find it strong meat." But nobody bit, and Yardley, abandoning it, sought as a coauthor the man under whom he had studied the novel and short story by correspondence in 1915.

Carl Henry Grabo, an associate professor of English at the University of Chicago, was seven years older than Yardley, born and raised in Chicago, and an instructor at the university since 1907. He had published short stories and articles in various periodicals, a novel, some juvenilia, and books on Percy Bysshe Shelley, philosophy, world peace, and nineteenth-century Romantic prose. He was perhaps the "very fine critic" who had suggested that Yardley complete a dozen stories before selling them. But what brought Yardley back to him were his *The Art of the Short Story* and *The Technique of the Novel.*

They worked together first in 1933 and 1934 on an untitled play that was to be a "Dramatization of the American Black Chamber" but that metamorphosed into a novel expanding the characters and plot of the "H-27" story. Greenleaf heads the American Secret Service codebreaking unit. His antagonist is Countess Thorlund, the wife of the Swedish ambassador and, it turns out, J-37, a German spy. Her shimmering golden hair gives the novel, *The Blonde Countess,* its name. The Germans discover the American troopships' midocean rendezvous with Allied escorts and radio this in cipher to Germany so the U-boats can torpedo them. Greenleaf foils the plot by developing, through the iodine vapor test, a message in an invisible ink that had been impregnated into the countess's scarf and by solving a much simplified version of the German World War I ADFGVX field cipher.

The novel, 314 pages, was published in April 1934 by Longmans, Green of New York at $2. Yardley, credited on the title page with *The American Black Chamber,* was listed as the sole author; his picture formed the frontispiece. Grabo's name appears nowhere. Yardley's hand appears in the technical descriptions and in an occasional phrase. Very characteristic is his use of "for" to mean "because": "He worked swiftly, for he was excited with the hope of discovery." He uses "must" in the past tense: "he summoned Blane and Jake to his apartment. He must talk, must ask their advice, must look to them to be reassured." Other phrases repeat some in *The American Black Chamber:* "He had, to Joe, the air of one who fenced with his accusers" mimics his saying that Victorica "fenced cleverly" with her accusers. In Yardley's writing, doors are always ajar.

But despite these bits, nearly all the book is by Grabo. He claimed to have written 99 percent of it, and although portions could have been written by either, many items could have come only from Grabo's pen. In none of his writing does Yardley allude to literature or music. *The Blonde Countess* does so several times. Greenleaf remarks that the figure of speech about sifting the sheep from the goats is biblical. A scene at a reception has a tenor bursting into "Celeste Aïda," a soprano singing the mad scene from *Lucia,* a pianist beginning a Chopin nocturne. Many other phrases and descriptions in the book are alien to Yardley's experience and personality: at one point Greenleaf wordplays on "dodo" and "lulu"; a character misquotes the French revolutionary Danton; the countess philosophizes on whether a woman who is not beautiful can occasionally seem so. Grabo betrays his literary bent when, in a description of a U-boat chase, instead of using the technically correct "the beat of a screw," he adopts the title of the Henry James story and writes "the turn of a screw."

These differences in style and content between Yardley and Grabo do not obtrude nor do they affect the plot. It moves rapidly and smoothly. But its characters do not come alive nor do they develop. The book is a potboiler—not that it pretended to be anything else. Grabo himself never claimed it as serious fiction, dismissing it as "such stuff as I wrote for Yardley."

Meanwhile, on 9 May 1934, "after weeks of negotiation," Yardley was pondering whether to accept an offer of "$12,000 and expenses to disappear for one year to do a job which is not only honest but will give me enough material to write for the rest of my life." It was almost certainly a proposal to work as a cryptanalyst for a foreign country. He told Bye that "I'm inclined to say yes for I need the money" but that "During the year I would have no time to write." He asked Bye's advice and told him to "*Please destroy this.*" In the end, he did not accept the offer, perhaps because, as he wrote to Bye, he would do better "to keep going while I'm having this run of luck. Would two novels coming out one in early fall and one late fall be too many? I can do four a year if you want them. Or even six for that matter, if there's money in it."

He apparently felt so confident because he was just completing another novel, *Red Sun of Nippon,* which he mailed to Bye in mid-June. It tells the story of a young half-American, half-Chinese beauty who is compelled to spy for Japan and must therefore break with her boyfriend, an American diplomat. Once again Nathaniel Greenleaf, now a counterespionage master, solves the Japanese code (using the planted-name ploy devised by Yardley in 1921), enabling the young diplomat to prevent a Russo-Japanese war and to be reunited with the beauty, who accepts her dual heritage. Greenleaf and the diplomat's attractive sister plan to marry. The book is inferior in every way to *The Blonde Countess.* That the matter is oriental, not Western, and that the few external references are historical, not literary, suggest that Yardley wrote it practically without Grabo. Unlike *The Blonde Countess*'s relatively fluid style, with occasional touches of psychological insight, *Red Sun* clunks along. Yardley's prose indeed flowed wonderfully in *The American Block Chamber*, but this ability deserted him when he was writing fiction. *Red Sun* is over-plotted and loaded with events that would never happen. He had asked Bye to "Please be good to little *Red Sun*," and Longmans, Green were, for they accepted it with an advance "even better than *The Blonde Countess*." It was published, at $2 in November 1934. The *New York Times* said that "Despite its wild improbabilities, the tale is engrossing," but the *Saturday Review of Literature* dismissed it as "below par."

At about this time, D. Thomas Curtin, a Harvard graduate, three years older than Yardley, an experienced writer of radio dramas who had adapted the Charlie Chan film character for the air, heard that Yardley wanted to produce a spy program for the radio. Curtin knew of *The American Black Chamber* and, as a correspondent for the London *Times* during World War I, had dealt with Captain Hall, head of British naval intelligence, and with Basil Thomson, head of Scotland Yard. After the war he lectured, wrote books, and, during the Depression, worked happily in radio. He and Yardley interested friends in the McCann-Erickson advertising agency in Yardley's spy radio idea. But rivals in the highly competitive radio business, hoping to intimidate potential sponsors, incited complaints from the German embassy, who feared the program might reignite anti-German sentiment, and from the American military, who were concerned that it might violate the espionage laws. The attacks got so hot that Curtin had to fly home to New York from a lecture in Cleveland to meet with McCann of the advertising agency. McCann said that unless the uproar could be quieted, the proposal would be canceled. Curtin called an acquaintance, Secretary of War George H. Dern, who had army brass attend an audition. Using actors from other shows, Curtin and Yardley "put the audition across big." The officers were enthusiastic and said that the show would dramatize patriotism.

Yardley and Curtin celebrated. It was bitter cold in New York as they walked from the NBC studio in Radio City to Sixth Avenue.

"Let's go over there and have a drink," Yardley said. "Thaw us out."

"I'd rather get a drink on the opposite corner," said Curtin.

"But that's only a drug store."

"Sure. A place to think coldly over an ice cream soda, maybe."

"What are you driving at, Tom?"

"We still have obstacles, and I'm sure you can give me some information that will keep us clear with sponsor and ad agency."

STORIES OF THE BLACK CHAMBER

"THE SPY EXCHANGE"

EPISODE 3

(Friday, March 15, 1935)

SIGNATURE   WIRELESS BUZZER HISSES BC...CLG, WITH-DASH-DOT-DOT-DOT....
DASH-DOT-DASH-DOT...DASH-DOT-DASH-DOT...DOT-DASH-DOT-DOT...
DASH-DASH-DOT...

VOICE   (METALLIC TONE) Black Chamber...Calling...Series of V's...
DOT-DOT-DOT-DASH.

WIRELESS BUZZER HISSES BC...CLG, WITH DASH-DOT-DOT-DOT...
DASH-DOT-DASH-DOT...DASH-DOT-DASH-DOT...DOT-DASH-DOT-DOT...
DASH-DASH-DOT....

VOICE   (METALLIC TONE) Black Chamber....Calling...Series of V's...
DOT-DOT-DOT-DASH...(FADING OUT).

ANNOUNCER   There's the signal for you to listen to "The Spy Exchange",
a story of the Black Chamber, by Major Herbert O. Yardley,
and Tom Curtin. Tonight's story opens with a battle between
two rival detectives for the possession of a secret message.
This message is not written in invisible ink, but in what
is known as cipher.

(CONTEST DETAILS TO COME HERE)

Opening of a Yardley-Curtin radio script

They drank sodas. "Out of their chill a warm friendship developed," wrote Curtin. And they had no more trouble with people sniping at the show.

Stories of the Black Chamber was broadcast on the National Broadcasting Company network in the winter, spring, and summer of 1935. In New York, it aired from 7:15 to 7:30 P.M. Mondays, Wednesdays, and Fridays on radio station WEAF, 660 on the dial, in three series: "Secret Ink," which adapted the plot of *The Blonde Countess,* in twenty-one parts, "The Spy Exchange," in twenty-two, and "The Girl from Soho," in twenty-nine. Opposite it ran three comedy shows: *Lum and Abner* on WOR, *Tony and Gus* on WJZ, and *Just Plain Bill* on WABC. Forhan's toothpaste sponsored the program but also plugged Yardley's secret ink—a package of a bottle of ink, a bottle of developer, and a round-tipped nub, enough for five hundred messages of fifty words each for games and stunts. "To get this secret ink, all you have to do is write your name and address on a box from a tube of Forhan's toothpaste, and mail the box to the Forhan Company, New York City." The final episode was broadcast on Friday, 12 July. On Monday, a comedy, *Uncle Ezra,* took its slot.

The programs are slick and professional. Each episode ends suspensefully; the characters have individuality. Again Yardley had someone do the work for him: Curtin, in New York, handled the writing and the production while Yardley, in Hollywood, "had a good sense for plot and loved to spin situations out of his head," Curtin said. They collaborated by telephone—though on Yardley's terms. He liked to call Curtin at 11 P.M.–2 A.M. in New York. Yardley was meticulous about details. In one such call, he was careful about state lines and kidnapping. "We mustn't get mixed up with the new law. Can't risk it. But we've got to figure out a way to slide around that law," he mused.

One day, when renewal of the show was being considered, Yardley informed Curtin, "I can't take time off this movie to go to New York."

"And I can't leave three shows a week to go out to Hollywood," responded Curtin.

Unable to work out a meeting at a halfway point, they finally agreed that one would have to go to the other.

"How can we decide which of us goes?" asked Curtin.

"Let's match coins," Yardley replied. "I'm matching you, Tom. Got a coin?"

"A quarter," Curtin said, breathing hard.

"Same, a quarter."

Clank went Curtin's coin onto the table. "Heads," he said.

A clink from three thousand miles away.

"Hell, tails. All right, Tom. I'll be at your home Saturday evening. Will fly back Sunday night. OK?"

"OK," agreed a relieved Curtin. Their conference went well—though apparently the renewal proposal failed—and Yardley flew from Newark Airport back to Hollywood. The incident endeared Yardley to Curtin more than ever. He could have cheated. But he didn't.

Curtin, who often appeared on the show as an announcer to add color, was accosted after it one evening by three serious, polite men, more formally dressed than the usual summer audience. They wanted to speak to him in confidence. He joined them in their hotel on Madison Avenue. They wanted Yardley to come to Colombia to break codes for that country, which had been arguing with Peru over the border city of Leticia. Yardley, in Hollywood, had replied to their note that they were to deal through Curtin. Curtin told them that they'd have to prove to Yardley that the job was good. They promised to pay well. Several meetings ensued. With his Hollywood work completed, Yardley agreed to go to Colombia—for $25,000 plus housing. The delegates' faces fell.

"It is too much. We can't pay him more than the president gets," they said.

Yardley would not cut his rates. "Couldn't you raise the president's salary?" he asked.

They couldn't, he wouldn't, and he never went. The boundary dispute was finally settled without war.

But it was not the last time Yardley's cryptologic free lance would be requested.

15

A Law Aimed at Yardley

In the months following the publication of *The American Black Chamber*, while Yardley was trying to exploit its success, he conceived another book idea. It would expand on his best work and best story: the solution of Japanese intercepts at the Washington disarmament conference. And best of all, he wouldn't have to write it: it could be produced, as *Yardleygrams* had been, by a hired hand. By October 1931, he had his ghostwriter. Marie Stuart Klooz, a native of Pittsburgh, was a 1923 graduate of a Virginia women's college, Sweet Briar. She had been a member of its International Relations Club, had majored in social science, and had, the yearbook said, "clicked out her A.B. on typewriter keys." Klooz had become a freelance journalist and had acquired an agent. The new book would disclose many more Japanese intercepts than the twenty-nine in *The American Black Chamber*. Yardley asked Chambers of Bobbs-Merrill to send Klooz "the Japanese telegrams that are in your safe." Since that story had already been told, Chambers warned that "It seems a bit doubtful whether we would be interested in publishing the book you plan about the Disarmament Conference, but," he hedged, "we shall certainly be interested in seeing the outline."

In seven months, Klooz produced a 970-page manuscript titled "Japanese Diplomatic Secrets." It is a bore. The book consists of hundreds of intercepted Japanese diplomatic dispatches with scraps of connecting text—impersonal, technical, dry. Moreover, Klooz's prose is dreary: her first chapter title is "Who Killed Cock Robin?" Her discussion of what Yardley had called "the most important and far-reaching telegram that ever passed through its doors" flattens its significance and drama: "From the following cable we gather that the Washington delegates had presented at least four possible courses of action." This, the culmination of the story, appears a quarter of the way through. The rest of the book skids downhill anticlimactically through Japan's promise to return Shantung to China, a multiparty agreement not to further fortify Pacific island possessions, and cable rights on Yap. Instead of answering questions, it asks them: "Picture for yourself what would have happened . . . If Kato had refused to concede status quo for Ogasawara? . . . If there had been no American Black Chamber at all?" Ten years after the conference, it fails to analyze the effect of codebreaking on American policy or of the conference on world events. It suppresses what might be the most valuable information by being "careful to reject any [telegrams] that might embarrass either the United States or Japan, and any that by the remotest chance could cause ill feeling between the two nations"—although that damage had long been done. Marie Klooz was not the writer Yardley was.

Bobbs-Merrill needed only two weeks to turn it down. "Our [in-house] readers . . . do not regard it as offering assurance of widespread popular interest," Chambers wrote on 1 August 1932. He suggested trying "Macmillan or some other publisher with a large direct-by-mail business."

Then the War Department heard of the manuscript. It was to be offered to Macmillan. War alerted State, which was managing relations with Japan that had grown tense since Japan had occupied Manchuria. The United States had angered the empire by refusing to recognize this. In June, a Japanese official warned that Japan might have to go to war if the United States "ever attempted to prevent Japan's natural expansion"; on 10 September, the American ambassador in Tokyo cabled that "the anti-American press campaign is becoming more intense" and that the military elements controlling the government view the United States as their "potential enemy." So on 12 September Stanley K. Hornbeck, State's senior adviser on Japan, warned the undersecretary "that, in view of the state of excitement which apparently prevails in Japanese public opinion now, characterized by fear or enmity toward the United States, every possible effort should be made to prevent the appearance of this book."

It was not the first time a government had considered suppressing, or actually had suppressed, a book on, or with information about, cryptology. In 1926, the head of the Austrian Cipher Group obtained the proofs of a book on codebreaking by Colonel Andreas Figl, the founder of the Austro-Hungarian cryptanalytic bureau and one of its World War I aces. This was to accompany his volume on codemaking, *Systeme des Chiffrierens,* published earlier that year. The proposed book was deprecated as "specially detrimental to the interest of the state." Figl, then a cryptanalyst in the Cipher Group, was threatened with a disciplinary action if he did not withdraw it. The work never appeared. The publisher, who had set the type, was indemnified with 3,500 schillings.

A memoir and an extensive historical study by the head of France's World War I army headquarters cryptanalysis, General Marcel Givierge, were never published. British officials anguished over revelations about codebreaking in several naval histories, including those by Admiral Lord John Fisher, builder of the dreadnought navy, and by Winston Churchill, former first lord of the Admiralty, but were unable to prevent their publication. A British crypt-analyst expressed the official rationale for secrecy after Sir Alfred Ewing, founder in 1914 of the Royal Navy's codebreaking establishment, Room 40, revealed its existence and successes in a 1927 lecture:

> If those officials in foreign countries who are responsible for the safety of their own communications or for the organization of the cryptographic bu-reaux which they certainly employ are unintelligent enough not to have learnt the lessons of the war or if having learnt them once are on the high road to forgetting them, then incalculable harm will be done by the publication by a scientist of European celebrity of his war experiences in this particular line. A fresh impetus will be given to all Code and Cipher Schools [meaning foreign cryptanalytic agencies], because their demands for greater efforts for security and more money and material for investigation will receive greater consider-ation. As a result the work of G.C. and C.S. [the Government Code and Cypher School, the cover name of the British cryptanalytic unit] may be rendered more difficult.

At about the same time that Hornbeck wanted to suppress Yardley's book, the Admiralty was telling Admiral Sir Reginald Hall that "In Their Lord-ships' opinion, it is undesirable on naval grounds that any references should be made in a book of this nature to . . . Intercepts." And though that former director of naval intelligence had to repay an £855 advance and £250 to a writer for the partial manuscript and to forgo likely sales in the thousands of pounds, he acceded to their requests. Later, when Britain's attorney general, under political pressure, allowed a shorthand typist in the World War I Naval Intelligence Division, Hugh Cleland Hoy, to publish a book about Room 40, the cryptanalyst who wanted secrecy said, "I was allowed to stipulate omissions and made it as difficult as I could for the publishers by insisting on these being on as many different pages as possible so that the whole had to be reprinted."

Hornbeck's similar antagonism to Yardley's book led State to notify the Justice Department. The U.S. attorney in New York urged Klooz's literary agent and Macmillan not to publish. Both promised to tell him when they received the manuscript. The army sent a couple of captains to Worthington and had them demand Yardley return all government documents in his possession. Yardley retorted that he wanted to talk the matter over with the attorney general—but he never requested an interview, and the documents seem never to have been returned.

In the middle of February 1933, Macmillan advised the chief assistant U.S. attorney, Thomas E. Dewey, the future governor and presidential candidate, who was handling the matter, that it had just received "Japanese Diplomatic Secrets." State and the army's chief of staff, General Douglas MacArthur, agreed that they should act jointly, and one of State's specialists on Japan was sent to New York to examine the manuscript. He telephoned the undersecretary of state that "it was as bad as could be, just the kind of thing which might be more than the Japanese could stand." The undersecretary spoke to the secretary, Stimson, about the book's charging Charles Evans Hughes, then chief justice, "with being the moving spirit in all this business of securing and decoding cables" during the conference. Stimson said at first that Hughes "stands too high to be touched by slander," but conceded the danger when the undersecretary, William R. Castle, pointed out that State had supported the Cipher Bureau and that Hughes was then secretary. "What if he denied any knowledge of Yardley? What if he denied having seen the telegrams? Only those who know him will believe him, and in these days when the Supreme Court is the only section of the Government which is not under constant fire [for not ending the Depression], we cannot afford to have the Chief Justice himself dragged through the mud." Castle saw Hughes on 19 February. Hughes "was profoundly disturbed . . . he saw the danger as fully as I did. Whatever is done now he must not be consulted as he cannot be put in the position of defending himself in advance. He must not appear to be afraid of any revelations." Castle conferred with the head of military intelligence and the public relations officer of the War Department, "the result being absolutely nil in either information or inspiration."

In New York, a U.S. marshal appeared at Macmillan's office and ordered its president to go, with the manuscript, to the Federal Building. Bye was also summoned. The government seized the document under the Espionage Act of 1917, which it had not used against *The American Black Chamber*. Dewey escorted the publisher and the agent before the federal grand jury. They testified about their connection with the book and were released, but the authorities retained the manuscript. No indictment ensued, Justice feeling that the act would not block publication. In March 1933, soon after Franklin D. Roosevelt was sworn in as president, high State Department officials discussed suppressing the book. Soon the new secretary of state, Cordell Hull, a former senator, called the department's legal adviser to his office and instructed him to talk to Representative Hatton Sumners, a Texas Democrat and chairman of the House Judiciary Committee, about a bill to prevent the publication. Sumners explained that the bill would have "to avoid the necessity of proving that the documents had been taken from a government officer or agency, since admission that the documents were in the government's possession would be as bad as publication of the documents." The next morning the legal adviser, Green H. Hackworth, brought his draft to Sumners, who felt it was not broad enough. A few minutes later, the full committee met. Though Hackworth explained what State wanted without mentioning Yardley, the members—many of whom had read *The American Black Chamber*—recognized the situation. They displayed considerable interest. To draw up the bill, Sumners appointed a subcommittee, which met immediately after the full committee meeting. It had Justice and State draft a bill, which committee members discussed at some length at a later meeting and changed here and there. On Monday, 27 March 1933, Sumners introduced H.R. 4220, "For the Protection of Government Records."

Roosevelt and the Congress were then struggling with the monumental task for which they had just been elected: to pull the nation out of the Great Depression. One of every ten people in the country was out of work. Men sold apples to feed their children. Others, without hope, jumped from windows. A thousand homes a day were being foreclosed on. Farmers abandoned their land. Refrigerators stood empty. It was in these Hundred Days of the New Deal, as the administration dealt with the Federal Emergency Relief Act, the National Industrial Recovery Act, the Agricultural Adjustment Act, the Farm Credit Act, the Emergency Banking Relief Act, the Banking Act, the Securities Act, the Tennessee Valley Authority Act, and still others, that Washington took time to discuss a bill to prevent Yardley from publishing a book that it felt might do irreparable harm to the republic.

The day after H.R. 4220 was introduced, the Judiciary Committee considered the bill. It made a few wording changes, some at the suggestion of State's legal adviser and an official of Justice. Then it reported out the bill, stating that "The executive branch of the Government has requested the enactment of this legislation at the earliest practicable date, and has satisfactorily demonstrated to the committee the need for it." The proposed law stated that "Whoever shall willfully, without authorization or competent authority, publish or furnish to another any matter prepared in any official code; or whoever shall, for any purpose prejudicial to the safety or interest of the United States, willfully publish or furnish to another . . . any matter which was obtained while in process of transmission from one public office . . . to any other such public office, . . . or . . . which was in process of transmission between any foreign government and its diplomatic mission in the United States . . . shall be fined not more than $10,000 or imprisoned not more than ten years, or both."

The House debated the bill on 3 April. Loring M. Black Jr., a New York Democrat, asked, "Under the terms of this bill, does the gentleman think that if the newspaper offices believe that in a certain department in the Government there was corruption and the editor sent a reporter into that department and he got certain information and furnished it to his editor that department could then harass him and intimidate him under the terms of this act?" Louis T. McFadden, a Pennsylvania Republican, added, "I am also fearful that if a member of Congress obtains information in that same manner he may be subjected to the terms of this act." Committee member Jacob B. Kurtz, another Pennsylvania Republican, replied, "If the House will examine the law as it exists at the present time, it will discover that there is very little difference between the law that is on the statute books of the United States today and the law that is to be enacted, with the exception of that portion of the second paragraph in the bill which reads as follows: 'Whoever shall willfully, without authorization or competent authority, publish or furnish to another any matter prepared in any official code—.' That is absolutely new, and that is the particular portion of this bill which every member of this committee is anxious to see enacted into law." He conceded that "It is true the committee is not disclosing some of the information that was brought before the committee, for it is deemed unwise to do so, but there is no member of the committee who does not realize the absolute necessity and importance of this legislation." The House then passed the bill.

Within an hour, protests poured in. The part about transmission was too broad. The State Department hastily issued a press release contending that "The bill is in no wise intended as a muzzle or censorship of the press."

Administration spokesmen in the House refused to disclose the real purpose of the bill, saying only that the executive branch wanted it. Officials there remained silent, but the reason was soon known. Though one House member declared, "The circumstances under which this bill was drawn up were so serious that my lips are sealed," others claimed that evidence showed that immediate passage was essential. Some screamed that it was potentially the most drastic peacetime censorship measure since the Alien and Sedition Acts of 1798. The objections intensified so quickly that a few hours later Sumners said he would seek changes in the House bill.

The Senate Foreign Relations Committee held closed hearings on it. Hornbeck, State's Far Eastern specialist, and Hackworth, the legal adviser, testified. An official declined to say why the bill was needed or how State knew about Yardley's new book. Yardley was not called. The committee entirely redrafted the bill to eliminate the objections—chiefly, that the bill would impede the Congress and the press in obtaining information. It inserted the cryptologic element and aimed the bill directly at Yardley. Its version read: "That whoever, by virtue of his employment by the United States, shall obtain from another or shall have custody of or access to, or shall have had custody of or access to, any official diplomatic code or any matter prepared in any such code, or which purports to have been prepared in any such code, and shall willfully, without authorization or competent authority, publish or furnish to another any such code or matter, or any matter which was obtained while in the process of transmission between any foreign government and its diplomatic mission in the United States, shall be fined not more than $10,000 or imprisoned not more than ten years, or both." It proposed striking the House wording and replacing it with its version.

On 10 May, the Senate debated this. Key Pittman, a Nevada Democrat and chairman of the Foreign Relations Committee, argued that "it is unconscionable for trusted employees to publish private correspondence between foreign governments which they obtain by virtue of their office." The bill was needed, he said, because "If . . . one through virtue of his office, or through his ability to crack a code which he had been taught by our Government," reveals a foreign coded message, "it might be found almost impossible to prove that it was a code of the foreign government without placing the representatives of that foreign government on the witness stand."

Homer Bone, a Washington Democrat, wanted to know "what it is that we have managed to go along from the First Congress to the Seventy-third without this sort of legislation."

"I will state," said Pittman, "that in the past our Government apparently has been very fortunate in having trusted employees in these extremely confidential positions. It has, however, recently found, or believes it has found, that there are grounds for suspecting that that confidence has been violated, and may be violated again."

"Is this bill designed to punish someone who has already committed some such offense?" lawyer Bone asked, smelling the rat.

"I think not," lied lawyer Pittman, "because in that event it would be an ex post facto law."

He placed in the record a letter from Secretary of State Hull, stating that any infringement of the freedom of the press was "not remotely contemplated by myself."

Then the great California Republican Hiram Johnson, short, stout, twice governor of that state and in 1912 the Bull Moose Party's vice presidential candidate under Theodore Roosevelt, an opponent of Asiatic immigration, joined the debate. When a constituent had sent him a copy of *The American Black Chamber* in 1931, he said that he would read it with great interest. Now Johnson laced his indignation with humor.

Upon its face the bill is as conventional as a wedding and as respectable as a funeral. . . . But, Mr. President, it is not quite so innocent as it appears at first blush, and it does not accomplish the result that was sought. . . .

It happened that on a certain day young gentlemen from the State Department rushed into the Capitol here, and said that as a matter of emergency, in order that guns should not rumble at our doors, we should forthwith pass this measure. Indeed, so persuasive were they with the House that the House considered it without ever telling its Members why it was presented. . . . That emergency was a month and a half ago, and the bill has been pending ever since, but nobody has heard of any of the dreadful and terrible things occurring that it was asserted were going to happen unless this bill should forthwith become the law of the land. So the reason for the passage of the bill first so vehemently asserted does not exist now, and, calmly scrutinizing the past, never did exist. . . .

I dare state the facts because they have been published throughout this country and there is no use in further concealment. They are these: Somebody, whose name escapes me for the moment, was in the employment of the government as a secret service man or as the head of one of the secret-service departments during the late war. This individual was a master of the breaking of codes. Until 1929 every first-class government had in its employment in its secret service an individual who broke the codes of every other country, and every other country on the face of the earth that considered itself a first-class power through its secret-service agents would, we will say, appropriate—we will not say "steal," but would appropriate—the code messages that would come into that country from another country, sent to the other's diplomatic agents. The nations employed individuals to break those codes and, then, of course, after they had been broken, they were read and digested by the officials of the country thus translating the codes of other nations.

Be it said to the credit of the government of the United States and to the credit of the secretary of state who came into office in 1929 that when that practice was found existing in our country he stopped it forthwith and he closed the particular office that was devoted in our country to that sort of business; and probably—I do not speak, of course, with exact knowledge—but probably, sir, ours is the only first-class power in all the world not doing this sort of reprehensible thing that has been done for many years in the past. But remember, always, that the other nations of the earth are doing it probably with our despatches sent to our diplomatic agents in their particular countries. So that was the situation in 1929.

An individual whose name I do not recall—it was published in all the newspapers, however, after the particular intelligence department was dispensed with in 1929—saw fit to publish a book called "The Black Chamber."

MR. CLARK: If the senator will permit me, the name was Yardley.

MR. JOHNSON: Yardley, that is the name. I thank the senator from Missouri. Mr. Yardley published a book called "The Black Chamber." In that book he purported to set forth certain despatches that had come from the Japanese during the Disarmament Conference in 1922. I read the book at the time of its publication. There was nothing particularly startling about it; it was more or less interesting; and we all had the like feeling, I assume, and there could be no difference of opinion among any of us concerning the publication of the despatches set forth in the volume. He published code despatches from the Japanese Government to its representatives that had come into his hands in 1922 while working for the United States Government. But remember also that in 1922 when those despatches were received which Yardley published in his book, they were decoded at the request of our own high officials and put upon the desks of distinguished gentlemen who represented the United States of America, and they unquestionably were familiar with them and used them. All right!

Yardley committed his offense against good taste, against every rule that related to fiduciary relations that we can suggest. I have nothing but indignation for that sort of act upon any man's part, and no sympathy whatsoever with him. After the publication of the book referred to he undertook recently to publish another containing despatches of the 1922 Disarmament Conference and relating, as had his first book, to that period. There were communications from the Japanese Government to its diplomatic agents here.

In 1932, or perhaps in the early part of this year, he was about to publish his second book. It was then that the great "emergency" arose. His manuscript, as I understand, was confiscated; and after its confiscation, then into the halls of Congress came these frightened gentlemen to say that it was such a delicate, perilous, and immediate emergency that they had to have a new criminal statute. That was the 1st of April or thereabouts of this year. So this proposed statute was born.

Immediately upon the bill being passed by the House—and it was passed in such fashion that no one knew anything about it until it had been passed—the members of the press set up the usual howl of the press about the freedom of the press and how this sort of a statute would interfere with them. The result was that, of course, everybody ran to cover and the bill was amended in the twinkling of an eye in order that the press should not be interfered with and the freedom of the press at all hazards should be preserved. Then the original bill was reframed and the new measure is before us.

That is the story of the amendment. The amendment is infinitely better than the original bill, I grant, although, of course, as will be demonstrated during the progress of the afternoon doubtless by the distinguished senator from New England [New Mexico—Bronson Cutting], the amendment is not in good English and makes no sense, but perhaps for that very reason it is infinitely better than the bill as originally presented. [Laughter] . . .

Let us look at the bill as presented. I am speaking more or less academically in respect to this matter. I do not believe in creating unnecessary crimes. . . . Here is a bill designed to fit a particular case. It is a misfit and never will touch that case. It will rest upon the statute books, a criminal law with harsh penalties, until—far in the future, when its original purpose will have been forgotten—it will be used for another purpose for which it was never intended and may do gross wrong.

This has ever been the story of this kind of law made to fit some past particular offense. . . . This measure provides: "That whoever, by virtue of his employment by the United States, shall obtain from another" is guilty of a crime. Under the plain import of the language of this particular measure, he is guilty of a crime for obtaining from another. But, sir, when we go further—

MR. [GEORGE] NORRIS [REPUBLICAN FROM NEBRASKA]: Mr. President, should he not be guilty? If he does such a terrible thing as that, should he not be guilty of a crime?

MR. JOHNSON: Obtaining from another?

MR. NORRIS: Yes.

MR. JOHNSON: Yes, I think so. In these days anybody that obtains anything from another ought to be condignly punished if he gets it, but the difficulty is with most of us that while we strive we do not succeed. [Laughter] . . .

We say, "which purports to have been prepared in any such code." There is an implication, it seems to me, that ought not be written in a criminal statute. . . .

The proposed statute is one made for a particular and specific case. Statutes of that sort are always doubtful. Sometimes they are necessary, I am willing to concede; . . . I am not interested in the individual who is sought to be reached by this kind of a measure, . . . but keep in mind, sir, that we are not only touching him with this measure, but we are touching anyone else from whom he obtains something. . . . We may be striking at the very fundamentals that we would preserve in this country untouched and unharmed.

Arthur R. Robinson, a Republican from Indiana, Yardley's state, told the Senate, "I did my best in the interest of fair play to have the Senate committee hear Mr. Yardley, but the committee refused to call him." He said Yardley indicated that he would be glad to call on Secretary of State Hull and discuss the matter but that Hull had refused. Nor had Robinson been able to get the details from "any authoritative source." He said the fact that this so-called emergency legislation had languished had convinced him "that there are other motives behind this proposed legislation, and entirely unrelated to Mr. Yardley."

He then read a telegram from Yardley that he had solicited. It rehearsed the reasons for publishing *The American Black Chamber* that Yardley had given in his previous apologias—mainly, to improve American codes—and concluded that "This Government's fear of the unpublished manuscript now in its hands is, in my opinion, due to false sensational rumors originating in New York. It is a dull treatise for scholars and students of history. The ordinary person would fall asleep while reading it. Whether it is published or not is of no consequence to me. As a matter of fact, I am too busy in my laboratory completing my experiments on a commercial invisible secret ink for children and adults to write their letters with to be at all concerned about anything else." Robinson then veered into a vehement denunciation of the president—"We have made Mr. Roosevelt a dictator—a dictator. . . . Now we propose to gag the American people with reference to all foreign relations." He went on: "Not a convincing reason has been suggested by any member of the Senate for the passage of this gag law. . . . A member of Congress in either House would not dare to put and publish any vital information he might get. . . . Even though it were to save the nation, though the republic's life were in danger, it would be impossible to publish it in any way, shape, or form under this infamous thing, and it would be impossible for a newspaper to publish it without violating the law."

Tom Connally, a Texas Democrat, asked, "What is there so wrong about this measure? . . . Where is the senator who approves pilfering private records? If there be such let him rise. Senators who become outraged because of a man's stealing a spotted calf and want to put him in the penitentiary would seem to entertain the idea that a man could steal a public record and sell it for money to the newspapers and that would be an act of patriotism and public service. I do not so regard it." Later, after a dispute flared, though in the courteous senatorial manner, between him and Robinson over what Connally claimed was Robinson's always dragging Roosevelt into any debate on any bill, Connally returned to the subject and pronounced "It is a bill in the interest of peace by preventing the publication of unauthorized diplomatic matter in order that our foreign relations may not be disturbed."

When Simeon D. Fess, an Ohio Republican, inquired why the phrase "or which purports to have been prepared in any such code" should not be struck out, Connally explained. "If we strike out that language, the government would have to prove that he used the genuine code, and in order to do that would have to reveal the code, which would be the identical thing we are trying to prevent. It would give publicity to our own code and to a foreign code." Fess, a former professor of history, replied, "I think the point of the senator is well taken. I had not seen that side of the question." The Senate, which had been debating the matter for several hours, then passed the bill by voice vote.

But it differed from the version passed by the House of Representatives. A conference committee discussed it. On 22 May, the committee recommended that "the House recede from its disagreement to the amendment of the Senate and agree to the same." The grammar was cleaned up, a few other changes were made, and on 7 June the Senate approved the corrected bill. The next day, Representative Emanuel Celler, a New York Democrat, explained to the House for the first time that Yardley "now threatens to publish another book containing other dispatches thus decoded, and it is feared by the State Department, in the light of the coming International Economic Conference [in London], that the publication of this book might seriously embarrass this government, because it may contain certain decoded messages

Seventy-third Congress of the United States of America;
At the First Session,

Begun and held at the City of Washington on Thursday, the ninth
day of March, one thousand nine hundred and thirty-three.

AN ACT

For the protection of Government records.

*Be it enacted by the Senate and House of Representatives of the
United States of America in Congress assembled,* That whoever, by
virtue of his employment by the United States, shall obtain from
another or shall have custody of or access to, or shall have had custody
of or access to, any official diplomatic code or any matter prepared
in any such code, or which purports to have been prepared in any
such code, and shall willfully, without authorization or competent
authority, publish or furnish to another any such code or matter, or
any matter which was obtained while in the process of transmission
between any foreign government and its diplomatic mission in the
United States, shall be fined not more than $10,000 or imprisoned not
more than ten years, or both.

Speaker of the House of Representatives.

Vice President of the United States and
President of the Senate.

Approved
June 10 — 1933

Franklin D Roosevelt

Act of Congress, signed by President Roosevelt, blocking Yardley's second book

that would be derogatory to the Government of Japan, whose representatives
will sit around the table with our own representatives in a few weeks."
Representative James W. Mott, an Oregon Republican, asked,

What is the difference between this proposed law and the present law? In
other words, is not this prohibition contained in the present law?

MR. [JAMES] RUFFIN [DEMOCRAT FROM MISSOURI]: There is some

doubt as to whether it is in the law or not. I think even though it may be construed to be in the present law, there is justification for passing this bill.

MR. MOTT: That is not my understanding. It was not the argument made when the bill was argued in the House. It was argued at that time that existing law covered this particular code situation.

MR. RUFFIN: I know, but there was some question about it.

MR. MOTT: And that, in the opinion of the Secretary of State, it should be broadened to contain all of these provisions.

MR. RUFFIN: That is the reason.

The House then agreed to the conference report. This passed the bill in the form that the Senate had approved. Two days later, on Tuesday, 10 June 1933, Roosevelt signed it as Public Law 37. It was published on page 122 of volume 48 of *Statutes at Large* as the law of the land and it lives today in the United States Code as Section 952 of Title 18.

As the code bill was wending through Congress, Yardley "received a couple dozen letters from my friends wanting to know why in the hell I did not defend myself." So in May he wrote an article on what he called the "gag" bill, telling Bye with his enthusiastic salesmanship that it was "a tale which I think is a 'knock out.' Since Cosmopolitan telegraphed me about the book I think it might be the smart thing to try to sell it to them." He hoped Bye would consider it "in good taste" and sent him corrections by mail and by wire, changing, for example, "dark eyed diplomat" to " 'poker-faced diplomat' or 'almond eyes' which ever you like better." When Bye said that the article "went a bit too far," Yardley conceded that he "did rub it in a little strong" about Dewey but "would be only too happy" to tone it down. Later, he reminded Bye that the article "will lose its commercial value after a short period." A few weeks later, Bye wrote with bad news.

My lawyer, the same lawyer who advised against the "American Black Chamber," says it was a grave responsibility for you and me and the magazine to let this get out in type. He insisted on waiting until after the bill had been signed. Cosmopolitan did not even want to consider the article until I had this lawyer's report. Now it seems that it is an even more dangerous chance. Danger be damned, but we can not damn public esteem. So far your position has been fine. It is not necessary for you to maintain the dignity of a maharajah. I think everybody is pretty well convinced that you are a devil-may-care human being. To that impression I should not like to have added an opinion that you are thumbing your nose at constituted authority.

Yardley was not happy at the rejection. Referring to the lawyer, he observed that "the American Black Chamber would never of been published if he had had his way." However, he told Bye, "please return the manuscript and I will put it away in camphor for my grandchildren to read."

The government had blocked the publication of "Japanese Diplomatic Secrets." Neither Yardley nor Klooz nor Bye nor Macmillan asked for that hot potato back, and the Justice Department simply filed the manuscript, jammed into seven manila envelopes. But Bobbs-Merrill feared that the law would prevent the sale of the forty-five hundred copies of *The American Black Chamber* that Blue Ribbon Books had printed and recently distributed. It also worried that booksellers might be arrested. So it petitioned the State Department for "authorization to sell and dispose of copies of" the book. The acting secretary of state, William Phillips—who, ironically, knew Yardley from having released him to the army in 1917—replied that "it is not clear" whether the new law applied to "materials published before the enactment" and whether State would be the body to authorize or to object to distribution. This didn't satisfy Bobbs-Merrill, and it renewed its petition. But, Phillips said,

> The granting by this Department of such a permission would imply that the Department felt no objection to the publication and distribution of the book and would in a measure associate the Department with action on the part of the author and the publishers upon which it has not at any time looked with approval. I therefore find it impossible to grant the permission which the Company requests. However, it is no part of the desire of the Department to contribute unnecessarily to the causing of embarrassment or loss to the publishers or the author. . . . The most that I can do is to state that the Department will take no action against the publishers or the author in connection with the distribution of such copies of this book as were actually printed before the date of the petition under reference, June 14, 1933.

Bobbs-Merrill still wasn't happy, however, because the contract called for 10,500 more books, to be sold at $1 apiece. It asked State not to move against the sale of these books, which had already been printed. But Phillips declined to make that promise, on the ground that this "additional concession . . . would be inconsistent with the spirit of the Act of June 10, 1933, and contrary to the best interests of the United States." On receiving this letter, Bobbs-Merrill's lawyer informed his client that "you have no course except to comply with the department's ruling." No more books seem to have been printed, and State did not stop the sale of those already printed.

16

Hollywood

In the spring of 1934, Hollywood summoned Yardley again. The moviemakers wanted fresh ideas (not too fresh, of course). Spy stories had been done. Greta Garbo put her mark on *Mata Hari*. In *Dishonored*, Marlene Dietrich played X-27, a Viennese widow who spies effectively until she falls for a Russian officer. Code, however, was a story that hadn't been done before—though X-27 had spent a night enciphering Russian war plans into music. And little wonder. Cryptology slowed the action. It was dry. It was boring. It needed explaining. The best it could project onto the screen was a pencil marking paper. No shootings. No seductions. Yet a bestseller had been written about it. Perhaps this was an idea the movie magnates could use. Fact had been improved on before. And the author had written a pretty good tale. What was its name again? Who was the author?

They remembered the title; they found the author. The office that passed on works for their moral suitability for films—the Motion Picture Producers and Distribution Association of America, headed by former postmaster general Will H. Hays—had *The American Black Chamber* read. R. B. Willis summarized it in seven pages. Though he thought that the secretary of state who closed the agency was Frank B. Kellogg, he said that while "Such a book may well have helped along the recent ill-feeling toward us in Japan, nobody blames Mr. Yardley at all, he's a genius" and "a swell story teller." On request, the Hays office forwarded the book on 29 May 1934 to Louis B. Mayer, the head of MGM, adding that the federal administration had no objections but expected that MGM would get approval for any material of which the United States or other governments might disapprove. By then, however, the studio had already made Yardley an offer.

On 6 April, Yardley wired his Hollywood agent, Frank Orsatti: "Am free to come out My suggestion is that you get them buy American Black Chamber and Blond Countess and pay for my services separate STOP With this material and if necessary adding other material am confident can develop either war time or modern topical story of espionage that will be both dramatic and different STOP As for price offer must come from them STOP For your confidential information my literary agent in New York has nibble from another movie Regards H O Yardley." Orsatti replied about a screenwriting job, the two books and two stories, one of them apparently "H-27, The Blonde Woman from Antwerp," then two weeks from publication in *Liberty:* "MGM offered me ten thousand dollars American Black Chamber and Blonde Countess This is absolutely best I can do STOP Seventyfive hundred is the price for the two stories STOP Guarantee of ten weeks at two fifty a week Transportation both ways Please confirm acceptance."

Yardley accepted the afternoon he received the telegram but—ever pressing—urged Orsatti to "Please try to get three hundred per week as my expenses will be heavy as will bring family with me." The next day, to ensure that he would not be stuck paying for a fruitless trip, he exaggerated to Orsatti that "Have thriving national secret ink advertising business here My absence will mean inevitable loss STOP Must go to expense to hire sales manager carry on business STOP Therefore although recognizing reputation your agency cannot outlay necessary expense to arrange for my absence unless I get telegram direct from Metro STOP Their telegram should state price for movie rights of two books COMMA guarantee salary for ten weeks COMMA and payment traveling expenses Worthington to Los Angeles and return STOP Not necessary wire transportation as may remain here until last moment and come by airplane STOP Please advise quickly so can arrange my affairs." On 11 April, an MGM vice president dispatched a page-long telegram of boilerplate offering to buy all rights except those of publication of the book and the H-27 story for $7,500, to employ him at $250 a week for ten weeks starting 20 April, and to pay for a round trip by rail between Worthington and Los Angeles. The $10,000 offer was not mentioned. Yardley wired his acceptance two days later.

He reached Hollywood as quickly as he could by rail and was "deemed" to have begun work on 19 April. On the 25th he signed contracts with Metro-Goldwyn-Mayer, giving it for $7,500 "all now or hereafter existing rights of every kind and character whatsoever" to *The American Black Chamber, The Blonde Countess,* and *Stamboul Quest,* a movie to be based on his H-27 story. At $250 a week, he was for ten weeks to "create, write, and prepare all material assigned to you hereunder."

He was put to work on *Stamboul Quest.* Publicists claimed the film was based on the activities of Fräulein Doktor, the agent controller in Antwerp whom they wrongly dubbed a master spy and whom Yardley erroneously thought was "more or less a myth." He began by checking a script for facts and plausibility. He wrote a memo on it, noting, for example: "Scene 144 and following scenes here and there: Sturm refers to Anne Marie as 'the Fraulein.' The identity of Fraulein must be kept secret. Therefore she must not be referred to openly as such." The job was beneath him.

He had been hired mainly as a screenwriter. The H-27 story turned in part on codebreaker Nathaniel Greenleaf's solution of a cryptogram that revealed that German submarines knew of the midocean rendezvous between American troopships and British escorts. The original tale never explains how the information saves the transports from being sunk but shifts instead to the use of a wide-angle lens in a ceiling that enables the capture of a "voluptuous" spy; she then commits suicide by taking poison. Before Yardley began writing, however, screenwriter Joe Sherman had concocted a couple of plot summaries. Though titled "The Black Chamber," they dealt instead with a wealthy young drunk involved with escaped Russian nobility; Robert Montgomery was suggested for the part. Sherman had not the faintest idea about a black chamber. He envisioned it as a laboratory for a potion that would make a person appear as if he or she were dead but would let him or her awaken in twenty-four hours—an idea less original in 1934 than when Shakespeare used it in *Romeo and Juliet.*

When Yardley took over, cryptology returned to the film: "During the World War the Black Chamber at Washington fights a war behind the trenches that is as dramatic and as fraught with danger as a conflict in the front-line trenches." Yardley described the offices of MI-8, drew up some charts of the contacts of letters with one another (a statistic important for some solutions), and wrote a "Tentative Wireless Sequence." In its four pages, a character named Harry explains to hero Greenleaf about wavelengths, signal strength, and goniometry (direction-finding). Later that Friday, 18 May, Yardley condensed the sequence into two pages. Still later that day, he wrote a "Tentative German Sequence" on the interrogation of a

German radio operator, a prisoner of war. On Monday, he wrote a fourteen-page memorandum about the ADFGVX, the preeminent German field cipher of 1918, explaining how it could be solved on the basis of identical repetitions in three cryptograms, as his French colleague Georges Jean Painvin had done in World War I. "For picture purposes," he proposed enlarging a small cryptanalytic display "to four or five feet in height." He conceived a cryptographic close-up in which "We see only the hand and [enciphering] square as he talks." All of this was a sure narcoleptic for film magnates, who don't get rich making cryptologists' training films.

During that summer or fall of 1934, Yardley returned to Worthington, picked up Hazel and Jack, then nine, and drove back out to Hollywood with them. He was learning about that town. "I like the climate and I like the work but I doubt if I could stick at it for it is a political game and I'm not very diplomatic. I usually say what I think and that is dangerous. Anyway it's swell while it lasts." And he was learning about screenwriting. "Story here going none too well—they of course want something completely different from what they bought," he told Bye. "As a result two treatments [scene-by-scene outlines] have been done and discarded and another will be done next week. Great life." Screenwriter Robert Presnell was even then writing a twenty-five-page "Continuity Outline for 'The Black Chamber.'" Though that title capitalized on the name of Yardley's best-seller, its plot sprouted from that of The Blonde Countess, and the studio changed the film's working title to that.

A few weeks later, C. Gardner Sullivan was writing a different treatment for The Blonde Countess. Yardley was also drafting a ninety-two page treatment. It set the stage in the melodramatic manner of 1930s films: "Mexico—1917. In a ramshackle building on a lonely hill a wireless is busily at work—at the door stands a heavily armed guard—within, the young operator, blond Teutonic, stripped to the waist, for it's a close sultry night, bends over his key. The messages, crackling, hissing, leap above the sleepy villages to the coast, cross the dark Atlantic where they are intercepted by a fleet of prowling U-boats, sweep over the Channel and come to rest like homing pigeons in the war office in Berlin." Yardley's hero perhaps fulfills some of his own wishes: "Major Nathaniel Greenleaf, an easy going, easy spoken young man recruited from the State Department, is considered the most able cryptographer in Washington—few people know that he is actually head of the Military Intelligence and as such directs the espionage activities of the American secret service. Beneath his lazy manner and bantering drawl he's a man to be reckoned with." Greenleaf's solutions of the German messages from Mexico prevent the U-boats from sinking American troopships.

But the treatment, dated 19 June 1934, bears somebody's blunt notation: "Wrong opening."

Some writer produced a full script. Three times as long as the previous effort, it reduces the technical details and focuses more on human matters; its tone is more polished but less energetic. It went nowhere. Yardley and screenwriter Howard Emmet Rogers wrote six pages describing an episode at an embassy reception in Washington.

During the summer, Yardley persisted with his technicalities. He provided a transposition rectangle with a message giving a midocean rendezvous with latitude and longitude. Greenleaf's assistant, Professor Morrison, modeled on Manly and his solution of the Waberski cryptogram, explained about transposition. Yardley burdened pages 20 to 20H of this draft with cryptologic details. He recapitulated some of his Paris experiences by having Greenleaf go to "one of the numerous intimate expensive dancing joints that sprang up in all the capitals during the war" and dance with a "cutie." He proposed changing the name of the film to *Rendezvous*. In August and September, he and Rogers—whose byline preceded Yardley's—wrote an eighty-three-page script that opens on a street scene in wartime Berlin, with soldiers marching in the background and a newsboy selling extras of the *Berliner Tageblatt,* whose headline dissolves into an English translation: "United States Declares War Against Germany."

Someone else's script begins with the city room of the Washington *Star.* Its puzzle editor, Greenleaf, has been conscripted to the Black Chamber, which resembles no cryptanalytic office ever seen.

It is a large room, the walls of which are lined with heavy draperies from ceiling to floor. The room is soundproof and lighted by square prize-ring type floodlamps. . . . It . . . contains about thirty-five flat-topped desks skirted with steel filing cabinets. About twenty-five cryptographers (most of them enlisted men) are seated at the desks, attempting to decode intercepts and making frequency tables. These latter are working at adding machines, the others calculating equipment. Over the whole place is an air of human wills fighting sleep, fighting exhaustion, fighting a strenuous and baffling mental problem. The whole force has been working all night, to solve the baffling and mysterious German wireless intercepts.

As the camera pans around the room, it picks up tired faces, faces *drawn* with exhaustion. Here and there some person has collapsed, and is sleeping with head in arms on the table or desk before him. The nationalities in the room are varied—Japanese, Indian, Arabian, etc.—one translator for almost every language existent.

Greenleaf tells his girlfriend, Joel Carter, who enters the room without anyone's checking her for security, that "There's only one thing I've got to do and that is, solve this cipher—it means getting away to France, where there's an honest war; honest enemies armed with bayonets, grenades, and bullets." To Greenleaf, codebreaking is neither honest nor important. Cryptologic color is provided by a private's putting a frequency table on the blackboard and by an enlisted man's erroneously referring to a substitution cipher as "a transpositional cipher." The call sign of the German radio station is HSI— the same call sign given in *The American Black Chamber* for a clandestine station in Mexico sending apparently to Germany. But neither the German codemakers nor the American codebreakers prove very smart. The crypt-analysts try solving the message on the theory that the Germans had cleverly replaced each plaintext letter with the previous letter in the alphabet, so that *b* in German became A in cipher, and so on. When that fails, several enlisted men discover that the Germans were not even that ingenious. They had merely replaced each letter of the German plaintext with the next letter in the alphabet, so that German *b* became cipher C. Presumably, Yardley had recognized that any more complicated cipher would unacceptably impede the narrative. In the end Greenleaf gets to go to France—but in the intel-ligence service. On the last page of the 142-page script, Yardley firmly wrote and underlined "The End." Except for the call sign, none of this ever appeared on the screen.

Yardley was retained on the MGM payroll after his original ten weeks expired. He helped a little with the screenplay of *The Great Impersonation,* a spy movie, and with that of *Stamboul Quest,* whose title seemed to have nothing to do with Fräulein Doktor, but mostly worked on *The Blonde Countess.* These jobs filled the autumn. Throughout the winter, spring, and summer, a bewildering parade of writers then wrote notes, synopses, scenes, script fragments, and scripts, either alone or in collaboration, once or several times. Among them were Samuel and Bella Spewack, later famous for the Shakespeare adaptation *Kiss Me Kate,* Monckton Hoffe, E. A. Dupont, Mi-chael Fessier, Horace McCoy, George Auerbach, Lynn Starling, John C. Higgins, Jules Furthman, Florence Ryerson, Howard Emmet Rogers again, C. Gardner Sullivan again, J. W. McGuinness, and others. P. G. Wodehouse, author of the Jeeves books who had been brought to Hollywood in 1931 at the then fantastic salary of $2,000 a week, described the system: "A gets the original idea, B comes to work with him on it, C makes the scenario, D does the preliminary dialogue, and then send for me to insert class and what not, then E and F, scenario writers alter the plot and off we go again." It all validated veteran screenwriter Ben Hecht's description: "Movies were seldom written. They were yelled into existence in conferences that kept going in saloons, brothels and all-night poker games"—venues not entirely unknown to Yardley. George Oppenheimer, a member of the Algonquin literary round table and a screenwriter, substantiated this with an anecdote about his bizarre resolution of a blockage in the *Rendezvous* plot:

Lawrence Weingarten, [legendary director Irving] Thalberg's brother-in-law, was producing a film called *Rendezvous,* a spy story of World War I with William Powell in the lead and Rosalind Russell, a newcomer to Hollywood, playing opposite him. A raft of writers had been on the picture and had succeeded in locking Powell and Russell so securely in a Washington hotel room—a hotel, incidentally, that seemed to cater exclusively to German spies—that now they could not get them out. The picture had been shot up to that point and then production had halted. As far as it went, it was exciting and entertaining, with Powell in top form and Russell revealing a richly comic gift as an influential lady who, having fallen for Powell, wanted him kept in Washington. . . . [They are lured and locked into] that room with costs mounting daily as the actors and crew stood by waiting for an ending.

George [S. Kaufman, the playwright and director], with more faith than I had, suggested that I might be the man to get them out and, as a result, Thalberg released me temporarily from [the Marx Brothers'] *A Day at the Races.* By this time *Rendezvous* had more producers than writers. In addition to Weingarten and director Sam Wood, Bernie Hyman, a man of great good will and charm, Thalberg when he could spare the time and any number of assistants were concentrating on the problem. Herman Mankiewicz was the only surviving writer until I came to join him. . . .

Herman could write extremely well when the mood was on him. (It was on full force when he wrote one of the best screenplays of our time, *Citizen Kane.*) However, he was definitely not in the mood for *Rendezvous* and, rather than get Powell and Russell out of their scrape, he got into one of his own. This left me holding the writing bag, mornings, afternoons, evenings and Sundays.

Then one day when we were all down at Bernie Hyman's beach house in Santa Monica, going over the same marshy ground that we and so many others had gone over before, I had an idea. It wasn't logical or even sensible, but by this time the producers were so desperate they were willing to accept any new solution. They would even have agreed to let Powell betray the United States and turn over the secret code to Germany in order to get him and Russell out of that room and Metro out of the red.

Suddenly I was a savior, albeit a reluctant one. While they were acclaiming me, I was already probing a gaping hole in my solution. I tried to point it out to them, but they didn't want to look at holes. They had seen too many of them in the past months. Amid cheers and hosannas I was sent home to write the saving scene.

Deep into the morning I labored, so worn out that I hardly knew what I was writing. Finally I finished and fell asleep on my way to bed. Next morning I awoke, reached for the script, and read what I had written. It made no sense, but its nonsense was mildly amusing. If it were directed fast enough an audience just might laugh and, in doing so, overlook its implausibility.

It worked. At the sneak preview logic was lost in laughter. A day or so later I was given the long-awaited raise and a three-year contract, complete with options (the studio's, not mine). I was a hero. . . . Louis B. Mayer called me by my first name; even my agent phoned me!

None of this appeared in the film.

William Powell and Myrna Loy had been scheduled to star because they had teamed so well in *The Thin Man*. But Loy was on strike for more money, so Rosalind Russell was chosen as the female lead—her first lead, having played "the other woman" in several other films, one (*Evelyn Prentice*) with Powell and Loy. She was self-conscious, knowing that they had been such a hit. She tried to apologize to Powell:

"I know you don't want me, you'd rather have Myrna."

"I love Myrna, but I think this is good for you, and I'm glad we're doing it together," Powell replied gallantly.

He played Greenleaf, now called William Gordon. Russell played Joel Carter, his girlfriend. Binnie Barnes, who had starred as Katherine Howard, the fifth queen in Charles Laughton's *The Private Life of Henry VIII*, was Olivia, an undercover enemy agent; Cesar Romero was Colonel Nieterstein, a soldier of indeterminate Allied nationality secretly loyal to Germany. Mickey Rooney, not yet famous for his Andy Hardy films, had a bit part as a country boy. After a postponement, shooting began 24 June with William K. Howard directing. On 29 July, production was halted for two weeks to await Binnie Barnes's return from an appendectomy. The film was again retitled, this time as *Puzzle Man*. That lasted about a fortnight, and then *The Black Chamber* moniker was restored. On 23 August, Hollywood was surprised to read on the front page of the *Hollywood Reporter* that "With only a few scenes to be shot to complete 'Black Chamber,' MGM has decided on a complete rewrite and re-shooting of the spy story." A new director and writers had been assigned, it reported. The next day, perhaps because the story had embarrassed the studio, the trade daily wrote, "The story in these columns yesterday that 'Black Chamber' was to be entirely remade was in error." The delay was caused, it said, by the fact that "from the start the production never had a satisfactory ending, but shooting continued and a better ending awaited reaction of review audiences. Another ending is being written and all shooting held for that." Filming began again 6 September under a new director, Sam Wood. One of forty-odd pictures in production, it was to be shot over the next two weeks; seventeen new sets were built for scenes yet to be shot. After eleven days—many of them half-days—of shooting, the film wrapped up on 26 September. By then it had been definitively titled *Rendezvous*. Yardley had long been completely marginalized.

Before the movie could be released, however, it had to pass the scrutiny of the Hays office. The office's moral arbiter, Joseph Breen, requested changing the script's reference to Newton D. Baker, who had been secretary of war during World War I. Then it got down to the real issues. "Pages 74 and 75: Great care must be taken in handling the scenes of the examination of Olivia and her undressing. Her clothes should not be thrown over the top of a screen. Greenleaf should not be shown examining them. The close shot of Olivia's legs should not be used. Page 134. Greenleaf's use of the expression 'Oh, my God!' should be dropped." In October, Breen wrote to Louis B. Mayer, "We had the pleasure yesterday of witnessing a projection room showing of your feature entitled *Rendezvous*. It is a thoroughly enjoyable picture of outstanding merit and is acceptable under the provisions of the Production Code, with the understanding that the shot showing Mr. Powell kicking the posterior of Miss Russell will be eliminated from the final print. Mr. Weingartner [*sic*] has assured me that this elimination has been made, and, on this basis, I am happy to send you herewith our formal Production Code certificate of approval, numbered 1656." In black and white, *Rendezvous* ran ninety-one minutes.

It is an amusing film with a clever and complicated plot that bears little relation either to Yardley's books or to the scripts he worked on. Powell is urbane and funny as Gordon, no longer a puzzle editor but now a foreign correspondent who once wrote a manual, "How to Encipher and How to Decipher," which he says sold five copies—a depressing thought for the authors of books on cryptology. He wants to fight at the front but is pressed into boring codebreaking duty. Russell, with the right touches of mugging, plays the girlfriend, Joel Carter, who wants to keep him in Washington. In the story, the Allies need to conceal the American transports' rendezvous point with British escorts. They radio it in an unbreakable code. But the inventor of the code is involved with an elegant blonde spy for Germany, who steals it and then kills him when he discovers the theft. Her colleagues, obtaining the rendezvous point from the code, radio the information in their own cryptosystem to Germany. The Americans intercept it, but their code-breaking bureau, crowded with women typists and suited men hustling to and fro, and with a shirt-sleeved supervisor shouting out letters to men at a blackboard, cannot solve the intercept.

Gordon does, in the liveliest cryptanalysis ever shown on the screen—perhaps the liveliest ever. Prancing back and forth along a row of five over-sized cipher disks, each set to a different key letter, he loudly converts each ciphertext letter into its plaintext original. Secret-ink messages lead Gordon to the spies' hotel rooms; Joel follows him. Instead of Oppenheimer's twist about the locked room, the evil German spies machine-gun their way into the room. They are shot by American agents, who have been summoned by a cryptosystem devised under duress by Gordon as a message to the submarines: it disguises 37 15th Street Northwest in Washington as latitude and longitude. The German radioman is prevented from transmitting the rendezvous data. As Gordon is finally boarding a train for embarcation to the real war in France, he is recalled to codebreaking in Washington. That battle is won by Joel.

Metro-Goldwyn-Mayer, the producer, mimeographed a publicity and advertising manual. Powell, it shouted, "gives you a new type . . . an unforgettable devil-may-care delineation of another unsung Washington hero . . . the Bureau of Intelligence Man . . . 'The Cryptographer' . . . Yes . . . *Powell* for star value! That and the unusual twist of the story—are your top merchandising mediums in *Rendezvous.*" It proposed as an advertising line "He could solve the most intricate puzzle—unless they were dressed in skirts." The story, the manual promised, offered "a behind-the-scenes view of 'the black chamber.' . . . Unsung branch of the Intelligence Department . . . where wars are fought on a silent battlefield."

Where was Yardley in all this? Mostly out. "Do not hesitate to use Major Yardley's name in your publicity and advertising," urged the publicity manual. It pointed out that his " 'Stories of the Black Chamber' have enjoyed a coast-to-coast broadcast over the NBC network." It mentioned his articles in the *Saturday Evening Post* and *Liberty* and his book *The Blonde Countess,* on which the film was allegedly based. Curiously it never referred to *The American Black Chamber,* even though the credits said the film was based on that book, exploiting its fame and seeking to give the film a factual foundation it did not have.

The film premiered at New York's Capitol Theatre on 25 October 1935. The *New York Times* called it a "lively and amusing melodrama." Yardley's hometown paper, the *Worthington Times,* mislabeled it as "The startling, dramatic story of the famous American Black Chamber, as told by the man who organized and headed it throughout the World War." The *Hollywood Reporter* said it was a "comedy as fresh and delightful as the drama is engrossing. . . . An especially arresting item is the inside picture presented of the Code work of the Secret Service. The author of the story, Herbert O. Yardley, was in this service and knows his stuff. . . . The laboratory and decoding rooms are marvels of authentic detail"—as if the writer knew. And a study of American films in the 1930s called *Rendezvous* "the first American spy film with a sense of humor."

In Hollywood, Yardley had become friendly with a couple from Worthington, Abe and Lelia Brewer. He played golf with Brewer for 10¢ a hole and one summer they rented a cabin in the mountains at Pinehead near Los Angeles. In 1936, three adult Worthingtonians and their daughters, ten and thirteen, drove to California in a 1936 Ford to visit them and another daughter. They spent a week's vacation at nearby Arrowhead Lake, horseback riding and swimming in a pool fed by melted snow. One day Brewer and Yardley shot a deer, skinned, butchered, and roasted it.

About that time, some men with a million-dollar sure shot somehow hooked up with Yardley. They had an option on five hundred barrels of concentrated orange juice from which they were going to make orange wine. They needed only $150 to hold the option. He gave it to them. Then they needed $50 here, $100, $500 for filters. Yardley, using his movie money, gave it to them. Then they decided that the juice could not be filtered and that the only way to make money was to turn it into orange brandy. For that a still was needed. Yardley put up the money to buy a controlling interest in a distillery in Colton, California, sixty miles east of downtown Los Angeles, owned by the Nolder family of San Bernardino. Brewer said that "the orange juice boys were slickers, but they could not carry water to the distillery crowd—they were *smart slickers.*"

Brewer looked over the plant at Yardley's request and found that it needed a steam boiler, a cooker, a cooling tower, slop tanks, brass piping, fuel storage tanks, and a few other little things. When Yardley asked him what he thought should be done, "My answer came the closest to causing friction with Herb and myself we ever had." But, Brewer thought, Yardley "never worked, played poker, golf, fished or did anything else for fun. Whenever he did anything he did it to *win.* . . . It was not a question of the dollars he had in the deal, but a question of making a go of it, so there was no quitting." Brewer moved to Colton; Yardley took a hotel room. They managed to get the distillery operating. By July 1936, Yardley wrote to Bye with reserved enthusiasm on the letterhead of M. J. Nolder Distilleries Inc. that "We are going along pretty good now—making about 1100 gallons a day." He said he was saving Bye "a nice barrel of the first gallon I make and will deliver it to you in person in December." Bye wondered whether Yardley was "the official tester in that distillery." But whiskey prices were falling. Friction developed with the stockholders. Yardley had to keep putting money in. Nothing went right. One night that fall he told Brewer that he was leaving the next day for Worthington. The San Bernardino crowd took over the distillery. Brewer rescued $2,700. Yardley never got a cent.

In March 1937, Yardley and Hazel returned to Jackson Heights. But fights broke out between them and they separated in September. Hazel and Jack went back to Worthington. Yardley claimed to be supporting them, but neighbors there believed differently: Jack, a slight, withdrawn boy with eczema, seemed abandoned by his father, who would appear, bring a few presents, and depart. Jack had no coat when he graduated from high school and had to borrow one from a teacher, Max Adkins; all Worthington talked about this. Jack never spoke about his father and seemed to resent him for the way he treated his mother. Hazel, by then a woebegone, sweet woman, returned to work as a librarian—the job she had had before she married—but never complained about Herbert. Six months later Yardley was living at 314 Roosevelt Avenue, Hasbrouck Heights, New Jersey, a suburb of New York, with Edna Ramsaier. He reconnected with Willis and Company, real-estate brokers in Rego Park, Queens. He neither bought nor sold property but seems to have worked only as a broker.

His writing went nowhere. Despite Bye's efforts, a play, "Eleven o'Clock," never sold. Bye told him he could write two thousand words on codes and ciphers for *Modern Mechanix* at 10¢ a word, but Yardley alibied that the file dealing with the subject was in Worthington and that he could not get it until he returned to Indiana for the fall quail shoot. From time to time people wrote asking for permission to reprint bits of his writings. It didn't enrich him. In May 1936, for example, the American Book Company wanted to reproduce a few lines in a book by August Dvorak called *Typewriting Behavior*. Bye granted permission without a fee.

Yet like many authors who, no matter how many times they get slashed by reviewers and battered by publishers, write yet again, Yardley wanted to do another book. He began "Shadows in Washington" in March and finished it in eight weeks. At George Bye's suggestion, he visited Bobbs-Merrill's New York editor, who promised "a quick reading," saying "We want a book from you." Then Yardley wrote to Chambers of Bobbs-Merrill in Indianapolis:

I've written it with the same attention and concentration that I did the Amn Black Chamber—I mean I've done nothing else but write and think of it—business was slow so I just locked myself up and went to it—and incidently *[sic]* have had a swell time. It is a peace time spy tale laid in Washington. The man and woman are not tossed in. They are essential to the tale. I create love—then love conflict in the first chapter (also mystery). The conflict between the two is so great that they cannot be brought together until the end of the tale. The actors are presumably commercial spies—they buy and sell secrets as the corner grocer buys and sells vegetables. But the particular thing they are after is in itself so terrible that the story has the menace of a war time spy tale. Incidents are novel and at least four major situations hair raising. Cameron [Bobbs-Merrill's New York editor] said he wanted to read it. I promised it to him the first of this week. But over the week end a critic friend of mine made a suggestion that is so swell that I'm going to incorporate it so I'll be a bit delayed. The tale will run about 65,000 words. All this just in case Bobbs Merrill needs a book at this time. I thought if you did I should tell you about it as well as Cameron.

He sent a copy to his Hollywood agent, H. N. Swanson, who said that he liked it, and another to Bye, who also said that he liked it but added that Yardley had been lazy here and there, that the book wasn't literature, but that it was a tale. Yardley called that "high praise from Bye." Bye sent Cameron the book. After two weeks, Yardley rang him. In the supercilious manner of some editors dealing with authors they don't think will provide them with a best-seller, he said, "I never read anything these days." Then he quit Bobbs-Merrill. Meanwhile, Jessica Mannon wrote Yardley that the book had been turned down but not in the Indianapolis office where she worked, so she could not say why. "I wish I might have had the opportunity to read it," she wrote. Yardley, infuriated at Cameron and the whole situation, fired off a letter to her, saying he was sending his copy of the novel to her because "I want you people to publish this tale."

He then told her what he had not divulged to anyone else—except perhaps Edna Ramsaier: he had agreed to go to China for a year to solve Japanese military messages. He said that when he returned he wanted "to turn out about three novels of adventure a year—adventure and mystery for I cannot write strictly mystery—nor can I read it." Mannon apologized for Cameron's behavior and said, "I know I shall enjoy reading your story and I'll hope to have a different answer for you." But in an internal memorandum to Mannon about "Shadows in Washington" one editor noted, "There may be a thread of a story here, but it's pretty ragged. I won't attempt to list my object[ion]s or to say what it needs—certainly a new start from scratch, or several of them, wouldn't hurt it. But one thing it *doesn't* need, as it stands now, is a publisher." Another added, "That there may be a market for it—an ultimately disappointed market—or that sales possibilities are not altogether lacking, is, I believe, beside the point at this writing." Faced with this, Mannon on 8 July soothed Yardley, "I shivered and shook as I read SHADOWS IN WASHINGTON even though the thermometer hovered about 90 degrees in the moonlight. You've a rattling good tale here," before sandbagging him, "which makes it all the harder to tell you that we think the chances of a decent book sale are mighty slim." She concluded, "Good luck to you, fella, and let me know if you set sail for China."

And set sail he did.

17

China

Japan had invaded China in July 1937, and after several months China's intelligence chief, Dai Li, wondered whether he might improve his position within the bureaucracy by obtaining help in solving Japanese cryptosystems from a man who had made his reputation by doing just that. The intelligence chief's man in America, the assistant military attaché, was instructed to find out whether Herbert Yardley might want to come to China. Despite his knowledge of Yardley's success, he checked him out. He did not consult Friedman, but Yardley's old wartime buddy, Ambassador J. Rives Childs, gave him the highest recommendation. On 18 May 1938, the attaché, Major Hsin Ju Pu Hsiao, addressed a letter to Yardley, asking him to lunch with him. As soon as Yardley saw it, he knew that the Chinese wanted him to break codes for them. He was offered $10,000 a year in a contract for six months with an option to renew for a year and, though it was less than the $25,000 he had wanted from Colombia several years earlier, he accepted. The money was probably the primary motive for his acceptance, but other elements perhaps contributed: the lure of travel, his sympathy for the heroic resistance of the Chinese people, and his disgust over such Japanese brutalities as the sinking of the American gunboat *Panay* and the rape of

Nanking. He disguised himself by dropping his last name—though not on his passport—and calling himself Herbert Osborn.

Preparations took three months, but he finally sailed from New York shortly after midnight on Saturday, 4 September, aboard the *Britannic.* After Le Havre he steamed through the Strait of Gibraltar to Marseilles, Malta, and Port Said, through the Suez Canal to Aden, through the Indian Ocean to Bombay, Colombo, Penang, and Singapore, then through the South China Sea to arrive at Hong Kong on 12 October—quite a trip, halfway around the world, for a man who had probably first heard some of those exotic names in a small Indiana high school class.

From Hong Kong, Yardley was to fly to Hankow, but the Japanese were reported entering the city. So he waited two weeks for instructions, while he indulged his Western curiosity about Asian women. "I did go to a naughty place and watched a couple of girls," he wrote to friends. "It *does not* run cross wise but there is not hair on it—and really they are built differently— there is a sort of large dimple and I suppose their sex is concealed within." He visited the "girl market," where *amahs* walked up and down with little girl prostitutes available for the equivalent of 15 American cents. "I know you will say I'm a liar but it is a fact that I am still a virgin," he wrote. While in Hong Kong, he had a blue suit custom-made and told the tailor who asked him on what side he carried his "water tap" that his was so small it didn't make any difference.

In the last week of October, Yardley and his government translator, Yen Shih, boarded the SS *Kiangsu,* a fifteen-hundred-ton freighter, bound for Haiphong in French Indochina. One of eight first-class, one hundred second-class and three hundred deck passengers, Yardley sat in undershirt and shorts, dripping with perspiration, as they steamed through the South China Sea. He perhaps feared a repetition of the pirate attack of a couple of years earlier, when two officers were killed and the passengers robbed. He complained that he departed New York under a full moon, sailed under another in the Red Sea, and now saw a third: "nearly two months and I have not yet reached my destination." He docked at Pakhoi, a little Chinese port, which Yardley called "my first *real* Chinese city." It differed from Worthington, New York, and Washington: "pigs running in the street, roosters crowing—I saw a wedding with the bride in ancient Chinese bridal carriage . . . homes with dirt floors and the inevitable pig lying on the ground— tiny chapels where they worshiped—streets only 10 feet wide—naked children . . . a leper colony where we saw lepers spinning beautiful things which are sterilized before being shipped away. . . . The people terribly poor but healthy—happy—yet on three occasions the Japanese warships have stood off

Envelope of a letter to Edna from Yardley, en route to China

and shelled the city." He believed "I shall be a real service to this lovely nation." After waiting three days in Haiphong for the narrow-gauge train to China, he rode it twenty-four hours to Kunming. From there he flew to Chungking, the temporary headquarters of Chiang's Nationalists, landing 5 November on a sandy island in the Yangtze River. Chungking, on the latitude of New Orleans, hangs on cliffs that overlook the junction of the Yangtze and Chialing Rivers. The riches of the semitropical province of Szechuan—fruit and flowers in profusion, scowloads of rice, squealing pigs with their eyelids sewn shut as they were carried to slaughter—poured into the wartime capital, as did the displaced but heroic bureaucrats who kept China alive and unbeaten. The sea was fourteen hundred miles away, the Japanese four hundred—beyond the mountains and the three gorges that were impassable for troops, but not for bombers.

Put up at first in an apartment house, Yardley was moved on 13 November 1938 to a tile-roofed twenty-room stone chateau atop the highest point in the city, with the Yangtze four hundred feet below. The chateau had been the home of the mayor, who, Yardley said, "was mysteriously and quickly dispossessed just before my arrival." Underneath was a cave chiseled from rock called the Grotto of Divine Immortals. To reach the house, Yardley rang a bell at a gate with the Chinese characters for "Pleasant Home," waited for a Chinese boy to unbar it, climbed stone steps to a garden with stone walks, palms, hedges, and stone tea tables, passed a spring called "Sweet Spring," and climbed forty steps to the chateau. Its address was Shen Shien Tung Gai 94. It had neither a bath nor running water nor heat; for a toilet he used a can whose contents were sold each day for fertilizer. With the indoor temperature forty to fifty degrees and fog outside, he had a charcoal stove jerry-built that dried out his twenty-by-forty-foot combined bedroom and office. This had a modern desk, a chaise longue, two chairs, two native rugs and a two-hundred-watt bulb, required because the current was so weak. It cast little light and hurt his eyes frightfully. He was not happy. Chungking, "a scurf of mud and bamboo huts and low, dull-colored stone buildings," means Heavenly Residence, he said, "but I would have given a good deal to be in Worthington, Indiana, which was never so characterized." He quickly learned that things were not like at home. "When I flicked an unfinished cigarette into the street, a half-naked ricksha coolie snapped it up as a fish rises to a fly, scarcely breaking his stride."

Fogs that come from the west dampen and chill Chungking's winter. The depressing weather of his first months, the worst cold he'd ever had, the frightening loss of almost all the sight of his right eye through a choroiditis for several weeks, and homesickness drove him almost to despair. He envied his correspondents at home, who he said were warm and happy. Several times he crawled into bed with his gun, ready to commit suicide. The bombings didn't help. On 15 January 1939 an air raid demolished several buildings near the Nationalist headquarters. Yardley rushed to take pictures but so many Chinese there were weeping with handkerchiefs to their eyes as the dead were being taken out that "I did not have the courage to take pictures." When the Japanese communiqué boasted that "Our brave air forces bombed Chungking today," he said, "I really felt ill." After another air raid a few months later, he saw an old man seated on the curb, his shirt ripped from his chest, muttering that he wanted to go home. The man struggled to his feet. His whole left side was torn open and Yardley could see his heart beating. The man took a few steps and fell dead.

Yardley hated the apparent callousness toward life. Once his interpreter read from a Chinese paper that bombing in Kweilin had set fifteen hundred homes on fire, and then turned the page. Yardley asked how many dead. The interpreter turned back the page and said, about fifteen hundred. Why didn't you tell me that, Yardley asked. "He said they are only poor people and of no importance," Yardley quoted him, "they are better dead—I did not think you would be interested—and so on and on and on." He abominated the un-democratic social system. He felt the Chinese were shiftless "monkeys." They couldn't understand what the hurry was. Tomorrow would do. Men had been working for three weeks on a bath and toilet for him and still hadn't gotten it done. Three requests hadn't brought him a Hong Kong daily. The handmade rat traps wouldn't work: the rats ate the two pounds of ham that was the bait. Springs to keep the doors closed finally arrived but the doors scraped the floor, nullifying much of the effect. The shortwave radio wouldn't operate because the voltage wasn't great enough. Once his boy had not boiled the water that Yardley was to drink with his orange juice. He poured the luke-warm water over his hand and shouted that he could piss warmer than that.

He put it about that he was in Chungking to trade in hides and leather, then settled into an unbusinessmanlike routine: he worked every night until 5 a.m., got up at 10 or 11, had some hot orange juice in bed while his boy built a fire, breakfasted, then—in the early days—composed lessons on crypt-analysis for his future students. He worked until 6, went downtown, had a small glass of what he called "vile" Chinese brandy, dined on what he thought was sometimes "good" Chinese food or in what he called a "stink-ing" restaurant, and returned around 11 to work through the night. His amusement consisted of running his rat traps—the place was infested with the rodents; sometimes they ran over him as he slept—and seeing out-of-date movies, usually twice. The theater was just then showing eighteen-month-old newsreels of Britons setting jewels for the 1936 coronation of King George VI. He did no cryptanalysis in part because his staff was still in the interior, in part, he believed, because his boss, the intelligence chief Dai Li—whose bureaucratic position Yardley was to enhance—wanted to talk to him before establishing a headquarters for the work. Toward the end of Novem-ber, desks for the students were installed; fifteen cryptanalysis students and fifteen radio operators arrived in December. Eventually, he had them work-ing from 8 a.m. to 10 p.m. They were not allowed to quit, and the general who oversaw them, while a prince to Yardley, tormented them.

Yardley had been brought to China to further empower Dai Li by improv-ing China's cryptanalysis. In modern times in China, that form of intel-ligence had begun during the chaotic civil wars of the 1920s when Chiang Kai-Shek was trying to unify China under his Nationalist Party. T. V. Soong, a Nationalist leader and Chiang's brother-in-law, thought that solving the secret messages of the numerous rebelling semi-independent military com-manders would help Chiang subdue them. His nephew and fellow Harvard graduate, Yu Ching Wen, who had collected As and Bs in mathematics on his way to his Ph.D. in physics, might do the cryptanalysis. Soong pulled the thin, thirtyish Phi Beta Kappan out of the Peking Tax Academy and turned him to codebreaking. The Chinese transmitted their ideograms telegraphically by replacing each with a number from a standard codebook. The numbers could be enciphered for secrecy. Many of the warlords' cryptosystems proved primitive enough for Wen to break, and his solutions indeed helped Chiang gain the ascendancy and establish the Nationalist Government in 1928.

Three years later, Japan occupied Manchuria and drove the Chinese troops south of the Great Wall, assisted in part by fake radio messages. When Japan next grabbed the northern provinces of Hebei and Suiyuan, Chiang on 1 March 1936 reorganized and renamed Wen's office, now the Midian Jianyi Suo, or the Inspection and Cryptanalytic Office of Secret Telegrams. He authorized him to attack Japanese cryptosystems. Within three or four months, Wen and his colleagues had cracked a low-grade code of the Japanese Foreign Ministry. Chiang, who controlled his cryptology tightly ever since his personal cipher clerk had betrayed his codebook to the Communist leader Zhou En-lai, was delighted and enlarged the Midian Jianyi Suo.

But at least two rival radio intelligence organizations had grown up during the 1930s. Chiang's chariness with intercepts had led the army chief of staff to establish his own radio intelligent unit. And Dai, brutal, utterly loyal to Chiang, always wearing the blue-black high-collared uniform of the Nationalist Party, wanted to increase his power base. In 1933, he assigned a radio expert, the shrewd and reticent Wei Daming, whose wife was said to be one of Dai's former mistresses, to train bright young men in radio intelligence. Eleven classes had graduated by 7 July 1937, when a clash between Chinese and Japanese troops at the Marco Polo Bridge near Peking gave Japan its excuse to begin aggression, China its need to solve Japanese military cryptograms, and Yardley his oriental job.

A Chinese scholar, recently returned from Germany, who spoke better English than Yardley's interpreter, translated the course Yardley had prepared. But Yardley was disappointed in the students. He complained, in one of his depressed moments, that they were not worth a damn. But since his analyses showed that the Japanese were "none too careful" in their cryptography, he nevertheless hoped for "a huge success." This was despite his difficulty in obtaining collateral material that would help in solution, such as captured messages. Once he wanted to talk to the Japanese officer from whom ninety-six documents had been seized. The reply was: "Chinese soldiers very mad at Japanese prisoners. They buried officer alive!" He had the prison camps scoured for signal officers but found none. In fact, Yardley learned, very few prisoners were taken. Most were killed, often by burying alive—apparently a common custom, even for disobedient sons. Once, however, when a Japanese bomber had crashed, one of Yardley's superiors flew to the town and rescued the bombardier, who told the Chinese the meaning of many Japanese abbreviations they did not understand.

As the school was gearing up, Dai visited, and so did his signals chief, Wei, who had been promoted to command the army's Department 4, while Dai headed Department 2, under which Yardley fell. Soon, the fifteen students and fifteen operators had grown to fifty students and one hundred operators at fifty intercept posts—though Yardley said his examination of operator handwriting found only seven. Later he had some seven hundred to eight hundred men and women working for him. In its first eighteen months, his team snared two hundred thousand intercepts, of which twenty thousand were analyzed. One of Yardley's early analyses seemed to show that the Japanese were using about twenty different codes, each enciphered. He sent samples of them to three of his former coworkers—Edna, Mendelsohn, and Wilson.

One day in February 1939, while studying a series of kana messages transmitted every day at 6 a.m., noon, and 6 p.m., he noticed that of the forty-eight kana only ten were used, perhaps representing numerals, and that the messages were extremely repetitious in format, perhaps therefore meteorological. He arbitrarily converted the kana into figures and studied them. His team's rough direction-finding indicated that the messages were being sent from near Chungking and Yardley concluded that the first group of all the messages, 027, stood for *Chungking*. He further observed that all the messages sent at 6 a.m. had, as their second group, 231, those sent at noon, 248, and those at 6 p.m. 627. The third group in nearly all the messages was 459—except for a message of noon that day, where it was 401. Yardley noted that the light rain of several days had cleared at noon and he concluded that 459 meant *rain* and 401 *fair weather*. It was 1 p.m. He called in his Chinese liaison officer and told him that he believed Chungking would be bombed that afternoon. While he was explaining his analysis, the sirens wailed. Yardley's reputation was made.

By mid-1939, he and Wei had solved a Japanese air force code. This enabled China to be warned of bombings and to avoid other air disasters. Chiang was delighted.

Cryptanalysis did not keep Yardley from other endeavors—any more than it had at the Cipher Bureau. To make what he called "a small fortune," he constantly proposed—and in a few cases drafted—articles for *Cosmopolitan* magazine and the *Saturday Evening Post.* He at first suggested articles and photographs about atrocities, obtained from Japanese dead or from the Chinese who stole them, and about the execution of spies, which he said happened every few days. Once a politician was executed, but Yardley "was a bit disappointed—I thought a soldier would cut his head off with a big sword but instead he was shot." He wrote at least two drafts of one article and occasionally sent photographs. He was willing to do more. If Bye gave him "any encouragement on article will knock out about 60,000 words of franker stuff for a book—a non fiction book about trip here and ordinary experiences dramatized a little and over written of course—having nothing to do with official work of course." Since these did not sell, he proposed an exclusive series with photographs for the *Saturday Evening Post* on what he called China's new South West Empire—completed roads, railroads under construction, munition factories, and so on. It didn't sell. He grew depressed—and perhaps more realistic—about his abilities: "Now do not class me as a writer. I have written so much unpublished stuff that I have none too much courage left except for stuff non fiction. Am working on article now—but I could never make a living writing—a book or so—yes—but not as a money making profession."

He felt he could sell "tons" of an American rodenticide that killed and deodorized rats in a land where they were "as thick as flies." He considered a plan to "steal any Am[erica]n formula," such as Bayer aspirin, import it in concentrated form, and make it into tablets with local rice flour. He proposed researching for a physician friend of Mendelsohn's why the Chinese had such remarkably good teeth. He offered to buy stamps for his former colleague, Victor Weiskopf. None of the ideas went anywhere.

He seemed always to need more money even though he was treated like a king. He was an "American adviser" who was helping the Chinese fight the Japanese invaders. His bosses did everything possible for him. They had the stove, bath, and toilet put in. They brought a foreign cook from Hong Kong. They gave him cases of whiskey, wine, and brandy. They put a car at his service. They supplied him with translators. They gave him two boys to look after him. They kept a kettle of water boiling on the stove because he was afraid of drinking the local water unsterilized. They sent him telegrams of thanks and praise. They introduced him to Chiang. He didn't like the coddling. "I said I was from a generation of pioneers who fought in the revolutionary war, the civil war—I knew what hardships and war meant—he [the Chinese] must not do this." They did it anyway.

Yet they limited his freedom and kept strict watch over him because, they said, they feared his being kidnapped. It may not have been overprotective: every day, Yardley wrote, there were murders, kidnappings, robberies. A guard accompanied him when he went out. He carried a pistol. He felt cooped up. He protested but it didn't help. Even when he slipped away, he didn't gain much liberty. Once, when he sneaked out alone to his favorite restaurant, he was rushed upstairs to the manager's office, the desk was cleared, and he was served there. "What's the idea?" he asked. The head waiter said that if anything should happen to your honorable self, he would be held responsible, cut into a thousand pieces, and made into mince pie. Yardley offered the waiter $5 in Chinese money to say nothing the next time he came. The waiter refused, saying he had a wife and baby. Yardley offered $20. The waiter kowtowed and again declined. And when Yardley left, his guard was waiting outside.

By the end of 1939, Yardley had begun hanging around the Chungking Hostel, where foreigners assembled. Built cheaply of wood, plaster, and brick originally as a hospital, it offered a dining room, a lounge, some rooms for private parties, and a number of unheated bedrooms. Drinks were available, as was a poker game. Yardley loved poker and played it well; he had improved his interpreter's game. He despised the sloppy play of the others in the hostel: they discarded face up, disregarded percentages, bet wildly. This enabled Yardley, who played by the percentages and had, as he said many cryptologists do, a photographic memory, to guess the hole card of the other players. When, with the aid of some fake shuffles, he beat a British code clerk, Morgan Crofton, who disliked Yardley intensely, Crofton flew into a rage, tore up the cards, sought to destroy Yardley's transparent cover by calling him "Mr. Herbert Osborn Yardley," and stalked out with his girl-friend, Emily Hahn, a reporter Yardley described as "striking but more than plump." Hahn returned the compliment, calling him "an American with a loud manner of talking."

Among the others in the hotel was a diminutive, owl-like American, Theodore H. White, aged twenty-three, a propagandist for the Chinese, who later became a correspondent for *Time* magazine, the author of the best-selling *The Making of the President* series, and the model in the *Star Wars* films for the Jedi master Yoda. He and Yardley took to each other. White described him as "a balding middle-aged little fellow with the attractive and happy garrulousness of a country storekeeper . . . an extremely witty man."

> Yardley was a man of broad humor and unrestrained enthusiasms, and among his enthusiasms were drink, gambling and women. He decided after we had become friends that he should teach me poker, which he did by letting me

stand over his shoulder and watch him unfold his hands and sweep up the pots. He also felt I should be taught sex, and tried to persuade me to sample that experience by inviting some of the choicest ladies he knew to a banquet in his house. I would not learn; Boston was still strong in me. But he did teach me something more important than anything I have learned since from any official American adviser or wise man: how to behave in an air raid. Yardley's theory was that if a direct hit landed on you, nothing would save you. The chief danger of an air raid, he said, was splintered glass from windows. Thus, when one hears the siren one should get a drink, lie down on a couch and put two pillows over oneself—one pillow over the eyes and the other over the groin. Splintered glass could hurt those vital organs, and if the eyes or groin were injured, life was not worth living. It was good advice for any groundling in the age before atom bombs; and I took it.

Sex was, as White observed, one of Yardley's preoccupations. The American military attaché reported that "Sex is a major obsession with him and his conversation is filled with vulgar and bawdy references to women." Hahn likewise said his conversation "was mostly about women." His letters often mentioned sex. A week after he arrived he discovered that "downtown for one dollar Chinese (15 cents gold) I can get a lovely room and a bath tub for one hour. Also the boy tells me a girl thrown in for one dollar gold. . . . I told my guard OK send for a girl at the baths. Here came a little thing no more than 13. I tried to get her to pose for some pictures but she was too shy." Later: "15 year old kids can be called in . . . will send you picture of Chinese pussy when I get proper film. But I can tell you they are not sliced side wise—also there is practically no hair on pussy. . . . Had a date a few times with Chinese girl but too slow for an American. I give up. Yen Shih, my interpreter, has 17-year-old sweetheart (he is married) but doesn't fuck her. I said what do you do? He blushed. I said You finger fuck? He actually got red. He said Americans finger fuck? I said yes. He said 'Everywhere crows are black,' I said 'why no fuck.' He said She be ruined."

Despite Yardley's repeated disclaimers that the girls at the baths "certainly are beautiful but I am scared to death of disease" and that there was "Very nice looking pussy here but I am afraid of it for I never could use a cundrum or how ever you spell it," many Chinese women—but no foreign women— visited his apartment. He was said to have purchased Chinese girls as his sex slaves, to have organized orgies in his house, gaining popularity among foreign journalists and diplomats, to have lent his flat for use by a prostitute, and to have forced Dai to let him keep a "comfort" college in downtown Chungking. Indeed, Dai's greatest headache with Yardley was said to be maintaining security without limiting his urge for sex—although, as far as his work was concerned, despite his having written *The American Black Chamber* and even though the officers of the American gunboat *Tutuila* knew about his work, Yardley was generally security-minded, less for patriotic than for economic reasons, since he did not want to make his job harder or end it altogether.

Edna had refused to come to China, dissuaded by the very attaché who had recruited Yardley. Yardley's letters to Edna, back in Washington working for the Signal Intelligence Service and not yet his wife, were businesslike and demanding. "Dear Edna: You must be pretty sick of questions by now but here are still more. . . . Pls write Tracy and ask where we can purchase 'Lie Detector' and the price." Next month: "First—I am not scolding—you who have been so kind and so energetic in carrying out my requests—I cannot scold BUT now and then, because you are INTELLIGENT, you do not do as I request." The letters were not tender. He typed them and signed them "As always HOY," with no little hearts or Xs and Os or SWAKs. They completely lack romance, surprisingly for a man in so alien a country so far from home. Though Edna's letters to him do not survive, she was so besotted with him that she seems not to have complained.

After Yardley's original contract expired, he signed the option to stay another year as long as his students' working conditions were improved. By early 1940, however, all his work had been suspended pending a consolidation of what had grown to be the five or more agencies doing cryptology; he was to be in charge of eight hundred people. The situation had not been resolved by the spring and the work had not been resumed. He was restless and lonely, and drank a great deal interspersed with periods of abstinence. Although talkative while drinking, he said nothing about his code work, complaining only that his hides and casing business was bad. In March, the American assistant military attaché told him discreetly that the War Department wanted information about Japanese military codes. Yardley bargained. He offered to give it complete technical information in return for Edna's being given a government job at $6,000 a year—not knowing that she was already working for Friedman's Signal Intelligence Service. He would not give the government the material for patriotism alone since "the patriots working in Washington for the government were well paid." Moreover, he felt that Friedman, whom he disliked because he felt Friedman had undermined him, would sabotage any efforts to establish connections with the War Department. No agreement was reached.

His desire to leave grew stronger, though Dai wanted to keep him another year because, Dai said, his work was not complete. That may have been a polite way of saying what the attaché had heard from other sources: that the Chinese were not particularly pleased with his accomplishments. And indeed American advisers two years later concluded that his work had been superficial and that Yardley was getting money for doing nothing—a charge that echoed one made about his work for the Cipher Bureau. But perhaps no result would have sufficed. As a former chief of German espionage once remarked: "It will always be a certain tragedy of every intelligence service that even the best results will always lag behind the clients' desires."

Yardley finally told Dai that he could stay no longer. He had lost forty pounds since his arrival in China and his health had deteriorated. "Though I should like to remain to complete the work I have begun, I feel that to do so may permanently injure my health." He conceded that "I shall remember my stay here as one of the most interesting experiences I have ever had. I came here to help this nation and I myself feel that I have done a good job."

He summarized his efforts in a progress report of 11 March 1940 to Dai: he had solved seven two-figure codes, three three-figure codes, two transposition systems, three so-called tana codes, and systems called kwantung A, two-kana B, German five-letter, and fifty-indicator. His students had written reports on how most had been broken. The American military attaché doubted that the Chinese would "willingly permit him to leave China before the end of the war." And, in fact, for weeks, whenever he sought an interview with Dai, he was put off. Finally he bribed an official to sell him air passage over the Japanese lines to Hong Kong, whence he planned to take the China Clipper to the States. When he was told that no one could board the airplane without approval from headquarters, he bluffed. He told the officials that if he were not given clearance he would go to the airport accompanied by a newspaperman and the attaché. It worked. Dai came to see him. He arranged the usual round of farewell parties and a final interview with Chiang. Yardley got to Hong Kong and Pan American World Airways' China Clipper. He touched down in Manila on 18 July and Honolulu on 22 July, both arrivals noted by Japanese diplomats and in Hawaii by the press. In Honolulu he visited with a colleague from MI-8, Lieutenant Colonel George W. Bicknell, assistant intelligence officer of the Hawaiian Department. He did not reply substantively to newspapermen's questions about his work in China. He said only that he was out of the code business for good and was taking home notes for a novel set against the background of the Sino-Japanese War.

18

Canada

Yardley returned to America in the summer of 1940 with a great desire to be home, to see Edna Ramsaier (she had divorced and resumed her maiden name), and to exploit his information about Japanese military ciphers—greater, he claimed, than that of any other white man. He stayed briefly at Washington's landmark Cairo Hotel before moving to an apartment on F Street just north of the Munitions Building on Constitution Avenue, though he gave his address as 1789 Lanier Place, in the funky Adams-Morgan section, which was Edna Ramsaier's apartment.

He tried to get rehired as a cryptanalyst, but *The American Black Chamber* had made him persona non grata and his overtures were rejected without hesitation. But in 1938 or 1939, the army's small Signal Intelligence Service under William Friedman had begun receiving Japanese military intercepts from the Philippines. It could use the information about Japanese army and air force cryptography that Yardley had brought home. The Signal Intelligence Service stood under the Signal Corps, whose head was a World War I acquaintance of Yardley's, Major General Joseph O. Mauborgne. At the suggestion of the head of his war plans and training division, Colonel Spencer B. Akin, Mauborgne contracted with Yardley for a report on Japanese military cryptography for $4,000. But since Friedman and Yardley disliked each other, he assigned Friedman's senior assistant, cryptanalyst Frank B. Rowlett, as the inspecting officer for the report. Rowlett visited Yardley eight or ten times during the work to discuss whether what Yardley was producing was what the Signal Intelligence Service wanted.

Rowlett arrived around 10:30 or 11 in the morning, for he knew that Yardley liked to work late at night and slept late. Yardley usually greeted him in a sleeveless undershirt, somewhat dirty in front, in which, Rowlett thought, he had slept. He would sit down at his dinette table, where his papers were spread around his typewriter. He would pull out a bottle and a couple of glasses.

"Can I offer you a drink, Mr. Rowlett?"

"No, thank you."

"You don't mind if I have one?"

"Absolutely not. Go right ahead."

Yardley would pour himself about two-thirds of a glass of whiskey and sip it while they talked. When the glass was empty he would refill it. On the few times that the liquor showed, Rowlett excused himself to return the next day. During their interviews, Yardley readily answered Rowlett's questions about what he was writing, and sometimes he talked—with his considerable verve and authority—about the Cipher Bureau. He showed Rowlett pictures of Japanese atrocities—one sequence showed two Japanese soldiers holding a kneeling Chinaman by his queue and shooting him. Rowlett found Yardley easy to talk to and with a good sense of what he wanted to say. He had the feeling that Edna, who was then working for the Signal Intelligence Service, was feeding Yardley information. Rowlett disliked the SIS's paying Yardley for information it had, even unwittingly, given him. He discussed his suspicions and his irritation with Akin, who reckoned that, even if this were so, it might stimulate Yardley to remember more details and Yardley's information would tend to confirm what the SIS had ascertained about Japanese cryptography through the intercepts. So he permitted the game, if such it was, to continue. During the fall of 1940, while Yardley was writing, and despite their mutual antipathy, he and Friedman met to discuss technical matters. They did not fight. Friedman perhaps enjoyed these encounters, for he was now on top whereas in the past Yardley had been, and Yardley, who respected Friedman's technical ability, never badmouthed him to Rowlett. As the work was nearing completion at the end of December, Yardley met with Mauborgne and Akin as well.

He titled his report "Japanese Military Codes and Ciphers in Occupied China: Period 1938–1940" and divided its 224 pages into six "brochures" bearing such titles as "Japanese 3-Figure Field Codes" and "Solution of Encipherment of Japanese 3-Kana Codes." He explained the systems—mostly enciphered codes that used three- and four-figure codenumbers—and their solution clearly and in detail. He used no modern terminology except the word "monoalphabetic," introduced by Friedman in 1923, and no higher mathematics for his solutions—which, in fact, did not need it. The reports sound as if they were written entirely on the basis of Yardley's experiences; they do not seem tinged with any outside information, as Rowlett suspected.

Yardley spiced his writing with personal observations. Some of these were racist—"To the Occidental mind the message [at this point] has been subjected to enough hazards for errors, but not to the Oriental." Some were amusing—"And when the bombers are over their objectives, this radio silence is broken with a single dash as each bomb is released from the racks. (This is a good time to duck.)" Mauborgne later reportedly said that Yardley's brochures, which Yardley held "contained all the information about Japanese Secret Military Communications that was known at that time," were "invaluable." But Friedman thought that the army had not got its money's worth from the work, and Rowlett that it "was about as good as we [already] had and it wasn't good. It was trifling, trivial." It wasted cryptanalysts' time in answering Mauborgne's questions about whether it was useful. But Rowlett felt that in the end the brochures served a purpose: they "conditioned" the army cryptanalysts to deal with the much more difficult Imperial Japanese Army cryptosystems a few years later.

The war had reached the Western Hemisphere by the time Yardley returned home. Canada was fighting Nazi Germany. Though the country showed its independence by not declaring war until a week after the United Kingdom had, many Canadians still looked to Britain for leadership.

These attitudes extended particularly to codebreaking. Britain all but kept its commonwealth partners out of the field, and no cryptanalytic unit existed in Canada. Still, Canada intercepted hundreds of messages from its telegraph censorship, its Pacific radio station at Esquimalt, on Vancouver Island, and its Atlantic post at St. John, in Newfoundland. The Royal Canadian Navy forwarded these to the British Admiralty, which passed them to the codebreaking Government Code and Cypher School at Bletchley, sixty miles northwest of London, which urged that Ottawa "be informed of the increasing value of this material." But then Canada began work of its own. When Italy declared war on Britain and France in June 1940, Canadian censorship obtained the Italian order of battle. The army's sixteen operators in the basement of the Signal Corps radio station at Rockliffe Airport, Ottawa, likewise determined the Spanish army's order of battle late in 1940, as Hitler was trying to persuade Spain to join him in the war and take Gibraltar. Using a spy cipher given to it in September 1940 by the U.S. Federal Bureau of Investigation, the Royal Canadian Mounted Police read more than two hundred messages intercepted by the army.

These successes made Captain E. N. (Ed) Drake, who ran the Rockliffe station and headed the signals experimental section, think that, if this much information could be gleaned from plain language messages, much more could be reaped from coded ones. On 19 November 1940, he visited Mauborgne to discuss this. The general agreed to give him copies of the army's six cryptologic manuals, detailed the organization of a cryptologic agency, and urged that Canada create one, saying that it could produce information of the highest value to a country. On his return, Drake proposed such an agency. But the chiefs of staff "felt that we should continue to use the United Kingdom facilities for this work." They added that "a similar organisation exists in the U.S.A. which would be available to assist in the event of the United States' entry into the war" and that "the cost of such an organisation in Canada could not possibly be justified at the present time."

Drake remained a believer, however. A way out of the financial difficulty appeared when the government's National Research Council unexpectedly received $1 million from several wealthy individuals. Its War Technical and Scientific Development Committee included a representative from Canada's Department of External Affairs, who thought, like Drake, that codebreaking might be a useful wartime endeavor. Since the chiefs of staff weren't interested, External Affairs might handle it. That representative, Hugh L. Keenleyside, an able forty-one-year-old who had organized the triumphal 1939 tour of Canada by the new king and queen, suggested looking for persons interested in cryptology. On 23 January 1941 the acting president of the research council wrote to deans, mathematicians, and engineers at fourteen Canadian universities to ask whether they knew of "people who have had experience or are expert in the special work of codes and ciphers."

Many responded, including two professors of mathematics at the University of Toronto. Gilbert deBeauregard Robinson, thirty-five, a Canadian, had received his Ph.D. from Cambridge University; Harold Scott Macdonald Coxeter, thirty-four, a Briton, had also received his Ph.D. from Cambridge and in 1931 had won the Smith Prize, sometimes called the mathematics Nobel. Several years earlier, Coxeter corresponded with one Dr. Abraham Sinkov in Washington about their mutual interest: group theory. They collaborated on a couple of articles and, when Sinkov, a cryptanalyst with the Signal Intelligence Service, learned that Coxeter was preparing a new edition of W. W. Rouse Ball's classic *Mathematical Recreations and Essays*, he offered to update its chapter on cryptology. Coxeter agreed, and Sinkov wrote an entirely new chapter. The research council letter impelled Coxeter to write to Sinkov about cryptology. The American replied that he believed training texts were being sent to Canada. Drake was not mentioned.

On 17 March 1941, the council approved $10,000 for Project G-1003, the establishment of a cryptologic bureau under External Affairs. The acting president, Chalmers Jack Mackenzie, arranged for the two mathematicians to visit Washington and to obtain as much information as they could about the organization of a codebreaking agency, current cryptology, and American successes.

Robinson and Coxeter met Sinkov and Mauborgne on 1 May. Mauborgne was surprised. Were they following up Drake's visit of six months ago? They were embarrassed to confess that they knew nothing about it. Mauborgne explained that he had already answered most of their questions during his talk with Drake and that the training material and organization plan Drake had wanted had been collected and were merely awaiting an official request to be sent to Ottawa. Though he refused to give them any information about his own cryptanalytic organization or lend anybody for instruction, Mauborgne could suggest a man who might set up a codebreaking organization for Canada. This man had blundered once, for which he had "perhaps suffered unduly." Mauborgne had been acquainted with him for more than twenty years. He was experienced; he was a fine organizer; he was in Washington; and he was free. His name was Herbert O. Yardley.

Robinson and Coxeter telephoned Yardley as soon as they left Mauborgne's office. He met them that afternoon at the Canadian legation. There he impressed the academics mightily. This was not surprising: people who knew Yardley conceded that he "was a good salesman of his own ability and his own services" and was "unusually skillful in this respect." He agreed to come to Canada to head a codebreaking unit if asked. The next day they telephoned Mackenzie concerning a possible visit by Yardley to Canada. They reported that Mauborgne said he was "the best expert in America—was with the American Army in the last war and has been a specialist with Chiang for some years." Mackenzie suggested that Robinson try to get Yardley to come up the first of the week. In their written report the next day, the mathematicians likewise urged a visit. "In our opinion he is expert in the highest degree."

Despite a warning from the legation's first secretary that Yardley was "in disfavor" in some Washington circles because of *The American Black*

Chamber, the authorities accepted Coxeter and Robinson's recommendation. Yardley entrained on the Montrealer to Ottawa—after the minister in Washington asked External Affairs to notify Customs that the confidential document he was carrying "should not be subjected to examination." He arrived on Monday, 12 May. External Affairs put him up at the elegant Chateau Laurier, the best hotel in Ottawa. Keenleyside scheduled a meeting for 3 p.m. that day and sent an officer of the department to call for him.

The conference took place in the department's Room 123, illuminated by two pointed-arch windows, of East Block, the heavy stone gothic office structure near the Parliament building. Present were Keenleyside, Drake, service officials dealing with intelligence, the censorship official who had run the Italian order-of-battle program, and a representative of the National Research Council. Yardley acted almost as if he had been given the job, indicating, for example, that he would like to start on both diplomatic and spy communications. He said that financial and personnel support of the bureau would depend on its first achievements and suggested that certain classes of Japanese diplomatic material would make a good beginning, since he was familiar with them and the Japanese were represented in Canada, meaning that interception would be easy. He listed the kind of workers he would need for breaking Japanese, adding that success would come more quickly if he could have someone experienced working with him. He mentioned a woman who had worked with him for a decade helping him break Japanese systems and was now in army codebreaking—but he did not name Edna Ramsaier. He sagely remarked that the Canadians should train someone to take over from him because they would probably prefer one of their own to head the department. He was told that the Canadian Bureau of Statistics leased machines that could be used for cryptanalysis, but he said that he preferred not to work with them, though he conceded they were faster for a big bureau. The meeting agreed "to start on as small a scale as possible with a couple of definite tasks."

Another meeting the next day recommended the formation of the codebreaking unit, to be financed by the National Research Council for $10,000 with links to External Affairs, the services, and the Royal Canadian Mounted Police. Its head was to be Yardley.

He contracted to work six months for $550 a month Canadian—$500 American. The term could be extended. For security's sake, he would use—as he had in China—the cover name Herbert Osborn. His mail from Canada would be posted in Washington by the Canadian legation; it would pick up his incoming mail. Back briefly in Washington, he obtained a promise for a dozen copies of the army's six cryptologic booklets to be used for training and gained Mauborgne's reluctant consent to release Edna Ramsaier for six months. The legation would send his documents by diplomatic bag, so that he could cross the border with only his personal effects to declare. He returned to Ottawa around Thursday, 5 June, to find a place to live.

At 11:30 Wednesday morning, 11 June, he met again in Room 123 with a dozen officials and officers to organize a codebreaking agency for the Dominion of Canada. Edna attended. A committee, chaired by T. A. (Tommy) Stone of External Affairs, would supervise it. "Examination Unit" was selected as a name that was obscure, accurate, and proper to the research council. Yardley arranged to get needed documents from the services, which would henceforth submit all encrypted interceptions to the unit. He said that he planned to devote at least an hour a day to instructing his staff on cryptology and that he intended to concentrate at first on the traffic of suspected German agents and the Japanese intercepts. The organization was given Rooms 202 and 203—one large, one small—in front of the wind tunnel in the National Research Council Annex on Montreal Road. Yardley rented a room to live in; Edna, a living-bedroom. They were appointed without competitive examination because the project "necessitates the appointment of persons thoroughly trained and experienced in a highly specialized field in which there is little or no possibility of competition." They, Robinson, and six others comprised the staff.

Yardley jumped off to a quick start. Intercepts began to arrive on Monday, 16 June. They consisted of suspicious letters intercepted by the postal censorship, old and current Japanese diplomatic messages from the telegraph censor and the navy, and intercepted radio messages from "unauthorized" stations. Drake sent more Tuesday and Wednesday. On Thursday, Yardley reported his analyses of them. Three of six German Air Force intercepts would not be worked on until the Examination Unit was requested to do so. It would attack the other three, apparently enciphered by transposition. It would determine whether other intercepts were code or polyalphabetic substitution and proceed from there. So fast-moving was Yardley that the chairman of the supervisory committee, Tommy Stone, was able to say, in a letter Monday to the Washington legation confirming the delivery to Yardley of the textbooks from Mauborgne, that the unit "has already produced some very interesting decyphers." Stone, who was married to an American, reported, "Some of them will be of interest to the United States authorities I am sure, and I am trying how to work out a channel to get them down."

The Monday after that, 30 June, Yardley—signing his name Herbert Osborn—added two members to the unit, said he had requisitioned office equipment, and noted that the staff had taken oaths of secrecy. He wrote that "As preliminary preparation, intensive study is being made of types of ciphers which we may encounter." Some of the Japanese intercepts—apparently plaintext—could be read "with the help of an experienced Japanese linguist." Of his staff, he wrote that "The entire personnel has shown a most commendable eagerness to learn and a willingness to accept the drudgery necessary for success. No one could ask for a more loyal and industrious group."

Two days later, at a meeting with Stone and four other members of the supervisory committee, Yardley happily announced that, of thirty messages intercepted from the unauthorized radio stations, the unit had solved all but two. In a semisubtle bid for more personnel, he complained that "With our small force we are swamped." He wanted to continue to send copies to military and naval intelligence by hand instead of by mail and hoped "to get organized so that I will be able to deliver the cyphers in the afternoon." In the never-ending struggle between those who wish to protect sources and those who want to use the information, Yardley pressed to keep distribution limited while an air officer wanted some material to show the chief of air staff to demonstrate why a flier should be in the unit. After the meeting, Stone wrote to Yardley that four numbered copies of the unit's output were to be made: one for military intelligence, one for naval, one for External Affairs, and one for the files.

The messages Yardley was solving were to and from German spies in South America. They were encrypted in a transposition cipher. Because it had to be easy enough for spies to use, the cipher was so simple that code puzzlers had long amused themselves with it. The great majority of the intercepts dealt with ship arrivals and departures at South American ports and with agents' assignments, movements, and payments. On 16 July, Yardley listed arrivals and departures by 169 ships in seven South American ports. Those messages were forwarded to the Admiralty, but, though they appeared sensational, they were actually pretty useless: the Admiralty already knew the sailing dates of Allied vessels and Germany did not forward the spy reports to its U-boats because the freighters' courses were unknown and pickings were richer in the North Atlantic. The intercepts did little more than demonstrate the industry of the German spy rings. A few did reveal political or military intelligence. One, of 7 July, reported "OTIS has offer of an invention of Argentine officer for new bomb sighting device. State if interested." Another revealed that "Panair"—probably Pan American World

From: Rio de Janeiro (—)
To: Hamburg (UOY)

Type: RCCS Ref. No. 25-1-1   Date 13-9-41   Time 17.19

Received: September 15, 1941.
Deciphered: September 15, 1941.
Translated: September 15, 1941.

Message No. 265. Date 13-9-41   Time 14.00

MOUNT LYCABETTUS....5-9-41   Arrived at Quequen
                             from Lisbon.

MOUNT LYCABETTUS....9-9-41   Sailed for Buenos Aires.

NAGARA.............9-9-41   Sailed from Rio Grande
                             for England.

MARQUESA...........9-9-41   Arrived at Rio Grande
                             from Liverpool.

BUENOS AIRES.......9-9-41   Sailed from Buenos Aires
                             for New York.

BAYARD............9-9-41   Sailed from Buenos Aires
                             for Barranquilla.

Examination Unit,
National Research Council,
September 15, 1941.

Type: GA (cipher)
File No. 166

Intercepted German spy message, solved in Canada by Yardley's codebreaking Examination Unit

Airways—had received some emergency instructions; a Canadian official forwarded this to the legation in Washington because American authorities might want to know that this information had been sent to Germany.

Yardley began widening his net. Helped by Edna's recent work on low-grade Japanese codes in Washington, the unit began solving Japanese codes. Yardley named the first one LA, after its indicator, and soon was boasting that three-quarters of each message could be read. He didn't mention that LA was only a variation of a code that Japan had been using since the 1920s, nor that it was the lowest Japanese code, little more than an abbreviation system, used mostly for administrative trivia. And even though, owing to the inadequate knowledge of one Japanese translator's English and of her Canadian husband's Japanese in interpreting the intercepts, "no one was ever sure how accurately they conveyed the meaning of the original," the solution impressed Canada's officials.

More important to the government of a country with many ties to France were the solutions of the codes of the government at Vichy. By mid-September, Edna, aided by two typists, had broken enough of one cryptosystem to get intelligible French. In September, Yardley observed that many of the French intercepts referred to editorials and articles in two Montreal dailies, *Le Canada* and *La Presse*—a sign, which he did not mention, of a low-level code. In November, only one French code remained unbroken. And by 19 August, the Examination Unit had solved a Colombian code. With Rockliffe being replaced by a new monitoring station, and with better radio reception anticipated in the fall and winter, Yardley expected a "huge increase in traffic." In October, he solved intercepts from a circuit in the Near East; one message dealt with the disposition of British troops and requested explosives for sabotage.

Robinson felt that these successes were mainly attributable to Yardley. He regarded Yardley as "an excellent organizer" and a man who "could inspire those with whom he worked with his own enthusiasm." The staff liked him and felt he was doing a good job. He instructed them well—using Friedman's excellent *Military Cryptanalysis* textbooks—and under his direction the unit showed considerable originality in attacking the problems presented to it. In mid-September, a new method for solving transposition ciphers had been "thought out and planned exclusively by the Examination Unit." They were making more rapid progresses than had been hoped. Yardley pleased his bosses. He "has done and is doing good and useful work," said one. Intelligence officers in Ottawa felt that Canada "had made a good move in bringing Yardley up here." An External Affairs official maintained that "the

Unit is producing results of high value to our Intelligence Services." Another agreed that "our Unit has been producing good results." And after visiting Yardley, the National Research Council's Mackenzie was "very much impressed with what is being done. This is another project which is proving very successful."

Yardley sought some goodies and some money for himself. He did not want to make a nuisance of himself, he said, but perhaps he could be extended the same privilege as American servicemen in Canada in being allowed to import U.S. cigarettes. He was smooth. As an official quoted him, "He was hopeful that after a certain length of time he might be able to smoke Canadian cigarettes with some pleasure but up until now he said that the education of his taste has been a very slow progress." But the request was turned down because the order in council exempted only servicemen. Stone, perhaps with a bit of schadenfreude, wrote to him: "I venture to suggest that you will have to go through the necessary training period so that eventually you will derive satisfaction from a Canadian smoke." Yardley also sought more money for himself and Edna based on what he claimed was a question about income tax, the imposition on his salary of a defense tax that he had not known about, currency conversion, and the greater cost of living in Ottawa. But before that issue was resolved, a more serious matter arose.

It had been simmering even before Yardley had started work. On 5 June, the secretary of state for External Affairs had dutifully informed authorities in Britain that Canada was hiring him. But External Affairs was using an older form of code that did not exclude codenumbers with transposed adjacent numbers. This meant that the recipient was not alerted if such a garbled codenumber was received. In the Canadian cable, the codegroup for *yard*, 6792, was received in London, as 6972, which stood for *eme*, and was not recognized as an error. So what should have been decoded as *Yardley* was read as *Emeley*. The British did not at first question this but, a month later, asked whether Emeley was Yardley, whose book "was very harmful to United States cryptographic organization." External Affairs at once responded that the cryptologist was indeed Yardley and that it knew he was the author of *The American Black Chamber* and consequently "was not, for a period, persona grata with either the United States or the British Intelligence services." But, it added, "it was found that Major Yardley had made his peace with the United States Intelligence Services and was working closely with them. Since he has come to Canada, in fact, General Mauborgne has furnished him with copies of their highly secret books of instruction for his use here in giving courses in cryptography (which he does for an hour or so each day) to the members of our Unit." Moreover, "Both Yardley and Miss Ramsaier have taken an Oath of Secrecy, which was carefully composed and administered by the Assistant Clerk of the Privy Council with a certain amount of pomp and circumstance."

The British didn't buy it. On 16 August, Commander Alastair Denniston, the diminutive Scot who ran Britain's Government Code and Cypher School, was visiting American codebreakers in Washington. A decade earlier, he had wanted to keep *The American Black Chamber* from publication in Britain. Now, during a discussion about cooperation with other countries, he contended that the "cooperation of his organization with the cryptanalytic section recently established by the Canadian Government at Ottawa would be wholly dependent upon the elimination of Mr. Yardley from the latter organization." He reiterated this to the Canadians in Ottawa on his way back to Britain. When the assistant undersecretary of state for External Affairs who dealt with intelligence, Lester Pearson, protested that Yardley had been recommended by Mauborgne and had received training aids from him that had previously been turned down, Denniston replied that Mauborgne's views about Yardley were his own and were not shared by any other U.S. intelligence officials. In any event, as a consequence of a fight with the Army Air Corps over signal equipment matters, Mauborgne had been relieved of his duties in August, six weeks before his term was to end. And although the Canadians wanted a codebreaking unit and believed that the one built up by Yardley was well trained and efficient, they held that "coöperation between cryptographic and intelligence officers in Ottawa, Washington and London is of the highest importance." Moreover, Denniston promised he would send over a good cryptologist.

Canada bowed to the mother to the east and to the giant to the south. Pearson told the high commissioner, "We propose, therefore, not to renew our arrangements with Yardley at the expiration of the six months' period for which he was originally brought here," which was 9 December. Before telling Yardley he was to be fired, however, Ottawa wanted "to have definite assurances from the United Kingdom that a cryptographic expert of high qualifications and capable of taking charge of our unit will be made available to us" and "that the collaboration will be forthcoming." Britain vowed to lend Canada an "experienced cryptographic expert" and assured "closest collaboration." It wanted Yardley out before their man arrived.

Not everybody was pleased with ousting Yardley. Mackenzie said so at a meeting of the supervisory committee, thinking that "it may mean the crippling of our effort for a diplomatic and unreal reason." It didn't matter. The Government Code and Cypher School wanted Yardley out. On Friday, 21 November, the day after the cable arrived from Britain, Yardley and his assistant Robinson were told that he was to be replaced by "one of our own people"—just as he had suggested at his opening meeting but had apparently forgotten. Mackenzie thought the two men were "both very much cut up" and Stone and Pearson were given "a most unpleasant half hour" by Yardley. By Pearson's account,

> Yardley took the news very hard and was most insistent in his demands for a full explanation of the circumstances which gave rise to our decision to terminate our arrangement with him when, in fact, his Unit was just getting under way and was doing most excellent work. He said that there must be something more behind it than the mere desire to put a British subject in charge and he thought that he had a right to know. It was explained to him that for many reasons it was considered desirable now to have the whole organization in our hands and further than that by way of explanation it was not possible to go. Yardley accused us of bringing him up here and picking his brains dry and turning over into other hands various new methods of approach to cryptographic problems which he had developed since he had been here. He was told that this was hardly a fair statement and he withdrew it.

The next morning, Robinson brought Stone a letter supporting Yardley and urging that the organization not be changed "unless under gravest necessity. For, like a plant, through uprooting it, it may perish."

Stone himself felt that "there must be something more" "as to why Yardley is not trusted" than the "vague and unsatisfactory references to the book which he published." "A very embarrassing situation has developed and I feel that it is important that we should have complete information as soon as possible on the views of the United States authorities." So on Monday, the supervisory committee reconsidered the matter. It dispatched Pearson and Lieutenant Commander C. Herbert Little, a tall, competent, energetic reservist who had helped start Canadian naval radio intelligence, to Washington to see whether Yardley should not be retained.

They arrived at 1:30 p.m. Wednesday, 26 November. It was not Pearson's first encounter with American cryptology: as a junior External Affairs officer in 1934, he opposed—though unsuccessfully—American solutions of bootleggers' cryptograms supporting U.S. arguments that the Canadian rumrunner *I'm Alone* was legally sunk by the U.S. Coast Guard while in hot pursuit. Pearson and Little heard first from a Royal Navy intelligence officer assigned to Canada and sent to the Washington legation, Captain Edward Hastings. He reported that American cryptanalytic circles felt Yardley "was unreliable and untrustworthy" and more interested in publicity and money than in the work. He was "technically no more than an ordinary cryptanalyst." Hastings was sure that neither the United States nor the United Kingdom would cooperate with the Ottawa unit as long as it was headed by Yardley. The reason was their general but strong dislike and distrust of him because of his having written *The American Black Chamber.* This was not due to professional jealousy or irritation at Yardley's having given away secrets of the craft, Hastings felt, but was an honest suspicion. To Hastings's remark that the Americans were very glad to have him go to Ottawa since this solved the difficult problem of what to do with him, Pearson retorted that Robinson and Coxeter's enthusiastic report in the spring did not sound as if Mauborgne had recommended Yardley just to get rid of him.

At 11:30 the next morning, Pearson and Little heard Rear Admiral Leigh Noyes, the director of naval communications, under whom naval codebreaking stood, vehemently declare that the Navy Department would not touch Yardley with a ten-foot pole. The man was untrustworthy and unreliable. At 2:30, Edward A. Tamm, assistant director of the Federal Bureau of Investigation, likewise stated that Yardley was untrustworthy and that the bureau would not use him under any circumstances. He gave Pearson and Little a five-page report on Yardley. It recounted the widely known outline of Yardley's public life and added a few tidbits, some old, some new, some correct, some less so, and some rewritten press reports. At 3:30, the pair heard Mauborgne's successor, Major General Dawson Olmstead, say that Yardley was unreliable and untrustworthy and that the Signal Corps would not employ him in any capacity. Brigadier General Sherman Miles, the director of military intelligence, and Colonel Otis Sadtler, chief of the operations branch of the Signal Corps, under whom army codebreaking fell, echoed the sentiment. And when Little and Pearson asked Olmstead if Canada could expect any cryptanalytic cooperation from the United States if it employed Yardley, he replied with a categorical "No!"

At 5:15, they spoke informally but at length with Friedman. He traced the history of army cryptology and Yardley's relation with it and with State. Friedman maintained that Yardley had published *The American Black Chamber* in part because he was aggrieved at those who destroyed his work by closing his bureau but mainly because he was "almost down and out." He said that the book caused Japan to improve its almost juvenile cryptosystems and other countries to tighten their cryptosecurity—the first only partly true, the second not true, though he probably thought it to be. Friedman felt the case against Yardley was based almost entirely on the publication of *The American Black Chamber.* Though he personally believed that Yardley would not betray the American or the Canadian government if he were in its employ, he affirmed that the authorities' refusal ever to trust him again was justified. The contract for the brochures on Japanese army cryptography was not employment; the authorities would never bring him back in any capacity. Friedman appraised Yardley's abilities very fairly. He was a fine organizer and a good craftsman, industrious and energetic, with a gift for inspiring loyalty in his staff. However, his methods were somewhat old-fashioned and behind the times: he had little experience with modern machine ciphers and people in Washington and London had advanced far beyond him. Friedman concluded by wondering whether Yardley could not stay in Canada, where he seemed very happy, doing the work he had begun—much of which was similar to the counterespionage cryptanalyses the FBI was doing. But he too agreed that Washington would not cooperate with Ottawa in the field if Yardley stayed.

The next morning, Pearson and Little met with a "high official" of the State Department who had worked with Yardley—almost certainly Frederick Livesey, who had broken Japanese codes with Yardley during the Washington naval disarmament conference. He felt that Yardley had "a very definite genius for this work" but that his book "quite justified" the government's attitude toward him. In the end, Pearson got "the definite impression" "that the attitude of London toward Osborn had been largely determined by the attitude of Washington." He submitted a nine-page report. It was fair. It was thorough. It changed nothing. At 3 P.M. Monday, 1 December, the Examination Unit's supervisory committee decided that Yardley would have to go. The unit would be placed under a Briton.

Yardley's replacement was Oliver Strachey, sixty-seven, a British codebreaker who, like Yardley, had been solving German spy messages. Lanky, good-looking, pipe-smoking, charming when he wanted to be, Strachey was a graduate of Eton and Oxford, an older brother of the eminent biographer Lytton Strachey, the nephew by marriage of the philosopher Lord Bertrand Russell, and a neighbor of the economist John Maynard Keynes. His father, the chairman of the East India Railway Company, gave him a job as a district railway traffic superintendent with an office in Allahabad. Disappointed and frustrated at his inability to become a concert pianist, he took a series of mistresses—and compelled his young wife to serve them morning tea in the marital bed. After their divorce, he married the suffragette daughter of the wealthy esthete Bernard Berenson's second wife and returned to England and the life of books, music, and conversation that he had missed in India.

When World War I broke out, Strachey joined the War Office's cryptanalytical unit and found, like many musicians, that he was good at codebreaking. After the war, he continued in the Code and Cypher School. His salary was supplemented by his mother-in-law; the couple needed it because of their sociability—Strachey was always the last to leave a party. Early in World War II, he specialized in the ciphers of the Abwehr, the German armed forces' espionage agency. His solutions were distributed under the acronym ISOS, for Intelligence Services Oliver Strachey. This work paralleled much of Yardley's; moreover, Strachey had technically retired from the codebreaking agency on 17 December 1939 and was therefore easily transferred. He arrived in Halifax with his assistant, Margaret Rogerson, around New Year's Day 1942, but traveled first to Washington and New York.

Yardley did not go gentle into his new night, however. His literary agent, George Bye, was also the agent of the First Lady, Eleanor Roosevelt. On behalf of Yardley, he wrote her a letter early in December beginning, "I don't believe I have ever taken up your time with an unworthy problem." He explained that the Signal Corps' General Olmstead had given Yardley "a black eye so that the Canadian authorities hesitate to renew the contract fearing that the value of cooperation between the two bureaus might be lost." He asked whether she could see Yardley for a few minutes the next evening or Sunday, 7 December 1941. Greater events claimed her attention.

Yardley fought in Canada as well. He pressed External Affairs. He pointed out that Pearson had promised to give him time to clear up the matter in Washington. He had discovered that Strachey was to sail 12 December and he requested that his own departure be postponed thirty days. "I was given a job to do in Canada and I did it well. It would seem to me that the least the Canadian authorities can do is give me another thirty days in this matter." When no one responded to that appeal either, he made one final effort. It came after Pearl Harbor, when Canada, like the United States and the United Kingdom, had declared war on Japan. In a seven-page memorandum, Yardley boasted that he was "the only white man who is thoroughly conversant with every type of Japanese Battle Communications." He explained some of the tricks needed to understand telegraphic kana and listed various Japanese cryptosystems. He offered to impart his knowledge to Canadian authorities, which would take "a minimum of sixty hard and grinding working days" before "my return to the United States." Captain Drake, the *spiritus rector* of communications intelligence in Canada, recommended "very strongly" that Yardley be hired. The recommendation was not accepted. Yardley's last chance had evaporated.

The Canadians, who felt that Yardley had been treated shabbily, were generous. They assigned Yardley and Edna to fictitious "special duty" in Washington for two and a half months at their Canadian salaries—$1,325 for Yardley, $500 for Edna. They tried to get questionable taxes returned.

They paid expenses for the move back to Washington. They facilitated movement through customs. And—though this cost nothing—they wrote both handsome letters of thanks.

There remained only the sad duty of farewell. After lunch on Friday, 16 January, Yardley went to Mackenzie's office to say good-bye. Mackenzie patted himself on the back for handling the matter "reasonably well" because, he thought, Yardley was leaving "in the best of good will." Edna felt bad. She compared their departure from Ottawa to Napoleon's from Moscow, with both parties leaving in snow and defeat.

At 4:30, a few hours after Yardley left Mackenzie's office, Strachey entered to be presented. Mackenzie was skeptical. "I may be prejudiced but I would never have selected a man of his age (67) to head an organization of this kind." And, still annoyed about Yardley's dismissal, he said bitterly, "Time will tell whether we have been sold out or not." Canada recovered. Yardley did not.

19

A Restaurant of His Own

Though Yardley was out of sight during his tours in China and Canada, he was not out of mind. People remembered him. With a war on in Europe and Asia, the State Department was getting two or three letters a week about him, presumably urging that he be re-employed; the War and Navy Departments may have received such inquiries as well. An FBI newspaper informant reported in February 1941, between Yardley's time in China and then in Canada, that "The working press in New York City is intensely interested" in him. The informant said that Yardley was working in a "confidential capacity" for the War Department and that none of the reporters could understand why he would be hired "after the disgraceful manner in which he sold out the Federal Government." They were "all carefully watching each other on this story, each one anticipating that someone else will break the story, after which everybody will 'go to town.'" FBI director J. Edgar Hoover passed this along to the army chief of intelligence.

None of this was bringing Yardley any money, however. Soon after his return from Canada, he asked Hoover for an appointment. He said he wanted to offer the bureau some new methods of solution. Hoover would not see him. But he did set up a meeting for him with three subordinates. On

3 February 1942, Yardley met with Stanley J. Tracy, the prim, humorless assistant director in charge of the identification division; Charles A. Appel, a document specialist and the founder of the FBI laboratory; and W. G. Blackburn, a laboratory scientist.

Yardley began by asking what they wanted to know about cryptology. When they replied that they had no specific questions, he told them that "we"—never specified—had worked out a simplified superior method of calculating probabilities, especially for solving grille ciphers, a transposition. This consisted of multiplying the normal frequency in English text of one letter, say e, by the frequency of another, say s, and then dividing that product by the frequency of the digraph, es. Despite considerable discussion about the value of this, it remained "a mysterious calculation" to them.

The conversation then turned to Yardley's recent work. He bragged that he had had "a great deal of success in solving [Japanese] codes" in China, talking "at great length but without particularity." Tracy concluded that Yardley was merely boasting to impress "the Bureau with the need for his services" because Tracy believed that "Codes are not solved in this way by mathematics or original thought. Solutions actually depend upon luck, investigative work, and the procurement of a code book." Yardley made some racist comments about the Chinese, basing them, he said, on his two years as the only white man ever to serve in Chinese intelligence. Near the end of the conference, he indicated he would like to take five minutes more to discuss a personal matter. He wanted to be removed from the black list of the War, Navy, and State Departments and the FBI. He rehearsed his grievances against Friedman and about how State had blocked publication of the "entirely harmless" "Japanese Diplomatic Secrets." He said the FBI had participated in this through its representative in New York, Thomas Dewey. Tracy stiffly explained that Dewey was employed by the U.S. Attorney's office in New York and was not an agent of the FBI. This surprised Yardley. He apologized for making the accusation and for thinking that the FBI had played a role in the prosecution.

Yardley then told them that he had been unable to get work in the War, Navy, or State Departments and that he had heard that Assistant Director Edward Tamm doubted that the bureau would be able to use him. He asserted that he was not seeking a job in the FBI because he did not need one—he professed to be "financially independent"—but wanted to offer whatever talents he had to the government for the war. The agents were not fooled. Tracy told Yardley that he would not meet the age requirements and that the bureau hired new employees only at the minimum salary. "He is a good talker," Tracy reported, but "It was apparent that Mr. Yardley's attempts to see the Director were for the purpose of getting himself off the 'black list' as he called it. He is on a fishing expedition to find out all he can concerning his inability to secure a position with the Army, Navy, or State Department. It is also obvious that he would like to be in charge of a Cryptographic Section during the present emergency." Appel and Blackburn believed that "he does not have too deep a knowledge of his subject." They thought erroneously that Edna had been "carrying on the detailed cryptographic analysis work for him." On departing, Yardley offered his service to the bureau at any time and any place and left the agents with his address—he was then living in a house at 819 Kentucky Avenue, Southeast, Washington. Nobody called.

Yardley's claim of financial independence was based on the $1,600 he then had in the bank—the remnants of the two-and-a-half-months' salary the Canadians had given him. But money goes fast, especially when none is replacing it. And Yardley seemed to spend whatever he had, as quickly as he got it. For example, though in the seven months from August 1940 to February 1941 he lived on less than $2,000, after he got $4,000—probably from the Canadians—at the end of March, he spent nearly $3,000 of it in two months. During the second half of 1941, he deposited $1,600 and spent $2,100. His balance fluctuated wildly, from the low four figures at which it customarily stood to $1.99 and even to 1¢. The bank occasionally covered small overdrafts and Yardley wrote some checks for $1. To make money, he planned to write an article, perhaps on Pearl Harbor, for the *Saturday Evening Post*. But when an editor there told him that the magazine never bought articles sight unseen, and his argument that it had previously done so for him—unlikely, at best—failed to persuade, he refused to write the piece. At the same time, Bye suggested that he turn his radio scripts into a comic strip. While he was considering this, Columbia Pictures offered him $2,500 for the movie rights to those scripts. He asked for $5,000, thinking that a movie would enhance the worth of the comic. He didn't get even the $2,500. He ended a letter to Bye by noting, "I can at least console myself that so long as I ran the show there were no Pearl Harbors!!!!!" Bye replied that "So many people, including Stuart Rose of The [Saturday Evening] Post, believe that Pearl Harbor wouldn't have happened if you had been on the job."

Yardley also considered what appears to have been a proposal to work with an amateur cryptologist, the New York architect Rosario Candela. A pepperpot of a man, Candela had in 1938 self-published a charming book puffing his solution of a not-too-difficult challenge cryptogram by the great pre–World War I French codebreaker, Commandant Etienne Bazeries. During the war, Candela taught a course in cryptanalysis at Hunter College, and in the spring of 1942 asked Yardley for some cryptograms for his students to work on, apparently holding out the possibility of Yardley's teaching with him. On 5 May 1942, Yardley sent him some of the German cryptograms he had solved while in Canada, saying that he hoped "this is sufficient to get us started." But whatever was intended did not materialize, for he never taught or collaborated with Candela.

To make money, he bought a restaurant on 15 March 1942 from Good-Acres Coffee Pot, Inc. He paid $10,000—$5,000 in cash and $5,000 in a chattel trust against the business, payable at $100 a month. The cash was probably borrowed from Edna, for at that time he never had more than $1,000 in his Riggs National Bank account, and the business was put in her name. The restaurant occupied a downtown storefront on H Street, Northwest, a main artery, at 1308, near another main thoroughfare, 14th Street. Its entrance was flanked on the right by a display window with crossed American flags. Inside, behind the window, stood a cashier's stand with a cigar counter. Six booths lined the right wall; nine tables filled the center; a steam table and a counter with stools ran the length of the left wall. Rent was $350 a month; the staff—cooks, waitresses, countermen, cleaning persons—numbered about six per shift, for the restaurant was open day and night, in part because employees of the Washington *Times Herald*, whose office was across the street, came in around 3 a.m. Yardley named the restaurant the Rideau, perhaps for an elegant club in Ottawa, itself named for a lake in Ontario. He thought the place would net him "close to $10,000 a year."

He moved with Edna into the apartment above the restaurant. On opening day, a Sunday, he bragged, seven hundred customers—an unbelievable number— were coming in for the "finest Bean Soup in town." It was a red-letter day for another reason as well: Bye had just written to him that Pocket Books was trying to get out a paperback edition of *The American Black Chamber*. It looked as if the State Department would consent as long as Yardley made certain changes—for which Pocket Books would pay him. Yardley was "thrilled at the prospect." Bye hoped to eat at the restaurant "the next time I go to Washington," but added a sardonic note of realism: "I dread to hear if you are going to have a liquor department. Please don't." The publishing euphoria died quickly. Bye wrote a week later that "It is awfully hard for me to think of anything but bean soup, but it seems to me that somebody said today that Bobbs-Merrill and the Pocket Book publishers are having trouble with the State Department." He was right. Though Bye, a faithful friend, assured he "would do everything he could to help him along," and though the publishers had been trying for a month, in April

State said the matter had "been given the careful consideration of several agencies of the Government especially concerned with problems of the national defense. I regret to have to inform you that it is the unanimous view of the agencies participating in this consideration of the matter that a republication and a further distribution of this book at this time would not be in the best interests of the United States." It never appeared.

That summer, military intelligence, suspecting Yardley of "disaffection and harboring pro-German sympathizers" in the Rideau, began investigating him. It described Yardley: "Present Age: 53. Height: 66″; weight, 185 lbs.; round head; gray eyes; bald headed; wears glasses; mole one inch above right extremity of right eyebrow; prominent forehead; straight nose; double chin; stout build; cultivated accent; short steps while walking; light brown hair; short neck." The surveillance began on 6 August 1942, when Special Agent Frederick A. Tehaan of the Counter-Intelligence Corps entered the Rideau at 1:15 P.M. and sat at the counter. About fourteen patrons were present; Tehaan said they were "of middle class caliber" and having "ordinary conversation." He ordered a beer and "was served by a man who appeared to be in charge of the employees. (approx. 6) Said man observed everyone entering the said establishment." After chatting with Edna, at the cash register, Tehaan left at 2:15.

He and other agents visited the restaurant eleven times in August, sometimes twice in one day, at various hours of the day and night. Only a handful of customers were ever present. One agent, noticing a new waitress and a new counterman, observed that the pay at the Rideau "is evidently very small as there is a continual change of employees." Though Tehaan came to be recognized as a customer, he only exchanged a few words with Edna at the cash register and was rebuffed by Yardley, who wanted to read his paper when the two sat side by side at the counter. The agents were thorough. They examined Yardley's files at the State Department (both documentary and passport), the Civil Service Commission, the army, the morgue of the *Times Herald,* the FBI, the Department of Justice, and the Metropolitan Police Department (finding nothing at the latter three). They studied the restaurant's file at the District of Columbia's Alcoholic Beverage Control agency and obtained a financial report from Dun and Bradstreet. One agent read *The American Black Chamber,* from which he learned only that "The book revealed that Subject was employed . . . in a secret capacity . . . in New York." Agents interviewed persons at and around his former addresses, including the house at 542 Shepherd Street in which he had lived in 1914 when he and Hazel married (a housewife had "no knowledge of anyone . . . who answers to the description of Subject"). A neighbor at 819 Kentucky said that during the month he lived there, a woman, who she thought was Yardley's wife, stayed with him several times a week. The manager of a garage on nearby New York Avenue, who had eaten at the restaurant rarely under its former owners but now went twice a week, thought that the restaurant did not make enough money to meet the rent. The agents got information from the town marshal of Worthington ("it is recalled to this day by faculty members that YARDLEY was one of the most brilliant students"). They copied his account at Riggs National Bank.

And they spied on Yardley and Edna. At 1 P.M. on 16 August, Tehaan went to the third floor of the Mutual Life Insurance Company and, using binoculars, peered into their apartment. No one was there, but he diligently listed the furniture. The view was not so good, however, so he got permission from the purchasing agent of the *Times Herald,* whose offices were across H Street at 1317, to use its fifth-floor conference room. From there he obtained a more detailed inventory of the furniture—a valuable clue in an investigation to see if the occupant was a spy. Six days later, in the morning, he returned to the newspaper office, this time to the third floor. He waited almost an hour until, at 10:25, Yardley appeared in the rear of the front room wearing shorts. A medium-sized woman, whom the agent could not recognize, followed, wearing a housecoat. Yardley seated himself briefly at a couch; then, as the woman set up an ironing board, he went into the back room, came out dressed, and went downstairs to the restaurant while the woman ironed shirts and lingerie. He bought some newspapers and returned to his apartment to read them, sipping a beer and talking to the woman, occasionally glancing up at her. Tehaan reported that "From the above indications this Agent believes that the Subject is living in the above second floor apartment with the woman mentioned herein." This dynamite constituted the total information obtained from the spying.

Tehaan sought to justify the investigation by warning "that YARDLEY is a very shrewd man and that he is capable of performing subversive acts . . . It seems difficult to believe that this man, with his background of cryptography, codes and ciphers is satisfied to remain inactive during the present world crisis. It is highly possible for YARDLEY to use the above restaurant as a front to pursue some other endeavor." He besmirched Yardley: he sometimes failed to pay debts—a charge based on a claim from the *Worthington Times* that he owed it $200—and his character was "doubtful as he is not living with his wife, but has been seen in a domestic surrounding with a woman." Still, Tehaan had to admit that he saw nothing suspicious, that nothing

Place Washington, D. C.
Date August 28, 1942
Case No. VIII

MEMORANDUM FOR THE OFFICER IN CHARGE

Subject: HERBERT OSBORNE YARDLEY
1308 H Street, N.W.
Washington, D. C.

Re: Undercover Surveillance.

On August 28, 1942, between 3:50 p.m. and 4:12 p.m., this Agent conducted an undercover surveillance of the Rideau Restaurant, 1308 H Street, N.W., Washington, D. C., regarding HERBERT OSBORNE YARDLEY.

3:50 P.M. This Agent obtained a stool at the counter of the restaurant and was served by a counterman. The restaurant was occupied by six employees and two customers. Preparations were being made to handle the supper customers and chairs were stacked on tables in order to facilitate scrubbing of floors

3:58 P.M. YARDLEY entered the establishment attired in paint covered clothes with a fly sprayer in his hand and proceeded to kill the flies in said restaurant.

5:05 P.M. Subject finished the above work, obtained a glass of beer and seated himself in the adjacent stool to the left of this Agent. This Agent greeted him and then inquired whether or not an article in the Washington Daily News concerning the achievements of a Russian girl soldier was propoganda or the truth. YARDLEY merely said that the achievements may or may not be true, then turned his back on this Agent, finished his glass of beer and commenced supervising the employees..

4:15 P.M. YARDLEY left the restaurant and this Agent closed the surveillance.

Agent's Comments: This Agent noticed a new waitress and a new counterman in the restaurant. The pay is evidently very small as there is a continual change of employees.

jaw

MEMO
(EXHIBIT .... X ....)

(Signed) ....
(Name typed) Frederick A. Tehaan
Special (Agent, CIC)

16—20072-1   U. S. GOVERNMENT PRINTING OFFICE

FBI agent's surveillance report of Yardley and his restaurant indicated subversive activities. Yardley and Edna "seem intent upon operating a good restaurant." On 7 September Tehaan recommended that the case be closed, and it apparently was.

The restaurant did not last much longer. Yardley found that his thirteen employees had "got so expensive and so difficult to deal with" that he sold it. He believed that an owner needed to have his family working at the restaurant if he wanted to make it a success. Edna and he were not enough. So he sold the Rideau and got a job on 9 November 1942 as a legal investigator for $2,600 a year at the government agency set up to prevent price-gouging during the war shortages, the Office of Price Administration (OPA).

He and Edna continued to live in the upstairs apartment for a while. After she broke her leg by slipping on a mat in front of an H Street restaurant 20 April 1944, she moved into a boardinghouse at 210 Tuckerman Street in far northwest Washington run by an old friend who took care of her, Bea Brink. Among the other boarders was a couple in their midtwenties, Frank Fordham, who worked in navy communications intelligence at Nebraska Avenue, and his wife, Layton. Yardley visited Edna on weekends and played cards and chatted with the Laytons, and other boarders or visitors. When her leg had sufficiently mended, he took her and the others on outings to nearby Beverly Beach.

"We were always happy to see him because he did things with us," said Fordham. "He loved to go to the beach and we'd never have gotten there without a car." They were impressed because they knew who he was and they were just a bunch of kids in their twenties; they thought he was great not because he was famous but because he was generous. He was friendly and talkative. He told jokes. He played cards. He drove them places. Layton thought he was articulate and refined: he never used bad language. Edna called him Hoy. He and she obviously enjoyed one another's company, but in an undemonstrative way. They seemed very much in love. Edna, with blue eyes and strawberry blonde hair, always seemed to have her head tucked in coyly. The Fordhams thought she was a very attractive woman.

Yardley was glad that the Republican Thomas E. Dewey, to whom he felt personally connected since the seizing of "Japanese Diplomatic Secrets," had been elected governor of New York and hoped he would run for president. "The dope here is that the only Democrates [*sic*] who will be felt [left] in Washn after 1944 are life time members of the Supreme Court. Thank God for that," he wrote Bye. He added that he had "plenty of time on my hands and little or no responsibility so my mind is turning back to putting something down on paper. . . . I don't plan any non-fiction. I'm keeping my mouth shut." But he accepted a sale of ten thousand copies of *The Blonde Countess* to the British armed forces at one guinea (about $5 at the rate of exchange then) per thousand copies—a patriotic, not a moneymaking, gesture.

At the OPA, he dealt with meat, apparently trying to block black-market sales. He called the job "just Ham and Eggs" and felt he'd made a fine record there. But "the outfit is so small and Congress is so sore at O.P.A. that there will be few opportunities for advancement—so I'm looking around." He mentioned the Far Eastern Department of the Office of War Information to George Bye, saying that he still got presents from his old boss in China, Dai Li, and was on good terms with the Chinese military attaché. "I believe I know China as well as most white men so that looks like something to me. Do you know anyone who counts in OWI and if so can you give me a letter to them?" Bye, who liked Yardley, promptly wrote to the head of the OWI, Elmer Davis, addressing him as "Dear Elmer." He reminded him of *The American Black Chamber* and of what he called the gag law and Dewey and asked him to see Yardley: "He is a most important man." Yardley went at once to see Davis, who "knew of me and really seemed to think he could use me especially since I have the most direct and trusted contact with those who count in China. The first question Davis asked was whether I worked for so and so and when I said that was my contact he replied that was the only faction that counted."

Davis referred him to a Dr. Taylor, a former teacher in China. "But when I talked with Taylor I knew I was licked. He like such men as Snow [Edgar Snow, author of *Red Star over China*] have popularized the eighth route army [the wartime name of Mao Tse-tung's Red Army], the worst thing they could do if they hope to be close to the present powers that be [Chiang's Nationalists], for the eighth route is Communistic and the boss [Chiang] hates all that the eighth represents." Yardley submitted ten pages of his experiences and connections in China, but a week later Taylor said that conditions made it impossible for the OWI to use him. Yardley was furious but consoled himself with the thought that he had the contacts that mattered. A couple of months later, though, Davis, having received confidential information that the OWI contacts in China were inadequate, had a subordinate tell Yardley that he wanted to confer with him because he respected his opinions. But the meeting was postponed, and the OWI people, saying that they were tied up with their budget, never scheduled another. "I am just as well pleased," Yardley told Bye, "for I have learned the whole OWI is full of crack pots. Therefore it may be just as well that I remain where I am well established."

And indeed, he did very well at the OPA, where, among other cases, he investigated one in which brothers who operated a slaughterhouse on the Bladensburg Road sold meat above OPA ceiling prices; they were fined $200,000. In other cases of his, price and rationing violators and black-market operatives were imprisoned. (Yardley was not above bending the law a little himself. In a time in which meat was rationed, he and Edna enjoyed good beef. And he had plenty of rationed gasoline.) He sometimes wrote twenty-five-page briefs in a single day. He liked the job. "I'm respected, liked, have my own way." In a reorganization in the spring of 1943, "I could have had the job as Chief Investigator but I preferred to remain the No. 2 man. I have more freedom this way." He kept getting promotions—from assistant investigator to associate investigator to investigator—with concomitant raises from $2,600 to $4,400. He explained regulations to large audiences, answered congressional queries, ran a team of ten investigators.

In November 1946, he transferred from Washington to the Baltimore field office and from meat to sugar. He spent half his time in the field making investigations and the other half supervising eight to twelve employees and replacing the chief investigator in his absence. His performance ratings were always "very good," once "excellent." Various supervisors rated him as "outstanding" or "satisfactory" in ability to organize his work, initiative, resourcefulness, directing, training and developing subordinates, meeting and dealing with others, attention to pertinent details, and accuracy of final results.

And he decided to divorce Hazel. They had lived apart since 1937. In China, he had relied on Edna, not Hazel, in financial matters. Edna, not Hazel, had gone with him to Canada. His son, Jack, was eighteen and no longer a responsibility. In the summer of 1944, Herbert went to Nevada. Hazel was notified by mail. On Friday, 25 August, Herbert swore in the First District Court of Storey County, in Virginia City, that he and Hazel had "separated on or about the fifteenth day of August 1937. That said separation has been continuous, without interruption and without cohabitation, for a period of time more than three consecutive years last past." Employees of the Hotel Senator in Reno and the owner of the house in which Yardley had stayed testified that Yardley had resided at those two places for the six weeks of the state's residency requirements. Yardley then perjured himself, swearing that he had no other home than the state of Nevada and was not contemplating changing his address to another state. The judge didn't question it. Hazel did not contest the action. On 28 August, Herbert and Hazel were divorced. He and Edna drove the twenty miles to Reno where, later that day, Washoe County District Judge William McKnight joined them "in lawful wedlock."

20

Playing Poker

Writing—or rather the money to be made from writing—had never been far from Yardley's thoughts. His film agent Swanson had written to him urgently saying that stories were wanted badly in Hollywood because all the writers had gone off to war. Yardley had several brewing, and sent Swanson the treatment of a script he called "False Passport," which he thought "a damned good tale." Swanson held it for a month and a half and then said it was overplotted and not material for the major studios; he would see if a minor studio wanted it. Yardley wondered whether the OPA would transfer him to Hollywood so he could get a short-time contract like the $500 and $750 a week he had gotten on previous visits "to whip the tale into shape" and write others he was working on. None of this happened, and he considered firing Swanson.

He compiled his letters from Chungking for publication. Bye called them "hot stuff" and said, "I am going to have to confess to my priest that I read them. I can understand now why China has such a large population." But Costain of the *Saturday Evening Post* turned them down, as did the publisher Appleton-Century, which reasoned, "We couldn't revise the China letters enough to suit the present demands of publishing diplomacy without spoiling them as lively and pungent documents."

This didn't discourage Yardley. He had "something absolutely unique. A spy story with a bizarre Chungking background" that he would not give to the movies. Rather "it is being written as a Novel with a background foreign to Pearl Buck [author of *The Good Earth*], Snow and all the rest." With his customary salesman's enthusiasm, he boasted, "It really is a whiz. Makes the Blonde Countess look like nothing." But the 1934 law had made him skittish. Were novels subject to censorship? If these were, he speculated, "I may leave my name off." Bye told him they were not unless they mentioned real people; he suggested Yardley write his novel and then deal with any censorship problems.

Which he did. He completed the work in a year, collaborating once again with Carl Grabo. He spent seven weeks in the West—perhaps in Albuquerque, to which Grabo soon moved—doing the third rewrite, riding a horse four hours a day, and losing seventeen pounds, enough to fit into his old dinner jacket. On Independence Day 1944 he told Bye, "I have a MMS which I think better than the American Black Chamber. Am mailing it to you under separate cover." He postscripted: "This means a lot to me. So Pls Pls read it. I ask this for I know you can sell anything if you *believe* in it. And I know also you will *believe* in this if you will only take time out to give it a trial." Within a week, Bye responded positively: "I like 'TINA' very much. It has a lot of atmosphere. It has a lot of the quality of 'AMERICAN BLACK CHAMBER.' I wouldn't be surprised if you were in the money again. . . . It's wonderful to find you in such fine writing form. I always knew that a lot of exciting melodramas lurked behind your mild eyes." Yardley was ecstatic. "Your letter made me so happy I didn't sleep a wink all night." He dreamed of lectures and films, scrupulously instructing Bye to "Be sure to include Grabo when you write out a moving picture contract! We're the original Siamese Twins." He suggested new story ideas, publishing plans, publicity angles. He was pleased with Bye's comparing "Tina" to *The American Black Chamber*, which he said "gave me an eerie feeling when after it was cold I'd pick it up and read a few pages. I could never convince myself that I had written it. Sounded strange and foreign to me. TINA also does this to me. And parts of it bring back such vivid memories of the horrors of Chungking that I find myself at night sometimes living it all over again in my dreams."

Doubleday and Bobbs-Merrill turned it down, but Putnam accepted it. The advance was $1,000, which Yardley and Grabo divided fifty-fifty. A new title was needed, and Yardley suggested one of his Chungking interpreter's favorite maxims: "Crows are black everywhere." It was accepted, and Putnam brought out its 247 pages in 1945. Codebreaking, spying, and murder swirl around an American woman reporter sent to Chungking by a newspaper chain as the good Chinese and Americans break up a Japanese espionage ring. The cryptologic diagrams reproduced in the book are in Yardley's handwriting, and the Japanese spy cryptosystem uses the same procedure as the German spies whose messages Yardley had solved in Canada—taking the last letters of the lines of a printed work to form a key. The *New York Times* damned it with faint praise: "Some of it—despite its swarming cast and their hopped up dialogue—is really exciting." The *New Yorker* offered advice: "Good material but it needs more orderly assembling." It did not make a fortune for its authors, and they abandoned the new melodrama they were beginning.

Yardley had wisely not quit his day job at the OPE. In 1946, he invested $1,400 in his Osborn Sales Company to sell small electrical appliances, kitchen supplies, and vacuum cleaners. In 1947, the OPA, a war baby, was terminated. Osborn Sales failed by 1948, and in January 1949 Yardley took a job as a salesman in the Public Housing Administration of the Housing and Home Finance Agency. The office, at 1200 Connecticut Avenue, Northwest, was filled with row upon row of desks. Seated to his right was Gordon Smith, a young fellow Hoosier just out of college working as a clerk-typist. He liked "the old gentleman." Yardley was affable and smiling, greeting him in a friendly way. He encouraged the younger man to take a test for a better job. They occasionally ate together, and though Yardley never mentioned the Cipher Bureau, he told stories about his time in China in a way that Smith found believable. Through Smith and one of his fellow roomers, Yardley was brought into touch with one Edward Hunter, who claimed to be from *Newsweek* but who people thought was from intelligence; Hunter, Yardley, and Smith went to lunch at a swank restaurant. Hunter asked, and Yardley told, about his experiences in China and more particularly about people to contact there. Yardley spun off names from the top of his head, saying go to such-and-such a street and go to the top floor and ask for so-and-so. All this impressed Smith, though naturally nobody knew whether any of these people were still there after the Communist takeover of 1949.

Of his duties, Yardley wrote in 1951: "I study, analyze and interpret housing legislation enacted by the Congress. I assemble material documenting need for the relaxation of occupancy to permit the admission of distressed immigrant workers of defense plants and installation to Lanham Act projects, and make appropriate recommendations. I do the same for conversions and reactivation of terminated units. I am actively engaged in the

Standard Form No. 51
August 1946
U. S. CIVIL SERVICE COMMISSION

Form approved.
Budget Bureau No. 50-R0123.

REPORT OF
EFFICIENCY RATING

MINISTRATIVE–UNOFFICIAL ( )
OFFICIAL:
REGULAR (x)   SPECIAL ( )
PROBATIONAL ( )

As of ___7-7-49___ based on performance during period from ___1-7-49___ to ___7-7-49___

Herbert O. Yardley   Sales Assistant, CAF-9
(Name of employee)   (Title of position, service, and grade)

HHFA-PHA   Disposition - Sales
(Organization—Indicate bureau, division, section, unit, field station)

ON LINES BELOW MARK EMPLOYEE	1. Study the instructions in the Rating Official's Guide, C. S. C. Form No. 3823A.	CHECK ONE:
V if adequate	2. Underline the elements which are especially important in the position. Director, Personnel & Planning Branch	Administrative, supervisory, or
− if weak	3. Rate only on elements pertinent to the position. a. Do not rate on elements in *italics* except for employees in administrative, supervisory, or planning positions.	planning ☐
+ if outstanding	b. Rate administrative, supervisory, and planning functions on elements in *italics*.	All others ☐

_____ (1) Maintenance of equipment, tools, instruments.
_____ (2) Mechanical skill.
_____ (3) Skill in the application of techniques and procedures.
_____ (4) Presentability of work (appropriateness of arrangement and appearance of work).
_____ (5) Attention to broad phases of assignments.
_____ (6) Attention to pertinent detail.
_____ (7) Accuracy of operations.
_____ (8) Accuracy of final results.
_____ (9) Accuracy of judgments or decisions.
_____ (10) Effectiveness in presenting ideas or facts.
_____ (11) Industry.
_____ (12) Rate of progress on or completion of assignments.
_____ (13) Amount of acceptable work produced. (Is mark based on production records? _____) (Yes or no)
_____ (14) Ability to organize his work.
_____ (15) Effectiveness in meeting and dealing with others.
_____ (16) Cooperativeness.
_____ (17) Initiative.
_____ (18) Resourcefulness.
_____ (19) Dependability.
_____ (20) Physical fitness for the work.

_____ (21) *Effectiveness in planning broad programs.*
_____ (22) *Effectiveness in adapting the work program to broader or related programs.*
_____ (23) *Effectiveness in devising procedures.*
_____ (24) *Effectiveness in laying out work and establishing standards of performance for subordinates.*
_____ (25) *Effectiveness in directing, reviewing, and checking the work of subordinates.*
_____ (26) *Effectiveness in instructing, training, and developing subordinates in the work.*
_____ (27) *Effectiveness in promoting high working morale.*
_____ (28) *Effectiveness in determining space, personnel, and equipment needs.*
_____ (29) *Effectiveness in setting and obtaining adherence to time limits and deadlines.*
_____ (30) *Ability to make decisions.*
_____ (31) *Effectiveness in delegating clearly defined authority to act.*

(over)

STATE ANY OTHER ELEMENTS CONSIDERED

_____ (A) This rating has been discussed with me.
_____ (B) H. O. Yardley
_____ (C)

STANDARD Deviations must be explained on reverse side of this form	Adjective Rating	Adjective Rating
Plus marks on all underlined elements, and check marks or better on all other elements rated	Excellent	Rating official Very Good
Check marks or better on all elements rated, and plus marks on at least half of the underlined elements	Very Good	
Check marks or better on a majority of underlined elements, and all weak performance overcompensated by outstanding performance	Good	Reviewing official Very Good
Check marks or better on a majority of underlined elements, and all weak performance not overcompensated by outstanding performance	Fair	
Minus marks on at least half of the underlined elements	Unsatisfactory	

Rated by _Everett T. Rice_   Sales Officer   7/15/49
(Signature of rating official)   (Title)   (Date)

Reviewed by _Walter Ashmun_   Sales Officer   7/18/49
(Signature of reviewing official)   (Title)   (Date)

Rating approved by efficiency rating committee _____ (Date)   Report to employee _____ (Adjective rating)

U. S. GOVERNMENT PRINTING OFFICE   16—26177-4

Yardley's efficiency rating as a salesman in the Housing and Home Finance Agency

liquidation of all bailee leases. . . . I prepare all letters in answer to Congressional enquiries and Department of Defense enquiries concerning the foregoing." Though Smith felt Yardley was just putting in his time, Yardley won promotion after promotion, rising from sales assistant to sales officer to management officer, and in salary from $5,232 to $6,940. But he resigned as of 11 April 1952 "so that I may devote full time to the construction business." Edna, who had become a secretary to an official in the administration, remained.

By then they had moved twice—from above the restaurant to 1741 Kilbourne Avenue, Northwest, in the spring of 1949, and then to a house Yardley had had built at 9813 Rosenstiel Avenue in Silver Spring, Maryland. There they took a boarder, Grover Batts, who worked in the housing agency with Edna. Living with Yardley for two years in his late twenties was one of the most interesting experiences of Batts's life.

I really admired Herbert tremendously. I liked to listen to him talk, especially about his time in China. He had a compelling way of expressing himself. When he spoke, it wasn't your ordinary boring thing. He talked in a way that made you listen to him.

I admired him very much for what he had done in his life. He kept forging ahead despite what happened to him. He had rough edges but he was always an interesting person to be around. He had a brilliant mind.

He was a good arguer. We would get in these terrible arguments. This was during the Army-McCarthy hearings. I was anti-McCarthy; he was pro-military and anti-communist. I could make him so mad. I enjoyed that. It is a wonder he didn't have a stroke.

He really had a vocabulary when it came to cussing. We didn't use any [vulgarities] in North Carolina, where I'm from. To me it was totally shocking. And I had been in the military. It didn't make any difference to Herbert who was there, what company he was in. He'd use that language just in general conversation. It would embarrass me to death. I think he did it almost for shock value. I have an idea that in his earlier years he was not like that.

I have the feeling that he was not treated well [by the government]. He never talked to me about being treated unfairly. It's my surmise. His attitude toward life was antagonistic. He was not a very happy man (at least then—I don't know what he was like as a younger man). I can't remember him ever really bubbling over with laughter. He was kind of dour.

I had $18,000 which Edna knew about because I had to file a form stating our assets. She said if they know about this you will never get a raise. So she took it out [of the form]. Later she broached the subject of using the money to help Herbert build houses. He needed the capital. So I lent it to him. For the time it was a lot of money. I got all the money back but didn't make anything on it. Herbert never cheated me. He was an honorable person.

I can't remember people visiting Herbert. I can't remember a living soul who was a close friend.

The least important thing to Herbert was dressing. He didn't care about clothes. If not for Edna he would have walked around in rags. When he retired, he looked almost shabby. I never saw him in a coat and tie.

Once Herbert went duck hunting locally and brought back a duck and cooked it. Herbert was so proud. Edna later said that the duck had been feeding on fish and it tasted of fish. Herbert thought it was great. Without a doubt it was the worst meal I ever ate.

I rarely ate with them. Herbert's table manners were ordinary. He did a lot of drinking but mostly at night.

He treated Edna well, courteously. He never was unkind to her in any way that I was aware of. Edna had such an attractive personality. A very warm, caring person. You felt that she really cared about you. It was really a sincere feeling—not put on. She had a strong personality and wouldn't have stayed around with Herbert if he wasn't worth something.

Batts was asked how so embittered a person could have led people so well and run so successful an organization. He said that as a younger man Yardley would have been different. "In pictures from that time he looks like a totally different person."

During the two years Batts lived with the Yardleys, Herbert worked as a general contractor building houses. He built three across Rosenstiel Avenue and three or four on lots he had bought in nearby Garrett Park. His organizing ability proved useful: when a contractor needed plywood or plumbing, Yardley had the supplies there. In December 1954, he and Edna moved to Orlando, Florida, living in a five-room rented house at 906 West Princeton Avenue with a Manx cat and what he said was an oversized Chinese alley cat. He may have planned to do some construction but found the duck hunting excellent in the fall and the fishing the same the rest of the year. In an interview with a reporter of the *Orlando Sentinel,* in what she called his "strong deep voice" with words clipped "as though biting on a cigar," he showed that he had not lost his tendency to exaggerate. He said that *The American Black Chamber* had sold more than a million copies and that when it was published "the embarrassed Japanese cabinet resigned."

In April 1956, he returned to Silver Spring. He resumed his friendship with a young man, Robert Mabie, whose sister's mother-in-law was Edna's sister, Lillian. She had urged him to look up the Yardleys when he went to Washington in 1950 to look for work. He and Yardley got along very well indeed. On weekends they rented a cabin on the Potomac in Fairfax County, Virginia, about a mile upstream from a locality called Cabin John in

Washington. There they hunted rabbits, squirrels, and ducks—and talked. Yardley talked a lot about women and sex and Mabie thought he had had a lot of affairs, including possibly one with Rosalind Russell, who had starred in *Rendezvous*. He told stories well, looking not at the listener but straight ahead, as if he were thinking all the time. The hunters took no food with them—though Yardley brought bourbon—so they cooked and ate what they shot. Sometimes he would cook a squirrel in wine. Yardley always came back with a bag, though he was not an exceptional shot with his 16-gauge Remington model 11 shotgun. He never had a hunting license or a duck stamp and hunters were supposed to shoot the waterfowl on the fly—but Yardley did not always follow the letter of the law.

After hunting, the two would go to a popular bar on 14th Street and New York Avenue, the Blue Mirror, for a drink. Yardley would drive up in his old Plymouth and sometimes park in front of a fire hydrant—he didn't care. They would go in wearing their hunting outfits and muddy boots. Mabie would have a beer; Yardley, two or three bourbons. Mabie enjoyed those weekends immensely.

When Mabie was about to marry a French woman, Elianne Jouen, who worked at the French embassy and who had no family in America, Yardley and Edna arranged the wedding. They took her in and were kind to him as well. For Mabie's birthday, Yardley "borrowed" his broken-down car—and returned it fixed as a present. Later, Mabie worked as a housepainter for Yardley while he was building houses. He thought Yardley "the greatest person. He loved life"—though Mabie could never understand how a person with such experience could be such a "redneck" as to water his lawn in his undershorts. Mabie, whose parents were divorced and who had never had a father at home, gushed of Yardley, "I loved him. I think I loved him more than my stepfather."

The two men played poker. Mabie felt Yardley was very methodical and had a good memory for the cards. Yardley usually won, but he drank while playing and this might have affected the game. Once Mabie brought home some poker players from his office and "They took Herb to the cleaners." Yardley also played poker from time to time at the National Press Club, though he was not a member and only members were supposed to play. The game room on the thirteenth floor had two large circular tables, the A table for those who got there first, the B for those who arrived later. Other tables were for chess, checkers, gin rummy, dominoes. Yardley would turn up around noon. But when he sat at one table, some members jumped to the other; they regarded him as too conservative a player—they called him Old

Adhesive—and they wanted action during their lunch hour. The games were five-card stud and five-card draw. Yardley would usually play about an hour, but occasionally all day. He concentrated on his cards and didn't talk much but would sometimes comment, "Well played, young man."

He decided to write a book on how to win at poker. *The Education of a Poker Player: Including Where and How One Learns* was published by Simon and Schuster in November 1957. A British poet and poker devotee who wrote on the game for the *New Yorker,* A. Alvarez, categorized it. "There are two types of poker books: the how-tos, which are more or less abstract and often contain a good deal of mathematics about probabilities and percentages, and the autobiographical, like Yardley's classic, in which examples and solid advice are sandwiched between racy stories about dramatic games." He said it concentrated "on simple guidelines designed to disabuse beginners of the idea that poker is a gambling game and to instill in them the principles of conservative play." The book includes tables in small type showing what players should do in typical cases. For example, in a game of five-card draw, one player draws a pair of nines, a pair of threes, and an ace; the next draws two sixes, a king, a jack, and a four. Yardley comments of the first, who has bet on his cards, that "This hand is too weak to play" and of the second, who stays in, "This is another sucker play. . . . I suppose he *hopes* to make Three Sixes. What he doesn't know is that it is 7 to 1 that he doesn't." Those details give the book its backbone.

What gives it its life are Yardley's wonderful anecdotes about poker in Worthington and China—how the saloon owner who ran the game outmaneuvered another player and won a pair of geldings, how knowing whether another player is a simpleton of the first or second degree will enable a person to beat him, how Yardley outplayed a distasteful British code clerk in Chungking to win a big pot. Yardley, who couldn't write fiction, hadn't lost his touch when it came to first-person narrative—the thrilling writing style that had catapulted him to fame in *The American Black Chamber.* He had an almost Dickensian ability to make up real-sounding names: Doc Prittle, Bones Anderson, Gravey Combs. Nor did he lose his capacity to exaggerate: he claimed that for the book he had analyzed two hundred thousand poker hands.

Its publication was preceded by an excerpt in the *Saturday Evening Post.* The issue, the *Post* said, broke all its records by selling 5.6 million copies. Though the *New York Times,* the *Saturday Review of Literature,* and other book-reviewing journals did not deign to review a how-to book about a card game, the public felt differently about it. *The Education of a Poker Player* took off, a Simon and Schuster editor wrote to Yardley, "like one big-assed bird." The publisher immediately went back to press for seven thousand more copies for Christmas. The book was continually reprinted and went through several paperback editions and British editions, still in print in the twenty-first century. Playwright David Mamet, an enthusiastic poker player, dubbed it, as had Alvarez, a "classic."

Yardley was flooded with mail. "I have never enjoyed reading anything so much." "I have read it three times already and keep it at the foot of my bed and brief it every nite." "I am only sorry that your book was not available while I was in the Army." "I only hope my opponents never read it." Most of the letters asked technical questions. A twenty-year-old from Brooklyn asked Yardley about his advice not to play with poor cards: "If I fold so often with weak hands, how will I be able to win money when I stay? . . . you mention this type of player who will bet on anything. My friends are all like that. I sure would feel bad folding on a pair of Kings while the winner takes the pot on a pair of Tens." Yardley answered many of them.

The impact the book had on many readers comes through best in a reminiscence by William Overend, an editor at the *Los Angeles Times,* formerly of the *Herald Tribune* in Paris:

> I was 15 when I got the Yardley book. I forget how I came across it. I was already playing poker with friends, but it was the Yardley book that put me over the top, turned me into a genuine teenage poker star, the best in my neighborhood, grownup or kid. This was Kansas City in 1957. The community of Westwood on the Kansas side. Before Elvis. Before virtually everything except Bill Haley and the Comets.
>
> I lived with my parents in a two-story white frame house and had most of the upper half to myself. I studied the book the way people study for physics. It was filled with so much practical advice, mixed with so many good stories, that it was hard not to pay attention to it. Night after night, month after month, I played out hand after hand in my bedroom, testing his advice, finding it almost always on the button. I forget the details now, all of them. But they boiled down to some pretty simple rules. Fold early if you don't have strong cards. Mix it up a bit in style and pace. Bluff rarely, but know that you can get away with a good bluff if you wait for the precise right moment. And the wilder the game, the easier the pickings for a player who knows the odds.
>
> A couple times a week, there was a poker game at Youngblood's house. Gary Youngblood was a friend of mine. His dad was a cigar salesman named Powder Ass. At least that's what we all called him. He had been a big golfer and one day he had a chapped backside, and somebody yelled out, "Hey, Powder Ass!" The

name stuck. He let us play poker and often played, too. And the kids could drink at his house. It was a wild scene compared to just about anything else in Kansas at the time. Enough people played that I could usually pick up ten bucks or so in a game, which kept me in expenses as I turned 16. That was primarily pizza at some mob pizza joint on the Missouri side of Kansas City and burgers at Winstead's in the Plaza.

None of this went over very well with my folks, who kept trying to get me to do chores around the house, like mowing the lawn, for fifty cents or whatever they were offering. I almost always managed to duck out of them because I had made enough money at poker not to have to do them. I don't think I ever lost at poker at Youngblood's, which built up my confidence for a huge poker showdown in the summer of 1958.

My mom and dad had divorced when I was four or so, and my dad lived in Phoenix. He was a bandleader. When I was 16, I went on a train trip out to Phoenix for a rare visit. And I ended up in the club car in a poker game with six adults. That was the scene, the 16-year-old kid who had memorized virtually every word Yardley wrote on poker versus six old guys. Big stakes at the time. I think you could bet up to five bucks on a card or something like that. We started playing early and I was winning from the start. I was up about 100 bucks by the time we approached the Texas border. The only other big winner and serious player in the group was an African-American Air Force sergeant, who was my chief competition. But this was 1958, and when we hit the Texas border, the conductor came along and told the sergeant that he had to leave the game and go sit in the back of the train by himself until we had crossed Texas. Even then, with not much of a raised sensitivity to racial issues, this struck me as pretty outrageous and disgusting. On the other hand, it left me alone in the game with five total chumps.

I think I walked away with about $175 before I finally quit. And the highlight of the game was pulling off a perfect bluff just the way Yardley had instructed. In those days, $175 was roughly the equivalent of $6 million today, or something like that. So I was one very cocky kid. And I owed it all to Herbert O. Yardley and his poker book.

In October 1957, just before *Poker Player* was published, Yardley suffered what he called "a mild stroke." He was home within a few weeks, though he was partially paralyzed. Edna wrote his letters for him. But he was famous again, and looked up to—adored totally, unlike *The American Black Chamber* and its indiscretions.

This was his life until he suffered a major stroke in the summer of 1958. Batts was called and was horrified at what he saw. "He was just lying there, looking at me with his eyes wide open, staring. He couldn't speak." The man whose talking and writing had charmed so many could not utter even a whimper. Seven days later, at home at 1:15 P.M. on 7 August 1958, Herbert Osborn Yardley died. And with his death there passed into history the most widely known, most inspirational, most colorful cryptologist of all time.

21

The Measure of a Man

Yardley was buried in Grave 429-1, Section 30, of Arlington National Cemetery. He lies on a slope in the company of several four-star generals. His will left his hunting gear and fishing tackle to his son, Jack, and everything else to Edna. What did he leave the world?

Of cryptologic techniques, nothing. In Washington, during World War I, his staffers—mainly Manly—had developed a few minor new methods. In New York, neither he nor his staff devised any original techniques. His triumph, the solution of the Japanese codes, utilized common, well-known methods. For Yardley was not an outstanding cryptanalyst. Friedman called his methods "old-fashioned." One navy contemporary, cryptanalyst Captain Joseph J. Rochefort, called him "a so-so cryptanalyst," and another, Captain Thomas H. Dyer, said he was "not particularly great." They were right. He did not advance the technology. He did not reach the levels of his World War I contemporary, France's Georges Jean Painvin, who wrung everything out of known techniques to solve the German ADFGVX field cipher, or of Friedman, who created powerful new statistical weapons, or of Poland's Marian Rejewski, who in 1931 used mathematics to crack the German Enigma machine. He did not devise tough new cryptosystems even by combining existing elements, as did Germany's Lieutenant Fritz Nebel to make the ADFGVX or America's Frank B. Rowlett in irregularizing the stepping of cryptographic rotors; much less did he originate pathbreaking new cryptosystems, such as the one-time tape of Joseph O. Mauborgne, the rotor machine of California's Edward H. Hebern, or the automated online encryption of Gilbert S. Vernam.

But such criticism misses the point of Yardley's contribution, which was broader than any technological advance. He gave America a new source of information. He did not care about new ways of making or breaking codes as long as the existing ones served his purpose. Of course, those new ways might have enabled him to do his job better, and he had to know cryptology to do it, but his job was bigger than the technology. France's General François Cartier, who headed the French Ministry of War cryptologic agency during World War I, put it well. He explained that the head of a cryptologic service has to be like an orchestra conductor: he doesn't have to be able to play all the instruments, "but he has to have a perfect knowledge of musical science and to know the peculiarities of each instrument well enough to make them play together harmoniously." He has to advise his staffers and pass around their studies and results, so that all contribute to the common task. He has to assign them jobs and not let them choose targets that offer easy success and its rewards. Because the most difficult analyses, which may not succeed, go to the best cryptanalysts, the chief "must have enough prestige to impose the conditions of work that he judges the best." He must inoculate his workers against discouragement. He has to provide the ancillary information such as captured documents and battle reports that will help them. Equally important, though Cartier did not specify it, the chief must deal with bosses and the users of information, who always want more of it.

Yardley, a charismatic, excelled in such administration. He organized and inspired his workers to get the information his chiefs wanted. Superiors and subordinates alike praised him. He was awarded the Distinguished Service Medal. He foresaw communications intelligence in America; his success convinced officials of its importance. He gave his country what it needed. That is his legacy to America.

But a character flaw kept him from consummating his life's work. His flaw was not as majestically fatal as those of tragic heroes, nor did it fell him; that disaster came from outside. Nor was it a lust for power. He did not seek to absorb Friedman's tiny Signal Intelligence Service and bring it and the navy's codebreaking unit into a national, State Department–run agency. Yardley's fault was his greed for money and the inattention to duty it entailed. It kept him from keeping his agency alive. That failure did not come because he failed to solve messages that might have altered American policy; in the late 1920s, none were to be had. Rather it came because he did not build his organization for the future. Paying attention to real-estate deals and commercial codes, he did not research new methods of cryptanalysis, adopt tabulating machines, investigate the new cipher machines as cryptosystems for soldiers or sailors or diplomats, recruit younger people, especially mathematicians, as staffers for the future, even train his existing people. If he had done all this, the army might well have decided to keep him, together with Friedman, even though State rejected him. But he did not, and he never enjoyed the lifetime pride and security his work could have given him. His weakness truncated his career.

An interesting question is, what would have happened had Yardley's Cipher Bureau not been disbanded in 1929? What if it had survived as the military and diplomatic cryptanalytic agency of the United States? Would Yardley, even with all his executive ability, have brought the United States to the commanding cryptanalytic position it was in by Pearl Harbor? In 1940, Friedman's cryptanalysts, who included mathematicians, had solved the Japanese diplomatic cipher machine called PURPLE. This enabled America to bring something of value to Britain in the 1941 exchange of cryptanalytic information and proved of extraordinary help later in the war, when the intercepted messages of the Japanese ambassador in Germany furnished details about Hitler's plans and the fortifications of the Atlantic Wall. In the cryptographic sphere, Frank Rowlett's rotor irregularization rendered American cipher machines unbreakable with the technology of the time. It is very unlikely that Yardley or his team would have either solved PURPLE or improved American cryptography so much. With Yardley at the helm, the United States would not have been as prepared cryptologically for World War II as it was with Friedman there.

Yardley's career paralleled the rise of intelligence to significance as a factor in modern state policy. That they coincide is no coincidence. Intelligence owes its importance in the modern world not to spying or interrogations or even aerial photography, but to codebreaking. It alone provides believable, high-level, unmediated, voluminous, continuous, cheap information. It first proved this in World War I. Yardley, whose field this was, soared as intelligence did.

The new national role of intelligence brought the United States face to face with the moral dilemma of intelligence for the first time. Neither George Washington's use of spies nor the infrequent Union tapping of Confederate wires during the Civil War occasioned any such introspection. But the expansion of intelligence meant that America's government, press, and public had increasingly to face that getting information would sometimes mean breaking laws, usually of the target country, sometimes of one's own. People understood, even without having read Immanuel Kant's criticism, that such activity was wrong in principle and sometimes counterproductive in practice. There stirred for the first time the conflict between idealism and realism that afflicts the American intelligence community to this day. Idealists hold that such practices betray the principles that make America what it is. Realists say that those practices are necessary to protect the nation, that without them it would not even exist. This conflict came into being in the 1920s when Yardley bribed cable employees to sneak him foreign messages and in the 1930s when the army chief of staff permitted the Signal Corps to violate a law and intercept Japanese radiograms. It expressed itself in the opposite direction in the 1920s and 1930s when Stimson closed the Cipher Bureau and when the army would not employ spies. It vanished as an issue during World War II, but reappeared during the Cold War, and then the two sides compromised their differences. The nation permitted clandestine operations as long as they were approved by a politically accountable person—the president—but it refused to sanction the assassination of foreign leaders. This conflict over the ethics of intelligence, which still roils American politics, first came to public attention in the work, the writings, and the ending of Herbert Yardley.

Three questions recur in Yardley's biography: Was he a drunk? Was he a womanizer? Was he a traitor?

Yardley drank a lot of liquor. He may have drunk too much. But no evidence even hints that his drinking impaired his ability or his judgment. He cannot be called a drunk.

It seems likely that he chased skirts. He took up with Jacqueline in Paris in 1918 and with Edna Ramsaier while he was still married and perhaps while she was. He went out drinking and perhaps had an affair with the wife of his friend and collaborator Klem Koukol. No conclusive evidence exists for this or for any other possible adulteries. But he had a strong sexual appetite, as he demonstrated in China, where neither the presence of friends nor Western mores inhibited him. He was attractive to people. He was energetic; he was self-confident; he was a boss, and he seized opportunities. So romantic liaisons with women may well have been among the opportunities he grasped.

Was Yardley a traitor? No. He never sold information to Japan or to anybody else, and he never worked against the United States. He cheated by working for himself while being paid by the government. Later, he was indeed a hired gun, an opportunist, and he breached the trust his country had placed in him when he published his book. The action was despicable. It was rightly castigated by many people. But it cannot be characterized as treason. Yardley was a rotter, not a traitor.

Apart from these questions lies his interesting relationship with Friedman. Friedman, though he knew he was a better cryptologist than Yardley, and though he planned better and carried Yardley's founding stroke of genius to completion, seems to have envied him. No documents substantiate this conclusion—though it may show itself in Friedman's excessive reaction to the publication of *The American Black Chamber*—but people who have studied the two sense it. Friedman's feeling of inferiority seems not to have stemmed from the facts that Yardley was older and Friedman's precursor and at first his idol, though these may have contributed to it. The feeling arises from their personalities. Friedman seems insecure. He always wore a tie, insisted on being addressed as Mr. Friedman, was punctilious. Yardley seems not to have been concerned about these things. He wore muddy boots when hunting, at least later in life didn't put on a tie, and watered his lawn in his underwear. But Friedman's envy probably came from the fact that Yardley appears to have succeeded with women and Friedman wanted to. Yardley had self-confidence, which Friedman lacked. Friedman's greater success did not compensate for this, and it permanently distorted his attitude toward Yardley.

The trajectory of Yardley's life lifts off at his formation of MI-8, peaks early at the Washington disarmament conference, sinks slowly through the 1920s, bursts into an amazed public's consciousness with the publication of *The American Black Chamber,* then spirals down through his other writings and his work in China and Canada to crash in misfortune and regret at the end of his life. But that misfortune did not eclipse his fame or obliterate his having done something that no one else had done.

The fame comes from his writing. *The American Black Chamber* humanized cryptology. Anecdotes fill its pages; people flit through them. Yardley drenched the arid letters and diagrams of cryptology in personality. More important, he showed the codebreaker turning knowledge into power. He showed the cryptanalyst as an oracle, a wizard, who foresees what is to come and helps victors. *The American Black Chamber* taught people that cryptology is significant.

Still, what Yardley did mattered more than what he said. He brought codebreaking to America. He endowed his country with the best kind of intelligence. He made America stronger. That is the immortal legacy of America's first professional codebreaker.

Notes

Abbreviations

SRH   Special Research History
WT   Worthington Times

Chapter 1   All-American Boy

Page

1   center of population: U.S. Bureau of the Census. The center was at Greensburg, forty miles southeast of Indianapolis.

1   Worthington: visit, 10 November 1996; Indiana Historical Society.

1   Robert Kirkbride Yardley: Helen Hannum Hoagland interview.

1   1703: Thomas W. Yardley, *Genealogy of the Yardley Family, 1402–1881* (Philadelphia: William S. Schofield, 1881), 9, 13, 75. The author claims that a Yardley was a signer of the Magna Carta. But the document has no signers.

1   from nearby Freedom; Mary Emma Osborn: This and other personal information about Yardley and his family, unless otherwise cited, comes from letters to Edna Yardley that she collected for a biography, which she never wrote. CAHA 00002:100 ff.

1   127 West Union Street: Greene County, Indiana, land records, showing Robert K. Yardley at Lot 46, 127 West Union Street, and A. L. Milam at Lot 45, 28 North Edwards Street. From Wilma McBride.

2   baby owls: *WT,* 1 April 1910.

2   13 April 1889: This is the date given by Yardley in all documents. No birth certificate can be found in the records of Greene County or those of neighboring Owen County, home of his mother's parents. But this was not uncommon for the time: no requirement existed for births to be recorded at the county courthouse, and physicians did not always want to ride to the county seat to record a birth. U.S. Census, 1900, Indiana, Greene County, Enumeration District 31 (Jefferson Township, Worthington Town), sheet 2, line 80 lists Yardley's birthdate as April 1889. The records of the 1890 census were destroyed in a fire.

2   dry, busiest: Indiana State Climatology Office, Comparative Observers Meteorological Record, Worthington, 13 April 1889; *WT,* 18 April 1889.

2   shoot at hat: Mark Hays interview.

2   "rhythmic figure": CAHA 00002: 142, Mina MacArthur undated letter.

2   blackbird pie: Hays interview.

2   janitor: MacArthur letter.

2   teachers, "smartest," "brilliant," "different level," word-building contest: CAHA 00002:109–110, letters; Fred Jewell interview; CAHA 00002: 107–108, Don Herold letter; *WT,* 13 September 1906.

2   mother died: *WT,* 10 February 1903.

2   Presbyterian church: *WT,* 29 August 1905. The newspaper had numerous stories linking the Yardleys to this church, but no records for the family were found in it by Wilma McBride.

2   poker: All from Yardley, *The Education of a Poker Player.* However, none of the names given in the book, such as Doc Prittle, Gravey Combs, and in particular James Montgomery, Yardley's mentor, appears in the 1900 census for Greene County, Enumeration District 31. Neither does the Worthington city directory for 1917 list those three names or any saloons (information from Lori Markle of the Worthington Public Library, 25 January 2001). Yardley nowhere says that the

names are fictional, and indeed they don't seem invented. But without any substantiation that they are real, I have not used them.

3 elected attorney: *WT,* 26 February 1907.

3 played Lemuel and Bob: *WT,* 28 November 1905, 12 March 1907.

4 *What a Young Boy Ought to Know:* By Sylvanus Stall, first published in 1897.

4 football: *WT,* 7 November 1905.

4 three out of four: *The Echo* (apparently class paper; December, probably 1910), 12.

4 second touchdown: *WT,* 23 October 1906.

4 "Clay Adkins and Herbert Yardley": *WT,* 9 October 1908.

4 Denver: *WT,* 15 May 1906, 23 August 1908; CAHA 00002: 123, John Owen letter.

4 "like I learned to talk": "Hoosier Author Gives Graphic Picture of Secret War Chapter," *Indianapolis News,* 1 June 1931, 8.

4 HOY: CAHA 00002: 143.

4 rivalry, flags: *WT,* 10 April 1906, 9, 16, and 26 April 1907; CAHA 00002: 123, Owen letter.

5 Eaton Rapids: HOYOPF, 2 January 1913, and University of Chicago Matriculation Application 54814, 17 March 1913. Eaton Rapids High School has no records of him, according to Robert Lange, principal, telephone interview, 10 May 1995, but this does not prove Yardley's nonattendance, given the brevity of his stay there.

5 12–8 victory: *WT,* 25 June 1907, 2 July 1907.

5 Yardley shot: *WT,* 29 June 1909, 17 September 1909, 26 November 1909; B-M, Authors' Questionnaire.

5 referee: *WT,* 14 November 1905.

5 never known to lie or cheat: CAHA 00002: 142.

5 railroad telegrapher: Thomas C. Jepsen, *Ma Kiley: The Life of a Railroad Telegrapher* (El Paso: Texas Western Press, 1997), 6–7, 8, 15, 16, 23, 25.

6 visited home: *WT,* 16 June 1911, 19 December 1911, 22 March 1912, 13 December 1912.

6 scored highest: HOYOPF, 22 November 1912.

7 clerk: HOYOPF, 22 November 1912, 23 December 1912; *WT,* 20 December 1912.

7 4 March 1889: U.S. Office of Personnel Management, Official Personnel Folder, Hazel Yardley.

7 Hazel: Hays interview; Harold J. Smith interview; Mary Ropp and Wilma S. McBride joint interview.

7 Milam: *WT,* 12 January 1900, 11 March 1904, 27 September 1904, 12 June 1912, 15 October 1920.

7 Hazel's life: *WT,* 9 August 1904, 7 March 1905, 20 July 1906, among others, and 1 July 1913.

7 Ellen Piel: *WT,* 23 June 1905.

7 raise: HOYOPF, 1 April 1914.

7 belle: Wilma McBride interview.

7 Hazel to Washington: *WT,* 15 May 1914, 19 May 1914, 22 May 1914.

7 married: District of Columbia Office of Public Records, Marriage License 65443.

Chapter 2   His Life's Work

Page

8   1009 Seventh Street: University of Chicago Matriculation File and Academic Record File (Home Study File) 54814.

8   honeymoon: They took a belated honeymoon in 1921. *WT,* 28 January 1921.

8   Worthington, brothers: *WT,* 22 September 1914, 20 July 1915, 10 October 1916.

8   typist: *WT,* 31 July 1917; Official Personnel Folder, Hazel Yardley.

8   542 Shepherd Street: HOYOPF, 11 July 1917.

8   correspondence courses, Grabo: University of Chicago Matriculation File and Academic Record File (Home Study File) 54814; University of Chicago, *Announcements* 16 (June 1916), Correspondence-Study Department, 1916–17, 42, 47; University of Chicago, Andrew S. Hannah, acting university registrar, letter of 29 June 2000.

9   Room 106: University of Chicago Matriculation File and Academic Record File (Home Study File) 54814.

9   "This spacious room": *ABC,* 17–18.

9   agency of its own, "As I asked": Ibid., 18–20.

10   books: Ibid., 20–21. In an undated paper in NA, RG 165, 10039-299 Yardley claims to know "English, German, Spanish," but "Historical Background of the Signal Security Agency," 2:11, indicates more accurately, I believe, that he knew no language but English.

10   manual: Parker Hitt, *Manual for the Solution of Military Ciphers* (Fort Leavenworth: Press of the Army Service Schools, 1916); NA, RG 457, SRH-004, Friedman, "Six Lectures," 143. Yardley's comment (*ABC,* 21) that "the types of cipher it explained were so simple that any bright schoolboy could solve them without a book of instructions" was not only ungracious but wrong.

10   Mauborgne: Mrs. Preston Corderman interview; H. H. Arnold, *Global Mission* (New York: Harper and Brothers, 1949), 40–41; "Joseph O. Mauborgne," *TEC TAC* [of the U.S. Army Signal School] (23 June 1961), 31 ff. at 34–35; Mauborgne, *An Advanced Problem in Cryptography and Its Solution* (Fort Leavenworth: Army Service Press, 1914).

10   "would wring your heart out": Kyle, "Divine Fire," 121, apparently quoting Mrs. Friedman.

11   Hitt and solutions: Kahn, *The Codebreakers,* 321–324; NA RG 165, Entry 65, 4131-22, 7579-180, 8532-20, and 8536-107; and Hitt papers in David Kahn Collection.

11   "undoubtedly the best," seven others: "Historical Background," 1:115–116.

11   "One night": *ABC,* 21–22.

12   renumbered: Weber, "State Department Cryptographic Security: Herbert O. Yardley and President Wilson's Secret Code," 576–579. In the House-Wilson system, page 739 became 113 and page 100 became 749, with the intervening pages renumbered respectively, except for page 734, a blank, and pages 735 and 736, giving spelling instructions. Other historians of cryptology, including me, said that perhaps Yardley had solved a mere jargon code (*The Codebreakers,* 351). Professor Weber went to the documents and found out what had happened.

12 RED, BLUE, GREEN codes, Haswell: Weber, "State Department Cryptographic Security," 554–558, 564–567; Weber, *Masked Dispatches,* 191–210.

12 concerned their weaknesses: This is my assumption. Though Yardley titled his paper "Solution of American Diplomatic Codes" and talks of "chiseling out words" (*ABC,* 23), he knew the codes well so he could hardly have *solved* them. The only explanation I can envision that does not contradict either Yardley's statements or common sense is that embodied in my text.

12 Salmon: Weber, *United States Diplomatic Codes and Ciphers,* 240–246; U.S. Department of State, *Register,* 15 December 1916, 23, 127; Rachel West, *The Department of State on the Eve of the First World War* (Athens: University of Georgia Press, 1978); NSA, CCA, 6; Rowlett oral history, 209.

13 "My fingers itched": *ABC,* 30.

13 March 1916, "first successful attempt": H. O. Yardley, "Theory and Practice of Enciphered Code," in George C. Marshall Library, Friedman Collection, item 17. In *ABC,* 31, Yardley says that he submitted his solution several weeks after the declaration of war and follows this with an account of his request to be released from State to join the army. But contemporary evidence is to be preferred. He may have collapsed his chronology to make a better story.

13 spoke to Salmon, Van Deman: *ABC,* 31–36.

Chapter 3 A History of American Intelligence before Yardley

Page

14 Nathan Hale: Miller, *Spying for America,* 16–19; O'Toole, *Honorable Treachery,* 22–24.

14 Washington as spymaster: Miller, *Spying for America,* 19; O'Toole, *Honorable Treachery,* 47, 49.

14 Culper spy ring: Morton Pennypacker, *General Washington's Spies on Long Island and in New York* (Brooklyn: Long Island Historical Society, 1939); Miller, *Spying for America,* 22–28; O'Toole, *Honorable Treachery,* 45–49.

14 "to remain in the City," "to no one," "intelligent": Pennypacker, *General Washington's Spies,* 46, 47, 72.

14 encoded, invisible ink: Kahn, *The Codebreakers,* 177–179.

15 Lovell: Ibid., 181–184.

15 Clausewitz: bk. 1, ch. 6.

15 Civil War: The best study of Civil War intelligence is Edwin C. Fishel, *The Secret War for the Union: The Untold Story of Military Intelligence in the Civil War* (Boston: Houghton Mifflin, 1996), with useful summaries in appendices 1 and 2. Like all studies of Civil War intelligence, it calls scouts "spies," confusing espionage with patrolling.

15 Greenhow: Ibid., 57–68, appendix 4; O'Toole, *Honorable Treachery,* 121–122; Miller, *Spying for America,* 94–98, 100–101.

15 Van Lew: Fishel, *The Secret War for the Union,* 551–553; O'Toole, *Honorable Treachery,* 157–160, 166; Miller, *Spying for America,* 147–151.

15 Pinkerton: Fishel, *The Secret War for the Union,* appendix 6; Miller, *Spying for America,* 93, 98–106; O'Toole, *Honorable Treachery,* 120–126, 168, 172.

16 balloons: Fishel, *The Secret War for the Union,* 84, 167; Peter Maslowski, "Military

Intelligence Sources during the American Civil War: A Case Study," in *The Intelligence Revolution: A Historical Perspective*, 39–70, ed. Walter P. Hitchcock, U.S. Air Force Academy (GPO, 1991), at 50–51.

16   tapped wires, signals: Maslowski, "Military Intelligence Sources," 52, 54–56.

16   polyalphabetic substitutions solved: Kahn, *The Codebreakers*, 217–218.

16   trivial contributions: Fishel, *The Secret War for the Union*, appendix 1. Secret intelligence—as distinct from scouting and cavalry reconnaissance—does not figure in the history of the war in Maurice Matloff, ed., *American Military History*, Army Historical Series, Office of the Chief of Military History (GPO, 1969), 184–280.

16   war plans: Paul M. Kennedy, ed., *The War Plans of the Great Powers* (London: George Allen and Unwin, 1979), 1.

17   exports: *Historical Statistics of the United States*, Series U189.

17   23 March 1882: Jeffrey Dorwart, *The Office of Naval Intelligence: The Birth of America's First Intelligence Agency, 1865–1918* (Annapolis: Naval Institute Press, 1979), 12.

17   Drum, 12 April 1889: Elizabeth Bethel, "The Military Information Division: Origin of the Intelligence Division," *Military Affairs* (spring 1947): 18–24; Bidwell, *History of the Military Intelligence Division*, 52, 53.

17   "for the pay": *United States Statutes at Large*, 26: 150. No such language appears in the appropriation statutes for the two previous or the two following years.

17   In three years: Bidwell, *History of the Military Intelligence Division*, 55–56.

17   attachés: Alfred Vagts, *The Military Attaché* (Princeton: Princeton University Press, 1967), 33.

17   secretary of war's bureaus: Matloff, ed., *American Military History*, 291, 347–348.

18   Wagner: Timothy K. Nenninger, "Wagner, Arthur Lockwood," in *Dictionary of Military Biography* (Westport, Conn.: Greenwood Press, 1984), 3:1146–1149; T. R. Brereton, *Educating the U.S. Army: Arthur L. Wagner and Reform, 1875–1905* (Lincoln: University of Nebraska Press, 2000); O'Toole, *Honorable Treachery*, 186–187, 194–195; Miller, *Spying for America*, 165–170; Matloff, ed., *American Military History*, 289; Weber, ed., *The Final Memoranda*, xi. Wagner's *The Service of Security and Information* (11th ed., 1903) deals mainly with scouting and protection against enemy scouting and has an appendix on spies but merely mentions tapping telegraph wires and seizing couriers.

18   June 1897: Weber, ed., *The Final Memoranda*, 4.

18   Van Deman: Marc Powe's preface to Weber, ed., *The Final Memoranda*, x–xviii; Harvard University Archives, Van Deman Biographical Folder, and *Harvard College: Class of 1888, Secretary's Report No. V* (February 1905), 91–93; *Secretary's Report No. VII* (June 1913), 155–157.

19   British, German, French staffs: Thomas G. Fergusson, *British Military Intelligence, 1870–1914: The Development of a Modern Intelligence Organisation* (Frederick, Md.: University Publications of America, 1984); Pierre Guinard, Jean-Claude Devos, and Jean Nicot, *Inventaire sommaire des Archives de la Guerre: Série N 1872–1912*, Ministère de la Défense, Etat-Major de l'armée, Service historique (Troyes: Imprimerie La Renaissance, 1975), 11–12; France, Ministère de guerre, *Journal militaire officiel: Partie réglementaire*, 1874 (230–231), No. 91, Décret portant réorganisation de l'état major général du Ministère de guerre; Germany,

Militärarchiv, Ober Kommando des Heeres, H/35, Stoerkel, "Die Organisation des Grossen Generalstabes," 35, 37–38.

19　copied numeration: U.S. Army, *Annual Report of the Secretary of War, 1903* (GPO, 1904), appendix D.

19　joined, cut: Bidwell, *History of the Military Intelligence Division,* 81–83; Nelson, *National Security,* 112, 222, 224; Weber, ed., *The Final Memoranda,* 16; Said, *U.S. Statutes at Large,* 39:167. In a letter to State's Harrison of 18 April, Van Deman said that "we have not yet succeeded in getting an organization for the Intelligence Section of the General Staff." His memoirs (Weber, ed., *The Final Memoranda,* 21–22) indicate that he enlisted the aid of the chief of the Washington police and a woman novelist to persuade the secretary of war to create a separate intelligence section over the objections of the chief of staff. But some of his dates contradict those in the record, and so I have omitted his story.

19　Aerial reconnaissance so good: William Mitchell, *Our Air Force* (New York: Dutton, 1921), 84; Baron von Löwenstern, "Bedeutung der Nachtluftaufklärung, in den Kriegsmonaten Mai bis Oktober 1918," *Militäur-Wochenblatt* 123 (19 May 1939): 3171–75.

19　radio intelligence: Kahn, *The Codebreakers,* 282–297, 346–347, 348–350, 622–633.

20　not yet known: U.S. War Department, Office of the Chief of Staff, *Field Service Regulations: United States Army* (1914, text corrections to 4 February 1916), War Department Document no. 475 (New York: Military Publishing Co., n.d.).

20　11 April, 3 May: Bidwell, *History of the Military Intelligence Division,* 109–110.

20　went by trolley, intensely interested: *ABC,* 34, 35–36.

20　"neither the State Department": NA, RG 59, Entry 349, Box 1, 18 April 1917.

20　"analyzing the enemy's codes": NA, RG 165, Entry 65, 639-142. Other memoranda: 639-129, -143, -145, -149, -150.

21　offer from private research organization: NA, RG 59, Entry 349, Box 1, 18 April 1917; RG 457, HOYC, Box 56, Folder Codes, Ciphers, Secret Inks, Radio Interception, and Goniometry, "M.I.8," 1.

21　29 June: "Historical Background of the Signal Security Agency," 2:10. Yardley's release from the State Department took place as of 19 July 1917 (HOYOPF, 18 July 1917). His commissioning came as part of the great wartime expansion and was authorized under the law of 18 May 1917 (*U.S. Statutes at Large* 40:76).

21　O-159744: CAHA 00010:2280.

21　5 July: "Historical Background," 2:10.

21　soon thereafter: Despite diligent search, with the help of archivist Mitchell Yockelson, I have been unable to find an order establishing MI-8. I can therefore fix no date for its founding. "Historical Background," 2:10, cites a 1919 memorandum to give 10 June as the founding date. NA, RG 165, Entry 65, 10039-299, a Van Deman memorandum of 22 February 1918 recommending that Yardley be promoted to captain, states that Yardley has been "in charge of the code and cipher Section since July 15th, 1917. This section was organized by Lieutenant Yardley." But both 10 June and 15 July were Sundays, when business was not transacted. So I believe both to be in error and am giving no date. The *Guide to Federal Records in the National Archives of the United States,* compiled by Robert B. Matchette et al., 2d ed. (Washington: National Archives and Records Administration, 1998), states, at

2:457-2, that "Army cryptanalytic origins date from April 28, 1917, when, by Chief of Staff (COS) memorandum, a code and cipher decryption unit was established as the Cable and Telegraph Section, MI-8, in the Military Information Section (MIS), War College Division (WCD), War Department General Staff (WDGS), headquartered in Washington, DC." However, the COS memorandum cannot be found, and when I asked about other evidence to support the 28 April date, I received a letter dated 31 July 2002 signed by Yockelson that states, in part, "the date of April 28, 1917 (457.2), cited in the Guide . . . is incorrect and the edition of the guide on our web site will be corrected with an approximate date." It further indicates that "Our staff conducted a thorough search of the correspondence and reports in the files of the War Department General Staffs (Chief of Staff, Military Intelligence Division, and the War College Division), Records of the War Department General and Special Staffs (Record Group 165), but were unsuccessful in locating the exact dates that MI.8 was established as an office of the Military Intelligence Division. Based upon various documents that were located in our holdings, we believe the office was organized around November 1917." But documents show Yardley working in MI-8 long before that.

21   balcony: "Historical Background," 2:15; visit, summer 1995.

21   twenty-eight, five feet five inches, 125: HOYOPF, 28 May 1921.

Chapter 4   A Rival

Page

22   Fabyan: Kopec, *The Sabines at Riverbank,* 4–5, 19–42; Elizebeth Smith Friedman, untitled autobiography; Fred W. Kranz, "Early History of Riverbank Acoustical Laboratories," *Journal of the Acoustical Society of America* 49 (1971): 381–384.

22   Wright remodeled: "George and Nelle Fabyan's Country Home," *Frank Lloyd Wright Quarterly* 6 (winter 1995): 4–11.

23   Fabyan offered, visited Van Deman: NA, RG 165, Entry 65, 4131-27; 9793-125, 18 April 1917.

23   "take immediate advantage": Ibid., 9793-125, 11 April 1917.

23   organizations participated: Ibid., 18 April 1917; "History of the Military Intelligence Division," 2:474–475.

23   Harrison, "mouselike": G. McMurtrie Godley, letter of 21 August 1995; U.S. Department of State, Personnel File, Harrison.

23   four men, three women: NA, RG 165, Entry 65, 10020-23, 31 May 1917.

23   Baconian, no knowledge: "History of the Military Intelligence Division," 2:475.

23   "finished," "We have had," 28 July: NA, RG 165, Entry 65, 10020-31, 22 June 1917; 10020-109 (1), 19 July 1917; 10020-30, 28 July 1917.

23   German, Spanish translators: E. S. Friedman, untitled autobiography, 12–13.

24   Specializing in agriculture: Cornell University Registrar's Office, Transcript. Earlier, he had attended Michigan Agricultural College, now Michigan State University. Michigan State University Registrar's Office, letter of 27 December 1998.

24   disliked Fabyan, Friedman: E. S. Friedman, untitled autobiography, 6, 9.

24   21 May 1917: Clark, *The Man Who Broke Purple,* 39.

24 "there is no fundamental": Norbert Wiener, *The Human Use of Human Beings: Cybernetics and Society* (Boston, 1950), 110.

24 "more than a helpmate," "They lived and ate": Riverbank Laboratories, Phyllis Fletcher (Riverbank worker 1917–18), undated interview.

24 department grew: NA, RG 457, HOYC, Box 1, Folder Correspondence involving Fabyan, Friedman, Yardley, and Van Deman, Friedman letter of 19 March 1924.

25 wrote technical papers: NA, RG 165, Entry 65, 10020-127, -139 (2), -171 (2). Fabyan was extremely proud of these papers.

26 Plett cipher machine: NA, RG 457, HCC, Box 777, Folder Mission and Function of MI-8, "MI-8: Codes, Ciphers, and Secret Writing," 6; RG 165, Entry 65, 10994-6; Donald W. Davies, "Charles Wheatstone's Cryptograph and Plett's Cipher Machine," *Cryptologia* 9 (April 1985): 155–160; Clark, *The Man Who Broke Purple,* 58–60. Riverbank Publication No. 20, *Several Machine Ciphers and Methods for Their Solution,* by Friedman, dealing in part with the Wheatstone system, had apparently been published early in 1918; I do not know why it did not warn of the dangers of the Plett system.

26 "lean back": E. S. Friedman, untitled autobiography, 29.

26 "that messages enciphered": NA, RG 165, Entry 65, 10994-6 (6).

26 fascinated four: Childs, *Foreign Service Farewell,* 3.

27 Riverbank accepted: NA, RG 165, Entry 65, 10020-86, -97, -145 (1); U.S. War Department, Special Orders No. 266, 14 November 1917. The four were Second Lieutenants J. Rives Childs, Robert W. Gilmore, John A. Graham, and Lee W. Sellers. Childs has described this briefly in "My Recollections of G.2 A.6."

27 Fabyan offered, Aurora Hotel: NA, RG 165, Entry 65, 10020-124 (12), -134 (29), 145 (1), -169; E. S. Friedman, untitled autobiography, 30.

27 a half dozen more: "Historical Background of the Signal Security Agency," 2:6.

27 Fabyan alienated: Kruh, "From the Archives: Riverbank Laboratory Correspondence (SRH-050)," 245–246; NA, RG 165, Entry 65, 10020-73, -78, -124 (26), -138 (32), (33), (35), (38), -159 (2), -172 (1), (4), (6), (8), -192 (6).

27 explosion, apology, no change: NA, RG 165, Entry 65, 10020-129 (9), (14), (16). Friedman says in a footnote on page 6 of RG 457, SRH-030 that the complaint that Fabyan was seeking publicity was not true but was merely Yardley's way of getting Fabyan out of the picture. The documents abundantly support the publicity problem and show no substantial Yardley dealings with Fabyan nor any machinations or intrigues by Yardley against Fabyan.

27 army's own: "Historical Background," 2:8, 9, 14–15.

27 intercepts from all departments to MI-8: CAHA 00011:2994.

Chapter 5   Staffers, Shorthand, and Secret Ink

Page

28 Altus E. Prince and subsection: "History of the Military Intelligence Division," 1:479 and Biographical Record; "Historical Background of the Signal Security Agency," 22, 29; *ABC,* 39–41. Yardley says that Prince came from the State Department code room. But the U.S. Department of State *Register* annual volumes from 1911 to 1917 list no Altus E. Prince. Prince says only that he was an attaché in missions abroad. He perhaps encoded and decoded there.

28 James E. McKenna and subsection: "History of the Military Intelligence Division," 1:474 and Biographical Record; "Historical Background," 2:13, 14, 59–61; *ABC*, 47–48; NA, RG 165, Entry 65, 10039-91.

29 Selective Service Act: Nelson, *National Security and the General Staff*, 224; *U.S. Statutes at Large* 40: 76–83, esp. §3.

29 "Judging from the letters": *ABC*, 98.

29 Holstein, Jensen: NA, RG 165, Entry 65, 10020-77, -124 (22) and (23). Holstein appears in cryptologic literature as the author of articles on the Vigenère and the Porta ciphers in *Scientific American Supplement* 83 (24 April 1917): 235, and in *Scientific American Monthly* 4 (October 1921): 332–334.

29 recruitment problem: As late as 4 June 1918, Yardley was seeking someone who could think in German to help solve some German four-letter traffic, which both the French and the British failed to do. Such a man would be paid $1,400 and could expect a captaincy, he said. NA, RG 457, HCC, Box 1029, Folder German Cryptographic Systems during the First World War, "German Cryptographic Systems during the First World War," 31.

29 Manly: *Dictionary of American Biography*, supplement 2; *American National Biography;* University of Chicago Biographical Files, "John M. Manly," memorandum by Robert Morss Lovett, 4; *ABC*, 38–39; NA, RG 165, Entry 65, 10020–68 and 13623, Special Orders 261.

29 Rickert: *Dictionary of American Biography*, supplement 2.

29 Beeson: *Dictionary of American Biography*, supplement 4. Cryptography of the *Etymologiae* is in book 1, xxiv and xxv.

30 Knott: *NYT*, 17 August 1945, 17:3.

30 Sturtevant: *NYT*, 2 July 1952, 25:5.

30 Luquiens: *NYT*, 18 April 1940, 23:1; Arthur W. Bell, ed., *Quarter-Century Record of the Class of 1897 Yale College* (New Haven: Class Secretaries Bureau, 1923), 232–233; *Bulletin of Yale University: Obituary Record of Graduates Deceased during the Year Ending July 1, 1940* (New Haven, 1941), 86–88.

30 Mendelsohn: *NYT*, 28 September 1939; University of Pennsylvania Archives and Records Center, and Van Pelt Library, Special Collections Department; City College of the City University of New York, Morris Raphael Cohen Library, Division of Archives and Special Collections; George C. Marshall Library, Friedman Collection. I am obliged to James Reeds for the information about the mathematics prize.

30 Weiskopf: "Victor Weiskopf, Inc.," *Mekeel's Weekly Stamp News* 44 (January 1930): 63; "Victor Weiskopf Passes Away," *Stamps* 20 (26 August 1939): 273; Connie Swartz of the American Philatelic Society, letter of 2 December 1995; Herman Herst interview.

30 Meeth: Arnold Voback interview; Maureen Crowley interview.

30 Benet: Charles A. Fenton, *Stephen Vincent Benet* (New Haven: Yale University Press, 1958), 73–74; Stephen Vincent Benet, "Breaking the Codes," *Saturday Review of Literature* 19 (1 April 1939), 11.

31 Burt: NA, RG 38, ComNavSecGru, 5750/87; "Historical Background," 2:25.

31 "What's this?": *ABC*, 48.

31 shorthand subsection: Ibid., 49–54; "Historical Background," 2:113–127.

32 Richards: *Dictionary of American Biography; American National Biography*.

32   Carver: Harvard University Archives, HUD 314.25, HUD 314.50, HUG 300.

32   "We have developed," "The only defect," "is still under," "No. 50": NA, RG 165, Entry 65, 10020-168.

33   laboratories, McGrail: NA, RG 457, HCC, Box 1124, Folder Outgrowth of Secret Inks Subsection, MI-8, Lt. Col. A. J. McGrail, "Outgrowth of Secret Inks Subsection, MI-8 (WWI), History," 1–2; "History of the Military Intelligence Division," 478; Harvard University Archives, HUG 300, HUD 313.20, HUD 313.50, UAV 874.269.

33   Collins, Iodine vapor: McGrail, "Outgrowth," 3; *ABC,* 79; "Historical Background," 2:110.

33   Two thousand letters, fifty instances: "Historical Background," 2:108.

33   "most daring," blonde: *ABC,* 90; Schragmüller, "Aus dem deutschen Nachrichtendienst."

33   Victorica: Doerries, "Tätigkeit," 42–43; *Deutsche Biographische Enzyklopädie,* s.v. Gustedt, Jenny von, and Braun, Lily; "History of the Military Intelligence Division," 1645–1661; NA RG 65, Microfilm M-1085, Roll 293; FBI File 2423, passim; *NYT,* 28 April 1918, 5:1; 29 April 1918, 20:1; 8 June 1918, 1:1; 21 May 1919, 17:3; 3 August 1920, 24:1; *ABC,* 90–119.

34   British: NA, RG 59, Entry 349, Box 1, Folder Misc. Edward Bell Letters Received, 17 January 1919. For an excellent study of how at least the Austrian black chamber of the 1700s and 1800s opened sealed letters, see Hubatschke, "Ferdinand Prantner," 1276–1281.

35   centavo: *ABC,* 86–89.

Chapter 6   The Executive

Page

36   "his device," "we should not": Kruh, "From the Archives: Riverbank Laboratory Correspondence" (SRH-050)," 245–246.

36   "outstanding": B-M, 4 May 1931.

36   "Yardley possessed": NA, RG 457, HOYC, Box 99, Folder Correspondence Regarding the Rehiring of Yardley, 12 December 1940.

36   Manly reconstructed, "the subject": CAHA 00004:884; NA, RG 457, HCC, Box 777, Folder Missions and Functions of MI, "MI-8: Codes, Ciphers, and Secret Writing," 7.

37   1 December, "deliberate steal": Kruh, "From the Archives," 243; 245, NA, RG 457, HCC, Box 777, Folder Missions and Functions of MI, "MI-8: Codes, Ciphers, and Secret Writing," 7. In addition, RG 165, 10020-172 (3) encloses an extract of a letter of 20 December 1917 by Lieutenant J. Rives Childs describing a method of solving a running-key cipher. The MI-8 solution led Mauborgne to suggest that the army be warned against the system's use. RG 165, M-1194, Manly, 16 March 1918 refers to a "memo re: erroneous view of many cipher experts maintaining messages enciphered with running key as long as message itself being indecipherable." Mauborgne's recognition that only a random, never-repeating key could be absolutely safe led in December 1917 or January 1918 to his devising the world's only absolutely unbreakable system, the one-time tape or pad. See Kahn, *The Codebreakers,* 397–400, 1044–1045.

37   Bazeries cylinder: NA, RG 165, Entry 65, 10020-192 (6).

37   "excellent work," "they have not": NA, RG 165, Entry 65, 10020-171, 23 March 1918.

37   State, stations, censorship: NA, RG 165, Entry 65, 10020-28; RG, 457 HCC, Box 793, Folder Instructions for the Interception of Messages between Points in Mexico and Central America; HOYC, Boxes 19, 20, 31.

37   navy abdicated: NA, RG 457, SRH-355, Appendix I, 3; SRH-029, 1; RG 38, ComNavSecGru 5750/87, 1918; RG 59, Entry 349, Box 200, Confidential File 117, 20 and 23 July 1918; RG 165, Entry 65, 10531-165 (7 February 1918), -182 (18 February 1918).

37   first target, 800, 28 January, "Advise when": CAHA 00011:1–10, 1008; "Historical Background of the Signal Security Agency," 2:97–99. I am indebted to Professor William F. Sater for the information about the Chilean submarines in New London (email, 21 June 2001).

38   Argentina, Brazil, Nicaragua, Cuba, Peru, Costa Rica, Ecuador, El Salvador: CAHA 00001, 00006, 00007, 00012, 00013; "Historical Background," 2:71–72, 96–102.

38   Norwegian code: CAHA 00013: 2272–2279.

38   Mexico: "Historical Background," 2:92; CAHA 00004:1210, 1222, 1374 ff., for some; NA, RG 165, Entry 65, 10531-143, -164, -181M, -194, -199, -200, for others.

39   G.2 A.6: Kahn, *The Codebreakers,* 333–339.

39   German intercepts: CAHA 00001 NA, RG 457, HCC, box 745; Mendelsohn, *Studies in German Diplomatic Codes,* 1.

39   German solutions: Mendelsohn, *Studies in German Diplomatic Codes,* 18–19; NA, RG 457, HCC, Box 1029, Signal Security Agency, "German Cryptographic Systems during the First World War" (Washington, 1945), 44; NA, RG 59, Entry 349, Box 3, Folder German Codes and Ciphers, 26 January 1918; David Kahn, "Edward Bell and His Zimmermann Telegram Memoranda," *Intelligence and National Security* 14 (autumn 1999): 143–159.

39   sixty-four times, "preliminary amount": NA, RG 59, Entry 349, Box 4, Folder German Loan to Mexico (Carranza), 13 January, 23 February [1918]; CAHA 00011:2995; Friedrich Katz telephone interview, 21 April 1995. Curiously, although this intercept was forwarded to the State Department under a covering letter of 22 November 1918 that says it has been "recently" solved, it was solved much earlier by the British and forwarded to State. See Entry 349, Box 4, Folder Gehrman Delmar, etc., Including Sabotage, 28 February 1918.

39   never mentioned: Katz, *The Secret War with Mexico,* 396, 407–408.

40   horses, identical: Mendelsohn, *Studies in German Diplomatic Codes,* 80, 71.

41   Waberski: *ABC,* 140–171; Harris and Sadler "The Witzke Affair"; Doerries, "Tätigkeit," 32, 38, 44; *NYT,* 22 November 1923, 8:3; 30 November 23, 2:4.

43   put aside: "Historical Background," 2:86.

43   Manly: University of Chicago Biographical Files, John M. Manly, Robert Morss Lovett, "John Matthews Manly: An Appreciation," David H. Stevens (also of MI-8), "Tribute to Manly," *University of Chicago Magazine* (November 1940), 17–18; University of Chicago Archives, David Stevens file, letter to Rosenthal, 16 August 1973.

43 "There was a": George C. Marshall Library, Friedman Collection, 811.1 (Manly's report on Waberski); "Historical Background" 2:86–88; U.S. Federal Records Center, Records of the Mixed Claims Commission, Volume 321, Exhibit 321 (transcript of Witzke's court-martial). I am grateful to Drs. Harris and Sadler for telling me of this transcript. After the war ended, President Woodrow Wilson commuted Witzke's sentence to life imprisonment. In 1923, his bravery in saving the lives of fellow inmates after a boiler explosion at Fort Leavenworth led to his repatriation. Back in Germany, he returned to the sea, and in 1932 he joined the Nazi Party as member number 1168089. During World War II, he served in the Kriegsmarine and worked as a businessman in Hamburg. From 1952 to 1953, he served as a member of the Hamburg parliament. He died 6 January 1962. Berlin Document Center; Frei- und Hansestadt Hamburg, Senat, Staatsarchiv, Handschriftensammlung, Bürgerschaftsmitglieder 1859–1959, No. 601. I am indebted to Dr. Reinhard Doerries for alerting me to the Hamburg documents.

44 *Dresden* sank: Another member of the crew, who also escaped from internment on the *Dresden,* was Lieutenant Wilhelm Canaris, head of the German military espionage organization, the Abwehr, during World War II.

45 25 February 1918: NA, RG 457, SRH-038, 11.

45 Yardley to visit: Ibid., 28; *ABC,* 207.

45 agency at largest: "Historical Background," 2:21.

45 Ritz, Comeraugh, Savoy: NA, RG 165, Entry 65, 10039-299.

45 "received no": *ABC,* 212.

46 War Office, "finishing": Ibid., 215–216. See also John Ferris, *The British Army and Signals Intelligence during the First World War* (Stround, Gloucestershire: Alan Sutton, 1992).

46 "stood next to": *ABC,* 217.

46 "anathema": NA, RG 59, Entry 349, Box 3, Folder German Codes and Ciphers, 5 and 8 April 1919.

46 refused admission, to France: *ABC,* 218, 220.

46 "worth four divisions": Ibid., 219.

46 Van Deman kicked over: Joan M. Jensen, *The Price of Vigilance* (Chicago: Rand McNally, 1968), 123–124; William J. Corson, *The Armies of Ignorance* (New York: Dial Press / James Wade, 1977), 62–63.

46 French repeated: *ABC,* 221–230; Givierge, "Etude historique," 699–700; Association des Réservistes du Chiffre et de la Sécurité d'Information, Archives, Painvin Papers, No. 1, Dossier Notes sur les travaux cryptographiques du Capitain Painvin, 9. Yardley seems not to have known that the Interior Ministry also solved diplomatic codes (Andrew, "Déchiffrement et diplomatie").

47 Spanish codes, "wouldn't have parted": NA, RG 59, Entry 349, Box 1, Folder Misc. Edward Bell Letters Received, 14 November and 5 December 1918; also Box 3, Folder German Codes and Ciphers, 21, 26, and 29 January, 7, 9, and 14 May, and 4 June 1919; and Folder 1.

47 Livesey, Childs: "Historical Background," 2:180.

47 Paris work, parties: University of Virginia, Special Collections Department, Childs Papers, Autobiography, 308, 309–317, 320–321, 330–332; Childs, *Let the Credit Go,* 41. I thank Donald and Susan Newhouse for examining 18, rue Gustave Zédé, for me.

47 French and British hadn't either: CAHA 00013:2471. See also Givierge, "Etude historique," and Alan Sharp, "Quelqu'un nous écoute: French Interpretation of German Telegraphic and Telephonic Communications during the Paris Peace Conference," *Intelligence and National Security* 3 (1988): 124–127.

47 press reports: CAHA 00002:2363 ff.

48 home via Italy: NA, RG 59, Entry 349, Box 198, Confidential File 83, 15 March 1919.

49 sailed from Genoa: NA, RG 457, SRH-038, 50, 51.

Chapter 7   Morning in New York

Page

50 10,735 messages: NA, RG 165, Entry 65, 10994-20, I.3.

50 50, 541: "Historical Background of the Signal Security Agency," 2:69–70. The estimate of fifty is mine. I calculated that the number of Mexican systems was thirteen and added that figure to the thirty-seven other systems listed.

50 "The chief value": NA, RG 165, 10994-20, II.

50 Britain, Germany, Italy: PRO, ADM 1/8637/55; Germany, Bundesarchiv-Militärarchiv, Faszikel 5708.II.9.3, Faszikel 5709.II.9.4; Cesare Amè, *Guerra segreta in Italia, 1940–1943* (Rome: Casini, 1954), 5–6, 8; Franco Maugeri, *From the Ashes of Defeat,* ed. Victor Rosen (New York: Reynal and Hitchcock, 1948), 31; Alvarez, "Left in the Dust," 389, 403.

51 "desirable," Fabyan, "at least": NA, RG 165, Entry 65, 10020-97.

51 navy: Ibid.; NA, RG 59, Entry 349, Box 3, Folder German Codes and Ciphers, 2 May 1919.

51 "I consider": NA, RG 165, Entry 65, 10039-299.

51 "should handle": NA, RG 165, Entry 65, 10020-97.

51 Harrison, Churchill: NA, RG 59, Entry 349, Box 200, Confidential File 121, 29 January 1919.

51 "Just at present": NA, RG 59, Entry 349, Box 3, Folder German Codes and Ciphers.

51 Burleson law: *U.S. Statutes at Large* 40:1017–1018. It was in effect under a congressional resolution of 16 July 1918 (*Statutes* 40:904) giving the president the power to assume control of wire communications during the war and under a presidential proclamation of 22 July 1918 (*Statutes,* vol. 40, part 2, pp. 1807–8), taking control and devolving this power on the postmaster general. For Burleson, see *Dictionary of American Biography,* supplement 2; *American National Biography.*

52 Yardley drafting: My assumption. The memorandum sounds like him.

52 "If it is": NA, RG 165, Entry 65, 10994-20, II.3, III, IV.

52 corollary information, "Therefore after," civilians, "Men and women," $100,000, salaries, two-thirds, funds: NA, RG 165, Entry 65, 10994-20; "Historical Background," 3:39.

53 $60,000, $40,000: NA, RG 457, HOYC, Box 99, Folder Yardley New York Correspondence 1919–1927, 4 May 1920; *ABC,* 240; "Historical Background," 3:50.

53 quarter of a percent, hundredth of a percent: U.S. Department of Commerce, Bureau of Foreign and Domestic Commerce, *Statistical Abstract of the United*

States, 1930. Table 189, "Expenditures of the Government" gives for 1922, a year by which the swollen wartime expenditures had abated, expenditures of $455 million for the War Department and $9.6 million for State.

53 16 May: NA, RG 165, Entry 65, 10994-20.

53 "OK," "Approved": Ibid.

53 $60,000: NA, RG 457, Box 99, Folder Yardley New York Correspondence 1919–1927, 4 May 1920; *ABC,* 240.

53 not District of Columbia: *U.S. Statutes at Large* 39:78, 40:770, 41:1224. U.S. Department of State, Office of the Historian, letter of 18 December 2000.

54 8 July 1919: NA, RG 457, SRH-038, 70.

54 Hazel quit: U.S. Office of Personnel Management, Official Personnel Folder, Hazel Yardley, 23 July 1919.

54 17 East 36th, 3 East 38th: "Historical Background," 3:46. Kahn, *The Codebreakers,* 355, errs in stating that the 38th Street town house was that of socialite T. Suffern Tailer. He never lived there.

55 P.O. Box, phones: David Kahn Collection, Livesey memoirs, 76; NA, RG 165, Entry 65, 10994-28, 3 October 1919.

55 women's fitting room: Kahn Collection, Yardley Talk before Los Angeles Athletic Club, August 1934.

55 personnel, salaries: "Historical Background," 3:49, 57–60; NA, RG 457, HCC, Box 777, Folder Origin of MI-8, 1919, 22 July 1919; Kahn Collection, Livesey memoirs, 75.

55 Edna Ramsaier: NSA, CCH, Edna Yardley and history, 1–2.

55 Yardley's $6,000: NA, RG 457, HCC, Box 777, Folder Origin of MI-8, 1919, 22 July 1919; *U.S. Statutes at Large* 41:1224.

55 4 June 1920: "Historical Background," 3:118.

55 lease sold, 141 East 37th, 1 July 1920: George C. Marshall Library, Friedman Collection, Item 840; NA, RG 457, HOYC, Box 99, Folder Yardley New York Correspondence 1919–1927, 4 May 1920; SRH-03, 73, 91.

57 Code Compiling Company: Kruh, "Tales of Yardley," 333, 334; Friedman Collection, Item 840.

57 Tanners' Council: Livesey in Annotated ABC, 250. Copy, bound with the *Universal Trade Code,* in the library of the National Cryptologic Museum.

57 "under the supervision": *Universal Trade Code* (New York: Code Compiling Company, 1921), iii; "Historical Background," 3:48.

57 honorable discharge, commission: NA, RG 457, SRH-038, 83, 86, 97.

57 challenge: *ABC,* 241; NA, RG 59, Entry 349, Box 3, Folder German Codes and Ciphers, 2 May 1919.

57 repeal of congressional resolution: *U.S. Statutes at Large* 41:157.

57 Mann-Elkins act: Formally, An Act to Create a Commerce Court, *U.S. Statutes at Large* 35:539. The relevant portions are at 545 and 553. The Transportation Act of 1920 slightly rewrote some definitions but left the prohibitions intact (*Statutes* 41:474). It was codified in the Code of Laws of the United States of America . . . in Force December 7, 1925 (*Statutes* 44:1650, 1662).

The United States never adhered to the International Telegraph Convention of St. Petersburg of 10–22 July 1875 (it is omitted from Charles I. Bevans, *Treaties and Other International Agreements of the United States of America, 1776–1949*

[GPO], vol. 1, *Multilateral, 1776–1917* [1968]). Its Article 2 states that its signatories "bind themselves to take all the necessary measures for the purpose of insuring the secrecy of the correspondence" (*League of Nations Treaty Series* 57:213). "Historical Background" 3:73–77, cites, as support for its view that the interception of cable traffic was illegal, statutes dealing with communications not by wire but by radio. These consisted of two treaties and two laws: the International Wireless Telegraph Convention of 1906, proclaimed for the United States on 25 May 1912, the International Radiotelegraph Convention of 1912, proclaimed for the United States 8 July 1913, the Act to Regulate Radio Communication of 13 August 1912, and the Act for the Regulation of Radio Communications of 23 February 1913 (respectively *U.S. Statutes at Large* 37:1570, 1584, 1602; 38:1710, 1721, 1740; 37:307; 44:1172). None of these applied to the cable messages with which Yardley was chiefly concerned.

Curiously, neither the 1925 codification of Title 47, on telegraphs, telephones, and radio (*Statutes* 44:1549–1555, which title does not include the Transportation Act), nor the laws up to 1921 granting telegraph companies the right to lay cable to foreign countries (*Statutes* 11:187, 13:340, 14:44 and 221, 15:10, 19:201 and 232, 22:371, based on a list in U.S. Congress, Senate, Committee on Interstate Commerce, *Cable-Landing Licenses,* Hearings before a Subcommittee . . . , 66th Congress, 3d Session [GPO, 1921], 251–253) required that messages be kept secret or permitted the government to examine messages.

58   "For fifty years": U.S. Congress, House of Representatives, Committee on Interstate and Foreign Commerce, *Cable-Landing Licenses,* Hearings . . . on S. 535 (GPO, 1921), 53.

58   Interception: NA, RG 457, HOYC, Box 99, Folder Yardley New York Correspondence 1919–1927; RG 59, Entry 349, Box 3, Folder German Codes and Ciphers, 2 May 1919; Yale University, Sterling Memorial Library, Manuscripts and Archives Division, Polk Papers, Group 656, Series I, Box 10, Folder 339, 23 and 27 March 1919; NSA, CCH, Edna Yardley oral history, 7–8, 60; Harvard University, Houghton Library, Castle diary, 23 December 1931; NA, RG 59, DSDF 894.727/22. Early on, at least, some Mexican messages were intercepted by radio. RG 457, HCC, Box 777, Folder History of Certain Radio Tractor Units, Folder Operations of the Field Units of the Radio Intelligence Service, Folder Operations of the Radio Intelligence Station at Houlton, and Folder Military Intelligence Division Control of Intercept Stations.

58   "The government can have": NA, RG 457, HOYC, Box 99, Folder Yardley New York Correspondence 1919–1927, 15 April 1920.

58   Postal Cable: Ibid., 22 April 1920.

58   Taff, Duncan: Ibid., 11 November and 6 December 1919, 22 and 24 April 1920.

58   "There are limits": Ibid., 21 November 1919, 23 April 1920.

58   Neville case: Ibid., 13 and 14 November 1919.

60   German codes: Ibid., 22 and 24 September 1919, 2 March 1920; "Historical Background," 3:125–129.

61   Spanish, Chilean, Mexican: NA, RG 457, HOYC, Box 99, Folder Yardley New York Correspondence 1919–1972, 24 and 29 September 1919, 17 May 1920; RG 59, Entry 349, Box 2, Folder Chilean Code, Folder German Codes and Ciphers; *FRUS, 1919,* 2:545.

61 "My plans": NA, RG 457, HOYC, Box 99, Folder Yardley New York Correspondence 1919–1927, 4 May 1920.

Chapter 8 Yardley's Triumph

Page

63 "characteristically": Library of Congress, Rare Book Room, D639.S7Y3, David H. Stevens, "Appendix," 396 (typescript pasted in).

63 "enough codes": "Historical Background of the Signal Security Agency," 3:64.

63 effective, fair, looked ahead: NSA, CCH, Edna Yardley oral history, 5, 41; NA, RG 165, Entry 65, 10039-299, Herbert S. Spencer, letter of 12 December 1940, and Ford, efficiency report.

63 conflict with Japan: E. S. Miller, *War Plan Orange,* 3; Walter LaFeber, *The Clash* (New York: Norton, 1997); U.K. Foreign Office, *Documents on British Foreign Policy,* 1st series, 14 (London: Her Majesty's Stationery Office, 1966), 435. An excellent succinct explanation of Japan's likely belligerency.

64 "to the unraveling": *ABC,* 251.

64 MI-8 failed: Ibid., 250–252.

64 "a solution or my resignation": Ibid., 251.

64 German and British cryptanalysts: Schauffler, "Erinnerungen eines Kryptologen," 11–13; Denniston, "The Government Code and Cypher School," 55–56. In 1904–5 and later, both the Russians and their allies, the French, solved Japanese diplomatic messages, some of them in English, the language of much Japanese diplomacy. Inaba, "Franco-Russian Intelligence Collaboration"; Givierge, "Au service du chiffre," 21; Andrew, "Déchiffrement et diplomatie." The French were intercepting coded Japanese telegrams at the time of the Washington disarmament conference (Archives Nationales, F^{90} 13710), but I have not seen any Japanese solutions in the archives of the Foreign Affairs ministry. Tatiana A. Sobolyeva errs when she says, on page 334 of *Tainopis v istrii rossii* [Secret Writing in the History of Russia] (Moscow: Myezhdunarodnye Otnoshyeniya, 1994), that the Russians began to break Japanese cryptosystems only in 1927.

64 "most difficult," kana, count, group length: *ABC,* 252, 255–262. Schauffler disparages Yardley's remark, saying that "So simple a cipher method was naturally easy to solve even without a compromise." He later became the Japanese specialist in the German Foreign Office cryptanalytical agency.

65 "a special talent": NA, RG 165, M-1194, Roll 134, s.v. Livesey.

65 Livesey, BA IL LY, dictionary: Livesey memoirs, 74–78, quoted in Kahn, *The Codebreakers,* George C. Marshall Library, Friedman Collection, annotated *ABC,* 260.

65 Japanese consulate: *ABC,* 264. Four years later, the U.S. Navy stole into that consulate and photographed a Japanese naval code. Timothy J. Nenninger, "From the Archives: Japanese Codebook Find," *Cryptologia* 17 (July 1993): 283–284.

65 like Dreyfus affair: *ABC,* 266–268; "Historical Background," 3:89–92; Kahn, *The Codebreakers,* 259–261.

65 "And if it," people laughed, encouraging letters, "The damned stuff": "Historical Background," 3:94; *ABC,* 263–266.

66 "had worked so long": *ABC,* 268.

66 Livesey distracted, did the same: Friedman Collection, annotated, 263, 268, saying, "We've all been there."

66 AS FY OK: *ABC,* 270; NA, RG 457, HOYC, Box 99, Folder Yardley New York Correspondence 1919–1927, 15 December 1921. Interestingly, Schauffler, in Germany, also began his Japanese solution in late 1919 by assuming that AS FY OK stood for *owari.*

66 *beikoku, eikoku:* Friedman Collection, annotated, 270.

66 "one night": *ABC,* 269. Yardley gives additional details in less dramatic but more detailed form in NA, RG 457, HOYC, Box 99, Folder Yardley New York Correspondence 1919–1927, 9 December 1919.

67 1 a.m. 13 December 1919: "Historical Background," 3:93.

67 Livesey's *kuan, jooya:* Friedman Collection, annotated *ABC,* 272.

67 "like a world champion": Livesey memoirs quoted in a letter 7 August 1963 from his widow, Vera Livesey.

67 reported success, "I may": "Historical Background," 3:93, 96.

67 Willson: Personal Papers from National Archives and Records Administration, National Personnel Records Center, obtained by Jennifer Wilcox, National Cryptologic Museum staff.

67 Ja: *ABC,* 279.

67 five hundred letters: *ABC,* 274.

67 Correll: NA, RG 457, HOYC, Box 99, Folder Yardley New York Correspondence 1919–1927, 9 and 18 December 1919; Archives of the Episcopal Church; *NYT,* 18 June 1926, 23:5; *Spirit of Missions* 91 (July 1926): 446; 92 (August 1926):514; *ABC,* 274–279; Friedman Collection, "The Annotated *ABC,*" 277.

68 "with a great deal," "the most remarkable," "eventually surpass": NA, RG 457, HOYC, Box 99, Folder Yardley New York Correspondence 1919–1927, 28 February and 1 March 1920.

68 Jb: Friedman Collection, "The Annotated *ABC,*" 279.

68 dispatch of 16 February, about a $7 million loan: NA, RG 457, HOYC, Box 99, Folder Yardley New York Correspondence 1919–1927, 1 March 1920.

68 Jc, Je: Ibid., 4 May 1920; "Historical Background," 3:97, 98, though this study errs in calling Je a kana code.

68 Japanese codes: "Japanese Codes and Ciphers," a post–World War II list of those solved, "Japanese Diplomatic Cryptanalysis," and a historical retrospective, appear in NA, RG 457, HOYC, Box 2, Folder General Correspondence.

68 Jg: More than half of what proved to be its approximately seven hundred code elements were three-letter codegroups in the basically two-letter code. But the three-letter codegroups all turned out to begin with V (as VAB, VAC, . . . VUZ, etc.), W, X, Y, or Z, so once they were detected the decoding clerks could separate them out without difficulty. CAHA 00013:10025-6; "Historical Background," 3:100.

69 "All of the material," Ji, Jh: "Historical Background," 3:101–102; CAHA 00013:1036. The date of this fairly complete reconstruction is 25 September 1922.

69 18 July 1921: "Historical Background," 3:102.

71 "24 different small codes": The supposition about what Yardley meant by twenty-

four small codes is mine, based on an examination of Jp in CAHA 00013:1040–1042. In *ABC,* 290, Yardley states that the difficulty in solving Jp was caused by the fact that "three-letter codewords were interspersed throughout the messages." He is confusing Jp with Jg (CAHA 00013:1025–1026). Jp does not have three-letter codewords.

71   two- and four-letter codewords: Examples range from the Renaissance to the Cold War. See Aloys Meister, *Die Geheimschrift im Dienste der Päpstlichen Kurie* (Paderborn: Schöningh, 1906), 71, and David Kahn, *Kahn on Codes* (New York: Macmillan, 1983), 150–151. Some Renaissance systems, however, incorporate the ambiguity of Jp, as Meister (331) demonstrates.

71   solution of Jp, 23 August: CAHA 00013:1040–1042; "Historical Background," 3:101–103.

Chapter 9   The Fruits of His Victory

Page

72   Washington conference: Buckley, *The United States and the Washington Conference;* Goldstein and Maurer, eds., *The Washington Conference;* Asada, "Japan and the United States"; William Reynolds Braisted, *The United States Navy in the Pacific, 1909–1922* (Austin: University of Texas Press, 1971); Roger Dingman, *Power in the Pacific: The Origins of Naval Arms Limitations, 1914–1922* (Chicago: University of Chicago Press, 1976).

73   venues: Buckley, *The United States and the Washington Conference,* 35, 36, 37; Pusey, *Charles Evans Hughes,* 466.

73   intelligence advantage: Britain's codebreaking agency, the Government Code and Cypher School, indeed produced fewer and less significant solutions during the conference than Yardley's agency. PRO, HW 12/28, /29, /30, /31, /32.

73   Congress of Vienna: August Fournier, *Die Geheimpolizei auf dem Wiener Kongreß: Eine Auswahl aus ihren Papieren* (1913); Harald Hubatschke, "Die amtliche Organisation der geheimen Briefüberwachung und des diplomatischen Chiffrendienstes in Österreich (Von den Anfängen bis etwa 1870)," *Mitteilungen des Instituts für Österreichische Geschichtsforschung* 83 (1975): 352–413 at 372–373.

73   Continental Memorial Hall: On 17th Street between B and D Streets, this is the headquarters of the Daughters of the American Revolution.

73   Hughes's address: *FRUS, 1922,* 1:53–61; *NYT,* 12 November 1921, 1:1–8; 13 November 1921, 1:1–8.

73   "slightly staggered," "turned," "straight ahead": Diary of Theodore Roosevelt Jr., quoted in Erik Goldstein, "The Evolution of British Diplomatic Strategy for the Washington Conference," in Goldstein and Maurer, eds., *The Washington Conference,* 27, and in Asada, "Japan and the United States," 229.

74   10:7, 10:6: I am indebted to Edward S. Miller for this insight, pointed out in his *War Plan Orange,* 32. The Lanchester equation, sometimes called the N^2 law, uses the square of the number of guns. I have simplified that to the square of the number of ships. Lanchester's article is reprinted in James R. Newman, ed., *The World of Mathematics* (New York: Simon and Schuster, 1956), 4:2138–2157.

David C. Evans and Mark R. Peattie, *Kaigun: Strategy, Tactics, and Technology in the Imperial Japanese Navy, 1887–1941* (Annapolis: U.S. Naval Institute Press, 1997), 143, describe how Japan evolved the 10:7 ratio in 1907–9.

74 British communication security: PRO, FO 371/5620.

75 1272 = experts, four two-part codes: CAHA 00004:3390, 66.

75 couriers: NSA, CCH, Edna Yardley oral history, 5.

75 typists decoded: Ibid., 24–25; George C. Marshall Library, Friedman Collection, annotated *ABC,* 318.

75 fair copies, "I can't play golf either": NSA, CCH, Edna Yardley oral history, 25, 11, 2.

75 day received, longer, volume: Examination of intercepts in CAHA 00015:3822 ff.

75 Hurley, couriers, Lay: Harvard University, Houghton Library, Castle diary, 21 February 1933; Farago, *The Broken Seal,* 27; NSA, CCH, Edna Yardley oral history, 5; U.S. Department of State, Personnel Files, Hurley, Lay; NA, RG 457, HOYC, Box 99, Folder Yardley New York Correspondence 1919–1927, 28 February 1930.

75 no markings: NSA, CCH, Edna Yardley oral history, 14.

76 few to Hughes, too busy: Castle diary, 20 February 1933; Pusey, *Charles Evans Hughes,* 475.

76 Japanese report of meeting: CAHA 00015:3836–7.

76 auditor mentality, $30,000: CAHA 00014:413, 00014:559; 00015:3937.

76 "very difficult," "almost never," "members": Castle diary, 21 February 1933. The remark makes no sense to me. The messages are perfectly clear. Many of the intercepts bear the initial "M"—probably for John V. A. MacMurray, head of the Far Eastern Division—or "WH," for William Hurley.

76 Japan resolute, change: *NYT,* 25 November 1921, 3:3–4; 26 November 1921, 1:5–6; 28 November 1921, 1:7. Tomosaburo Kato is not to be confused with Kanji Kato, also an admiral but a staunch supporter of 10:7.

76 "the ratio of": CAHA 00015:3862; also in *ABC,* 308.

77 front-paging, "Crisis": *NYT,* 29 November 1921, 1:5–8; 30 November 1921, 1:6–8.

77 2 December: *FRUS, 1921,* 1:76, 82.

77 telegram of 28 November: Description of the message from the photograph facing p. 312 in *ABC.* Because the solved plaintext is lighter than the codetext, I suspect it may have been typed in red. *ABC,* 312, says the telegram was solved on 28 November. This makes the Cipher Bureau look more efficient than it was, for it suggests that, at the 2 December meeting of Hughes, Kato, and the Balfour, Hughes already had this intercept, which revealed that Kato would yield on the 10:7 ratio in return for an agreement on Pacific fortifications. In fact, CAHA 00015:3935 shows that the message was not solved until 2 December. It probably was not in Hughes's hands until the next day. My text reflects this.

79 "the most important," "first sign," "shows," "With this information": *ABC,* 312, 313.

79 "made it clear," "stiffened": MacMurray in Castle diary, 21 February 1933.

79 "they put pressure," "even British," "appear to desire": CAHA 00015:3994-5 (solved 4 December), 4010, 4012 (solved 6 December), 4315 (solved 10 December).

79   Japan capitulated: The cablegram of 10 December, J6507, that instructed Kato
      "to accept the ratio proposed by the United States" was solved on 14 December
      (CAHA 00015:4409, cited in *ABC,* 317), after Kato's agreement with the 10:6
      ratio on 12 December. It therefore had no effect on the negotiations. Kato agreed:
      FRUS, 1921, 1:90–91.

79   bonuses: Kahn, *The Codebreakers,* 164; CAHA 00011:2777ff. The precise
      amount of each person's bonus was 2.5 percent of annual salary.

80   "by personal regards": *ABC,* 317.

80   save hundreds of millions: Hyde, "Charles Evans Hughes," 247.

Chapter 10   The Busy Suburbanite

Page

81   nightmares: *ABC,* 318, 320–321.

81   "daily contact": CAHA 00011:2792-3, 24 May 1922.

82   "out of a practically": U.S. War Department, General Orders No. 56, 30
      December 1922, 43.

82   Weeks: *Dictionary of American Biography.* He was the Weeks of the Hornblower
      and Weeks investment firm.

82   "the wink": *ABC,* 323; NA, RG 457, SRH-038, 100–102.

82   War, State, military intelligence budgets: U.S. Department of Commerce, Bureau
      of Foreign and Domestic Commerce, *Statistical Abstract of the United States, 1930,*
      table 189, "Expenditures of the Government"; Bidwell, *History of the Military
      Intelligence Division,* 258 and note p. 260.

82   lost 30 percent: "Historical Background of the Signal Security Agency," 3:71.

83   Bogel as "a nice old duck": U.S. Naval Institute, Dyer oral history, 76–77.

83   bonuses, another clerk: "Historical Background," 3:69–71. Fifteen received the
      bonus after the Washington conference. Victor Weiskopf was transferred from the
      Justice Department to the War Department.

83   remaining staff: NSA, CCH, Edna Yardley oral history, 23–24.

83   stamp business: Herman Herst interview.

83   Wilson, O'Connor, Dillon, Hackenberg: NA, RG 457, SRH-038, 120.

83   burglary, 52 Vanderbilt: University of Pennsylvania, Van Pelt Library,
      Mendelsohn Collection, annotated *ABC,* 331.

83   raise, housing allowance: "Historical Background," 3:70–73; U.S. *Statutes at
      Large* 42:598 for salary of undersecretary of state.

83   move to suburbia: *Jackson Heights News,* Christmas 1924, 13:1, lists Yardley
      among new neighbors of the past twelve months.

84   Britain: 10 and 11 Geo. 5 (23 December 1920), 495; Ferris, "Whitehall's Black
      Chamber," 63–64, 69; Denniston, "The Government Code and Cypher School,"
      64–66. The results of this interception are in PRO HW/12. The British lied to
      the United States about doing this (*FRUS, 1920,* 1:142) but American cable
      officials suspected it (U.S. Congress, Senate, Committee on Interstate Commerce,
      Cable-Landing Licenses, 63d Congress, 3d Session, 129–131, 182–187, 196–
      197, 317–318; U.S. Congress, House of Representatives, Committee on
      Interstate and Foreign Commerce, *Cable-Landing Licenses,* 67th Congress, 1st
      Session, 53–55).

84 Germany: Paschke, "Das Chiffrier- und Fermeldewesen," 22; Schauffler, "Erinnerungen eines Kryptologen," 9; Weimar Constitution, Article 117.

84 France: The French *Bulletin des lois* (1850): 685–687, "Loi sur la correspondance télégraphique privée," no. 2567 (3 July, 18 and 29 November 1850), states, in §3, that "The director of telegraphs may, in the interest of public order and of good morals, refuse to transmit dispatches." I am grateful to Colonel André Cattieuw for help in this matter. Givierge, "Au service du chiffre," 21, indicates that this law was used to legalize the interception of cipher messages. Yet Bernard Warusfel, *Contre-espionnage et protection du secret: Histoire, droit et organisation de la sécurité nationale en France* (n.p.: La Vauzelle, 2000), 18, states that the cryptanalytic services "appear never to have had a public law" authorizing their work.

84 bribed employees: NA, RG 457, SRH-048, 139; NSA, CCH, Edna Yardley oral history, 7–9; Harvard University, Houghton Library, Castle diary, 23 December 1931, quoting Friedman; *ABC,* 368–369; RG 59, DSDF 894.727/22, 18 March 1931, a letter of Yardley's; David Kahn Collection, MS of ABC, 19:4.

84 what was he doing: NA, RG 38, Entry CNSG Library, Box 104, Folder COMNAVSECGRU, History of Comint Operations 1917-1950, 14–16, gives a partially accurate report about Yardley's work.

84 Mexico, Nicaragua, Peru: *ABC,* 351–356.

84 China: CAHA 00011:2777; Hannah, "The Many Lives of Herbert O. Yardley," 9.

84 "We have temporarily," "very little success," "We have only": CAHA 00004, Signal Security Agency, "French Codes Studied by MI-8 in 1921–23," 3.

85 "The City of Tokio": CAHA 00013:1575–1601.

85 French press reports: CAHA 00013:1602, 439, 440.

85 "There were practically," Jn, Jq, Jr: NA, RG 457, HOYC, Box 56, Folder Memoranda and Letters Concerning H. O. Yardley 1919–1940, 31 January 1923, and Box 2, Folder General Correspondence, "Japanese Codes and Ciphers"; "Historical Background," 3:109–111.

86 Edna's solutions, "brain was expanding": NSA, CCH, Edna Yardley oral history, 25–26; NA, RG 457, HOYC, Box 99, Folder Yardley New York Correspondence 1919–1927, 22 September 1924, 24 January 1925, and undated later letter; "Historical Background," 3:113, 114.

86 Kowalewski: Waclaw Jedrzejewicz interview; *Polski Slownik Biograficzny,* trans. Christopher Kasparek; Hanyok, "Before Enigma," Mieczyslaw Sciezynski, *Radjotelegrafja: Jako Zrodlo Wiadowmosci o Nieprozyjacielu* [Radiotelegraphy as a Source of Intelligence on the Enemy] (Przemysl: Headquarters of Corps X, 1928), 16–25, trans. Christopher Kasparek. The cryptanalysis seems to have been neither omniscient nor decisive, however: the Polish commander, Marshal Joseph Pilsudski, complained that at a critical moment he regretted not having "a glimpse of the secret plan of campaign" of his Russian enemy (Viscount d'Abernon, *The Eighteenth Decisive Battle of the World: Warsaw, 1920* [London: Hodder and Stoughton, 1931], 133). The Stalin telegram is in the Pilsudski Institute, New York. On Kowalewski's instruction, see Takahashi, "A Case Study: Japanese Intelligence Estimates of China and the Chinese, 1931–1945," 204; Chapman, "The Polish Labyrinth and the Soviet Maze," 68; *ABC,* 280–282. Yardley says

that this system was instituted by the Polish cryptologist before the Washington conference. But Kowalewski did not go to Japan until almost a year after the conference ended.

87   in a "Bulletin": "Historical Background," 3:84–85.

87   Hurley: U.S. Department of State, Personnel File.

87   Lane: Ibid.; *American National Biography;* NA, RG 457, HOYC, Box 99, Folder Yardley New York Correspondence 1919–1927, 1 October 1924. During the time he served as liaison, he was assistant to Undersecretary Joseph Grew, who handled the Cipher Bureau for State.

88   Jackson Heights: Daniel Karatzas, *Jackson Heights: A Garden in the City* (n.p., 1990), 29, 32, 38, 40, 45, 54, 60, 72, 79, 84, 85, 91–92, 98, 100–101; Robert A. M. Stern, Gregory Gilmartin, and Thomas Mellins, *New York, 1920: Architecture and Urbanism between the Two World Wars* (New York: Rizzoli, 1987), 479, 481–482.

88   addresses in Jackson Heights: NA, RG 165, Entry 65, 10039-299, 28 August 1928, 7 March 1929.

89   golf practicing, temper: CAHA 00002:107–108, Don Herold letter; Fred Jewell interview.

89   golf tournaments: *Jackson Heights News,* 23 May, 20 June 1924; 22, 29 May, 19, 26 June, 31 July, 7, 14, 21, 28 August, 4, 18 September, 23 October 1925; 18 June, 26 August 1926. Yardley is not mentioned as golfing in any earlier or later issues than those cited.

89   winter carnival, Koukols: *Jackson Heights News,* 23 January 1925; 11 May 1928; 15 March 1929.

89   "Twenty-foot building lots," real-estate work: HOYOPF, 1 December 1948. Further proof of his real-estate work comes indirectly in a letter of Nat Willis of Willis and Company real estate, who said, "I never could understand why you rushed to Washington so often." B-M, 24 July 1931.

90   hour a day: Harvard University, Houghton Library, Castle diary, citing Friedman, 23 December 1931. Livesey, in Annotated ABC, 273, says that after the Japanese solution Yardley "lived the life of Reilly, turning his attention to his private fortunes."

90   dealt in land: City of New York, Borough of Queens, Department of Finance, Office of the City Register, Deed-Liber Books and Land Block Books, 2811:107641, 2813:109014, 2960:115329, 3065:67469, -70, -71, -79, 3079:81877, 3080:83147, -48, 3103:105675, 3125:127536, -37, 3145:11937, 3256:117803, 3323:58645.

90    $5,000, profiting: Castle diary, citing Friedman, 23 December 1931.

91   Bulletin every few days: "Historical Background," 3:145; Friedman, "A Short History of the Signal Intelligence Service," 266.

91   intercepts hard to get: Friedman, "A Short History," 265.

91   Friedman trying to intercept: NA, RG 457, HCC, Box 781, Intercept/Crypto Correspondence 1927-1941, 27 April 1929.

91   "By the end": Paschke, "Das Chiffrier- und Fermeldewesen," 29. By "range of cryptographic elements" he means the size of a code or the period and number of cipher alphabets of a cipher machine.

91 Great Britain, Germany: Ferris, "Whitehall's Black Chamber," and Chapman, "No Final Solution: A Survey of the Cryptanalytical Capabilities of German Military Intelligence Agencies, 1926–35." Both studies are first-rate.

91 worldwide shift: Recognized in 1927 by Friedman. NA, RG 38, Entry CNSG Library, Box 14, Folder Army-Navy Collaboration in Sigint (6 of 6), 20 May 1927.

91 "sixteenth-century codes": *ABC,* 358–366. The criticism was expressed to Leland Harrison, by then an assistant secretary of state.

91 "When it came": Kahn, *The Codebreakers,* 371.

93 Friedman reconstructed the settings: His work was printed later in William F. Friedman, *Analysis of a Mechanico-Electrical Cryptograph* (GPO), part 1 (1934), part 2 (1935).

93 *Elements of Cryptanalysis:* The superiority of Friedman's taxonomy and nomenclature may be seen clearly by comparing it with such contemporary works as Marcel Givierge's solid *Cours de cryptographie* (1925) and Andreas Figl's "Systeme des dechiffrierens" (1926). The latter exists only in manuscript and in proof.

93 mathematicians: Schauffler, "Erinnerungen eines Kryptologen," 10; Wladyslaw Kozaczuk, *Geheimoperation Wicher,* trans. Theodor Fuchs (Koblenz: Bernard und Graefe, 1989), 24–25; "Historical Background," 3:203.

93 Hollerith machines: Geoffrey D. Austrian, *Herman Hollerith: Forgotten Giant of Information Processing* (New York: Columbia University Press, 1982), 51. Germany may also have had some in the 1920s (Schauffler, "Erinnerungen eines Kryptologen," 11). Charles J. Bashe et al., *IBM's Early Computers* (Cambridge, MIT Press, 1986), provides technical details.

93 Hooper: Burke, *Information and Secrecy,* 382. Navy cryptanalysts began using such machines in 1931 and Friedman in 1934, so they perhaps first dreamed of using them while Yardley was not.

Chapter 11　End of a Dream

Page

94 Albright work, responses: NA, RG 165, Entry 65, 10039-299, 24 March 1931; RG 457, HCC, Box 777, Folder Correspondence re Permanent Organization for Cipher Work, 18 March and 4 April 1929; NSA, CCH, Rowlett oral history, 206. I cannot find Albright's own memorandum.

95 "Things are moving": George C. Marshall Library; Friedman Collection, Friedman to Yardley, 23 April 1929.

95 Changes No. 1: "Historical Background of the Signal Security Agency," 3:182.

95 cryptology "bible": NA, RG 165, Entry 65, 10039-299, 27 May 1929.

96 new parley: *ABC,* 368–369.

96 Childs: Childs, *Foreign Service Farewell,* 5.

96 "take full advantage," "My plan," "The newspapers": David Kahn Collection, MS of ABC, 20:2–4. This has material not in the printed book. With minor excisions, the Hoover quotes are accurate. *Address of President Hoover at the Annual Luncheon of the Associated Press at New York City, April 22 1929* (GPO, 1929), 2, 4–5.

97   "before a galaxy": Yale University, Sterling Memorial Library, Stimson diary, 158.

97   "moral," "He is never," "there will be," "the most profound": Quoted in Kruh, "Stimson," 71, 69.

97   Admiralty: John Ferris, "The Last Decade of British Maritime Supremacy," in *Far-Flung Lines,* ed. Greg Kennedy and Keith Nelson (London: Frank Cass, 1997), 162.

97   started his secretaryship: Stimson, diary 158–159, 162; Morison, *Turmoil and Tradition,* 303.

97   both worked: 12458, NA, RG 165, 2 June 1917. Both are also listed in "History of the Military Intelligence Division," Box 22, Biographical Record.

97   June: This is my estimate. Stimson himself said two years later "In the summer of 1929" (Stimson diary, 1 June 1931). An exact date cannot be fixed because Stimson was too busy during his first year and a half in office to make daily diary entries. Stimson diary, 10: "Memorandum of events since becoming Secretary of State. Dictated Aug. 28, 1920." The date of early May given by Friedman (in Kruh, "Stimson," 68) seems too early in view of Yardley's tranquillity in correspondence to Friedman at the end of May.

97   "a series," "to acquaint": *ABC,* 369.

97   exploded: Friedman, "A Short History of the Signal Intelligence Service," 268.

98   "The chief lesson": Morison, *Turmoil and Tradition,* 639.

98   "We will do better": Quoted in Kruh, "Stimson," 70, 81. These quotes are from the transcript of Stimson's replies to McGeorge Bundy's questions in preparation for Bundy's writing Stimson's memoirs.

98   Cotton: *American National Biography.*

98   "highly unethical": Friedman, "A Short History," 268.

98   "If we have to do it": Quoted in Kruh, "Stimson," 81, 79. Stimson contradicts himself at one point when he says that the results of military codebreaking "would have to be used by the State Department people" (81). His experience as secretary of war in World War II, when State used codebreaking results, may have caused this.

98   "The ambassador is," "absolute freedom," "are the only": Ibid., 70, 81. Stimson was correct in believing that diplomatic immunity gave envoys the right to communicate free from eavesdropping. See A. Miruss, *Das Europäische Gesandschaftrecht* (Leipzig: Engelmann, 1847), 1:169–170; Linda S. Frey and Marsha L. Frey, *The History of Diplomatic Immunity* (Columbus: Ohio State University Press, 1999), 247, 315. In 1930, a League of Nations committee ruled that under the 1875 St. Petersburg Telegraph Convention and the 1927 Washington Radiotelegraph Convention, both of which required carriers to keep messages secret, no government had the right to read telegrams that the league's committee on opium traffic wanted; League of Nations, *Official Journal* 11 (November 1930): 1547–1552, provides a brief legal history of these two prohibitions. Though Hugo Grotius, the father of international law, does not mention the immunities of diplomats or their correspondence in his works, the 1961 Vienna Convention on Diplomatic Relations, which codified long-standing rules, states, in Article 27, §2, that "The official correspondence of the mission shall be inviolable" (United Nations, *Treaty Series,* 500 [1965], 95–221). Of

course, nations had nevertheless for centuries copied and solved foreign messages with only occasional protests.

98   "Gentlemen do not": Stimson, diary 188.

98   Hoover: Herbert Hoover Presidential Library, Papers of Herbert Hoover, Post-Presidential Individuals Series, Truman Smith, 7 August 1954. In an unpublished, untitled article submitted to the *Saturday Evening Post,* Yardley wrote that he "learned" that he had "done Stimson a great injustice" because in fact not Stimson but Hoover had closed the Cipher Bureau (NA, RG 457, HOYC, Box 3, Unpublished manuscript by HOY). New York Governor Thomas E. Dewey said in 1944 that Stimson had told him that he, Stimson, was acting on President Hoover's orders when he closed Yardley's office ("From the Archives: Statement for Record of Participation of Brig. Gen. Carter W. Clarke, GSC, in the Transmittal of Letters from Gen. George C. Marshall to Gov. Thomas E. Dewery the Latter Part of September 1944," *Cryptologia* 7 [April 1983]: 119–128 at 127–128; this is SRH-043). But Hoover's account is of his own action and Dewey's and Yardley's are secondhand. I think Hoover's statement is the more accurate and am thus basing my text on it. I believe that Dewey is misremembering and Yardley is repeating him.

98   stop payments: Stimson diary, 1 June 1931; NA, RG 457, SRH-038, 140. RG 165, Entry 65, 10039-299, 3, an army memorandum of 24 March 1931, states that "Stimson, soon after he came into office in March 1929, informally notified the Military Intelligence Division that he considered the activities of Mr. Yardley's office unethical, and that the Department of State would discontinue the subscription of funds for that purpose after September 1929." Some historians have argued that the impetus to close Yardley's Cipher Bureau came from the army. Louis Kruh quotes several such arguments in "Tales of Yardley" at 335, 336, 338, as does Farago, *The Broken Seal,* 63. The record, given here, shows that they err. The army had no effect on the closing of the Cipher Bureau.

98   $23,000: CAHA 00011:2963. An undated memo signed by Friedman gives the payroll as of October 1929 as $19,630. NA, RG 457, SRH-038, 120, a letter from Major Albright, confirms this and adds that rent was $250 a month, or $3,000 a year. Salaries and rent thus total $22,630. Allowing $780 for supplies, light, and miscellaneous (petty cash on hand on 17 July 1929 was $15), $23,000 a year is a reasonable total. Albright says that when outside support—State's contribution—ceases, the communications branch will make available to the military intelligence division $833.33 a month, "which amounts to the full $10,000 per year." The remaining $13,000 presumably came from State.

99   compromised: NA, RG 457, SRH-038, 120; Kruh, "Tales of Yardley," 338.

99   six on payroll: NA, RG 457, HCC, Box 777, Folder Data on Personnel Assigned to the Military Intelligence Division 1919–1931, 17 July 1919; CAHA 00011:2963.

100   to train, not solve: NA, RG 457, SRH-038, 121–123.

100   three clerks: Kruh, "Tales of Yardley," 339; Hannah, "The Many Lives of Yardley," 10.

100   Yardley resigned: NA, RG 457, SRH-038, 128, 129.

100   "be offered": NA, RG 457, HCC, Box 777, Folder Data on Personnel Assigned to

the Military Intelligence Division 1929–1937, memorandum attached to letter dated 17 July 1929.

100 $3,750: Hannah, "The Many Lives of Yardley," 10. NA, RG 165, Entry 65, 10039-299, says Yardley had been getting $625 and "the highest the Chief Signal Officer would offer was $300 per month."

100 $230,404, $98,808.49: NA, RG 59, DSDF, 894.727/10.

101 less than one one-hundredth, less than half a penny: U.S. Department of Commerce, Bureau of Foreign and Domestic Commerce, *Statistical Abstract of the United States, 1930,* table 189, "Expenditures of the Government." I rounded 1921 to 1929 State Department expenditures to $114.5 million and War Department expenditures to $3.3 billion (counting 1921 as the same as 1922 to eliminate the overflow from World War I), for a total of $3.4 billion. I put the population at 110 million.

101 Honduran, Nicaraguan, Mexican: No evidence exists for any Cipher Bureau input into these.

101 Tacna-Arica: *ABC,* 351–356, reports the solution of a Peruvian cryptogram dealing with the Tacna-Arica dispute and CAHA 00015:3766–3793 discusses the solution of that message and its code.

101 "A thief is a thief": Martin Luther, *Werke: Kritische Gesamtausgabe* (Weimar: Hermann Böhlaus Nachfolger), 30:2 (1909), 29 ("Von heimlichen und gestohlenen Briefen").

102 no qualms: PRO, ADM 1/8637, 25 April 1921.

102 America's mission: Ernest Lee Tuveson, *Redeemer Nation: The Idea of America's Millennial Role* (Chicago: University of Chicago Press, 1968). Also Secvan Bercovitch, *The American Jeremiad* (Madison: University of Wisconsin Press, 1978).

102 1792 law: U.S. *Statutes at Large* 1:236.

102 "moral obligation," "liberation and salvation," "condemned spying": Arthur S. Link, ed., *The Papers of Woodrow Wilson* (Princeton: Princeton University Press, 1990), 63, 512, 43.

102 "a military attaché," "with the knowledge": NA, RG 165, Entry 65, 10560-993, "A Guide for Military Attaches," the Director, Military Intelligence Division, 21 April 1921. Army War College lectures, Col. Stanley H. Ford, 27 November 1928.

102 Philadelphia *Public Ledger:* 5 October 1931.

102 *Boston Post:* 3 June 1931.

102 Hiram Johnson: *Congressional Record* (1933), 77:3177.

103 best thing: Castle diary, quoted in Kruh, "Stimson," 87.

Chapter 12   The Best-Seller

Page

104 no money, George C. Marshall Library, Friedman Collection, Item 840, McGrail to Friedman, 8 April 1931.

104 in-laws had died: NA, RG 165, Entry 65, 10039-299, 3.

104 in-laws' money: Carol Vandeventer of Worthington, a friend of Hazel Yardley's,

said that Hazel frequently told her Herbert had spent all the money her parents had left them.

104   applied to navy: NA, RG 457, SRH-038, 128.

104   "I gave up": University of Chicago Library, Manly Papers, Yardley to Manly, 29 August 1930.

104   "I'm not at all": Ibid.

104   Northwestern: Arnold, "Herbert O. Yardley, Gangbuster," 62–64.

105   his secret knowledge: Yardley claimed that "One of the great powers learning through their secret agents of the abandonment of cryptography in the United States, approached me with a view to my creating such a bureau and training their subjects in the science of cryptography." He said he was offered twice his American salary of $7,500 plus expenses for his family and himself. "Though I have felt no hesitancy in revealing the secrets of the American Black Chamber, I did not feel that I could accept such a position for my knowledge would have been turned against my native country" (B-M, 6 June 1931). I don't believe this story. Somebody might have approached him in a general way, but, in view of the fact that Yardley was broke and that several years later he did work as a cryptanalyst for two other countries, I think that if such an offer had been made and he felt that it would not harm the United States, he would have taken it.

105   religious story: Manly Papers, Manly to Yardley, 5 December 1924.

105   "I believe I can be": Manly Papers, Manly to director of Military Intelligence Division, 30 June 1927.

105   "covering use": NA, RG 165, M-1194, Roll 143, Manly, 7-8-27.

105   FPA in military intelligence: "History of the Military Intelligence Division," Box 22, Biographical Record. FPA was in MI-1 and MI-4 and then in G-2 in the American Expeditionary Forces. Sally Ashley, *F.P.A.: The Life and Times of Franklin Pierce Adams* (New York: Beaufort Books, 1986) does not mention Yardley.

105   Viking: Columbia University, Butler Library, Bye and Brown Collection (hereafter cited as Bye), Bye to Chambers, 27 February 1931.

105   Bye clients: *Publishers Weekly,* "Obituary Notes" (9 December 1957), 31.

105   "It is my job," Shively: B-M, 18 December 1930.

105   "Bye may have," "more impressed," "up to your eyes": B-M 20 December 1930, [24 December 1930], 26 December 1930.

106   Apartment 14: B-M, 11 February 1931.

106   "I sat for days": Manly Papers, undated letter, probably spring 1930.

106   "Congratulations," "I cannot tell": Bye, both 11 February 1931.

106   "I do not approve": Bye, 1 April 1931; Hannah, "The Many Lives of Yardley," 12.

107   "could not very well": George C. Marshall Library, Friedman Collection, Item 840, 6 April 1931.

107   Albright, Yardley promised, "There is no law": NA, RG 457, SRH-038, 140–141; RG 165, Entry 65, 10039-299.

107   "whoever, lawfully or unlawfully": U.S. *Statutes at Large* 40:218.

107   Ford, Lane, records: NA, RG 165, Entry 65, 10039-299, 24 March 1931.

107   army discussed, decided: Friedman Collection, Item 840, 6 April 1931; NA, RG 457, SRH-038, 141.

107   resignation accepted: Bye, 1 April 1931.

108   "various individuals": Ibid., 12 January 1931.

108   "there should be no": B-M, 8 January 1931.

108   $500, $50, $75, $250, $375: B-M, 23 February 1931; Bye, 25 February 1931.

108   "Sorry I could not": Bye, 21 February 1931.

108   Kersey counted: B-M, 19, 21, and 24 February 1931.

108   "is proof," changes in copy: B-M, 25 February 1931; *ABC,* 177, 345, 374, compared with MS of ABC in Kahn Collection.

109   "This has hurt the book": Manly Papers, undated.

109   "The story hasn't been hurt": Bye, 12 March 1931 and undated.

109   "quivering with excitement": Bye, 21 March 1931.

109   "a hell of a scene," $3.50: Bye, Yardley to Bye, Thursday.

111   early spring, Stout: Bye, Yardley to Bye, Saturday.

111   "Secret Inks": *Saturday Evening Post,* 4 April 1931, 3–5, 140–142, 145.

111   "Codes," "Ciphers": *Saturday Evening Post,* 18 April 1931, 16–17, 141, 142; 9 May 1931, 35, 144–146, 148, 149.

111   "I have enjoyed": B-M, 4 May 1931.

111   Stevens, Wilson: Manly Papers, undated.

111   "interest-holding": Friedman Collection, Item 840, 4 June 1931.

111   "I approve," "you might incur," "I myself": Manly Papers, 30 January, 24 July 1931; Friedman Collection, Item 840, 28 August 1931.

111   "You did a fine job": Friedman Collection, Item 840, 21 April 1931.

111   "I started to read," "I have never seen": Manly Papers.

112   "The articles were": Manly Papers, undated.

112   "It's too bad": B-M, 26 May 1931.

112   black chambers: See the dissertations by Hubatschke and by Karl de Leeuw, "Cryptology and Statecraft in the Dutch Republic" (Universiteit van Amsterdam, 2000), as well as Eugene Vaillé, *Le Cabinet noir* (Paris, 1950), and Kahn, *The Codebreakers,* 156–188 and references.

113   "the beautiful," "for whom": *ABC,* 90, 117; Schragmüller, "Aus dem deutschen Nachrichtendienst."

113   "Fräulein Doctor is more or less a myth": University of Southern California, Cinema-Television Library, Archives of the Performing Arts and Warner Bros. Collection, *Stamboul Quest,* Folder 2, Yardley memo, 24 April 1934. Yardley perhaps confused Schragmüller with Victorica in part through ignorance and laziness, in part because Richard Wilmer Rowan in his *Spy and CounterSpy* (1928), who tells about her work in Antwerp, describes her as blonde. The most solid information about her is her memoir; see Schragmüller, "Aus dem deutschen Nachrichtendienst."

113   Waberski cipher: Yardley gives a slightly clearer exposition of this complicated cipher in a letter to Friedman in NA, RG 457, HCC, Box 775, Folder Lawther Witzke.

115   Nolan: See James J. Cooke, *Pershing and His Generals* (Westport, Ct.: Praeger, 1997), 95–105. Of course, breaking the codes of the Holy See did not faze other nations. See, for example, Alvarez, "Left in the Dust," 389–391, and Kahn, "Nothing Sacred: The Allied Solution of Vatican Codes in World War II," 217–

220, in *Gesellschaft und Diplomatie im transatlantischen Kontext: Festschrift für Reinhard R. Doerries zum 65. Geburtstag.* Michael Wala, ed. (Stuttgart: Franz Steiner Verlag, 1999).

116   "bunk," "hooey," "To write": Manly Papers, Yardley to Manly, 30 April 1931.
117   Mendelsohn review: Friedman Collection, Item 840.

Chapter 13   The Critics, the Effects

Page
121   front-paged: B-M, Hepburn letter, undated.
121   probed beyond: *New York Times,* 2 June 1931, 18:3; *New York Herald Tribune,* 2 June 1931, 21:5; *Chicago Daily Tribune,* 2 June 1931, A15; *Evening Star,* 3 June 1931, 1:4; *Washington Herald,* 7 June 1931, 7:1.
122   Hanson: *New York World-Telegram,* 1 June 1931, 23:1.
122   Gannett: *New York Herald Tribune,* 2 June 1931, 21:5–6.
122   *Philadelphia Ledger:* B-M, collection of quotes for publicity.
122   *New York Times Book Review,* 14 June 1931, 9.
122   *Saturday Review of Literature: Book Review Digest* (1931), 1173.
123   Morley, White: B-M, collection of quotes for publicity.
123   satire: "J. R. to Major H.O.Y.," in Corey Ford [alias John Riddell], *In the Worst Possible Taste* (New York: Charles Scribner's Sons, 1932), 68–83.
123   "amazing bunch of clippings": B-M, 6 June 1931.
123   advertisements, third printing, sales bulletins: B-M.
123   displays: George C. Marshall Library, Friedman Collection, McGrail to Friedman, 29 June 1931.
123   7,456 copies, $4,736.89: B-M, Chambers to Bye, 18 June 1931; B-M, Author's File, 20 August 1931.
123   Mail, cryptograms: B-M, 10 August 1931, undated to Dear Chambers; University of Chicago Library, Manly Papers, 30 April 1931.
123   Mark Ryan: B-M, 9 June 1931; U.S. Department of State, *Register, 21 October 1915,* 20, shows Ryan and Yardley next to one another in a listing by seniority.
125   "The more he talks": Columbia University, Butler Library, Bye and Brown Collection (hereafter cited as Bye, Yardley to Bye, Saturday [spring 1931].
125   "Yardley is crazy," "I trust": B-M, Dear Andy, 10 June 1931.
125   "betrays government secrets": *New York Evening Post,* 15 June 1931, 12.
125   strengthen its restraint: *Brooklyn Daily Eagle,* 2 June 1931, 20.
125   "We do not believe": *Boston Post,* 3 June 1931, 14.
125   *Japanese American:* NA, RG 457, SRH-038, 158–163.
125   "This fine gesture": Quoted in Miller, *Spying for America,* 213.
126   "The book is": NA, RG 457, SRH-038, 151–153.
126   "I cannot protest": Ibid., 149.
126   "dishonorable": Friedman Collection, Item 840, 17 October 1931.
126   "without question," "represents only": *ABC,* 43, 45.
126   Barnes: Twelve years older than Yardley, Barnes had studied at Georgetown University, had clerked in the Office of the Chief Clerk and in the Consular Bureau, and had represented State on the General Supply Committee. He served nineteen months in the London embassy, returning in June 1916. He never

served as a code clerk. I don't know why he was chosen for the code-production job. U.S. Department of State, *Register,* annual volumes from 1911 to 1917.

126 "did a very creditable": Friedman Collection, Item 840, 29 April 1931. Friedman first made the charge after the articles appeared in the *Post* and returned to it after the *ABC* was published.

126 "My best recollection," Ludendorff: Ibid., 3 June and 19 September 1931.

128 "every one," "he put it on": Manly Papers, letter to Moorman, 16 May 1931, copy to Manly. Childs's report is reproduced in William F. Friedman, *American Army Field Codes in the American Expeditionary Forces during the First World War,* War Department (GPO, 1942). Childs tells his story briefly in "My Recollections of G.2 A.6." His two pompous letters to Friedman add little. University of Virginia Library, Special Collections Department, Accession No. 9256-b, Box 24.

128 "had before us": Manly Papers, 24 July 1931.

129 "I can hear," Neff: B-M, 11 and 22 June 1931.

129 "what valid reason," "an airing": B-M, [19 June 1931], draft.

129 grocery bills: Friedman Collection, Item 840, memo of 26 February 1933.

129 "it was very questionable": Ibid., 29 February 1933.

129 "The only grounds": Ibid., 29 April 1931, 31 [*sic*] April 1931.

129 McGrail: Ibid., 21 April 1931; CAHA 00002, 25 April 1931.

129 "If you will look": Friedman Collection, Item 840, 25 April 1931.

129 Harvard Club: Ibid., McGrail letter, 2 May 1932.

129 "I sure got": Manly Papers, 29 August 1930.

130 "I wish I could," "whatever information," "Of course": Friedman Collection, Item 840, 16 December 1930, 27 February 1931, 21 and 29 April 1931.

130 "had always liked": Quoted in Kruh, "Stimson," 85.

130 *Buraku chiemba:* Information kindly supplied by Professor Chihuru Inaba.

130 charges and countercharges: NA, RG 59, DSDF 894.727/9, /11.

131 cryptanalysis in 1921: Takahashi, "Case Study," 204.

131 false accusation: Library of Congress, Microfilm UD Series, Item 52, Reels 29–30:02–03, 05. The story of Yardley's alleged betrayal was first made public by Farago, *The Broken Seal,* 57–58. As a consequence, Fred C. Woodrough Jr., a Japanese linguist who translated messages for American cryptanalysts during World War II, was directed to investigate the matter, using captured Japanese records. He submitted a report on 28 November 1967 to Vice Admiral Rufus L. Taylor, deputy director of central intelligence, agreeing that the betrayal had taken place (photocopy in David Kahn Collection). Both he and Farago based their belief on a memorandum by the chief of the Japanese Foreign Office telegraph section dated 10 June 1931—ten days after the publication of *The American Black Chamber.* The chief states that the Japanese ambassador to the United States, in telegram No. 105 of June 1930 (no day is given), reported that Yardley had sold him a large volume of solved Japanese messages for $7,000. But though two Japanese scholars—Ikuhito Hata, a World War II historian who translated an abridged version of *The Codebreakers* into Japanese, and Sadao Asada, a specialist in Japanese naval policy whose Yale University dissertation dealt in large part with the Washington naval conference—have independently searched for telegram 105, both report that it does not exist in the files, though a listing summarizes it as "cryptographic leak." Hata wrote in a 14 May 2000 letter to Dr. Edward Drea

that the "telegram itself cannot be found." Asada examined the six-hundred-plus-page Yardley file in the Foreign Ministry archives but said, in a letter of 27 June 1998, that "it contains no world-shaking new discoveries," deals mainly with "the Foreign Ministry's reaction to Yardley's book," and includes no materials prior to 1 June 1931, the book's publication date. In a 10 July 1998 letter, he wrote, "The fact that I could not find the dispatch No. 105 or pre-June 1931 telegraphs on the Yardley incident in the Foreign Ministry archives can mean that they were destroyed, given the very delicate nature of the subject. My conclusion is that Japanese archives do not substantiate the story of Yardley's betrayal, although the Japanese ForeignMinistry leaders believed in it for one reason or another." Moreover, the files contain no internal memoranda about the proposal (Is it a trick? If it is legitimate, should the decrypts be bought? How much should we pay?), no payment vouchers, and—most significantly—no documents from Yardley. These would have existed if the deal had gone through. The charge of betrayal rests on a post–*American Black Chamber* allegation for which great motivation but no evidence exists. Consequently, I believe that Yardley never sold any documents to the Japanese and that the story was fabricated to denigrate him and save Japanese face. Woodrough says this hypothesis is "super-intricate" and "outsmarting itself," but whatever he means, I think it is simple, coherent, and reasonable. I do not know whether the summary listing was contemporary and without this knowledge cannot agree that it supports the accusation. A revival of the betrayal charge, repeated uncritically in Rhodri Jeffreys-Jones, *Cloak and Dollar: A History of American Secret Intelligence* (New Haven: Yale University Press, 2002), 110, was disposed of by Louis Kruh in a letter to the editor, *Cryptologia* 19 (October 1995): 377–379.

131   33,119 copies: B-M.

131   Pangborn, Herndon: Friedman Collection, Item 840, McGrail letter, 29 November 1931; Hannah, "The Many Lives of Yardley," 11; *NYT,* 7 August 1931, 1:4; 8 August 1931, 3:1; 16 August 1931, 1:2.

131   foreign minister: Shigenori Togo, *The Cause of Japan,* trans. Fumihiko Togo and Ben Bruce Blakeney (New York: Simon and Schuster, 1956), 61.

131   Some writers: Kahn, *The Codebreakers,* 362; "Historical Background of the Signal Security Agency," 3:149, 152; Edward J. Drea, *MacArthur's ULTRA* (Lawrence: University Press of Kansas, 1992), 15; Burke, *Information and Secrecy,* 56; O'Toole, *Honorable Treachery,* 341; Norman Polmar and Thomas B. Allen, *Spy Book* (London: Greenhill, 1997), 608.

131   "every nation": Quoted in Kruh, "Stimson," 85.

133   training cryptanalysts: "Historical Background," 3:203–205; NSA, CCH, Rowlett oral history.

133   updating every couple of years: NA, RG 38, Entry CNSG Library, Box 104, Folder COMNAVSECGRU History of Comint Operations 1917–1950, 21 January 1931, 22.

133   "all the secrets": Cambridge University, Churchill College, Archives, CLKE 3, "40 O.B. and Secrecy."

133   number of Japanese solutions: My count of those listed as having been submitted to officials in PRO, HW 12/127 (January 1930) to HW 12/162 (December 1932); HW 3/32:3. This was consonant with the growth in Japanese traffic

volume and diplomatic activity. The Japanese Foreign Office lists the approximate number of telegrams received from embassies and legations as 19,200 in 1929, 18,600 in 1930, 23,400 in 1931, 28,500 in 1932, 15,900 in 1933. Figures for telegrams sent are missing for 1926 and 1932–35 so I do not give them. Information kindly provided by Chuharu Inaba. The *New York Times Index* may be taken as a rough indication of diplomatic activity. Under "Japan" and "China–relations with Japan," it listed 4 columns of stories in 1930, 20.5 in 1931, 55 in 1932, and 33.5 in 1933.

133 no cryptanalytic repercussions: NA, RG 242, Microfilm T-77, Roll 1575, E-Berichte der Chiffrierstelle, OKW 2309–OKW 2312.

133 "indiscreet, sensational": Schauffler, "Erinnerungen eines Kryptologen," 16.

133 Sawada: Farago, *The Broken Seal,* 59–60.

133 RED solved by Germans and Americans: Dr. Werner Kunze interview, 4 May 1962; NSA, CCH, Rowlett oral history, chs. 11–13.

136 "the great harm": Friedman Collection, Item 840, Friedman to Manly, 21 November 1931.

136 "more and more difficult," "losses of thousands": NA, RG 457, HOYC, Box 2, Folder General Correspondence, "Japanese Diplomatic Cryptanalysis," 4. In April 1945, he said essentially the same thing. RG 457, HCC, Box 1129, Japanese Army Systems, Unedited Source Document G20, 42–43.

136 "terrific": Rowlett oral history, 100–105. There is no evidence that the imperial army or navy changed their codes as a consequence of *The American Black Chamber.* Rowlett's remark applies to the diplomatic solutions, which themselves provided much valuable intelligence, as General Marshall himself acknowledged (Kahn, *The Codebreakers,* 605–607). But the experience gained in solving diplomatic codes perhaps also helped in solving military and naval codes.

Chapter 14   Grub Street

Page

137 payments: B-M, 1 October 1931.

137 "American subject," "early in his": PRO, HW 3/13, 16 June 1931.

138 266 pages, 15 shillings: B-M, 24 August 1931; back of title page of *Secret Service in America.*

138 "disappointing": B-M, 16 December 1931.

138 France: *Les annales politiques et littéraires* 17 August, 184–189; 24 August, 214–219; 31 August, 241–248; 7 September, 274–279; 21 September, 330–335; 28 September, 360–363; *Le cabinet noir américain* (Paris: Editions de la Nouvelle revue critique, 1935), 249 pp.

138 Swedish edition: *Amerikas Svarta Kammare,* Stockholm: Tidens Förlag, 1938, 280 pp. Reference to Gyldén appears on p. 254. I am indebted to Dr. Craig Graham McKay for this information and for that about the translator.

138 Norway: Norway Foreign Office, Boxes Cipher Committee 1935–39, 25 October and 19 November 1935, in which Captain Roscher Lund, who became the head of Norwegian cryptanalysis, refers to Yardley's work as an impetus to set up a similar agency in Norway. See also Alf R. Jacobsen and Egil Mork, *Svartkammeret: Den Innerste Hemmeligheten* (n.p.: J. W. Cappelens Forlag, 1989). I am much

obliged to Mr. Jacobsen for locating these memoranda and for telling me about them.

138   German, Chinese translations: B-M royalty book. Yardley never received any royalties from the Chinese edition (*CBC*, 45).

138   sales, royalties: B-M and Columbia University, Butler Library, Bye and Brown Collection (hereafter Bye) files. The estimates are mine.

139   "I had a burst": Bye, 15 April 1931.

139   "I wanted to get rid": Bye, 20 June 1931.

139   "cipher squibs:" Bye, 11 October 1931.

139    $100 apiece: B-M, 27 May 1931; Bye, 5 December 1931.

139   Yardleygrams: *Liberty*, 26 December 1931, 43. Solutions appeared the week following each cryptogram.

139   Koukol wrote: Kruh, "Who Wrote 'The American Black Chamber?' "

140   "too difficult": B-M, 28 October 1931.

141   "I have not," "to map out," "I'm such," "for the amount": Bye, 27 July 1931.

141   "cuts in": Bye, Thursday.

144   RKO Pathé contacted, "I think": Bye, 27 July 1931.

144   Bye made deal: Bye, 11 October 1931.

144   "report our studio": Bye, 9 October 1931.

144   "I sure as hell": Bye, 11 October 1931.

144   laid low: "B-M, 22 October 1931.

144   Shippey: "The Lee Side o' L-A," *Los Angeles Times*, 29 November 1931.

144   "Everyone here": Bye, 6 November 1931.

144   "Studio is cockeyed": Bye, 14 November 1931.

144   "That's Hollywood": Ibid.

145   "Story a complete flop": B-M, 1 December 1931.

145   "actually is working:" B-M, 2 December 1931.

145   "I am terribly": Bye, 2 December 1931.

145   "I have been after Yardley": B-M, 2 December 1931.

145   "positively" fill: B-M, 6 December 1931.

145   "This to your advantage," "finishing up cryptographic": Bye, 5 December 1931.

145   "type of cipher": Ibid.

145   lecture series: Bye, 24 December 1931; B-M, 6 January 1932.

146   "god dammed Jew," admitted, paid: Bye, Yardley to Bye, undated letter.

146   "Haven't had a drink": Bye, 18 August 1932.

146   secret ink: Wilma Shouse McBride interview and telephone interview; Anna C. Vandeventer telephone interview.

146   Experiments took until June: B-M, 13 June 1933.

146   "We are selling": B-M, 16 May, 13 June 1933; Bye, 23 August 1933.

146   "unreasonable," "25 to 30%:" B-M, 10, 12, 16, 22, 23 May 1933.

146   "Yesterday my wife": Bye, 10 May 1933.

147   ten days: B-M, 10 May 1933.

147   "I had a hunch," "has died," "what's": Bye, Sunday.

147   "Finger whittled": Bye, 21 May 1933.

147   still draining: Bye, 1 June 1933.

147   poison ivy: B-M, 10 July 1933; Bye, 11 July 1933.

147   "A discouraging angle": Bye, Sunday [1933].

147   Bye sent $250: Bye, 10 May 1933.

147   "You will receive": Bye, 21 May 1933.

148   "Spies inside Our Gates": Published in both magazines 8 April 1934.

149   "I shall feel": Bye, 27 May 1933.

150   "I will have": Bye, 1 June 1933.

150   "I don't NEED": Bye, Thursday.

150   "Just recovered": Bye, 25 August 1933.

150   "The Beautiful Secret Agent": *Liberty,* 30 December 1933.

150   "H-27": *Liberty,* 21 April 1934.

151   I shall be": Bye, 1 December 1934. There is no further reference to the manuscript in Bye's file.

152   Grabo: *National Cyclopedia of American Biography.*

152   "Dramatization of the American Black Chamber": Copy in David Kahn Collection. Both men are listed as authors.

152   Yardley's hand: *The Blonde Countess,* 50, 78, 111, 132, 281; *ABC,* 18, 29, 47, 55, 118.

152   99 percent: Carl H. Grabo Papers, 24 October 1935. By gracious permission of his daughter.

153   goats, "Celeste Aïda," Lucia, Chopin, dodo, screw: *The Blonde Countess,* 98, 101, 273, 289, 291, 293, 305.

153   "such stuff:" Grabo Papers, 9 October 1935.

153   "after weeks," "$12,000": B-M, Monday; Bye, 9 May 1934.

153   "to keep going": Bye, Tuesday.

154   without Grabo: In his two mentions of Yardley in his papers, Grabo refers only to *The Blonde Countess.*

154   "Please be good": Bye, Saturday.

154   "even better": B-M, Monday.

154   Curtin: *Who Was Who in America; Harvard University Archives, HUG 300,* Curtin.

155   *Stories of the Black Chamber:* The first series ran from 21 January to 8 March, the second from 11 March to 29 April, the third from 1 May to 8 July. Bound volume of scripts, kindly lent by Louis Kruh; *NYT,* "Radio Programs Scheduled for Broadcast This Week," 20 April; 1 and 3 May; 8, 12, and 15 July; 7 October, all 1935.

156   coin-tossing, $25,000 offer: Edna Yardley papers, memorandum by Curtin.

Chapter 15   A Law Aimed at Yardley

Page

158   Klooz: B-M, 22 October 1931.

158   "clicked out her A.B.": *The Briar Patch* (published by the Junior Class, Sweet Briar College, 1923, 35.

158   "It seems a bit": B-M, 22 October 1931.

159   "Our [in-house] readers": B-M, 13 July, 1 August 1932.

159   "ever attempted": "Ishii Bids Us Shun Interfering in Asia," *NYT,* 22 June 1932, 1:2.

159 "the anti-American press": *FRUS, 1932,* 4:240–241.

159 "that, in view of the state": NA, RG 59, DSDF 894.787/20.

160 Figl book suppression: Austria, Archiv der Republik, Bundesministerium für Heerwesen, Z1:49635-1/1926.

160 Givierge: Givierge, "Au service du chiffre," and "Etude historique."

160 officials anguished: PRO, HW 3/65/77.

160 "If those officials": PRO, HW 3/87.

160 "In Their Lordships'": Cambridge University, Churchill College, Archives, HALL 1/5, 4 August 1933.

161 "I was allowed": PRO, HW 3/82.

161 captains to Worthington, documents: NA, RG 165, Entry 65, 10039-299. Department of Justice agents were later reported to say that Yardley put the documents "in safe deposit boxes at various points in the country" ("Code Expert's Ms. on Japan Is Seized," *NYT,* 21 February 1933, 3:4). This seems unlikely.

161 act jointly: NA, RG 165, Entry 65, 10039-299.

161 "it was as bad": NA, RG 59, DSDF 894.727.

161 "with being the moving," "stands too high," "What if," "was profoundly," "the result being": Castle diary, quoted in Kruh, "Stimson," 86–89.

162 Macmillan president, Bye ordered: "Code Expert's Ms. on Japan Is Seized," *NYT,* 21 February 1933, 3:4.

162 testified, were released: NA, RG 60, Entry 112, Department of Justice Central Files, Straight Numerical File 235334, dealing with "Japanese Diplomatic Secrets," has nothing about any presentation to a grand jury or about why no prosecution ensued. The database of case files 1919–29, for the U.S. attorney's office for the Southern District of New York in RG 118 in the New York branch of the National Archives and Records Administration, has no listing for Yardley, Macmillan, or Klooz. Dewey said in 1944, "I am the man who stopped Yardley from publishing his second book. I met him in a speakeasy one night and persuaded him against publishing the book. He agreed provided Mr. Stimson write him a letter of apology for the abusive manner in which Mr. Stimson had fired him. Stimson did, too." Dewey said this to Colonel Carter Clarke, who was giving him a letter of General George C. Marshall asking him not to mention codebreaking in his presidential campaign. Clarke's report, SRH-043, is reprinted in *Cryptologia* 7 (April 1983): 119–128, with this quotation at 128. I don't believe it. Yardley and Dewey might have met—though it is questionable whether a law enforcement official would have gone into a speakeasy—but the threat of prosecution seems more convincing than a chat. No evidence exists for any Stimson letter to Yardley. Dewey was misremembering.

162 H.R. 4220: The account of the drafting and passage of the bill is assembled from NA, RG 59, DSDF 119.25/Official Secrets Act/2, /11, /12, /19, /20, and DSDF 894.727/26; RG 165, Entry 65, 10039-299, 17 February 1933; *Congressional Record* (1933), 77:1151–1155, 3125–3140, 3177–3190 (Johnson speech at 3177–3178), 5142, 5218, 5333–5334; RG 233, House of Representatives, 73d Congress, Minutes of the Committee of the Judiciary, 28 March 1933; House Reports 18 and 226 and Senate Report 21; "House Passes Bill to Guard Secrets," *NYT,* 4 April 1933, 6:2, "Senate to Revamp the Secrets Bill," *NYT,* 5 April 1933, 5:3; "Aim Gag Bill at Yardley," *Indianapolis Star,* 4 April 1933. The NA does not

have any unprinted transcripts of Senate Foreign Relations Committee hearings for 1933–36.

171   "received," "a tale which," "went a bit," "did rub it in," "My lawyer": Bye, 20, 22, 27 May; 1, 16, 19 June 1933; and undated.

172   Bobbs-Merrill petition: NA, RG 59, DSDF 894.727/22, /26, /28, /29, /32; B-M, 14, 30 June and 13, 26 July 1933.

Chapter 16 Hollywood

Page

Unless otherwise noted, all material about the scripts comes from the Academy of Motion Picture Arts and Sciences, Center for Motion Picture Study, Margaret Herrick Library, Turner-MGM Collection, joint file on *Rendezvous, The Black Chamber,* and *The Blonde Countess,* the file on Yardley in the H. N. Swanson Collection, and the *Rendezvous* Production Files, and from the University of Southern California Cinema-Television Library, MGM Collection, Box 251, Folders 1 and 2, "*Rendezvous.*"

174   get approval: MGM had nothing to fear from the government. On the very day that Yardley was signing contracts with MGM, Brigadier General Alfred T. Smith, the assistant chief of staff for intelligence, was writing to the State Department that *The Blonde Countess* "contains nothing upon which could be based any action" under the so-called Yardley law, since the characters and incidents "all appear to be purely fictitious." As assistant secretary of state, Wilbur J. Carr concurred after reading the book. NA, RG 59, DSDF 119.25/Official Secrets Act/21, /22.

174   Yardley negotiations and contracts: Turner Entertainment Co., Yardley files.

176   returned to Worthington, "I like the climate": B-M, Thursday, marked 21? June 1934 in brackets.

176   "Story here": Bye, Saturday.

178   *The Great Impersonation, The Blonde Countess:* B-M, Thursday, marked 21? June 1934 in brackets.

178   "A gets the original idea": Quoted in Ian Hamilton, *Writers in Hollywood, 1915–1951* (New York: Harper and Row, 1990), 50–51.

178   "Movies were seldom written": Hecht, *A Child of the Century,* 478.

179   "Lawrence Weingarten": Oppenheimer, *The View from the Sixties,* 127–129.

180   Loy on strike: Quirk, *The Complete Films of Powell,* 181.

180   "I know you don't want me": Russell and Chase, *Life Is a Banquet,* 56.

180   Barnes, Romero, Rooney: Hanson, ed. *The American Film Institute Catalog, Feature Films, 1931–1940,* s.v. *Rendezvous.* The synopsis of the film in this valuable work is not entirely accurate. At my request, Kevin Pawley, Mickey Rooney's agent, kindly asked him some questions about the film over the weekend of 13–14 January 2001. Pawley reported that Rooney, who said he had made some eight hundred films, could not remember *Rendezvous* at all.

180   postponement and other changes: *Hollywood Reporter,* 5 June, 2:3; 12 June, 6:4; 22 June, 4:2; 30 July, 8:3; 7 August, 2:3; 23 August, 1:2; 24 August, 5:2–3; 7 September, 3:3; 9 September, 6:2; 25 September, 10:1; all 1935.

181 "Pages 74 and 75," "We had the pleasure": Margaret Herrick Library, Hays Office, *Rendezvous.*

182 "lively and amusing": *NYT,* 26 October 1935, 12:2–3.

182 "The startling": *WT,* undated clipping.

183 "comedy as fresh": *Hollywood Reporter,* 23 October 1935.

183 *Rendezvous* "the first": Dooley, *From Scarface to Scarlett,* 103.

183 week's vacation: Gayle Owen interview; Gloria Love Jaffe (Yardley acquaintance from Worthington) letter of 3 August 1998.

183 distillery: David Kahn Collection, Folder Memories of HOY, letter dated Sunday Abe [Brewer] to Dear Edna; memo to Klem pinned to that letter. State of California, Department of State, Corporation No. 162719, Articles of Incorporation of M. J. Nolder Distilleries, Inc., 16 May 1935. These do not mention Yardley, but the Certificate of Amendment of 11 April 1938 lists him as the owner of 2812.5 shares by proxy, C. C. Nolder, the owner, of 92.75 shares. A spokesman at the California Department of Alcoholic Beverage Control said on 28 January 1999 that records such as those of the production of the Nolder Distilleries are shredded after five years.

183 "We are going," "the official tester": Bye, 5 July, 10 June 1936.

184 separated in September: U.S. District Court for the District of Columbia, Civil Action 20070.

184 Jack, Hazel: Gayle Owen postcard of 2 December 1996 and interview; Mary Ropp and Wilma S. McBride interview; Harold J. Smith interview.

184 *Modern Mechanix, Typewriting Behavior:* Bye, 15 May, 18, 19 May, and 5 July 1936.

184 "Shadows in Washington": B-M, 3 May, 15 June, 3 and 7 July 1938.

Chapter 17   China

Page

Letters from Yardley are filed in David Kahn Collection, Y, Folder China. They are cited here as letter, followed by the clearest reference, which is sometimes the date, sometimes a number, sometimes the addressee(s).

187 Childs: Childs, *Foreign Service Farewell,* 179–180; comment by Henry Schorreck in NSA, CCH, Edna Yardley oral history, 32.

187 18 May 1938: Edna Yardley oral history, 25. She apparently had the letter in front of her.

187 Hsiao: Yu, *OSS in China,* 37–38. In pinyin, he is Xaio Bo. For more on him, see Frederic E. Wakeman, *Spymaster: Dai Li and the Chinese Secret Service* (Berkeley: University of California Press, 2003).

187 Yardley knew: Edna Yardley oral history, 31.

187 $10,000, six months, option: Yu, *OSS in China,* 38; letter to Abe and Lil.

188 not on passport: NA, RG 457, HOYC, Box 100, Folder Yardley Contract, 10 May 1940.

188 4 September: *NYT,* 3 September 1938, 27.

188 12 October: Letter to Abe and Lil.

188 "I did go": Letter of 24 October [1938].

188 "water tap," *Kiangsu,* "nearly two months": Letter no. 1, 27 October 1938.

188 Pakhoi: Now Beihai.

188 "pigs running": Letter no. 1, 27 October 1938.

189 "I shall be": Letter from Hong Kong, 24 October 1938.

189 narrow-gauge, sandy island: *CBC*, 6, 7.

189 Chungking: Now Chongqing.

189 5 November: Letter to Abe and Lil.

189 wartime Chungking: White, *In Search of History*, 66–71.

189 chateau: Letter no. 4; letter to Abe and Lil; partial letter; *CBC*, 25–26.

190 Shen Shien Tung Gai 94: U.S. District Court for the District of Columbia, Civil Action 20070, Complaint, 2.

190 "a scurf," "When I flicked": *CBC*, 7, 9.

190 worst cold, choroiditis, homesickness: Letters 28 February and no. 3. I am indebted to ophthalmologist Dr. Cyrus Kahn for help confirming Yardley's ailment in his letter of 29 November 1998.

190 "I did not have," "I really felt ill," heart beating: Letters nos. 18 and 20; *CBC*, 94–95.

190 interpreter read: Letter of 31 December [1938]. Kweilin is now Kuilin.

191 "monkies," rats, radio: Ibid.

191 piss warmer: Letter of 22 or 23 December 1938.

191 routine: *CBC*, 101.

191 "vile," "good," "stinking," rat traps, movies: Letters nos. 3 and 9, to Abe and Lil, and 22 or 23 December 1938.

191 wanted to talk to him: Letter no. 3.

191 students, general: Letters nos. 4, 7, 9, and 28 February.

191 China's cryptanalysis: Yu, "Chinese Codebreakers," 201–213; Yu, *OSS in China*; Frederic Wakeman, "Dai Li's Communications System," a chapter from his book on Dai Li. I am grateful to Dr. Wakeman for letting me see this.

191 Yu Ching Wen: Harvard University Archives, UA III 15.75.12, UA III 15.88.10. In pinyin, Wen Yuqing.

192 Manchuria, fake radio messages, Japan grabbed: Jonathan D. Spence, *The Search for Modern China* (New York: Norton, 1990), 394–395, 420–422.

192 Dai Li: *CBC*, passim; Wakeman, *Spymaster*.

192 Chinese scholar translated: *CBC*, 10–11.

192 "none too careful," "huge success": Letter no. 6.

193 no signal officers, burying alive: Letter of 19 December 1938.

193 bombardier: *CBC*, 70.

193 Departments 2, 4: Letter of 22 or 23 December 1938.

193 one hundred, fifty, seven: *CBC*, 63.

193 seven hundred to eight hundred: Hannah, "The Many Lives of Yardley," 19.

193 two hundred thousand, twenty thousand, twenty codes, samples: Letter no. 9.

193 February 1939 solution: *CBC*, 53–55.

193 Japanese air force code: Yu, *OSS in China*, 38–39.

193 "small fortune": Letter no. 3.

194 articles: Letters no. 3 and 31 December.

194 "was a bit": Letter to Dear Kids (undated).

194 "any encouragement": Letter no. 9.

194 exclusive series: Letter of 31 December (to George).

194   "Now do not": Letter of 28 February (to George).

194   "tons," "steal any": Letter no. 15 (only half exists).

194   good teeth: letters no. 15 and 19 December. The friend/was Alice Bernheim.

194   stamps: Letter of 8 January 1939.

194   did everything possible: Letters to Abe and Lil, nos. 6, 7; and 4, 20, and 22 or
       23 December 1938, 14 January 1939.

194   "I said I was": Letter no. 6.

194   limited freedom, waiter: Letter no. 7.

195   Chungking Hostel: *CBC,* 173.

195   Crofton, Hahn: White, *Fire in the Ashes,* 173–176, 358; Hahn, *China to Me,*
       167–168.

195   "Yardley was": White, *In Search of History,* 75–76.

196   "Sex is a major obsession": NA, RG 457, HOYC, Box 100, Folder Yardley
       Contract, 10 May 1940.

196   "downtown for one dollar," "15 year old kids," "certainly are," "Very nice
       looking": Letter no. 3 and 20 December 1938.

196   many Chinese women: NA, RG 457, HOYC, Box 100, Folder Yardley Contract,
       11 March 1940.

196   "comfort" college: Yu, *OSS in China,* 82.

197   *Tutuila:* NA, RG 457, HOYC, Box 100, Folder Yardley Contract, 11 March
       1940.

197   Edna refused, dissuaded: Ibid. and 10 May 1940.

197   "Dear Edna," "First—I am not": Letters nos. 16 and 2.

197   signed option: *CBC,* 62–64.

197   in charge of eight hundred, restless, drank, War Department, "the patriots": NA,
       RG 457, HOYC, Box 100, Folder Yardley Contract, 11 March 1940, 10 May
       1940.

198   work superficial: Ted Wildman via George McGinnis interview, 22 December
       1995.

198   "It will always be": Gempp, "Geheimer Nachrichtendienst und Spionageabwehr
       des Heeres," vol. 2, pt. 7, p. 162.

198   "Though I should": NA, RG 457, HOYC, Box 56, Folder Memoranda and
       Letters Concerning H. O. Yardley, 1919–1940.

198   progress report: Ibid.

198   departure from China: *CBC,* 218–219; NA, RG 457, HOYC, Box 3,
       Unpublished manuscript by Yardley.

198   Manila, Honolulu, Bicknell: NA, RG 457, Japanese Master Diplomatic
       Collection, no. 077 (19 July 1940), no. 125 (23 July 1940); David Kahn
       Collection, Y, Folder Poker Book, Bicknell, 30 October 1958; Honolulu
       Advertiser, 23 July 1940.

Chapter 18   Canada

Page

Sources in this chapter listed with only dates may be found in NAC, RG 24, Vols.
20306, 20307, or 29163–29173, except 29165, 29166, or 29167.
"Memorandum" refers to Vol. 29166, File WWII, part 1, 0235–0243,

Memorandum on a Visit [by Coxeter and Robinson] to Washington to Enquire into the Situation Regarding H. O. Osborn, 26 November 1941; "History" means Vol. 29167, "History [of] Examination Unit."

199   F Street: NSA, CCH, Rowlett oral history.

199   overtures rejected: Memorandum.

199   Mauborgne contracted: David Kahn Collection, Y, Folder China, loose page headed "China—Herbert O. Yardley."

200    $4,000: NA, RG 457, HCC, Box 1129, Folder Signals Communications Systems, Unedited Source Document, Friedman interview, 4 April 1945, 42.

200   Rowlett assigned: Rowlett oral history.

200   "Can I offer you a drink?": Rowlett telephone interview.

200   meetings: David Kahn Collection, Y, Folder Japanese Military Codes and Ciphers in Occupied China, Brochure 2b, p. 2.

200   six "brochures," observations: David Kahn Collection, Y, Folder Japanese Military Codes and Ciphers in Occupied China, Brochure 2a, p. 16; Brochure 1, p. 14.

201   "contained all," "invaluable": CAHA 00002:4.

201   "was about as good," wasted time: Rowlett oral history, 403.

201   showed its independence: *Canada Gazette/Gazette du Canada,* 10 September 1939. See also J. L. Granatstein, *Canada's War: The Politics of the Mackenzie King Government, 1939–1945* (Toronto: Oxford University Press, 1975), 2–7, 15, 19, 42.

201   kept its partners out: Mauborgne said that, besides Canada, South Africa had come to him for help in codebreaking. "History," sec. 1, pt. 1, p. 1. And when the Australians asked the British in 1940 for assistance in setting up a signal intelligence agency to watch Japan, the British replied that the Australians could send a naval officer to Britain's cryptanalytic agency at Stonecutter Island near Singapore. Frank Cain, email of 27 July 1998.

201   no cryptanalytic unit: Elliot, *Scarlet to Green,* 126. The navy's not having a cryptanalytic unit is my supposition, based on lack of evidence for one.

201   Canada intercepted: PRO, HW 14/1, 14 and 17 September, 11 and 18 October, all 1939; HW 14/3, 9 January 1940.

201   "be informed": PRO, HW 14/1, 4 and 16 October 1939; HW 14/3, 6 February 1939.

201   Italian, Spanish orders of battle: Bryden, *Best-Kept Secret,* 14, 21, 27.

202   two hundred messages: "History," sec. 1, pt. 1, p. 2.

202   Drake visited Mauborgne, highest value: NA, RG 457, HCC, Box 798, Folder Canadian–U.S. Intercept Matters, 20 November 1940; "History," sec. 1, pt. 1, p. 3. The training manuals, all by Friedman and far superior to anything else, consisted of *Elementary Military Cryptography, Advanced Military Cryptography,* and *Military Cryptanalysis,* the fourth volume of which was then available only in mimeographed form. "History," sec. 1, pt. 1, p. 7.

202   Drake proposed: "History," sec. 1, pt. 1, p. 7.

202   chiefs of staff: Ibid., p. 9.

202   National Research Council, Keenleyside: Bryden, *Best-Kept Secret,* 44–45; Thistle, ed., *The Mackenzie-McNaughton Letters,* xiv.

202   "people who have had": 13 February, 28 January 1941.

202   Robinson, Coxeter: *Canadian Who's Who,* 2 (1936–37).

202 Sinkov collaborated, new chapter: Abraham Sinkov interview. The American edition of Ball's book was published in 1939 by Macmillan. Sinkov was listed as "a Cryptanalyst in the U.S. War Department."

203 The American replied: Bryden, *Best-Kept Secret,* 47.

203 $10,000: Ibid., 46.

203 Mackenzie arranged, meeting with Mauborgne: "History," sec. 1, pt. 2, p. 1; Memorandum.

203 "perhaps suffered unduly": Bryden, *Best-Kept Secret,* 49.

203 "good salesman," "unusually skillful," "best expert," "In our opinion": Memorandum; NAC, MG 30, B122, Mackenzie diary, 2 May 1941.

204 meeting at 123 East Block: NAC, RG 24, Vol. 29165, File WWII-20, part 1, Report of a Conference of the Interdepartmental Committee on Cryptography Held in Room 123, East Block, Dept. of External Affairs, 12 May 1941.

204 $10,000: "History," sec. 1, pt. 5, p. 5.

204 $550, cover name, Ramsaier release: 30 May and 3 June 1941.

205 11 June meeting: 11 June 1941.

205 offices: NAC, RG 24, Vol. 29165, File WWII-19, 000089.

205 rented room, living-bedroom: CAHA 00002:11, Edna undated letter to Klem Koukol.

205 Yardley reported: NAC, RG 24, Vol. 29165, File WWII-19, 000200 of 19 June 1941.

205 "has already produced": Ibid., 000088. On Stone: *Canadian Who's Who* 5 (1949–51); *NYT,* "Thomas Archibald Stone Dies; Former Canadian Ambassador," 27 July 1965, 33:1.

206 30 June report: NAC, RG 24, Vol. 29165, File WWII-19, 000090.

206 Yardley announced: Ibid., 201–205.

206 four numbered copies: Ibid., 206.

206 16 July: Bryden, *Best-Kept Secret,* 65.

206 not forwarded to U-boats: None of the U-boat logs I have read list messages from their commanders naming individual targets. In a few cases, ships reported by spies were sunk. But the sinking took place so much later and so far away that, even if the report had been transmitted to the U-boat that eventually sank the ship, it seems unlikely that the spy report led to the sinking. For example, the spies reported 7 July that the Panamanian tanker *Hanseat* had sailed 5 July from Rio for Caripito, Venezuela (NAC, RG 24, Vol. 29172, File WWII-40, part 5, GA-49). It was sunk on 9 March 1942 west of Haiti—eight months later and two thousand miles away (Jürgen Rohwer, *Axis Submarine Successes, 1939–1945* [Annapolis: Naval Institute Press, 1983], 84).

206 OTIS: NAC, RG 24, Vol. 29172, File WWII-40, part 5, GA-49.

206 "Panair": Ibid., GA-54.

208 Japanese codes: Report No. 5, 15 September 1941.

208 "no one was ever": "History," sec. 1, pt. 1, p. 19.

208 Vichy codes: Report No. 5, 15 September 1941; Yardley memo, 18 September 1941; Bryden, *Best-Kept Secret,* 69–71.

208 "huge increase": Bryden, *Best-Kept Secret,* 79.

208 Robinson felt: 22 November 1941.

208 "thought out": Bryden, *Best-Kept Secret,* 78–79.

208   "has done": NAC, RG 24, Vol. 29165, File WWII-19, Ibid., 221–222.
208   "had made a good move," "the Unit is producing": NAC, RG 24, Vol. 29165, File WWII-19, Ibid., 16.
209   "our Unit": 17 November 1941.
209   "very much impressed": Mackenzie diary, 6 August 1941; a similar comment on 19 August 1941. Yardley briefed Mackenzie on the unit's work on 10 September 1941.
209   cigarettes: 18, 22, 24 July 1941.
209   cost-of-living raise: 14 October 1941.
209   Emeley: Bryden, *Best-Kept Secret,* 345; Cable. no. 864, 5 June 1941. For the problem of transposed letters, see Kahn, *The Codebreakers,* 847. In a curious coincidence, Sinkov mentions this very form of codeword construction on pages 405–406 of his chapter in *Mathematical Recreations and Essays.*
209   "was not, for a period": 7 July 1941.
210   "cooperation of his": NA, RG 457, HCC, Box 949, File 2714, 16 August 1941.
210   Pearson protested, Denniston replied: NA, RG 24, Vol. 29165, File WWII-19, 221–222. Pearson won the Nobel Peace Prize in 1956 for devising a plan for a United Nations peacekeeping force to ease Britain and France out of Egypt after the Suez invasion. He served as Canada's prime minister from 1963 to 1968.
210   Mauborgne relieved: Dulany Terrett, *The Signal Corps: The Emergency (to December 1941),* United States Army in World War II: The Technical Services (Washington: Office of the Chief of Military History, 1956), 271–272.
210   "coöperation between," "We propose": NA, RG 24, Vol. 29165, File WWII-19, 221–222.
210   "definite assurances": 17 November 1941.
210   Britain vowed: 20 November 1941.
210   "it may mean": Mackenzie diary, 17 November 1941.
211   "very much cut up": Ibid., 21 November 1941.
211   "a most unpleasant," "Yardley took": Ibid., 22 November 1941. The date of the interview telling Yardley he was fired is given in the Mackenzie diary as 21 November and in this document as "this afternoon." But this same document refers also to Robinson's seeing Stone about the matter "this morning." I believe that the reference to "this afternoon" was written on 21 November, that the document was held back a day, that the Stone reference was then added and the "this afternoon" reference not corrected, and that the date of the firing interview was therefore Friday, 21 November.
211   "unless under gravest": Ibid.
211   Stone felt: Ibid.
211   Little: Bryden, *Best-Kept Secret,* 12–13, 45–46, 47; Mackenzie diary, 24 April 1941; C. H. Little, "Early Days in Naval Intelligence, 1939–41," *Salty Dips,* 2:111–118, and "Now It Can All Be Told," *Salty Dips* 3:213–237.
211   dispatched to Washington: Mackenzie diary, 24 November 1941.
211   *I'm Alone:* Pearson, *Mike,* 1:72; Kahn, *The Codebreakers,* 813–815.
211   Visit to Washington: Memorandum.
211   Hastings: *Canadian Who's Who* 2 (1936–37).
213   under a Briton: Mackenzie diary, 1 December 1941.
213   Strachey: [Julia Frances Strachey] and Frances Partridge, *Julia: A Portrait by*

Herself (London: Victor Gollancz, 1983), 17–27, 40, 42, 44, 45–46, 183, 187, 188; Barbara Strachey, *Remarkable Relations: The Story of the Pearsall Smith Family* (London: Victor Gollancz, 1981), endpapers, 251, 252, 265, 267, 272, 288, 289, 299, 303; Yigal Sheffy, *British Military Intelligence in the Palestine Campaign, 1914–1918* (London: Frank Cass, 1998), 227. References to Strachey in the Government Code and before he went to Canada in PRO, HW Cypher School 14/3, -/23, -/24, -/25, -/39, -/40. He left Canada in mid-1942, appreciated for his work and for "an unselfish and brave act on your part to take on that job in.the middle of winter." PRO, HW 14/38, 26 May 1942.

214   Eleanor Roosevelt: NA, RG 24, Vol. 29165, File WWII-19, 246–250; David Kahn, ed., "Nuggets from the Archives: Yardley Tries Again," *Cryptologia* 2 (April 1978): 139–143.

214   "I was given": NA, RG 24, Vol. 29165, File WWII-19, 244–245.

214   "the only white man," "minimum of sixty": Ibid., 255–261.

214   Drake recommended: 27 December 1941.

214   Canadians generous: 6 and 20 January 1942; NA, RG 24, Vol. 29165, File WWII-19, 132–134.

215   Compared to Napoleon: NSA, CCH, Edna Yardley oral history.

215   "I may be prejudiced": Mackenzie diary, 16 January 1942; PRO, HW 14/3, 5 January 1940; 14/7, 18 October 1940; 14/25, 19 December 1941.

215   Canada recovered: Bryden, *Best-Kept Secret,* chs. 5–14.

Chapter 19   A Restaurant of His Own

Page

216   two or three letters a week: HOYOPF, 15 September 1941.

216   informant reported: NA, RG 457, HOYC, Box 100, Folder Yardley Contract.

217   meeting of 3 February 1942: FBI, File 62-27581, 4 February 1942. I am grateful to former Special Agent Ray Batvinnis for his memorandum of 17 May 2000 about the FBI personnel.

218   finances: Ibid., 31 August 1942. I thank Joel Sieger, C.P.A., for analyzing the bank record.

218   "I can at least:" Columbia University, Butler Library, Bye and Brown Collection (hereafter cited as Bye), Yardley to Bye, Saturday night.

218   "So many people": Bye, Bye to Yardley, 10 March 1942.

218   Candela: David Kahn Collection, Yardley to Candela, letter of 5 March 1942.

219    $10,000: FBI, File 62-27581, 15 August 1942.

219   restaurant: FBI, File 62-27581, 6, 20, 28 August 1942.

219   "close to $10,000": Bye, Yardley to Bye, Saturday night.

219   "finest Bean Soup," Pocket Books: Bye, Yardley to Bye, undated; Bye to Yardley, 10, 12, 24 March 1942; B-M, 19, 21, 26 February, 6, 10 March, 9 April 1942.

220   "disaffection," description, investigation: FBI, File 62-27581, 6 August 1942, passim.

223   sold the Rideau: Bye, Yardley to Bye, undated; Lillian Meyer interview.

223   job at OPA: HOYOPF, 4 November 1942.

223   Edna broke her leg: U.S. District Court for the District of Columbia, Civil Action 26343.

223 210 Tuckerman Street, boarders, beach: Frank and Layton Fordham interview.

223 "The dope here," *Blonde Countess* sale: Bye, Yardley to Bye, undated; Bye to Yardley, 10 and 29 December 1942.

224 "I believe I know": Bye, Yardley to Bye, undated; Bye to Elmer Davis, 20 January 1943.

224 Dr. Taylor: Roger Burlingame, *Don't Let Them Scare You: The Life and Times of Elmer Davis* (Philadelphia: Lippincott, 1961), mentions neither Yardley nor any Taylor. I had thought that the Taylor to whom Yardley spoke was Edmond Taylor, a foreign correspondent who had worked for the Foreign Information Service, which began in William J. Donovan's spy agency, the later Office of Strategic Services, and moved to Davis's Office of War Information. But he had no doctorate and was in North Africa when Yardley spoke to Dr. Taylor in Washington. Edmond Taylor, *Awakening from History* (Boston: Gambit, 1969), 308–309, 321 ff. I have not been able to discover who Dr. Taylor was.

224 Yardley furious: Bye, Yardley to Bye, undated.

224 "I am just": Bye, Yardley to Bye, 28 May 1943.

225 Bladensburg Road: "Two Arrested in Black Market Quiz Here," [Washington] *Times Herald,* 18 February 1943, 1.

225 beef, plenty of gasoline: NSA, CCH, Edna Yardley oral history; Fordham interview.

225 "I'm respected": Bye, Yardley to Bye, 28 May 1943.

225 explained regulations, answered queries, ran a team of ten: HOYOPF, OPA and Housing File, "Memorandum for Economic Stabilization Agency," 22 February 1941.

225 performance ratings: HOYOPF, passim.

225 divorce: Nevada, Storey County, 1st Judicial District Court, 10982. I am indebted to David Reno for locating this record.

225 married Edna: Nevada, Washoe County, Marriage Certificate 178919.

Chapter 20   Playing Poker

Page

226 "False Passport": Columbia University, Butler Library, Bye and Brown Collection (hereafter Bye), Yardley to Bye, Thursday 5:30 p.m.

226 "I am going," "We couldn't revise": Bye, Bye to Yardley, 9 April, 2 June, 10 September 1943; Shively to Yardley, 10 September 1943.

227 "something absolutely unique": Bye, Yardley to Bye, undated.

227 real people: Bye, Bye to Yardley, 5 and 19 March 1943.

227 "I have a MMS," "Your letter": Bye, Yardley to Bye, 4 and 12 July 1944.

227 $1,000, "Crows Are Black Everywhere": Bye, Yardley to Bye, 19 August, 4 and 19 October 1944.

228 Osborn Sales Company: Edna Yardley, undated memo.

228 at Public Housing: Gordon Smith interviews.

228 "I study": HOYOPF.

230 "I really admired": Assembled from Grover Batts interview.

231 906 West Princeton Avenue, "strong deep voice": *Orlando Sentinel,* undated clipping.

231   Mabie, hunting: Robert Mabie interview.

232   poker at National Press Club: Paul Means interview. Though only members were
       supposed to play at the club, and Yardley's name does not appear in the extant
       directories (Gini Blodgett, archivist, email of 26 January 2001), members might
       have invited him to play (John P. Cosgrove, president of the club in 1961,
       telephone interview, 28 January 2001).

233   "There are two types": Alvarez, *Secret Messages,* 105, 106.

233   ability to make up names: To repeat a note to chapter 1, none of the persons
       named in the book, including their family names, appears in the 1900 census for
       Indiana, Greene County, Enumeration District 31, or in the Worthington city
       directory for 1917.

233   two hundred thousand hands: Yardley, *The Education of a Poker Player,* 70.

233   broke all records: David Kahn Collection, Y, Folder Poker Book, letter to Dear
       Pete, 27 November 1957.

233   did not deign to review: The book is not listed in *Book Review Digest* for 1957 or
       1958.

234   "big-assed bird": David Kahn Collection, Y, Folder Poker Book, Pete to Herb,
       20 November 1957.

234   "classic": Mamet, *Make-Believe Town,* 15.

234   mail: David Kahn Collection, Y, Folder Poker Book, passim.

234   "I was 15": William Overend, memorandum of 19 January 2001. I am grateful to
       Mr. Overend for this reminiscence.

236   1:15 P.M. on 7 August 1958: Maryland State Archives, Certificate of Death 9350.

Chapter 21   The Measure of a Man

Page
237   burial: Arlington National Cemetery. He was buried in a tie that Grover Batts
       gave Edna for the funeral, since Yardley did not own one.

237   "old-fashioned": NAC, RG 24, Vol. 29166, File WWII, part 1, 0235-0243,
       Memorandum on a Visit [by Coxeter and Robinson] to Washington to Enquire
       into the Situation Regarding H. O. Osborn, 26 November 1941, at 0241.

237   "so-so": U.S. Naval Institute, Rochefort: oral history, 36.

237   "not particularly great": U.S. Naval Institute, Dyer oral history, 216.

238   Cartier: Givierge, "Etude historique," 909.

239   Japanese ambassador's messages: Carl Boyd, *Hitler's Japanese Confidant: General
       Oshima Hiroshi and MAGIC Intelligence* (Lawrence: University Press of Kansas,
       1993).

239   intelligence, importance: David Kahn, "An Historical Theory of Intelligence,"
       Intelligence and National Security 16 (autumn 2001): 79-92.

240   Immanuel Kant: *Perpetual Peace,* §6, in *Kant's Political Writings,* ed. Hans Reiss,
       trans. H. B. Nisbet (Cambridge: Cambridge University Press, 1971), 96-97.

240   chief of staff permitted interception: U.S. Congress, Joint Committee on the
       Investigation of the Pearl Harbor Attack, *Pearl Harbor Attack,* Hearings, 79th
       Congress (GPO), 3:1100-1101, 1146.

240   no spies: Ibid., 2:785; Anthony Cave Brown, *Wild Bill Donovan: The Last Hero*
       (New York: Times Books, 1982), 176-177; Thomas F. Troy, *Donovan and the*

CIA: A History of the Establishment of the Central Intelligence Agency (Frederick, Md.: University Publications of America, 1981), 105–197.

240   presidential approval: *U.S. Statutes at Large* 88:1795–1820 at 1804 (§32).

240   no assassinations: *Federal Register* 41:7703 (Executive Order 11905, §5).

Bibliography

Repositories

Academy of Motion Picture Arts and Sciences. Los Angeles, Calif.

Center for Motion Picture Study. Margaret Herrick Library. Special Collections.
 Turner-MGM Collection. Scripts. *Rendezvous. The Black Chamber. The Blonde Countess.*
 Motion Picture Association of America [Hays Office] files. *Rendezvous. The Great Impersonation.*
 H. N. Swanson Collection. Yardley, (Major) Herbert O. and Files 67, 80, 80, 104.
 Gladys Hall Collection. Folders 415 and 416. Rosalind Russell interviews.
 Production Files. *Rendezvous.*
 Biography Files. Rosalind Russell.

Archives Nationales. Paris.

F^{90} 11152, 13709, 13710.

Association des Réservistes du Chiffre et de la Sécurité d'Information. Fort de Kremlin-Bicêtre, Paris.

Archives. Georges Jean Painvin Papiers.

Cambridge University. Cambridge, Eng.

Churchill College. Archives.
 W. F. Clarke Papers. CLKE 3.

A. G. Denniston Papers. DENN 1/2, 1/4.
W. R. Hall Papers. HALL 1/2, 1/3, 1/5, 2/2, 3/6.

City College of the City University of New York. New York, N.Y.

Morris Raphael Cohen Library. Division of Archives and Special Collections.
Mendelsohn Files.

City of New York. Borough of Queens. Jamaica, N.Y.

Department of Finance. Office of the City Register. Deed-Liber Books and Land Block
Books. Liber 2811: Page (actually deed registration number) 107641 (henceforth as
2811:107641), 2813:109014, 2960:115329, 3065:67469, -70, -71, -79, 3079:81877,
3080:83147, -48, 3103:105675, 3125:127536, -37, 3145:11937, 3256:117803,
3323:58645.

Columbia University. New York, N.Y.

Butler Library.
  Rare Book and Manuscripts Division. Col U 391. George Bye and James Oliver
  Brown Collection. Boxes 391, 396, 408, 415.
  Oral History Collection. Joseph O. Mauborgne.

Federal Bureau of Investigation, Washington, D.C.

File 62-27581. Herbert Osborne [*sic*] Yardley.
File 2423. Maria K. de Victorica.

Harvard University. Cambridge, Mass.

Archives. Files on Emmett K. Carver, Daniel Thomas Curtin, Aloysius J. McGrail, Ralph
Van Deman, Yu Ching Wen.
Houghton Library. William R. Castle Diary.

Indiana Historical Society. Indianapolis.

Bobbs-Merrill file on Yardley.

David Kahn Collection. Great Neck, N.Y.

Miscellaneous papers of Herbert O. Yardley, received from his sister-in-law, Lillian
Meyer. Includes manuscripts of published and unpublished writings; carbon copy of
original typescript of "The American Black Chamber," containing material not in the
printed book; his letters from China; letters from readers; his reports on Japanese ciphers
in China. In folders marked with a red Y.
  File of letters and photocopies on Carl W. Grabo, Yardley book collaborator.
  Papers collected by Samuel Snyder for Edna Yardley's proposed biography.
  Interview notes and correspondence about Yardley.
  Photographs of Worthington High School football team, from Virgil Rogers, and of
  Worthington, from various sources.
  Photographs of Yardley, family, and coworkers, from various sources.
  Photocopies of numerous documents dealing with Yardley and his work.
  Parker Hitt papers.
  Typewritten extracts from Frederick Livesey memoirs.

George C. Marshall Library. Lexington, Va.

William F. Friedman Collection. File on Yardley, annotated *The American Black Chamber,* individual papers.

Ministry of Defence Naval Historical Branch Library. London.

[W(illiam) F. Clarke and F(rank). Birch.] "A Contribution to the History of German Naval Warfare, 1914–1918." Typescript [1919–1920]. Vol. 1, "The Fleet in Action." Vol. 2, "The Fleet in Being," includes ch. 18, "German Codes and Ciphers." Vol. 3, [secret; not released].

Museum of the City of New York. New York, N.Y.

Prints and Photographs Department. Wurts Collection. Boxes 108–113.

National Archives. College Park, Md.

Record Group 38. Department of the Navy.
   ComNavSecGru 5750/15A, /86, /87, /88.
   Entry CNSG Library. Boxes 14 and 104.
Record Group 43. International Conferences, Commissions, and Exhibitions.
   Records of the Washington Conference on the Limitation of Armaments. U.S. Delegation.
      Entry 99. Informational Memorandums, 1921–22. Boxes 1, 2, 3, 4.
      Entry 100. Records of A. H. Miles, secretary of the delegation, 1921–22. Boxes 1–8.
Record Group 46. Senate.
   67th Congress. Papers Relating to Specific Bills and Resolutions. S. 505–590. Box 9.
   S. 535. An act to prevent the unauthorized landing of submaring cables in the United States.
Record Group 59. Department of State.
   Department of State Decimal File. 119.25/Official Secrets Act. 894.727.
   Name Index. Yardley.
   Source Cards. State Department Legal Advisor. 1 February–6 June 1933.
   Entry 349. Office of the Counselor. Leland Harrison's Classified Case Files.
   Entry 540. Office of the Counselor. Letters Received by Leland Harrison—Pro-German Activities. Boxes 1–5.
   Entry 541. Office of the Counselor. Leland Harrison's Correspondence with Edward Bell. Boxes 1 and 2.
   Entry 549. Office of the Counselor. Leland Harrison's General Correspondence. Boxes 1–8.
Record Group 165. War Department General and Special Staffs.
   Name Index File. M-1194.
   Military Intelligence Division.
      Entry 65. Correspondence 1917–1941.
         File 248-20-395.
         Files 4131-1 to -562/1300.
         File 7579-180.
         Files 8061-69 to -90.
         File 8532-20.

File 8536-107.
File 8930-120.
File 9793.
Files 10015-83 to -123.
Files 10020-1 to -169, -188 (1), -192, -195 (10).
Files 10039-91, -294, and -299.
File 10531.
Files 10560-103 to -152/231, -993.
Files 10994-3 to -28.
File 12458.
File 13623.
War College Division.
 Entry 296. General Correspondence 1903–1919.
  Files 639-93 to -150.
Record Group 226. Office of Strategic Services.
 Entry 99. History Office. Boxes 19, 85, 90.
 Entry 125. Field Station Files. Box 44.
 Microfilm 1642. Rolls 38, 123.
Record Group 233. House of Representatives.
 73d Congress. Minutes of the Committee on the Judiciary. Tray 12885.
  Folder for H.R. 4220.
Record Group 242. Foreign Records Seized.
 Microfilm T-77. Roll 1575. E-Berichte der Chiffrierstelle. OKW 2309–OKW 2312.
Record Group 457. National Security Agency.
 Herbert O. Yardley Collection. Boxes 1, 2, 3, 19, 20, 21, 31, 53–56, 59, 97–99, 100.
 Historical Cryptologic Collection. Boxes 23, 50, 153, 202, 279, 280, 745, 750, 775, 776, 777, 778, 793, 798, 949, 1019, 1029, 1124, 1125, 1129, 1430, 1432.
 SRH-004. William F. Friedman. "Six Lectures on Cryptology/Cryptography."
 SRH-030. "History of the Code and Cipher Section during the First World War."
 SRH-038. A Selection of Papers Pertaining to Herbert O. Yardley.
 SRH-050. Riverbank Laboratory Correspondence.
 SRH-134. Expansion of the Signal Intelligence Service 1930–7 December 1941.

National Archives of Canada. Ottawa.

Record Group 24. Vols. 20306, 20307, 29163–29173.
Accession 1983-84/167 Box 189. File 1310-6.
Manuscript Group 30, B122. C. J. Mackenzie Diaries. 1 December 1940–31 March 1942.

National Security Agency. Fort Meade, Md.

The Yardley files were microfilmed onto fifteen reels of microfilm indexed as CAHA and numbered 00001–00010, 10011–10015. I have examined all of these. Another cache of Yardley documents, only in photocopy, was discovered late in 2002. I have examined these, which consist mainly of 1919 and early 1920s Mexican and Japanese intercepts. The microfilm and these photocopies are available at the library of the National Security Agency. In addition, the documents that were microfilmed have been given to the

National Archives and Records Administration, where they are catalogued in Record Group 457 as Entry 9031.

Center for Cryptologic History.

Papers on MI-8 or Yardley being prepared to go to the National Archives. Ciphers sent by Mauborgne to Yardley and Riverbank 1917; MI-8 Test Messages Submitted to MI-8; MI-8 Chess Problems to Transmit Ciphers; MI-8 Substitution Ciphers WWI; Radio Tractor Intercept; Routing Slip MI-8 and Swedish Traffic 1918; Secret Japanese Communications—Diplomatic Intercepts 1921–22; Various Cables from Censors and Cable Companies 1917–19; Miscellaneous German Ciphers 1917–1918; Material from Cable Censors 1917–19; Data re Chile by F. B. Luquiens; Miscellaneous Private Ciphers of WWI.

Oral History of Frank B. Rowlett, 1974, 1976.

Oral History of Edna Yardley.

New York Public Library. New York, N.Y.

Manuscript and Rare Books Division. Bacon Cipher Collection. Boxes 4, 15, 16.

Princeton University. Princeton, N.J.

Seeley G. Mudd Manuscript Library. John V. A. MacMurray Papers. Boxes 23, 44, 49.

Public Record Office, Kew, London.

HW 1/2, /6; 3/1, /3, /8, /12, /13, /14, /16, /32, /33, /37, /65, /77 /82, /176, /178, /181; 7/20; 12/28, /29, /30, /31, /32, /127–174; 14/1, /3, /23, /24, /25, /38, /39, /40, /45, /62; ADM 1/8637; FO 371/5620.

Turner Entertainment Company. Atlanta, Ga.

Files on Herbert O. Yardley.

U.S. Department of State.

Personnel Files. Leland Harrison, William Lee Hurley, Arthur Bliss Lane, Tracy Lay.

U.S. Federal Records Center. East Point, Ga.

Records of the Mixed Claims Commission. Volume 321. Exhibit 321. Transcript of Manly's testimony in Witzke court-martial.

U.S. Naval Institute. Annapolis, Md.

Oral History of Thomas H. Dyer.

Oral History of Joseph J. Rochefort.

University of Chicago Library.

Special Collections Research Center. John M. Manly Papers.

University of Pennsylvania. Philadelphia, Pa.

University Archives and Records Center. Mendelsohn Files.

Van Pelt Library. Mendelsohn Collection.

University of Southern California. Los Angeles, Calif.

Cinema-Television Library.

MGM Collection. Box 251. Folders 1 and 2. *Rendezvous.*

Archives of the Performing Arts and Warner Bros. Collection. *Stamboul Quest.*
Regional History Center. Information Services Division. *Los Angeles Examiner* files for
Herbert O. Yardley.

University of Virginia Library. Charlottesville, Va.

Special Collections Department. J. Rives Childs Papers. Autobiography.

Yale University. New Haven, Conn.

Sterling Memorial Library. Manuscripts and Archives Division.
Frank L. Polk Papers. Ms. Group 656. Boxes 4, 10, 24, 28, 39.
Henry L. Stimson Diary.

The following depositories were searched for records on Yardley; none were found.

Archives du Ministère des Affaires Etrangères. Paris.

Intercepted telegrams.

Martin Luther King Jr. Library. Washington, D.C.

Washington Star Collection. YARD file.

National Archives and Records Administration. Northeast Regional Office, New York, N.Y.

Record Group 165.
Entry 122. Card Register [seeking seizure of "Japanese Diplomatic Secrets"].
Record Group 21.
Screened Bankruptcy Case Files. Eastern District and Southern District of New York.
Bankruptcy Dockets. Eastern District of New York. 1931–33.

State of New York. County of Queens. Jamaica, N.Y.

County Clerk. Records of Supreme Court, Civil Division. Docket of Judgments,
27 March 1919 to 31 December 1932, 1 January 1933 to 30 June 1934. Indexes for later
1930s are missing.

U.S. Army Military History Institute. Carlisle, Pa.

Ralph H. Van Deman Papers.
Dennis E. Nolan Papers.
G-2 [courses]. Lectures on Military Intelligence. 1919, 1926–27, 1927–28, 1928–29,
1929–30, 1932–33, 1933–34, 1934–35, 1935–36, 1936–37, 1937–38, 1938–39.

Author's Interviews

Interviews were in person, unless stated to have been by telephone.
Batts, Grover. Boarder with the Yardleys in 1950s. 20 October 2000.
Corderman, Mrs. Preston. Knew Mauborgne. 5 April 1998.
Coxeter, H. S. M. Investigated Yardley for Canada. 26 September 2001 (telephone).
Crowley, Maureen. Former daughter-in-law of John Meeth. 2 October 1995 (telephone).
Fordham, Frank and Layton. Lived in boardinghouse with Edna Yardley. 31 August
1995.

Grabo, Cynthia. Daughter of Carl W. Grabo. 28 March 2000.

Hahn, Emily. Knew Yardley in China. 1996.

Hannum, Dale. His aunt was Robert Yardley's second wife. 10 November 1996 and 3 January 1999 (telephone).

Hays, Mark. Knew Yardley in Worthington. 10 November 1995.

Herst, Herman. Knew Victor Weiskopf as fellow stamp dealer. 12 December 1995 (telephone).

Hoagland, Helen Hannum. Her aunt was Robert Yardley's second wife. 27 December 1996 (telephone).

Jedrzejewicz, Waclaw. Polish intelligence official who knew Kowalewski. 29 December 1979.

Jewell, Fred. Caddied for Yardley in Worthington. 25 June 1999 (telephone).

Mabie, Robert. Distant relative who hunted with Yardley. 3 November 2002.

McBride, Wilma Shouse. Worked with Yardley on secret ink. 11 November 1996, 9 December 1999 (telephone).

Means, Paul. Played poker with Yardley at the National Press Club. 5 February 1999 (telephone).

Meyer, Lillian. Edna Yardley's sister. 5 December 1995.

Owen, Gayle. Was visited by Yardley on family trip to California. 20 December 1996 (telephone).

Rogers, Virgil. Worthington resident and antiquarian. 7 March 1998 (telephone).

Ropp, Mary, and Wilma S. McBride. Long-time residents of Worthington who knew Yardley and Hazel. 1 November 1995. Joint interview.

Sinkov, Abraham. American link to Canadian cryptanalytic organizers. 13 September 1995 (telephone).

Smith, Gordon. Worked with Yardley at Public Housing Administration. 11 October 1997 (telephone) and 11 January 1999.

Smith, Harold J. Friend of Jack Yardley. 21 July 1997 (telephone).

Vandeventer, Anna C. Bought secret-ink business from Yardley. 6 December 1999 (telephone).

Vandeventer, Carol. Worthington librarian. 11 November 1996.

Voback, Arnold. Son-in-law of John Meeth. 1995 (telephone).

Yardley, Mrs. Jack (Barbara). Daughter-in-law of Herbert Yardley. 16 February 1999 (telephone).

Manuscript Works

Asada, Sadao. "Japan and the United States, 1915–1925." Ph.D. diss., Yale University, 1962.

[Friedman, Elizebeth Smith]. Untitled autobiography, covering Riverbank to Prohibition. Typescript. 99 pp. Photocopy in David Kahn Collection.

Gempp, Fritz. "Geheimer Nachrichtendienst und Spionageabwehr des Heeres." In Record Group 242, Foreign Records Seized. Microfilm T-77. Rolls 1438–1440, 1442, 1507–1509.

Givierge, Marcel. "Au service du chiffre: 18 ans de souvenirs, 1907–1925." France: Bibliothèque nationale, département des manuscrits, don 18899. 998 pp.

——."Etude historique sur la Section du Chiffre." France: Bibliothèque nationale, département des manuscrits, nouvelle acquisition française 24353. 932 pp.

"Historical Background of the Signal Security Agency." Army Security Agency, Assistant Chief of Staff, G-2, 12 April 1946. Vol. 1, "Codes and Ciphers Prior to World War I." 118 pp. + index. Vol. 2, "World War I." 218 pp. + index. Vol. 3, "The Peace 1919–1929." 323 pp. + bibliography + index. Cumulative index of 184 pp. This is SRH-001.

"History of the Military Intelligence Division." 8 vols. In Record Group 319, Records of the Office of the Assistant Chief of Staff, G-2, Intelligence. Historical Studies and Related Records of G-2 Components 1918–1959. Military Intelligence Division. World War I. Boxes 21 and 22.

Hubatschke, Harald. "Ferdinand Prantner (Pseudonym Leo Wolfram), 1817–1871: Die Anfänge des politischen Romans sowie die Geschichte der Briefspionage und des geheimen Chiffredienstes in Österreich." Ph.D., University of Vienna, 1975. Parts dealing with cryptology.

Kyle, Katie Letcher. "Divine Fire: Elizebeth Smith Friedman, Cryptanalyst." Typescript draft. 222 pp. Photocopy in David Kahn Collection.

Overend, William. Memorandum to David Kahn on learning poker from Yardley's book. October 2000.

Paschke, Adolf. "Das Chiffrier- und Fermeldewesen im Auswärtigen Amt: Seine Entwicklung und Organisation." VS-6025. 158 pp. In Auswärtiges Amt: Politisches Archiv. Berlin.

Schauffler, Rudolf. "Erinnerungen eines Kryptologen." VS-6025. 24 pp. In Auswärtiges Amt: Politisches Archiv. Berlin.

Turchen, Lesta VanDerWert. "Herbert Osborne Yardley and American Cryptography." Master's thesis, University of South Dakota, 1969.

Books and Articles

Some works, cited only once in the notes, are not listed here.

Alvarez, A. *The Biggest Game in Town.* Boston: Houghton Mifflin, 1983.

Alvarez, David. "Diplomatic Solutions: German Foreign Office Cryptanalysis, 1919–1945." *International Journal of Intelligence and CounterIntelligence* 9 (summer 1996): 169–185.

——. "Left in the Dust: Italian Signals Intelligence, 1915–1943." *International Journal of Intelligence and CounterIntelligence* 14 (fall 2001): 388–408.

——. *Secret Messages: Codebreaking and American Diplomacy, 1930–1945.* Lawrence: University Press of Kansas, 2000. Solid and scholarly, like all Alvarez's work.

Andrew, Christopher. "Déchiffrement et diplomatie: Le cabinet noir sous la Troisième République." *Relations internationales* 5 (spring 1976): 37–64. Original and basic.

——. *For the President's Eyes Only: Secret Intelligence and the American Presidency from Washington to Bush.* New York: HarperCollins, 1995. A thorough overview.

Angevine, Robert G. "Gentlemen Do Read Each Other's Mail: American Intelligence in the Interwar Era." *Intelligence and National Security* 7 (April 1992): 1–29.

Arnold, Jonathan P. "Herbert O. Yardley, Gangbuster." *Cryptologia* 12 (January 1988): 62–64.

Asada, Sadao. "Japanese Admirals and the Politics of Naval Limitation: Kato Tomosaburo vs. Kato Kanji." In *Naval Warfare in the Twentieth Century: Essays in Honour of Arthur Marder,* ed. Gerald Jordan, 141–166. London: Crown Helm, 1977.

Bidwell, Bruce W. *History of the Military Intelligence Division, Department of the Army: General Staff, 1775–1941.* Frederick, Md.: University Publications of America, 1986. Thorough, accurate, essential.

Bryden, John. *Best-Kept Secret: Canadian Secret Intelligence in the Second World War.* Toronto: Lester Publishing, 1993.

Buckley, Thomas H. *The United States and the Washington Conference, 1921–1922.* Knoxville: University of Tennessee Press, 1970.

Burke, Colin. "Automating American Cryptanalysis, 1930–1945: Marvelous Machines, a Bit Too Late." *Intelligence and National Security* 14 (spring 1999): 18–39.

——. *Information and Secrecy: Vannevar Bush, Ultra, and the Other Memex.* Metuchen: Scarecrow Press, 1994. A pathbreaking study.

Chapman, J. W. M. "No Final Solution: A Survey of the Cryptanalytical Capabilities of German Military Intelligence Agencies, 1926–35." *Intelligence and National Security* 1 (January 1986): 13–47.

——. "The Polish Labyrinth and the Soviet Maze: Japan and the Floating World of Signals Intelligence, 1919–1939." *Intelligence Studies* (1982): 66–87.

Childs, J. Rives. *Foreign Service Farewell.* Charlottesville: University Press of Virginia, 1969.

——. *Let the Credit Go.* New York: Giniger, 1983.

——. "My Recollections of G.2 A.6." *Cryptologia* 2 (July 1978): 201–214.

Clark, Ronald. *The Man Who Broke Purple: The Life of Colonel William F. Friedman, Who Deciphered the Japanese Code in World War II.* Boston: Little, Brown, 1977.

Denniston, Robin. "The Government Code and Cypher School between the Wars." *Intelligence and National Security* 1 (January 1986): 48–70.

——. "Yardley on Yap." *Intelligence and National Security* 9 (January 1994): 112–122.

——. "Yardley's Diplomatic Secrets." *Cryptologia* 18 (April 1994): 81–127.

Dewerpe, Alain. *Espion: Une anthropologie historique du secret d'état contemporain.* Paris: Gallimard, 1994. The sociology, psychology, and ethics of espionage; a tour de force.

Doerries, Reinhard R. *Imperial Challenge: Ambassador Count Bernstorff and German-American Relations, 1908–1917.* Chapel Hill: University of North Carolina Press, 1989.

——. "Die Tätigkeit deutscher Agenten in den USA während des Ersten Weltkrieges und ihr Einfluß auf die diplomatischen Beziehungen zwischen Washington und Berlin." In *Diplomaten und Agenten: Nachrichtendienste in der Geschichte der deutsch-amerikanischen Beziehungen,* ed. Reinhard R. Doerries, 11–52. Heidelberg: Universitätsverlag C. Winter, 2001. Very useful.

Dooley, Roger. *From Scarface to Scarlett: American Films in the 1930s.* New York: Harcourt Brace Jovanovich, 1973.

Elliot, S. R. *Scarlet to Green: A History of Intelligence in the Canadian Army, 1903–1963.* Toronto: Canadian Intelligence and Security Association, 1981.

Farago, Ladislas. *The Broken Seal: The Story of "Operation Magic" and the Pearl Harbor Disaster.* New York: Random House, 1967.

Ferris, John. "The Road to Bletchley Park." *Intelligence and National Security* 17 (spring 2002): 53–84. An important update.

——. "Whitehall's Black Chamber: British Cryptology and the Government Code and Cypher School, 1919–1929." *Intelligence and National Security* 2 (January 1987): 4–91. Fundamental.

Finnegan, John Patrick. *Military Intelligence*. Lineages compiled by Romana Danysh. Army Lineage Series. Center of Military History, United States Army. GPO, 1998.

Friedman, William F. "A Short History of the Signal Intelligence Service." *Cryptologia* 15 (July 1991): 262–272. This is SRH-049.

Goldstein, Erik, and John Maurer, eds. *The Washington Conference, 1921–22*. London: Frank Cass, 1994.

Hagerty, Alexander. "An Unpublished Yardley Manuscript." *Cryptologia* 23 (October 1999): 289–297. On Pearl Harbor. Manuscript is in HOYC, Box 3.

Hahn, Emily. *China to Me*. Garden City, N.Y.: Doubleday and Co., 1944.

Hannah, Theodore M. "The Many Lives of Herbert O. Yardley." *Spectrum* [of the National Security Agency] (fall 1981): 4–29.

Hanson, Patricia King, ed. *American Film Institute Catalog of Motion Pictures Produced in the United States: Feature Films, 1931–1940*. Berkeley: University of California Press, 1993.

Hanyok, Robert. "Before Enigma: Jan Kowalkewski and the Early Days of the Polish Cipher Bureau, 1919–1922." *Enigma Bulletin* 5 (June 2000): 25–32.

Harris, Charles H., III and Louis R. Sadler. "The Witzke Affair: German Intrigue on the Mexican Border, 1917–1918." *Military Review* 59 (February 1979): 36–50.

Hecht, Ben. *A Child of the Century*. New York: Simon and Schushter, 1954.

Hodgson, Godfrey. *The Colonel: The Life and Wars of Henry Stimson, 1867–1950*. New York: Knopf, 1990.

Hyde, Charles Cheney. "Charles Evans Hughes." In *The American Secretaries of State and Their Diplomacy*, ed. Samuel Flagg Bemis, 10: 221–401. New York: Knopf, 1928. Reprint, New York: Cooper Square, 1943.

Inaba, Chiharu. "Franco-Russian Intelligence Collaboration against Japan during the Russo-Japanese War, 1904–05." *Japanese Slavic and East European Studies* 19 (1998): 1–23.

Jeffreys-Jones, Rhodri. *American Espionage: From Secret Service to CIA*. New York: Free Press, 1977.

——. *Cloak and Dollar: A History of American Secret Intelligence*. New Haven: Yale University Press, 2002. All wrong in his chapter on Yardley.

Journal of the Telegraph. 1909–13.

Kahn, David. "The Annotated *The American Black Chamber*." *Cryptologia* 9 (January 1985): 1–37. Comments by Friedman, McGrail, Livesey, and others in a copy of the book, plus names of persons whose titles only are given in the book's text.

——. *The Codebreakers: The Story of Secret Writing*. 2d ed. New York: Simon and Schuster, 1996.

——. "An Historical Theory of Intelligence." *Intelligence and National Security* 16 (autumn 2001): 79–92.

——. "A New Source for Historians: Yardley's Seized Manuscript." *Cryptologia* 6 (April 1982): 115–118.

——. ed. "Nuggets from the Archives: Yardley Tries Again." *Cryptologia* 2 (April 1978): 139–143.

Karatzas, Daniel. *Jackson Heights: A Garden in the City*. N.p., 1990.

Katz, Friedrich. *The Secret War with Mexico: Europe, the United States, and the Mexican Revolution*. Chicago: University of Chicago Press, 1981. A rich, rewarding book.

Komatsu, Keiichiro. *Origins of the Pacific War and the Importance of "Magic."* New York: St. Martin's Press, 1999.

Kopec, John W. *The Sabines at Riverbank: Their Role in the Science of Architectural Acoustics.* Woodbury, N.Y.: Acoustical Society of America, 1997.

Kruh, Louis. "Another Herbert O. Yardley Mystery." *Cryptologia* 22 (October 1998): 370–375.

——. "From the Archives: Riverbank Laboratory Correspondence (SRH-050)." *Cryptologia* 19 (July 1995): 236–246.

——. "Stimson, The Black Chamber, and the 'Gentlemen's Mail' Quote." *Cryptologia* 12 (April 1988): 65–89. An outstanding, scholarly, and original article of fundamental importance.

——. "Tales of Yardley: Some Sidelights to His Career." *Cryptologia* 13 (October 1989): 327–357. Solid, useful explorations.

——. "Who Wrote 'The American Black Chamber'?" *Cryptologia* 2 (April 1978): 130–133.

Mahnken, Thomas G. *Uncovering Ways of War: U.S. Intelligence and Foreign Military Innovation, 1918–1941.* Cornell Studies in Security Affairs. Ithaca: Cornell University Press, 2002.

Mamet, David. *Make-Believe Town.* Boston: Little, Brown, 1996.

Mendelsohn, Charles J. *Studies in German Diplomatic Codes Employed during the World War.* War Department, Office of the Chief Signal Officer. GPO, 1935.

Meryman, Richard. *Mank: The Wit, World, and Life of Herman Mankiewicz.* New York: William Morrow, 1978.

Miller, Edward S. *War Plan Orange: The U.S. Strategy to Defeat Japan, 1897–1945.* Annapolis: Naval Institute Press, 1991. A pathbreaking study.

Miller, Nathan. *Spying for America.* New York: Paragon House, 1989.

Morison, Elting. *Turmoil and Tradition: A Study of the Life and Times of Henry L. Stimson.* Boston: Houghton Mifflin, 1960.

Nelson, Otto L., Jr. *National Security and the General Staff.* Washington: Infantry Journal Press, 1946. Extremely useful.

Ollier, Alexandre. *La cryptographie militaire avant la guerre de 1914.* Paris: Lavauzelle, 2002.

Oppenheimer, George. *The View from the Sixties: Memories of a Spent Life.* New York: David McKay, 1966.

O'Toole, G[eorge]. J. A. *Honorable Treachery: A History of U.S. Intelligence, Espionage, and Covert Action from the American Revolution to the CIA.* New York: Atlantic Monthly Press, 1991.

Pearson, Lester B. *Mike: The Memoirs of the Right Honourable Lester B. Pearson.* 3 vols. New York: Quadrangle Books, 1972–75.

Pusey, Merlo J. *Charles Evans Hughes.* New York: Macmillan, 1951.

Quirk, Lawrence J. *The Complete Films of William Powell.* Secaucus: Citadel Press, 1986.

Richelson, Jeffrey. *A Century of Spies: Intelligence in the Twentieth Century.* New York: Oxford University Press, 1995.

Rowlett, Frank B. *The Story of Magic: Memoirs of an American Cryptologic Pioneer.* Laguna Hills, Calif.: Aegean Park Press, 1998.

Russell, Rosalind, and Chris Chase. *Life Is a Banquet.* New York: Random House, 1977.

Schragmüller, Elsbeth. "Aus dem deutschen Nachrichtendienst." In *Was Wir vom Welktrieg nicht wissen,* ed. Friedrich Felger, 138–155. Berlin: Wilhelm Andermann, [1930].

Stimson, Henry L., and McGeorge Bundy. *On Active Service in Peace and War.* New York: Harper and Brothers, 1948.

Takahashi, Hishashi. "A Case Study: Japanese Intelligence Estimates of China and the Chinese, 1931–1945." In *The Intelligence Revolution: A Historical Perspective,* ed. Walter T. Hitchcock, 203–222. Washington, D.C.: U.S. Air Force Academy, Office of Air Force History, United States Air Force, 1991.

Thistle, Mel, ed. *The Mackenzie-McNaughton Wartime Letters.* Toronto: University of Toronto Press, 1975.

U.S. Congress. House of Representatives. 65th Congress, 3d Session. Document 1432. *War Department Annual Reports, 1918.* Includes *Report of the Chief of Staff, 1918.* GPO, 1919.

——. 66th Congress, 2d Session. Document 426. *War Department Annual Reports, 1919.* Includes *Reports of the Secretary of War, the Chief of Staff, the Commander in Chief of American Expeditionary Forces, 1919.* GPO, 1919.

U.S. Department of Commerce, Bureau of Foreign and Domestic Commerce. *Statistical Abstract of the United States, 1930.* GPO, 1930.

U.S. Department of State. *Register.* GPO, 1910 to 1918.

——. *Foreign Relations of the United States: Diplomatic Papers.* GPO, various dates.

U.S. Statutes at Large.

Wark, Wesley. "Cryptographic Innocence: The Origins of Signals Intelligence in Canada in the Second World War." *Journal of Contemporary History* 22 (1987): 639–665.

Weber, Ralph E. *Masked Dispatches: Cryptograms and Cryptology in American History, 1775–1900.* United States Cryptologic History. Series 1: Pre–World War I. Vol. 1, Center for Cryptologic History. Fort George G. Meade: National Security Agency, 2002.

——. "State Department Cryptographic Security: Herbert O. Yardley and President Wilson's Secret Code." In *In the Name of Intelligence,* ed. Hayden Peake and Samuel Halpern, 543–596. Washington: NIBC Press, 1994.

——. *United States Diplomatic Codes and Ciphers, 1775–1938.* Chicago: Precedent Publishing, 1979.

Weber, Ralph E., ed. *The Final Memoranda: Major General Ralph H. Van Deman, USA Ret. 1895–1951, Father of U.S. Military Intelligence.* Wilmington, Del.: SR Books, 1988. Important.

Westerbarkey, Joachim. *Das Geheimnis: Die Faszination des Verborgenen.* Berlin: Aufbau Taschenbuch Verlag, 2000. An original study of secrecy in its many forms.

White, Theodore H. *Fire in the Ashes.* New York: William Sloane Associates, 1953.

——. *In Search of History: A Personal Adventure.* New York: Harper and Row, 1978.

Woodeman, Nathan X. "Yardley Revisited." *Studies in Intelligence* 27 (summer 1983): 41–60.

Yanni, Nicholas. *Rosalind Russell.* New York: Pyramid Publications, 1975.

Yu, Maochun. "Chinese Codebreakers, 1927–1945." *Intelligence and National Security* 14 (spring 1999): 201–213.

——. *OSS in China.* New Haven: Yale University Press, 1996.

Writings by Yardley

Books

The American Black Chamber. Indianapolis: Bobbs-Merrill, 1931.

——. London: Faber and Faber, 1931 and 1937. 265 pp. Reprinted as *Secret Service in America,* 1940.

——. Laguna Hills, Calif.: Aegean Park Press, undated. Softcover, 8 ½ × 11 inch photographic reprint of the Bobbs-Merrill edition as no. 52 in A Cryptographic Series.

——. Espionage/Intelligence Library. With an introduction by David Kahn, xi–xvi. New York: Ballantine Books, 1981. Paperback. 250 pp.

——. Mattituck, N.Y.: Amereon House, n.d. 250 pp. Photographic reproduction of the Ballantine edition, with the byline of the author of the introduction deleted.

Amerikas Svarta Kammare. Trans. Johan O. Lilliehöök. Stockholm: Tidens Förlag, 1938. 280 pp.

Burakku Chienba: Beikoku wa ikanishite Gaiko Hiden o nusundanoka? Trans. Osaka Mainichi Shinbunsha. Tokyo: Osaka Mainichi Sinbunsha, 1931.

Burakku Chienba: Beikoku wa ikanishite Gaiko Ango o nusundaka? Trans. Hiratsuka Masao, ed. Kingendaishi Hensankai. Tokyo: Arachi Shuppansha, 1999.

Le cabinet noir américain. Trans. E. Rinon. Bibliothèque d'histoire politique, militaire et navale. Paris: Editions de la Nouvelle revue critique, 1935. 249 pp.

Ciphergrams. London: Hutchinson, 1932. 190 pp. British edition of *Yardleygrams.*

The Education of a Poker Player. New York: Simon and Schuster, 1957. Many reprints.

Universal Trade Code. New York: Code Compiling Co., 1921.

Yardleygrams. Indianapolis: Bobbs-Merrill, 1932. 190 pp.

[with Carl Grabo]. *The Blonde Countess.* New York: Longmans, Green, 1934. 314 pp.

[with Carl Grabo]. *Crows Are Black Everywhere.* New York: G. P. Putnam's Sons, 1945. 247 pp.

[with Carl Grabo]. *Red Sun of Nippon.* New York: Longmans, Green, 1934. 247 pp.

Magazine Articles

"Are We Giving Away Our State Secrets?" *Liberty,* 19 December 1931, 8–13.

"The Beautiful Secret Agent." *Liberty,* 30 December 1933, 30–35.

"Buraku chiemba: Beikoku wa ikani shite gaikohiden o nusunda ka?" *Osaka mainichi shimbun,* 1931.

"Ciphers." *Saturday Evening Post,* 9 May 1931, 35, 144–146, 148, 149.

"Codes." *Saturday Evening Post,* 18 April 1931, 16–17, 141, 142.

"Cryptograms and Their Solution." *Saturday Evening Post,* 21 November 1931, 21, 63–65.

"Double-Crossing America." *Liberty,* 10 October 1931, 38–42.

"From the Archives: The Achievements of the Cipher Bureau (MI-8) during the First World War." *Cryptologia* 8 (January 1984): 62–74.

"La guerre des chiffres: La chambre noire américaine." Trans. R. L. Claude of portions in *Les annales politiques et littéraires* 17, 184–189; 24 August 1934, 214–219; 31 August 1934, 241–248; 7 September 1934, 274–279; 21 September 1934, 330–335; 28 September, 1934, 360–363.

"H-27, the Blonde Woman from Antwerp." *Liberty,* 21 April 1934, 22–29.

"How They Captured the German Spy, Mme. Maria de Victorica, Told at Last." *Every Week Magazine,* 12 July 1931.

"Secret Inks." *Saturday Evening Post,* 4 April 1931, 3–5, 140–142, 145.

"Secrets of America's Black Chamber." *Every Week Magazine,* 26 July 1931.

"Spies inside Our Gates." *Sunday* [Washington] *Star Magazine,* 8 April 1934, 1–2, and *New York Herald Tribune Magazine,* 8 April 1934.

"Yardleygrams." These anecdotes with a puzzle cryptogram ran in *Liberty* from 26 December 1931 to 5 March 1932 on pages 43, 65, 65, 64, 64, and 67 of the respective issues, with answers from 2 January to 12 March 1921 on pages 25, 70, 50, 68, 58, and 58.

"Yardleygrams." This second series consisted of twelve squares of letters through which an unbroken line could be drawn to reveal a message. They ran weekly in *Liberty* from 27 May to 12 August 1933 on pages 28, 38, 26, 29, 27, 30, 26, 34, 28, 20, 18, and 22. The answers ran one week later, from 3 June to 19 August, on pages 46, 45, 32, 51, 52, 54, 52, 42, 17, 38, 46, and 55.

Unpublished Works

"On Pearl Harbor." 19 pp. NA, RG 457, HOYC, Box 3.

"Shadows in Washington: A Story of Intrigue." Typescript. 275 pp.

Stories of the Black Chamber. Bound volume of radio scripts. In collection of Louis Kruh. The first series ran from 21 January to 8 March, the second from 11 March to 29 April, the third from 1 May to 8 July, all 1935.

With Carl Grabo. "Dramatization of the American Black Chamber." Typescript. 108 pp.

With Charles E. Whittaker. "Eaters of Men." Whereabouts of manuscript unknown. Yardley refers to this work in a letter of 1 December 1934 to George Bye.

Illustration Credits

In Text

Photo Gallery

Edna Ramsaier: Courtesy Lillian Meyer

Ruth Willson: Syracuse University Archives

John Meeth and Marguerite O'Connor: Courtesy the Vobach family

Office building at 52 Vanderbilt: Museum of the City of New York, The Byron Collection, 93.1.3.1569

Washington naval convefence: National Archives and Records Administration, Signal Corps photo, 111-SC-80631

Frederick Livesey: National Archives and Records Administration

Irvin H. Correll: Courtesy Archives of the Episcopal Church, Record Group 106, Photograph Collection

Yardley with Jack: David Kahn

Yardley and Hazel on toboggan: *Jackson Heights News*, 23 January 1925, 8

Jackson Heights: Museum of the City of New York, Wurts Collection, 80543

Yardley with Georges Jean Painvin: David Kahn

William F. Friedman: National Security Agency

Henry L. Stimson: National Archives and Records Administration

George T. Bye: Bettmann/Corbis

Marie Stuart Klooz: Courtesy of Sweet Briar College

Carl Grabo: Courtesy of Cynthia Grabo

Chiffrierstelle: Courtesy of Walther Seifert (second from left in front row)

Yardley and Rosalind Russell: Courtesy of Turner Broadcasting System

Yardley with Chinese codebreakers: David Kahn

Yardley in Chungking: Courtesy of Lillian Meyer

Yardley in Los Angeles: Courtesy of Los Angeles Public Library, Herald Examiner Collection

Canadian codebreakers: Courtesy of the Canadian Security Establishment

Yardley and Edna in Reno: Courtesy of Lillian Meyer

Group at Beverly Beach: Courtesy of Frank and Lillian Fordham

Yardley and Robert Mabie: Courtesy of Robert Mabie

Yardley with gun: Courtesy of Robert Mabie

The poker player: David Kahn

Index

Yardley, Edna (*continued*)
32, 237, 240; Yardley fed information by,
200, 204, 205, 208, 218; Yardley letter to,
189

Yardley, Hazel Milam, 7, 54, 65; divorce
from Yardley, 225; marriage to Yardley, 7,
8, 55, 65–66, 83, 87–91, 104, 176, 184,
220, 240; separation from Yardley, 184,
225

Yardley, Herbert Osborn: as an author, 150–
57, 158–72, 184–85, 194, 218, 219,
223–24, 226–28, 233–35, 241; birth of,
2; "blacklisted" by government, 159–72,
209–14, 217–18, 219–23, 241; Canadian Examination Unit work and dismissal, 204–15, 216, 218, 241; character
of, 5, 21, 36, 63, 130, 144, 195–96, 203,
230, 238–42; childhood of, 2–5; in
China to solve Japanese codes, 185, 187–
98, 199–201, 216, 217, 224, 226–28,
233, 241; as Cipher Bureau chief, 53–62,
63–88, 90, 91–93; Cipher Bureau closing, 98–103, 105, 115, 130; Cipher
Bureau founded by, 51–53, 54, 113,
149–50; contribution to America, 9, 20,
21, 238, 242; cryptological limitations of,
91–93, 237–40; death and burial of, 236,
237; Distinguished Service Medal
awarded to, 81–82, **82,** 100, 238; divorce
from Hazel, 225; drinking of, 197, 200,
232, 240; early interest in cryptology, 9–
13, 21; education of, 2, 3, 4–5, 8–12;
failure of, as head of Cipher Bureau, 91,
93; false accusation, 273–74; as a father,
184; FBI and, 216–18, 220–23; fiction
writing, 149–54, 174–75, 184–86; finger amputation, 147, **149;** as freelance
cryptologist, 157, 187–98, 241; as general contractor, 230, 231; as government
telegrapher, 6, **6,** 7, 8–10, 20; greed for
money, 238–39; health of, 147, 198,
235–36; Hollywood and, 144–46, 156–
57, 173–86, 218, 226; Housing and
Home Finance Agency job, 228–30; Japanese codes and, 63–80, 84–87, 91, 115,
118–19, 130–36, 139, 158–72, 187–98,

199–201, 204–8, 212–14, 217, 228,
237, 239, 240; "Japanese Diplomatic
Secrets" manuscript and legal problems,
159–72; leadership abilities of, 63; lectures, 26, 141–43, 145–46; legacy of,
237–42; *Liberty* articles, stories, and
squibs, 139–43, **140–43,** 148–50, 174;
marriage to Edna, 225, 230–32, 237,
240; marriage to Hazel, 7, 8, 55, 65–66,
83, 87–91, 104, 176, 184, 220–21, 240;
as MI-8 cryptologist, 21, 27, 28–49, 50,
241; as Military Intelligence Reserve
Corps major, 57; 1920s Cipher Bureau
weaknesses, 91–93; OPA job, 223, 224–
25, 228; poker and, 232–35; post–World
War I period, 50–62; radio program,
154–55, **155,** 156–57, 182, 218; real-
estate and commercial code ventures, 88–
91, 100, 104, 184, 239; resignation from
Military Intelligence Reserve, 106–7; resignation from War Department, 100; restaurant of, 219–23; rivalry with Friedman, 37, 91–93, 100, 107, 126, 128–33,
197, 200, 212–13, 217, 237, 238, 239,
241; *Saturday Evening Post* articles, 109,
110, 111, 130, 182, 233; as screenwriter,
144–46, 173–86, 226; secret-ink business, 146–47, **147,** 148, **148,** 156; separation from Hazel, 184, 225; sexual
appetite of, 196–97, 232, 240; spymaster image of, 146; as telegrapher,
5–7; untrustworthy reputation of, 209–
14, 241; Waberski solution, 42–44, 113,
119; World War I cryptanalysis, 13, 20–
50. See also *American Black Chamber*

Yardley, Jack, 89, 146, 176, 184, 224,
237

Yardley, Mary, 1, 2

Yardley, Robert Kirkbride, 1, 5

Yardleygrams, 139–41, **140–41**

Yardleygrams (Yardley book), 139–41, 158

"Yardley symptom," 13

Yomiuri shimbun, 130

Zhou En-lai, 192

Zimmerman, Arthur, 20, 39, 46